Action Arcade Adventure Set

Action Arcade
Adventure Set

Diana Gruber

CORIOLIS GROUP BOOKS

Publisher	*Keith Weiskamp*
Developmental Editor	*Pat Vincent*
Copy Editor	*Jenni Aloi*
Technical Reviewer	*Phil Kunz*
Proofreader	*Diane Green Cook*
Interior Design	*Bradley Grannis*
Layout Production	*Rob Mauhar and Bradley Grannis*
Publicist	*Shannon Bounds*
Indexer	*Lenity Mauhar*

Distributed to the book trade by IDG Books Worldwide, Inc.

Library of Congress Cataloging-in-Publication Data

Gruber, Diana
Action Arcade adventure set / Diana Gruber
p. cm.
Includes Index
ISBN 1-883577-06-3 : $39.95

Printed in the United States of America

10 9 8 7 6 5 4 3 2 1

Acknowledgments

I would like to thank the following people for their contributions to this project: Keith Weiskamp for his guidance, Jeff Duntemann for his encouragement, Patrick Vincent for his composure, Eric Lund for his humor, Phil Kunz for his perseverance, and Dave Taylor for not sugar-coating it. Also, thanks to Brad Grannis and Rob Mauhar for the layouts and Jenni Aloi for copy editing. Special thanks to Eric Lund and Steve Blackwood for beta testing the software, and to Phil Kunz for testing it again. Another thanks to Eric Lund for contributing the palette fade program, and thanks to Dave Taylor for optimizing the sprite minimization function.

Thanks to Les Pardew of Cygnus Multimedia for the background artwork, and thanks to Alfred Woo and Mike Wall of Dub Media for the title screen and the Hedge Row background. Thanks to Chad Max for designing all the Fastgraph artwork, and thanks to Steve Brown for the cover art. Thanks to Shannon Bounds for organizing the contest. Thanks to Dan Linton for running such a cool BBS. Thanks to Ted for writing Fastgraph. Thanks to Karen Crowther for being there. Thanks to Joel Vaughan for creating some of the additional artwork included with the companion disk.

Thanks to the members of the CompuServe GAMERS Forum for their knowledge and encouragement. Thanks to all the authors who wrote the wonderful games that are featured in this book—you guys are the greatest! Thanks to all my customers and friends without whose support I could not have finished this project. Did I forget anybody? Oh yes. . . . Thank you for buying this book.

Dedication

This book is dedicated to all aspiring game programmers—without whom there would be no new games!

About the Author

Diana Gruber is the senior programmer at Ted Gruber Software, creators of Fastgraph. She has been writing computer games since 1987. Her articles on game programming and marketing appear frequently in *PC TECHNIQUES* and *Game Developer* Magazine.

Installation Guide

The companion disk for *Action Arcade Adventure Set* contains the complete game that we'll be discussing throughout this book, including all the source code, art files, and other support files required to rebuild and run the game. In addition, you'll find a complete game editor with source code for creating and editing the components of arcade games—background tiles, sprites, and so on. Last but not least, the disk includes the shareware version of a high-performance graphics library called Fastgraph. This library provides over 170 useful C functions that you can call for performing everything from moving the mouse around in VGA Mode X to drawing fast-action graphics. On disk, you'll find not only the Fastgraph/Light library and utilities, but the complete documentation (over 600 pages!) for using the library and utilities as well.

Requirements

To install all of the files you will need approximately 3.5 Mb of free space on your hard disk. If you don't install the documentation for Fastgraph, you'll only need 2.5 Mb of free space.

Files on the Disk

The files provided on the companion disk include:

EXC.ARJ	Example programs from the *Fastgraph User's Guide*
FADE.ARJ	Palette fade program from Eric Lund
FGE.ARJ	*Fastgraph Game Editor* program and data files
FGESRCE.ARJ	Source code for *Fastgraph Game Editor*
FGLIGHT.ARJ	*Fastgraph/Light* libraries, driver, and utilities
FILELIST.TXT	The list of files provided
HEDGE.ARJ	Game: *Hedge Row* with source code
INSTALL.EXE	Installation program—run this first!
LEVEL.ARJ	Level Editor and source code from Chapter 6
MAKEFONT.ARJ	Utility to make a character font header file

MANUALS.ARJ	*Fastgraph User's Guide* and *Fastgraph Reference Manual*
ORDER.FRM	Order form for *Fastgraph* and special offers
PALETTE.ARJ	Palette matching and reduction utility
PCX.ARJ	Utility to display any PCX file
QF.ARJ	*Quickfire* demo
READ.ME	Release notes
RIPPER.ARJ	Tile Ripper program with source from Chapter 4
TOMMY.ARJ	Game: *Tommy's Adventures*
TOMSRCE.ARJ	Source code for *Tommy's Adventures*
UNARJ.EXE	Unarchiving program
XTRA_ART.ARJ	Additional artwork to play with

Most of these files are stored in an .ARJ format. These files were archived using Robert K. Jung's ARJ program, and the individual files may be extracted from the archives using the UNARJ.EXE program, which is included on the disk. While you should be able to unarchive any of the files without difficulty, I recommend that you run the install program to unarchive all the programs into convenient subdirectories.

Installing the Game and Support Tools

To install all of the source and executable files for the game editor and the actual game, place the *Action Arcade Adventure Set* disk in drive A (or drive B depending on how your system is set up). Next, move to the drive, switch to the root directory, and run the installation program. Here are the three commands you'll need:

```
A:
CD \
INSTALL
```

The installation program creates a main directory named FG and eight subdirectories. The .ARJ files will be archived into the subdirectories shown here:

\FG\EXAMPLES\	*Fastgraph* example programs
\FG\FGE\	*Fastgraph Game Editor*
\FG\FGESRCE\	Source code for *Fastgraph Game Editor*
\FG\HEDGE\	*Hedge Row* game with source code
\FG\QF\	*Quickfire* demo

\FG\TOMMY\	*Tommy's Adventures* game
\FG\TOMSRCE\	Source code for *Tommy's Adventures*
\FG\UTIL\	Tile ripper, level editor, palette matching program, and makefont utility

In addition, the *Fastgraph/Light* files are installed in the \FG directory, including the FGDRIVER.EXE program, the various utilities, and documentation for Fastgraph. The Fastgraph/Light libraries are installed in the appropriate library subdirectory. The install program will suggest a default choice that you may override. For example, the install program may suggest the subdirectory C:\BORLANDC\LIBRARY, but you may prefer to put the Fastgraph/Light libraries in another subdirectory, such as C:\LIB. I recommend you put the Fastgraph/Light libraries in the same subdirectory where your compiler usually looks for libraries.

Similarly, the install program will suggest an appropriate subdirectory for the Fastgraph header file; for example, the C:\BORLANDC\INCLUDE subdirectory. If you have questions about library and header file paths, refer to your compiler manuals.

Running the Game

Before you do anything else, you'll probably want to run the game, *Tommy's Adventures,* that we'll be creating in this book. Go to the \FG\TOMMY\ subdirectory and enter this command:

```
TOMMY
```

That's it. If you need help playing the game, read the instructions in Appendix A.

Contents

Introduction

Have you ever played a side-scrolling action arcade game on your PC and wondered what it takes to program one? How do the programmers scroll their backgrounds so fast and make their sprites move so smoothly? And how do they learn how to design their games? Do they use custom development tools, or do they write all of their code line by line? Do they code up their fast-action graphics in C or C++, or do they have to drop down to assembly? Is there a correspondence course you can take to learn the mysteries of game programming? And where's the *secret* manual that explains everything?

These are the questions that used to keep me up late. Unfortunately, I had to learn the hard way. When I started writing computer games, there was virtually no information available. We were all stumbling around in the dark back then. Game development techniques were invented or discovered in a haphazard fashion. That situation has gradually improved. These days, many people share in the pool of knowledge that gaming technology has become. But it is shared as a verbal tradition—most of the fundamentals of gaming technology remain undocumented. This book is an effort to change that tradition. Throughout this book, I'll be showing you how action arcade games are created from the ground up. You'll learn what it takes to create one, how to work with artists, how to create useful support tools, how to code up fast VGA Mode X graphics, and how to debug and even market your games. If only I had a book like this when I was starting out!

Why I Wrote This Book?

Some of my friends who are game programmers aren't pleased that I wrote this book. These game programmers (gamers) share a certain mindset; they are willing to exchange information and coding secrets, but only up to a certain point. After all, some things are, by tradition, kept secret. If everybody knew how to write games, gamers wouldn't be valuable anymore. So why should I give away the secrets of gaming technology?

In general, I do not share the point of view that technological cards should be played close to one's vest. I am in favor of disseminating information, even over the protests of some of my colleagues. When Jeff Duntemann, editor of *PC TECHNIQUES* magazine, asked me to write a book on game programming for The Coriolis Group, I jumped at the chance. I believe the technology should be documented, and I am willing to be the one to do it.

I'm in a unique position because I don't rely on game programming as my primary source of income anymore. My husband and I sell a programmer's graphics library called Fastgraph. Since this toolkit is used by many programmers to write games, our interest is in helping our customers (gamers) write as many games as possible. The more game programmers there are and the more games that get written, the more customers we'll have.

So unlike other gamers, it's not in my best interest to keep gaming technology a secret. The best thing I can do is give it away and hope people like you can use it. So, here's your opportunity: Take whatever you can from this book—the tools, the knowledge, the programming and design tips. Create the best possible action arcade games that you can, and help spread the fun and commerce of PC gaming.

The code in this book represents a technology that has never been documented. There is no reference book to show you how to write a side-scrolling arcade game. The information is simply not available anywhere. In return for the privilege of presenting my product Fastgraph to you, I'll give you this information, and what was once undocumented will now be recorded.

What You Get

This book is the product of several years of work. The games and utilities in this book were written by me over a three-year period, but they represent a much larger investment in knowledge. The techniques for creating side-scrolling games were developed over many years by many people. I feel fortunate to have been a part of this community of knowledge, and now I am sharing what I have learned with you. You will find a lot of source code on the companion disk—over 12,000 lines! You will also find a complete tool set to help you build action arcade games, along with several example programs to show you ways to use the tools. There is also a powerful graphics library included on the disk to speed up and simplify the development process. This software, along with the ideas presented in this book, will give you everything you need to get started on your path to game development success. Here's what you get:

- A full-featured, side-scrolling arcade game engine with complete documentation and C source code.

- A game editor with complete C source code. The game editor includes a level editor, sprite editor, and other support tools that will help streamline the process of writing games.
- A palette matching/reduction program to aid in preprocessing artwork.
- A sample game called *Tommy's Adventures* with complete C source code that provides two levels of action and adventure.
- A continuous-running sample game called *Quickfire,* which demonstrates another application of the game engine. (I didn't include the source code for this game because of its size.)
- A bonus game called *Hedge Row,* which shows another way to use tile-based levels created by the game editor.
- All of the high-quality graphics for the games presented (sprites, level art, tiles, and so on).
- The *Fastgraph/Light* high-performance graphics library that includes over 170 callable functions.
- Over 600 pages of online manuals that describe how to use the Fastgraph/Light functions. The *Fastgraph User's Guide* describes graphics programming from the ground up, and includes over 140 example programs to help you learn how to use Fastgraph quickly. The *Fastgraph Reference Manual* is an alphabetical listing of all the Fastgraph functions.

Creating a Real Game Engine!

So, what exactly is a game engine? Most people think of a game engine as the underlying code to a computer game, plus the utilities used to create the game. Since we're treading onto uncharted territory here, I'll go out on a limb and define a game engine to be just that. In actual practice, a game engine is a rather nebulous concept. I've seen people write a few functions to perform 3-D projections and call their code a game engine. I've also seen systems that are so rigid that you can only write one type of game, within a few narrow parameters. These "engines" are sometimes sold commercially.

In my opinion, a game engine should be flexible enough so that it can be easily modified to accommodate a great number and variety of games. It should also be powerful enough to be significantly useful. That means that the developer using the game engine will have a major advantage over the developer starting from scratch. The game engine should give the developer extensive functionality without getting in the way when the developer wants to be experimental. The game engine should also be thoroughly tested, and should have practical, as well as theoretical, applications.

That's a tall order for the game engine developer! In this case, the developer is me, and I've done the best I can to write a game engine that fits that description. No game engine can be all things to all people, however. You'll surely find parts of my game engine that you want to work differently. The best part is that you can change it yourself since I'll be giving you all of the source code. Make it *your* game engine. Modify it, upgrade it, and use it as you see fit.

The Parts of the Game Engine

The game engine in this book consists of two parts: the game editor and the underlying game code, or *game template*. The game editor is actually a collection of tools for building games. You can use the game editor to create tiles, edit levels, import and edit sprites, and manage files. The second part of the game engine, the game template, should be thought of as a skeleton for creating side-scrolling arcade games. How much of this skeleton I should write proved to be problematic. I didn't want to write a whole game because it wouldn't fit in this book. But I did want to give you more than a handful of disjoint functions. So I wrote "almost" a game. The *Tommy's Adventures* game is designed to give you enough information about how such games work that you can use it as a model for your own games, without being overwhelmed by too many details.

How to Use This Book

I designed this book for programmers, but you don't need to be a rocket scientist to follow the discussions or the code presented. I've tried to present the key areas of side-scrolling arcade game programming in a step-by-step manner so that you can understand both the big picture concepts and the important details. Some of the programs, such as the game editor, are rather large (over 7,000 lines of code!), so I'll be presenting the code highlights in the book to help you navigate your way through the code. The first thing you may want to do is print all of the C source files that come with the companion disk. You might want to punch holes in the listings and put them in a binder for easy reference. But make sure you get a big binder!

Any C/C++ programmer can understand and use the code presented. No knowledge of assembly language is required for most of this book. There is a little bit of assembly-language code presented when timing considerations are discussed, but you should be able to use that code without modifications. While understanding assembly language will be useful to you in your gaming career, it's not a prerequisite to reading this book.

In addition, there's quite a bit of information in this book that requires no programming knowledge at all. This introduction, for example, contains no code. Similarly, Chapters 1, 18, and 19 are not just about programming games. They contain information about what side-scrolling arcade games are, how they work, and how to finish and market them. Publishers, distributors, producers, and curious game players may find these chapters interesting.

Neither Chapter 2 or 3 contains code, but they are directed more toward the developer. They discuss how to go about developing games and how to use the game editor. Usually, the programmer is the one who uses the game editor, but not always. I've heard of programming teams where a non-programmer is the creative impetus behind a game, and may take charge of level design.

Chapters 4 through 15 contain the meat and potatoes of game programming. We begin by discussing how to develop your tools. After all, you can't do a proper job without proper tools. Chapters 4 through 9 discuss the source code for the game editor. Some of the concepts in these chapters can be applied to other types of games. All games, not just side-scrolling arcade games, require pre-processing artwork. These days, artwork is bigger and more important than ever. Anytime you can write a program to manage the tedious job of importing artwork into your game you should.

Chapters 10 through 15 discuss the code that is very specific to side-scrolling arcade games. Our sample game, *Tommy's Adventures*, is dissected and the concepts of using tiles, sprites, scrolling, and animation are discussed in detail. Hard-core game programmers may want to skip ahead to these chapters. This is where the good stuff is.

Before you skip ahead, though, take a good look at Chapter 5. It is in this chapter that the concept of scrolling using *tiles* is introduced. This technique is the heart of side-scroller programming; it's the topic that gets the most discussion and generates the most interest. It was presented in the game editor section because, like the game, the level editor requires four-way scrolling. This material will be covered again in Chapter 11, where we look at game scrolling, which uses the same technology as level editor scrolling, but at a much faster pace.

Finally, the appendices offer you some useful resources, and the glossary will help to demystify some of the common game developer jargon.

Tommy's Tips

Throughout the book we'll highlight important terms and concepts with an icon that I call *Tommy's Tips*. Here's an example:

Tommy's Tip

What Is a Game Engine?

A game engine is the reusable, underlying code for a game, along with the collection of tools and utilities used to create the game. A game engine usually consists of two parts: a *game skeleton* that can be used as a template for other games, and a *game editor* for processing artwork.

About Fastgraph

Beneath the game engine, there is an even lower level of code. This code is the *graphics library*. All game programmers use graphics libraries, but not all of them use a commercial graphics library. Some game programmers prefer to write their own low-level graphics routines.

Writing a graphics library from scratch would definitely be beyond the scope of this book, plus it would not be nearly as interesting as the topics we'll discuss. Therefore, we'll use a commercial graphics library upon which to base our game engine. The library we'll use is called *Fastgraph*. It was written by my husband, Ted Gruber. It is well suited to the current task (and to many other tasks), and it has the advantage of being available in a shareware version.

We are including the shareware version of Fastgraph, called Fastgraph/Light, on the companion disk. This is a fully functional, fully documented version of Fastgraph. When you install it, you'll get the libraries and utilities, examples, and complete documentation. If you want, you can print out the Fastgraph manual and read it. If you prefer, you can scan the Fastgraph manual online, and just use it to fill in whatever gaps in your understanding are left unanswered by this book. To help you understand Fastgraph, we'll include Fastgraph boxes that define and explain Fastgraph's functions and programs. Here's an example of a Fastgraph box.

Fastgraph Tip

FGDRIVER.EXE

The FGDRIVER.EXE program is a TSR video driver for Fastgraph/Light. This program must be run once before any program linked with Fastgraph/Light can be run. It loads into memory in a manner similar to a mouse driver, and it will stay in memory until it is unloaded or until you reboot.

I recommend that you install Fastgraph/Light before you try any of the other code on the disk. (The installation instructions are included at the front of this book.) Read the installation instructions and experiment with the library a little to get familiar with it before you try to recompile and relink the game or the game editor. If you decide to use Fastgraph rather than Fastgraph/Light, there is ordering information in the back of this book. Fastgraph works the same as Fastgraph/Light, except there is no TSR driver. To upgrade your code to work with Fastgraph from Fastgraph/Light, all you need to do is relink. The code will be completely compatible.

What You'll Need

All of the programs on the companion disk were tested with Fastgraph and Fastgraph/Light, and work with current versions of Borland C++, Turbo C++, Microsoft C/C++ and Microsoft Visual C/C++. The programs probably work fine with other compilers too, though I haven't tested them all. I'll be working on that while this book is being printed, so be sure to read the release notes on the disk for the latest information on the software. Compiling instructions and batch files will also be on the disk as appropriate. Everything that you'll need to write your own games is included in this book and the companion disk except, of course, a PC equipped with VGA, a mouse, and a C compiler.

Restrictions on Usage

The license agreement for the software is printed on the last page of this book. My feeling about the code is that I want you to use it. Take my code and dissect it, change it, add your personal touches, and create great games with it. The only part of the game I want to hang onto is the artwork. The main character, Tommy, is my baby. Please don't write any games starring Tommy for commercial use (although you can feel free to use Tommy and any of the other artwork to create a game for the contest presented in this book). Create another character of your own. Similarly, the background art is proprietary. You can experiment with the tiles, use them to test the game editor, and create your own levels with them. But please do not release any games using my artwork. I may want to use that stuff myself someday, and it was mine first.

None of the code or artwork is public domain, and there are some time restrictions on how long you can use the unregistered version of Fastgraph/Light. So when you write your game, play fair. Use a registered version of either Fastgraph or Fastgraph/Light, and get your own artwork. If you do those things, you're welcome to use the game editor and the game engine code as much as you want.

Contacting Me

As you are reading this book and developing your own games, I'd love to hear from you. You can reach me on CompuServe as 72000,1642. I tend to hang out with the game developers in the GAMERS forum, so GO GAMERS, section 11, to join the party. Also, I operate a bulletin board for game developers and users of our Fastgraph product. You'll find many useful code examples and messages from other game developers. When you need to take a break from your programming adventures, call the board at (702) 796-7134. Finally, we've set up a special forum for readers of this book on the popular Software Creations bulletin board. This board serves as a clearing house for thousands of game programmers around the U.S. If you are serious about writing games, and you are not currently using the Software Creations board, I encourage you to call them at (508) 368-7139. I've included all the information you'll need for using bulletin boards and accessing game programming forums in the back of this book.

By the way, if you're still looking for the *secret* manual, I think you've come to the right place. Let's start the adventure!

Chapter 1

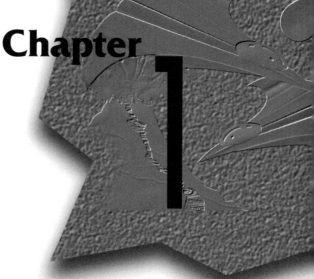

So you want to be a game programmer? Well, you've come to the right place.

The Adventure Starts Here!

Here's your chance to forget all those boring programming projects you've been working on lately and enter the fascinating world of action arcade game programming—a world where you can let your imagination soar! You can create your own scrolling worlds inhabited by creatures from your imagination. The possibilities in game development are endless, and the ideas presented in this book can be used as the building blocks of an infinite variety of action arcade games

As you've probably guessed by now, game programming is one of the most challenging areas of PC programming—you need to master animation, graphics programming, data structures, event-driven programming, sound effects, and much more. But with the right tools, the right strategy, and a little bit of luck, you'll be amazed at what you can do.

In this book, you will find everything you need to create your own action arcade games in C. Together, we'll explore how to develop and use game editing tools, create scrolling levels, add animated sprites and special effects, debug game code, and put all the components together to create a fast-action scrolling arcade game. We'll also take an insider's look at the state of the gaming industry, including tips for working with other gamers, finishing games, packaging and marketing games, what to expect as a game developer, and where to go for more information. Mostly, though, we will concentrate on the process of creating the game—assembling the necessary tools, building the code from the ground up, using a third-party library, selecting and processing artwork, and adding all the finishing touches that make an action arcade game great. But before we embark on our game programming adventure, let's take a look at what action arcade games are all about.

Getting Our Terminology Straight

For years, gamers have referred to the type of action arcade game we will be working on as a *platform game* or *side scroller.* As shown in Figure 1.1, an action arcade game contains animated sprites that move along a scrolling background. I originally learned to call these games "platform games" because they are based on the concept that sprites walk and jump on platforms. Originally, these platforms were blocky-shaped projections extending out of the back wall. Gamers used these platforms as a device to move the player through the level in a two-dimensional manner. Traveling from left to right on the screen in a straight path is rather boring. The platforms added an element of height to the player's path (as compared to depth, which is seen in 3-D games such as *Wolfenstein 3D*). The platforms eventually evolved into more interesting shapes. Sprites could jump up on rocks, branches and bridges, for example. But the name "platform game" stuck because the platform is a defining element of the game genre. We don't call them that any more, though. Unfortunately, the term "platform" has become such a buzzword in the computer industry that people get confused if we use that term to nail down this genre of games. It is not an adequately descriptive name.

But calling these games arcade adventure games isn't the best solution either. The arcade game genre is too broad and describes a number of games that do not resemble the game we will be working on in this book. Arcades are filled with games like Pac Man and Asteroids, which didn't have scrolling backgrounds, and games like Street Fighter and Mortal Kombat, which don't have platforms. We also don't want to call our scrolling games "adventure games" because the adventure game genre is well defined and specific. Here you will find games that are designed around a story that gradually unfolds as the player works through a graphics world. *King's Quest* is an example of a

Figure 1.1 *An example of an action arcade game: Epic's Jazz Jackrabbit.*

popular adventure game. In general, adventure games do not involve platforms or much in the way of hand-eye coordination. Rather, they involve problem-solving, similar to that involved in reading a good mystery novel. So an adventure game is not a side scroller, even though sometimes they scroll sideways. Are you getting confused yet?

To make matters worse, side scrollers don't always scroll sideways. Sometimes they scroll vertically or even diagonally! In fact, one of the games I've included on the companion disk, *Quickfire*, scrolls both horizontally and diagonally. So now you're probably thinking that all the names I've introduced don't really accurately describe the type of games that we will be creating. You are right, and it is a problem, but for lack of a better name, I'll go with the name "side scrollers" throughout the rest of this book.

Features of a Side Scroller

If the purpose of this chapter was to define the genre of side scrollers, we haven't gotten very far. We can't even agree on a good name! Fortunately, there are a few important features that all of these games have in common. The more visible components, such as sprites and platforms, are labeled in Figure 1.2. Other features, such as fast-action scrolling, are hard to show in a picture, but nevertheless, they are important. So, let's take a closer look.

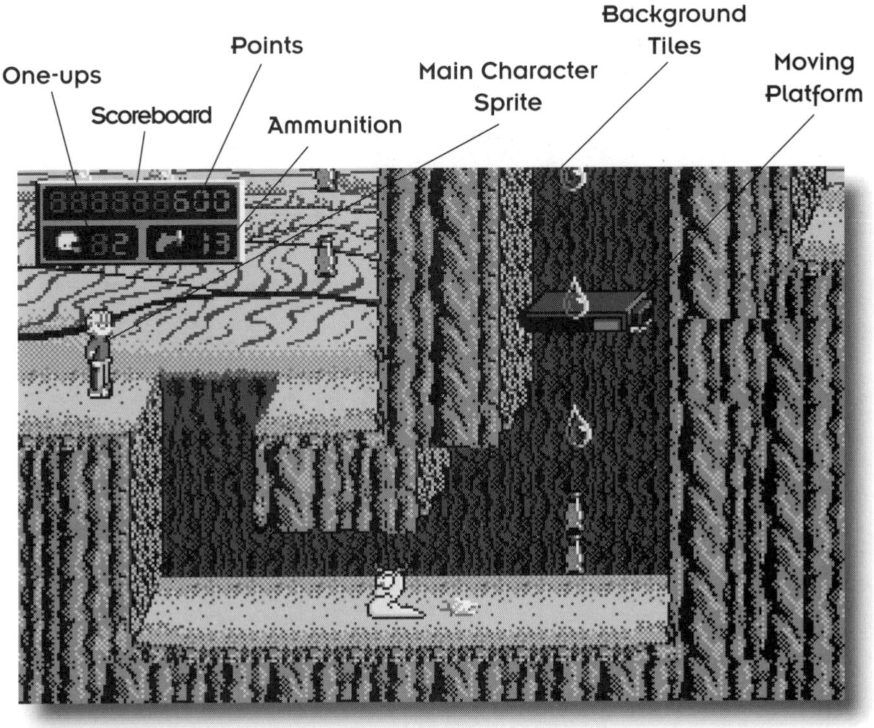

Figure 1.2 *The key components of a side scroller in Id's Goodby Galaxy.*

Tommy's Tip

You Gotta Play This Game

Before you get too far into this chapter, you should try out the game *Tommy's Adventures* provided on the companion disk. (This is not a complete game; it's a template game developed to demonstrate the functions of the game engine.) In fact, if you go play it now, you'll have a much easier time understanding the features I'm about to explain. To start this game, go to the directory where the game is stored on your hard disk and execute this command at the DOS prompt:

```
TOMMY
```

If you are running Windows, you should quit Windows before you start the game. Figure 1.3 shows what the game looks like. You can move Tommy around with the arrow keys, and make him jump by pressing the Ctrl key. When he encounters the scorpion, press the

Alt key to make Tommy shoot his gun. You can also make Tommy perform a spin kick by pressing the Spacebar. If you get tired of playing the first level, press the letter W to "warp" to the next level. To quit the game, press the Esc key and then press the letter Q. (I've included more detailed instructions for playing this game in Appendix A. So, if you get stuck, you know where to go.)

Introducing Levels

All side scrollers provide one or more *levels.* Most games usually provide between five and thirty levels. The level consists of the scene or background art that you scroll through. (The Egyptian scene in *Tommy's Adventures* is the first level for this game.) You can make your games more interesting and enjoyable by adding different types of levels. For example, if you are creating a side scroller named "Alien Invasion," you might provide a base level that consists of a mountain terrain. Then, you might add a level that takes you through an underwater adventure. To wrap up the game, you might even include a level that takes the player to the home planet of the invading aliens. When it comes to designing levels, anything goes.

The main goal in a side scroller is to navigate your way through a level until you "earn your way" way up to another level. This might involve locating a secret door, rescuing a princess, finding a power crystal, or defeating a boss enemy. This

Figure 1.3 *Taking Tommy's Adventures for a test drive.*

"level hopping" (or *warping* as gamers call it) is the key feature that makes side scrollers interesting and challenging. The ultimate thrill is to conquer a level and finally see what is waiting for you on the next one.

In designing side scrollers, you'll want to make your levels as visually interesting and appealing as possible. For example, Figure 1.4 shows the levels we'll be using to create our game, *Tommy's Adventures.* Notice here that we start in an Egyptian pyramid and end up in a space station platform—quite a leap, but this should certainly surprise our player and keep him or her interested in playing our game. The more you can catch your player off guard and dazzle him or her with your action-packed levels, the more popular your game is likely to be.

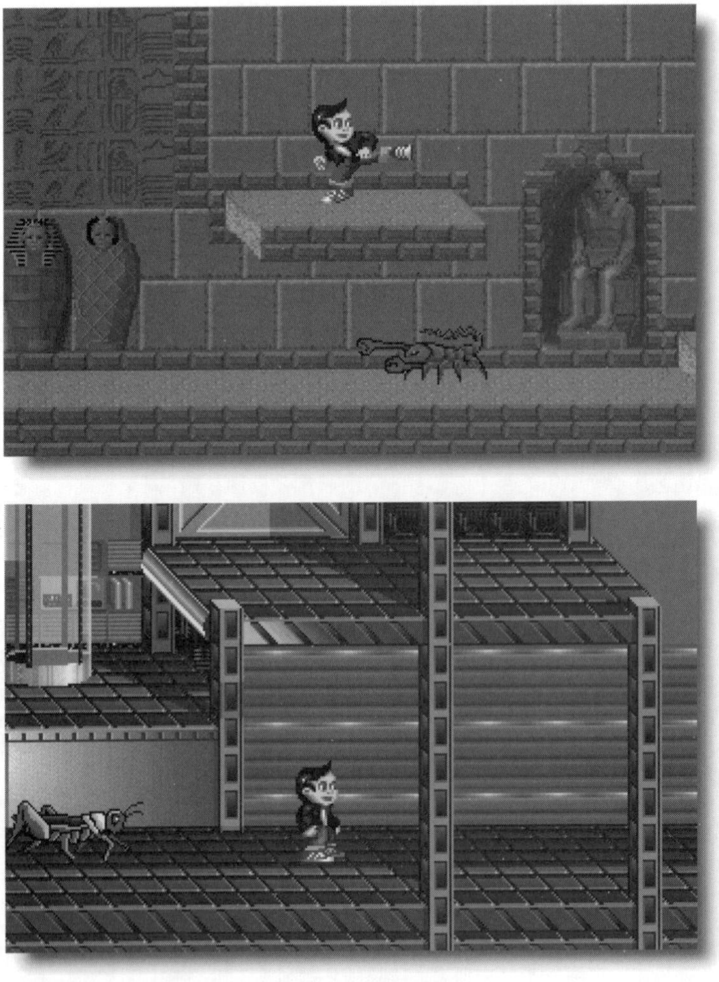

Figure 1.4 *The two levels used in Tommy's Adventures.*

As you'll see shortly, levels are actually constructed from distinct tiles and they are inhabited by animated creatures called sprites.

Sprites and Animation

Sprites are the characters that appear in the foreground. They interact with each other, the background, and sometimes with other foreground objects. They may run, jump, fly, swim, spin kick, or shoot. Usually, a game provides a single main character sprite controlled by the player. The other sprites could be monsters or creepy insects that chase after the main character. The goal in a situation like this would be to have your main sprite character wipe out as many of the enemy sprites as possible as you work your way up the levels. For example, in *Tommy's Adventures* our little guy Tommy serves as the main character. As he explores the Egyptian pyramid or the space station platform, he encounters the enemy sprites—the poisonous scorpion and the giant "boy-eating" grasshopper.

But one important point to keep in mind is that your sprites can be anything you want them to be. You don't have to create monsters or dangerous villains. You can easily use the side-scroller technology to create educational games. In such a case, you could design a main character sprite to move around and collect "non-threatening" animated sprites such as walking numbers or letters.

In many games, different sprites are introduced at the different levels. This approach can really keep the player of your game on guard at all times. For example, if the first level of your game takes place under the ocean, you might introduce sea monsters or clams that hide hidden jewels. Later, when you take your player to a dark underground cave, you could introduce giant carnivorous earthworms or blind newts. When it comes to creating sprites, anything goes.

The challenging part of sprites is animating them. You've got to be able to move them around and have them perform actions as smoothly as possible. This takes a lot of practice. To see what is involved in animating a sprite, let's return to Tommy. When playing *Tommy's Adventures*, you can press the Spacebar to make Tommy perform a spin kick. This is a tricky maneuver. Figure 1.5 shows how I did it. Here, I've created different versions of Tommy as he progresses through the spin kick. In the game, I simply cycle through these different versions of the sprite to create the appearance of a smooth moving karate expert.

When designing your sprites, you'll need to map out each character and then create the animated variations needed to bring your sprites to life. This is a tedious process but the sprite editor described in Chapter 7 can help you create new sprites quickly.

Figure 1.5 Animating sprites—making Tommy do the spin kick.

Tiles—The Building Blocks of Levels

I mentioned earlier that levels are created from distinct tiles. So what exactly is a tile? A tile is simply a re-usable, visual graphic building block. Side-scroller games have backgrounds that are constructed of re-usable tiles. In this way, a small amount of artwork can be used to create huge levels. The background for the level is usually much larger than the size of the screen, often many times larger. Since patterns in the background art are repeated, a single tile can be used over and over. For instance one tile can be used several times to represent many rows of bricks.

As an example, Figure 1.6 shows how the Egyptian level in *Tommy's Adventures* is divided into distinct tiles. If you design your levels carefully, you'll be surprised at how few tiles are actually needed to create attractive scenes. In Chapter 4, I'll show you how to create levels using the tile approach. I'll also show you how to create an automated "tile ripper" to reduce screens of level art into tiles.

Fast-Action Scrolling

Side scrollers, by their nature, scroll. Usually they scroll in conjunction with the movement of the main sprite. As he or she jumps up, the background scrolls down, so the sprite is roughly (but not exactly) centered. You can scroll a background up, down, left, right, or even diagonally. With some

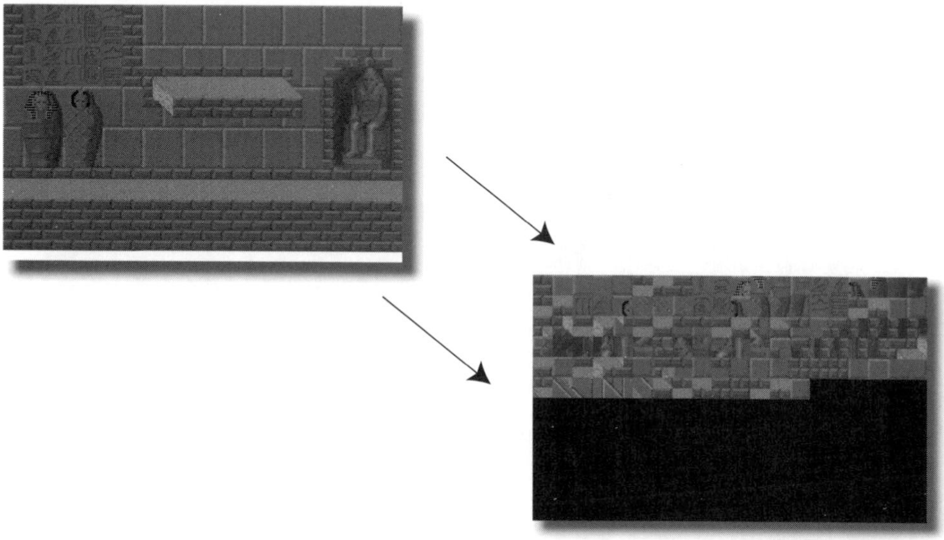

Figure 1.6 *Breaking a level into tiles.*

games, you can make the background scroll on its own so that it gives the player the feeling that the game is constantly in motion. The *Quickfire* game provided on the companion disk uses this technique. The sky background shown in Figure 1.7 continually scrolls to the left giving the player the illusion that the jet fighter sprites are constantly in motion. This is a useful technique to use if you want to create self-playing demos for your games.

Creating fast-scrolling backgrounds on the PC is a challenge. We use a tricky method that involves resizing video memory and simulating page flipping. This trick is made possible by setting the video mode to Mode X, an extended or "tweaked" VGA mode first publicized by Michael Abrash. The screen can be updated very quickly in Mode X, and tiles are used to rebuild the level as it moves around. In Chapter 5, we will discuss the theory behind the scrolling algorithm, and the code for scrolling in the game editor will be presented in Chapter 6. More scrolling code will be found in Chapter 11, where we soup up the scrolling algorithm to handle the high-speed animation we need in our game.

Platforms

I know, I told you I wasn't going to use the term *platform* anymore, but I can't help it. Platforms are an important part of a side scroller. After all, sprites jump on platforms, and usually they work their way to the end of a level by choosing the right platforms to jump on. Sometimes the platforms move. If you fall

Figure 1.7 *The Quickfire game with the continuous scrolling background.*

off a platform, watch out! You could land in something unpleasant, like a puddle of hot lava.

In creating side scrollers, you don't want to limit yourself to just moving your main sprite along the ground level. Most successful side scrollers use all kinds of platforms like rooftops, ladders, bridges, mountain trails, and so on. Figure 1.8 shows an example of a highly popular game called *Math Rescue,* by Karen Crowther. In this game, the main sprite travels around looking for numbers that were stolen by the troublesome Gruzzles. Notice that in the screens presented in Figure 1.8, a number of platforms are used to enhance the game.

Hand-Eye Coordination

The primary thing that differentiates a side scroller from an adventure game is the hand-eye coordination a player must have. In an adventure game, the player works his way out of a room by finding a key, opening a box, reading a clue, and so on. In this manner a true adventure game is like a puzzle. In a side scroller, the action tends to be fast and furious. The player must move quickly and accurately to avoid hazards and reach his or her destination.

In our game, we'll use the keyboard to control the action of the player. It is also possible to use a joystick to control a side-scroller game. The joystick is a

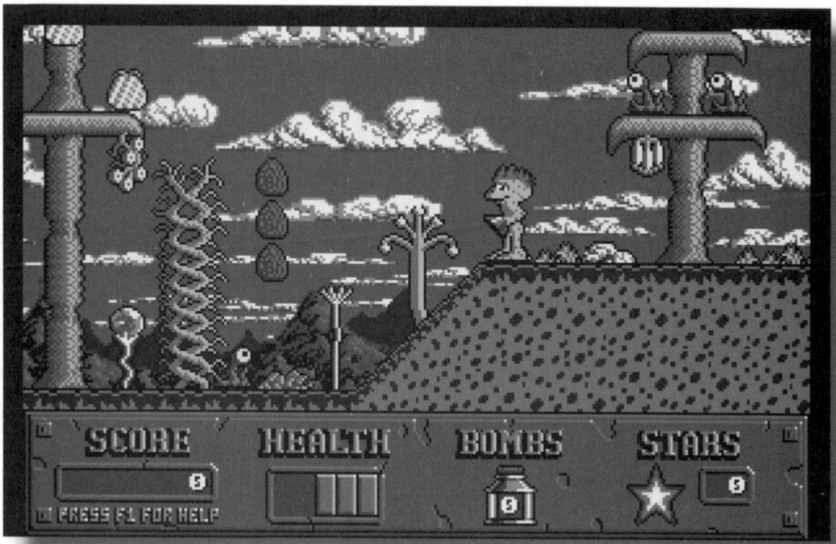

Figure 1.12 *My all-time favorite game, Cosmo.*

Cosmo was pretty, but it was outsold by Todd's other classic Apogee game, *Duke Nukem. Duke Nukem* is a more traditional violent game featuring Duke the war hero blasting his way through post-holocaust Earth. His mission is to stop the evil Dr. Proton and his army of Techbots. This award-winning game remains amazingly popular. Although I'm not a big fan of violence, most of the highly successful games sure have their ample share of it.

Evil mad scientists are a popular theme in Apogee games. In Jim Norwood's *Bio Menace*, a super agent named Snake Logan must battle the evil Doctor Mangle, who is unleashing hideous mutants upon the world. Another popular Apogee theme is zombies. In Frank Madden's *Monster Bash*, a small boy, Johnny Dash, runs a gauntlet of zombies and ghouls in an effort to rescue his pets. Armed with a slingshot, Johnny frees dogs and cats from their ghostly prisons, as he dodges through waterfalls, bounces on sofas, encounters strange and wonderful unworldly critters, and generally has a gleeful time on his spooky quest. Check out some of the level art shown in Figure 1.13 and you'll see what I mean.

Halloween Harry (Figure 1.10), by Sub-Zero Software is another popular zombie game, this time with a twist. Alien invaders have landed in New York City, kidnapping people (especially pretty girls) and turning them into mindless zombies. Harry must rescue the girls from the evil alien clutches, and his reward is watching them fall in love with him as he uses tactical nuclear weapons to set them free. (And you thought Steven King had a wild imagination!)

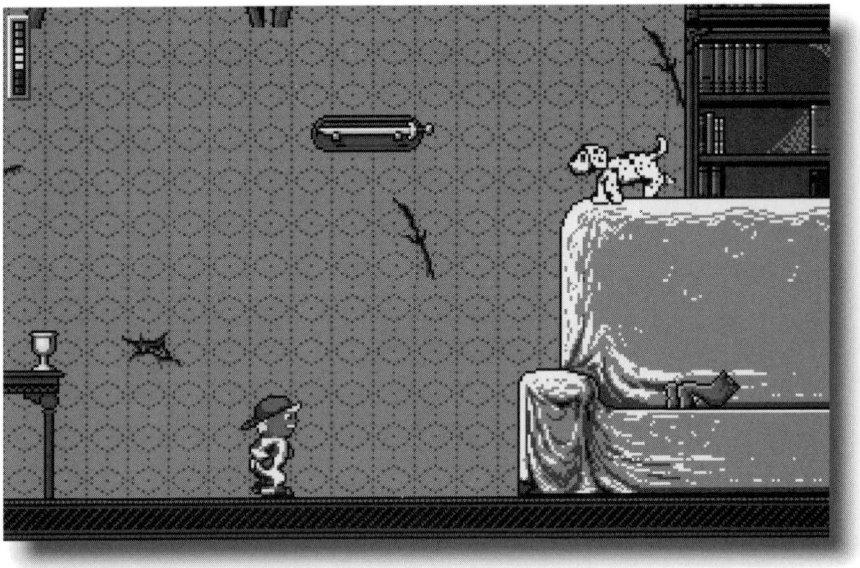

Figure 1.13 *The action packed Monster Bash.*

Not all of Apogee's games are violent in nature. Karen Crowther's games, *Math Rescue* and *Word Rescue*, as shown in Figure 1.14, are classic "edutainment" titles. The addictive quality of the side-scroller genre is used to hook kids into playing a game that is actually good for them. They have so much fun running and jumping their way through different levels, they don't even realize they're learning how to read and do simple arithmetic. These games have been highly successful in a tough market because of the way they were designed. Karen gave the enjoyment factor precedence over the educational element, with the result that kids love them, as do their parents. They are designed to be easy for young fingers, and nobody dies.

Figure 1.14 *Scenes from Word Rescue and Math Rescue.*

The side scrollers Apogee pioneered would probably have been successful in any marketing channel, but Apogee chose to distribute them through shareware, and in the process expand both the gaming industry and the shareware industry. Others have tried to follow in Apogee's footsteps and develop high-quality, side-scrolling games, but so far nobody has been able to duplicate Apogee's success. In later years, Apogee has moved away from side scrollers, in favor of the wildly popular 3-D games. *Wolfenstein 3D*, developed by Id and published by Apogee, set another standard, and Apogee continues to move forward into new technologies.

Personally, I'm nostalgic for the glory days of side scrollers. In my opinion, they have more to offer than 3-D games. The artwork is prettier, the story lines are more interesting, the characters are more lovable, and there is more variety in the levels. I find 3-D games to be vaguely repetitive, as if there are only a finite number of new ideas available; and someday soon, all those ideas will have been explored. Side scrollers, on the other hand, hold the keys to infinite new worlds of action and mystery. There will always be a new level to explore, another monster to fight, another puzzle to solve. I like being able to see the character's face, and I like to see other emotions expressed besides bloodlust. When the current craze for 3-D games dies down, I think we'll see a resurgence of side scrollers as gamers recognize the unlimited creative potential of the genre.

Built for Success

What makes side scrollers so successful? Is it the dazzling graphics, the heart thumping music, the engrossing (and sometimes ridiculous) story lines? Not exactly. Other types of games have great music and graphics, but they do not have the playability of side scrollers. There must be something about the design of side-scrolling games themselves that makes them so addicting.

What is the objective when we play a side scroller game? Is it to beat all the levels and win the game? I don't think so. After all, once we beat the game, we stop playing it, and the fun is over. So that can't be the primary goal. In fact, if we beat the game right away, we tend to get disappointed. We don't want to stop playing the game, we want to keep playing it for a long time. We want to participate in the imaginary world the game creates for us. We want to be part of that world, and revisit it again and again. So the goal is not to beat the game, but rather to play it over and over to the point of failure.

Why is that fun? It doesn't sound like a logical way to enjoy ourselves. Repeated failure sounds more discouraging than entertaining. Yet we keep going back and doing it again. Perhaps what we're trying to achieve is a personal best. We "win" each time we beat our previous high score. As we improve our skill, we move closer and closer to the end of the game. The game becomes more exciting in the higher levels. The experience of reaching the higher levels gives us a sense of accomplishment.

When we finally do reach the end of the game, the challenge is gone. We'll miss the hours we spent trying to beat the game. We'll miss the character we were playing as well. We got to know the character pretty well over all those hours of playing and failing and dying, and we're not quite ready to let go yet. In fact, we might miss the character so much that we'll shell out more money for another episode, if one is available.

So, what makes a side scroller so addicting? Perhaps it's the element of suspense. Each level is a whole new world. We can't wait to finish a level to see what the next one is going to look like. If the bad guys at the end of a level are especially gruesome, it makes you wonder what the bad guys are going to look like at the next level. Each level introduces new tiles, new enemies, new paths to follow, and new plot twists. Like a good book that you can't put down, you find yourself dying to see what is going to happen next. This feeling of anticipation keeps us coming back for more.

So the successful side scroller combines the elements of hand-eye coordination, competition, endless variety, anticipation, and suspense into a formula that perhaps we don't completely understand, but we know it works. Side scrollers are universally popular, and have become a standard among game-playing aficionados around the world.

Introducing Tommy and His Adventures

For the purposes of our discussion, we'll be dissecting a game called *Tommy's Adventures*. As mentioned previously, this is not a complete game, it's a template game developed to demonstrate the functions of the game engine. Figure 1.15 shows the different components that are provided for this game. Here you get two levels, a collection of sprites, a title screen, and an animated status screen.

As you can see, *Tommy's Adventures* has many of the key elements of a side-scroller game. It has scrolling backgrounds with platforms that are composed of tiles, it has sprites, and it has a main character sprite (Tommy), who you control with the keyboard. It also has enemy sprites that move independently and try to attack Tommy.

Tommy is a young boy about eight years old with a punk haircut and a black leather jacket. He's resourceful beyond his age, however. He's apparently accomplished at martial arts, being able to deck a giant grasshopper

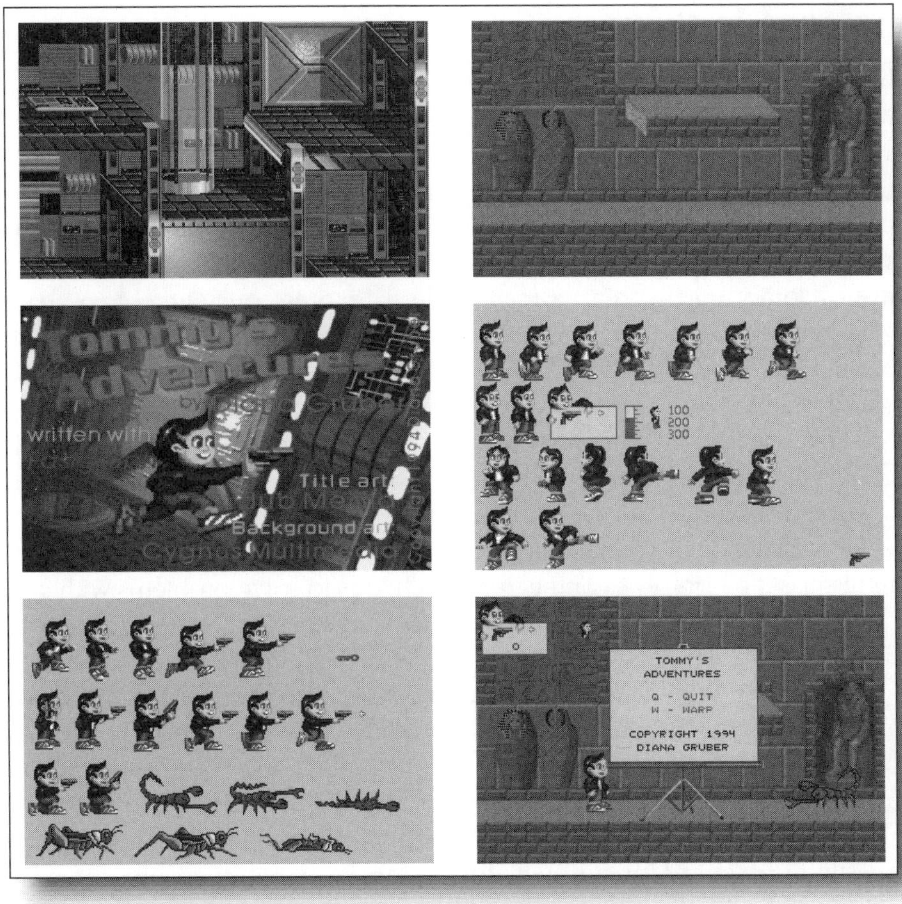

***Figure 1.15** The complete kit for elements of Tommy's Adventures.*

with a single-well-aimed spin kick. Since he doesn't always want to get close enough to his enemies to deliver a deadly kick, he also packs a gun.

This scenario is typical of side scrollers. Characters are designed to be endearing and empowered. A successful character is not somebody we could be, but somebody we imagine we want to be. A hip youngster strikes a chord in us. Who wouldn't want to dabble with green hair dye and shock the establishment? Tommy does things adults can't do. He has no apparent source of income, no bedtime, and no responsibilities. He dresses like James Dean. He dismisses danger with a shrug and a grin. These elements of the rebel hero appeal to us as game players. For a few minutes, or a few hours, we can play the game and become Tommy.

Violence in Games

The paradox of a kid with a gun shouldn't present us with any problems. It gives us the best of both worlds—a character we can love, and the ability to shoot things.

Like it or not, game players love to shoot things. With all the current controversy about violence in video games, it remains an undisputed fact that games containing violence sell well. The public craves them. It apparently satisfies some urge within us to be able to express our aggression against computer-generated foes. Tommy does not negotiate with his enemies. He does not placate them with gifts. He does not wait to see if their intentions are honorable. He sees them and shoots them, and by extension we see our problems and eliminate them swiftly and unambiguously. That simple reality is pretty far removed from the reality of everyday life, where problems must be worked out more carefully, often with less satisfying results.

The prevalence of violence in games is a complex subject. I don't think we can dismiss it by simply saying games teach kids to solve problems with guns. For one thing, it's obvious adults are buying and playing these games. And I think the adults who play them are well aware that guns don't solve problems in real life. But who hasn't had a yearning for simpler solutions? After a hard day at work, and the pressures of daily living, wouldn't it be a relief to go home and just shoot something? Expressing that urge on the computer is preferable to kicking the cat or yelling at the kids. It is also more fun.

I don't want to take sides in the controversy over violent games, because I honestly don't know for sure which side is right. Violent games may not be particularly healthy for children, but the bottom line is money—in the current market, violent games sell. I think there are certain levels of violence that sell better than others. Extremes in either direction do not seem to work as well. A truly gory game will turn off a significant portion of the audience, as will a totally non-violent game. *Tommy's Adventures* contains a medium level of violence, which is stylized, cartoon-type violence. Tommy is not shooting at other people, and he is not shooting at anything lovable. We wouldn't want Tommy to shoot at koala bears, for example. Tommy is shooting at giant insects, which are perceived to have no human emotions. I think this is key in game violence. You should shoot at things that are inhuman. That's why so many games contain mutants, aliens, robots, and zombies. When you shoot at a non-human enemy, you are not killing a sympathetic character. You are merely eliminating an emotionless hazard, so you do not need to feel remorse. This level of violence seems to be well accepted in the mainstream side scrollers.

Enough said about violence; let's go create our game.

Chapter 2

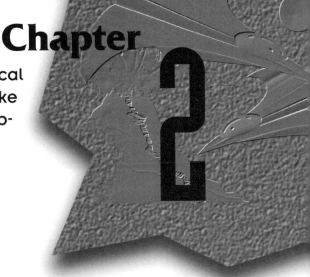

What is the mindset of the typical game programmer? Thinking like a gamer will speed the development process.

Let the Games Begin

As we begin our descent into the netherworld of game development lore, it is important to remember there is more to game development than programming. A computer game is not just a program, it is a software product. That means it needs all the auxiliary details of a marketable product—artwork, design, user appeal, documentation, packaging, and a marketing plan. We're going to touch on some of these issues in this chapter, and in Chapters 17 and 18. I've written this chapter to give you a good working overview of the key areas of game development. First, we'll look at some basic techniques for designing side scrollers, then we'll explore the game development tools that we'll be creating in this book in a little more detail. Then, we'll discuss some general game development strategies. In the next chapter, I'll introduce the complete Fastgraph Game Editor, which is used to process artwork for importing into your game.

As you read this book, keep in mind that the successful game developer must wear many hats and perform many jobs. Besides writing awesome code, you must also be good at collecting (and often modifying) artwork and music. You must be able to design levels and transition screens, and write a captivating storyline. You also need to thoroughly test your game, not just for bugs but for playability.

Incorporating all these elements into the game is a challenge, especially if you've never done it before. Sometimes you can get help—you may hire someone to compose your music or draw your sprites, for example. But to successfully bring a product to market, you must understand and be involved in all the aspects of game design.

Creating Side Scrollers

From a programming standpoint, there are two parts to the game development process. The first, and most obvious part, is writing the code for the game. Most of us start there—we dive in and try to get some kind of prototype of the game up and running right away. This strategy works great for some kinds of games, but when it comes to side scrollers, we soon discover many things slow us down. We need the artwork before we can write the animation code. Then, once we get the artwork, we must organize it in a format that can be used by the game. Organizing the artwork is a tedious process—backgrounds must be reduced to tiles, sprites must be stored in binary files, palettes in one picture must match those in another picture. By the time we get that organized, weeks have passed and we still haven't built the game prototype yet. About this time we realize we have approached the problem wrong—instead of starting with the game, we should have started with the development tools.

A suite of efficient development tools is an essential element in developing side-scroller games. Your work will be greatly simplified if you have tools to do the repetitive tasks of processing artwork for you. The better you become at finding or writing development tools, the better and faster you'll be at developing games. Because I believe the development tools are so important to the game development process, I am going to spend a lot of time discussing them in the next few chapters.

This book is organized so that the tools come first, then the game code. But in my experience, things don't usually work that way. In real life, I find that games and tools tend to be developed simultaneously. Sometimes you will not discover you need a particular tool until you are well into writing your game. When that happens, you need to stop working on the game and write the necessary tool. A professional game developer will be adept at creating tools, and will be able to hack out a simple utility in no time flat. The tools presented in this book will get you off to a good start, and you should be able to use the ideas presented here to build more tools.

The Tools of the Trade

While some tools can be bought "off the shelf," the tools we're going to need most are not available in any commercial package. Therefore, we will have to build them as we need them. If this task sounds daunting, it is. However, I will give you plenty of code to get you started. Most of this code is incorporated into one program, which I call the Fastgraph Game Editor, or FGE.EXE. We will examine both how to use the game editor and how the editor is constructed. An overview of the game editor code is presented in the next section.

Overview of the Game Editor Code

The Fastgraph Game Editor consists of five components:

- File Manager
- Level Editor
- Tile Editor
- Tile Ripper
- Sprite Editor

All of the .C and .H files needed to compile and link the editor are shown in Table 2.1.

Table 2.1 *The Source Files Used in the Game Editor*

File	Description
EDITDEFS.H	Main header file containing the declarations and definitions
FONT5.H	Header file containing data for bitmapped fonts
CHAR.C	Code for displaying bitmapped fonts
COMMON.C	Commonly used functions including initializations
FGE.C	Main source code file for Fastgraph Game Editor
LEVEL.C	Level editor code
MENU.C	Menu code (controls the user interface)
RIPPER.C	Tile ripper code
SPRITE.C	Sprite editor code
TILE.C	Tile editor code

Tommy's Tip

Compiling and Linking the Game Editor

If you make any changes to any of these files, you'll need to recompile and link the files. In general, to rebuild the program FGE.EXE, all you need to do is compile all the .C files, and link them together. You will need to link with the Fastgraph large model library, which is called FGL.LIB (or the Fastgraph/Light large model library which is called FGLL.LIB). To simplify the process, I have included batch files on the disk to use with current versions of the following compilers:

- Borland C++
- Turbo C/C++
- Microsoft C/C+
- Microsoft Visual C++

Run the batch files to compile and link all the source code. If you prefer, you can create project files and make files as appropriate. See the release notes on the disk for more information.

Overview of the Game Code

The game engine has two parts, the game editor, and a template for the game. Our game template is called *Tommy's Adventures.* The source code files for *Tommy's Adventures* are listed in Table 2.2.

Table 2.2 *The Source Files Used in the Game Engine*

File	Description
GAMEDEFS.H	Main header file containing declarations and definitions
FONT5.H	Header file containing data for bitmapped fonts
ACTION.C	Code for action functions needed to perform sprite animation (this file is embedded in the TOMMY.C code using the #include preprocessor directive)
CHAR.C	Code for displaying bitmapped fonts
EFFECTS.C	Code to produce special effects
MAP.C	Code to load levels, display and process tiles, and scroll backgrounds
MOTION.C	Code for supporting sprite animation and collision detection
TIMER.ASM	Code to speed up clock interrupts
TIMER.OBJ	Assembled TIMER.ASM
TOMMY.C	Main game code, including the code to initialize and load sprites and levels

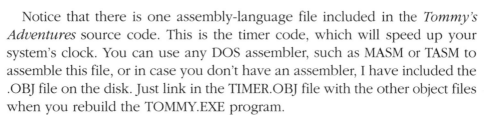

Notice that there is one assembly-language file included in the *Tommy's Adventures* source code. This is the timer code, which will speed up your system's clock. You can use any DOS assembler, such as MASM or TASM to assemble this file, or in case you don't have an assembler, I have included the .OBJ file on the disk. Just link in the TIMER.OBJ file with the other object files when you rebuild the TOMMY.EXE program.

Also, notice that ACTION.C is not compiled by itself, but is included as part of TOMMY.C, using the **#include** preprocessor directive. Briefly, this is done because we need to address the action functions as integer pointers, so they must reside in the same code segment as the functions that call them. We'll discuss this in detail in Chapters 12 and 13.

As with the game editor, batch files for compiling and linking the game are included on the disk, and instructions for using the different compilers are in the release notes.

A Labor of Love

What is the profile of a typical game developer? You must be dedicated, diligent, determined, and just slightly *deranged.* And hopefully your only motivation isn't to make a lot of money writing best-selling games. Game programming is a crazy field that takes a lot of creative energy and a desire to push the boundaries of traditional software development. It takes a sort of crazy genius to be successful at writing games, and if you don't start out that way, be warned, it's the way you are likely to end up.

If I haven't scared you off with that last paragraph, read on, and enter the marvelous world of side-scroller game development.

The Ten Steps to Development Success

So you probably now have a few ideas of your own and you're anxious to start writing your own side scroller. Maybe you've even sketched out a few levels or sprites on a napkin. But before you start writing code for your game, you'll want to make sure that you have a good master plan for the complete development process. Here is my top ten list, which should help to put you on the right track:

1. Make sure you have a good story.

As we learned in the previous chapter, side scrollers work best when they are designed around a great story. If you are not a great story writer, get together with someone who is. If you have a good story, your levels and sprites will fall out naturally. The plot in the story will help keep the game focused and heighten the player's interest. Let's explore an example.

One of my favorite games is Karen Crowther's *Math Rescue.* If you remember from the previous chapter, this is a kid's game that involves searching for numbers and then answering math problems. For this game, Karen came up with the following clever story to start out the game:

> A bone-chilling crisis has struck the world! Reports are pouring in from all corners of the globe: missing numbers! Numbers were missing from speed limit signs and the frantic highway patrolmen couldn't stop speeders. On Wall Street, stock brokers were throwing up their hands in despair. The Dow Jones wasn't down, and it wasn't up, it was gone!
>
> Your own mother has closed herself in the bathroom and won't come out because her paycheck is inexplicably blank. You start to call your best friend, but the buttons on your phone are blank, and you can't remember your friend's number! Where will it end?
>
> Glancing out the window, you suddenly freeze with horror. A creature that looks like a giant nose with arms is standing in your driveway! It's stealing the numbers off your street address and loading them into a robot controlled garbage truck! Speechless with shock and rage, you point a quivering finger...
>
> Before you can say "mystic intervention," a huge butterfly appears in the air and dumps a bucket of slime on the nose. In a flash, the nose disappears! You have discovered the secret to stopping the number stealers! Grabbing a nearby garbage can lid for protection, and hoping the butterfly will continue to help you, you embark on your mission to recover the stolen numbers and outwit the mysterious aliens.
>
> Yes, the fate of the world as we know it is in your hands!

As Figure 2.1 shows, the game even starts out with a screen that introduces the story line to the player before they start to play the game. This story works well because it helps set the stage for the adventures to come.

2. Plan out your levels in advance.

Once you have a good story in mind, start to plan out your levels. The levels should expand and enhance the storyline. You will want to have many levels in your game, perhaps between 10 and 30. These levels should somehow fit together and make sense in the context of the story. If Tommy suddenly warps from an Egyptian pyramid to a spaceship, you need to explain why. The explanation should be fairly simple—the pyramid was built by aliens, for example, or Tommy's dad has built a time travel machine. Remember, game players don't want to read a story, they want to act it out. Let the story unfold naturally as the levels progress.

You also need to think in terms of finding a creative balance between level variety and conserving artwork and disk space. If you have very elaborate levels, you will need to have fewer of them (unless you are writing a CD-ROM

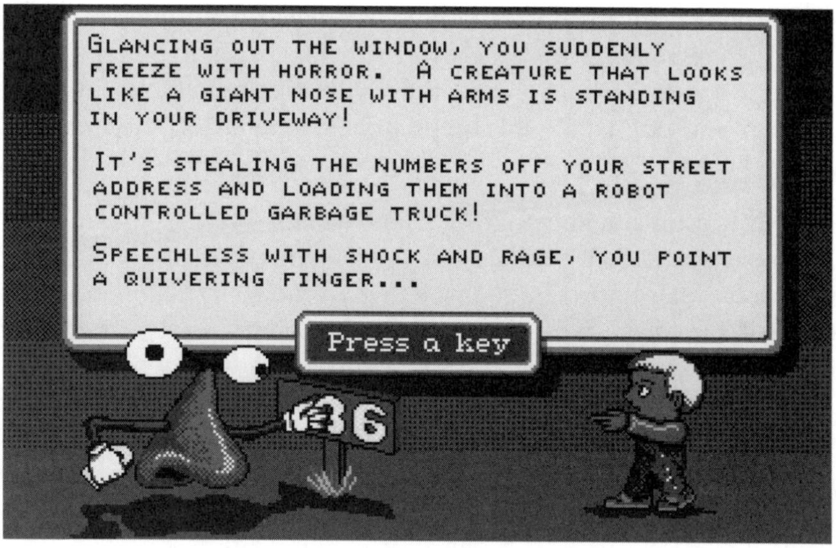

Figure 2.1 *The story introduced in the Math Rescue game.*

game, in which you'll have plenty of room for anything and everything). One way to conserve level space is to use the same tile library for more than one level. You can have two Egyptian levels for Tommy, for example, one inside a pyramid and the other inside a sphinx. Tommy encounters different sprite enemies on each level, and a must find a different path out, so the levels are unique and challenging, but the background art looks about the same.

3. Spend as much time as possible on your main character (sprite). You want to develop a main character sprite your players can identify with. They will be spending a lot of time with this character as they move him around the levels and try to keep him alive. Developing this character is more difficult than you might think. If you work with an artist, you will need to describe the character to him, in terms of his age, sex, hairstyle, facial characteristics, clothes, and personality. Your artist will probably give you back a character that looks nothing like you imagined him. At this point, you may need to modify the character yourself. Use a paint program or sprite editor to give your character the right look. Then give it back to your artist and let him touch it up. This process may require several iterations to get it just right. Once you have achieved the desired look for your main character, you will need all the different sprite positions for him—the running frames, jumping frames, shooting frames, and so on. It will take your artist a while to get this work done, so you better begin the sprite development process early in the game development cycle.

In some games, you may want to give the player the choice of selecting from a few different characters. Kids especially like to have different options. For example, the *Math Rescue* game allows you to choose between a boy or girl character. You can handle this by providing a character selection screen, as shown in Figure 2.2.

4. Don't skimp on the supporting cast.

Although the main character can make or break your game, the other characters are important also. Design enemies that are not only scary looking, but responsive. If possible, give them artificial intelligence—have them follow you, for example, or duck when you shoot at them. Also, put some creativity into killing enemies. In *Commander Keen: Goodbye Galaxy*, there are small dangerous bats that swarm around your head and occasionally land on the path in front of you. The only way to kill them is to squash them with your pogo stick. This action is not obvious, it takes a while to figure it out. (And I still haven't figured out how to get away from the giant fish!)

Enemy sprites are a bit easier to develop than the main character sprite, because they require fewer sprite frames (perhaps only three or four) and because they are not required to have the emotional impact of the main character. Usually it is a good idea to give your artist some creative license when working with the enemy sprites. Let your artist draw several different enemies, and choose the ones you like best.

Figure 2.2 *Selecting a character in the Math Rescue game.*

5. Plan keyboard control carefully.

Too many keystrokes will confuse your players. There should be one key to shoot, another one to jump, and possibly one more to kick or throw a punch. In addition to these designations, you should use the arrow keys to move your character around, the Esc key to provide a quick exit from the game, and the F1 key to access online help. That's about it. Do not expect the player to remember more keys than that. Requiring a player to press a combination of two or more keys to accomplish a simple task is a recipe for disaster. *Keep your keyboard interface as simple as possible.*

6. Find unique solutions to common problems.

Game designers use visual devices to represent certain events. The problem is, gamers use the same devices over and over. A successful game will incorporate new ideas for solving common problems. Examples of some common problems are:

- **The Key/Door Problem**—Exiting from a level involves finding a door (location on the level) and a key (device or event required before the door can be opened). In *Word Rescue*, the player is awarded a key when he finds all the words, and then must proceed to a door. That solution is so common it has become cliché. In *Goodbye Galaxy*, the key is replaced by a crystal, which is also a very common device. In other games, the key may be rescuing a scientist or defeating a boss enemy. Since most levels require unlocking some kind of door to exit, we need to find some new metaphorical keys. Use your imagination, but please, come up with something new.
- **The Longevity Problem**—Main characters have a finite amount of energy. The energy level goes up and down, depending on what hazards are encountered and what rewards are achieved. Often you will see some kind of visual health meter that graphically displays the amount of energy a character has left. When the character finds food (usually the same old hamburger and soda pop), the energy goes up. When he touches an enemy, the energy goes down.

  Can we come up with a new metaphor? In real life, people do not walk around with an energy meter that flows up and down. This device is so common (it is even in our *Tommy's Adventures* game) yet so completely nonsensical, it seems like we should be able come up with something a bit more original.

  An example of an uncommon energy device is the lamp in the popular *Aladdin* game. As Aladdin's energy goes down, the smoke wafting out of the lamp decreases. To make his energy go back up, Aladdin finds blue hearts. This is still nonsensical solution, but at least a little different.

7. Add some surprises.

Did you know you can make Commander Keen drop his pants in the Pyramid of the Moons? (You didn't hear that from me.) Players love stuff like that. When they play your game, they want to see things they have never seen before. Unusual enemies, hidden clues, secret rooms, special effects, humorous segues, and puzzles with non-obvious solutions are the special touches that will set your game apart from the rest. When it comes to game design, don't be afraid to try something new.

8. Conserve everything.

I will be stressing this point throughout this book. Plan on conserving disk space, RAM, video memory, code, array space, stack space, machine cycles, artwork, and everything else. If there are two solutions to a problem, choose the one that is less resource intensive. If you can re-use array space, do so. Similarly, re-use artwork whenever possible. Modern games can quickly become unwieldy, and the professional game developer will use every trick under the sun to keep things under control.

9. Don't take shortcuts with the beta test cycle.

Beta testers, also known as play testers, are an essential part of the game development process. Recruit and reward competent beta testers. One of the best rewards you can give a beta tester is to take the suggestions offered seriously.

10. Set time aside for the finishing touches.

Okay your game is done; everything works and the art looks great so you're ready to unleash it on the world. Stop right there. You still have work to do if you want to create a truly great game. Don't think of your game in terms of a program, think of it as a product. As I mentioned earlier, there is more to the game than just the code. Be sure you have all the elements of a complete product before you release your game. Don't skimp on documentation. Animate your transition screens. Use an attractive font. Pay attention to the details, and give your game a polished, professional look. I will give you more tips for finishing your game in Chapter 17.

Notes about Working with Other People

If you try to create a game completely by yourself, you might be limiting your chances for success. Most developers I know work in teams or they contract out part of their development tasks. For example, a developer might hire another programmer to write development tools, or two programmers may work together as partners to develop a game, each bringing some unique skills that make the game better than either one of them could do alone.

Cooperation speeds up the development process, and also usually results in a better product. There are some potential pitfalls, though. Be careful about choosing a partner to work with, and make sure the responsibilities and rewards of each partner are understood in advance. I have seen partnerships break up after both partners have invested heavily in developing a game. Try to foresee problems and protect yourself.

I have also seen successful teams that consist of one programmer and one non-programmer. The non-programmer may do the creative work of level design, artwork, packaging, marketing, and user support. Sometimes husbands and wives form this kind of a team, and it works out well. Be careful of forming a team where one person does all the development work and the other person is in charge of only "marketing." In my experience, such teams tend to be unbalanced. If you are capable of developing a really good game, you can always find someone to help you market it, but you do not need to make that person a full partner in your business. If you explore your options, you will probably find a more cost-effective way of getting the marketing done. As your company grows, you may decide to hire a marketing person, but that decision should be made carefully.

Keeping Secrets

Some developers are very secretive about what they do. They'll share information with each other, but only after certain dues have been paid. For example, if you've proven yourself worthy by releasing a game, then others will give you inside information. This information is not to be released to outsiders, however. To do so would risk saturating the market with low-end games, and diluting the value of any individual game.

Non-disclosure agreements (NDAs) are standard among gamers. In some circles, it's considered standard operating procedure to exchange NDAs before talking about anything. For example, before I let you see my new game, you must sign a paper that says you'll never tell anybody what you've seen. Similarly, if you give me a glimpse at your source code, I'll also sign an NDA for you. Only then will we whisper our secrets to each other, making sure nobody else is within earshot. The only way we'll find out about a competitor's technology is by espionage; and once we get it, we won't give it to anybody else. So even as the insider pool of knowledge increases, we discourage newcomers from entering the field. We protect our interests that way.

Must it always be like that? No, not really, and the gaming arena is starting to change. Despite the best efforts of the pioneers, new game programmers *have* entered the playing field. This new generation approaches the market differently. They are not as tight-lipped as their predecessors. They are less concerned with protecting the marketplace, and more concerned with furthering the technology. As the market has evolved, more programmers are beginning to discuss their methods in public forums. As a result, the market has expanded, and so has the number of titles available. A few development houses have released the top-selling titles, and hundreds of other developers have released less popular, but still marketable, games. The market has become flooded with titles, but it's turned out to be not such a bad thing. There are games available to suit almost any player's preferences. Every niche of the market is receiving coverage. The game market is expanding to fill every nook and cranny, and the players are emerging as the big winners.

There is still, however, some information that is not easy to get access to. While game programmers are less hesitant about sharing their information than they used to be, they are just as busy as ever. Not many game programmers worth their salt are writing books about game programming, because they're too busy programming games. You can find out how a game programmer does it by asking him questions on CompuServe or other networks, and he may tell you, but he'll be too busy to tell you in any detail. To really explain how to write a game, it takes a whole book—like this one, for example.

The Zen of Game Development

When I was first approached with the idea of writing a game programming book, my editor, Jeff Duntemann, suggested that I write a book for his popular *Zen* series—something like *Zen of Game Programming.* I don't think of myself as a Zen Master or a "Zen Mistress" for that matter, so the idea didn't really grab me. Actually, I'm not sure what a Zen Master is. My impression of a little old man who spends his life pondering the meaning of the sound of one hand clapping is probably not very accurate.

I think the idea behind "Zen programming" is that we programmers tend to develop a philosophy for writing software, and we train ourselves to think in ways that improve the development process. Game developers, especially, need to develop good habits, and need to understand why they write games the way they do. Some of these habits are inherent. Some game programmers are even born with them. Other habits are a bit more subtle. So here are some of my thoughts on the Zen of game development:

To begin with, game development should focus on beauty, speed, and functionality, but not necessarily all of those things at the same time. You need to know when to optimize, when to beautify, and when to hack out code in a hurry.

Allocate your time wisely. If it takes you a week to write a utility that shaves a month off your development cycle, then that's a good investment of your development time. If you spend a month optimizing and beautifying that utility, then it's a waste of time.

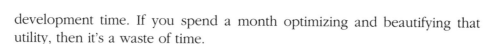

Write re-usable code. Volumes can be written on this subject, but I think most programmers need to develop a feel for how to design re-usable code. In general, write modular code. Don't mix general-purpose code with code that is specific to the current project. Plan on being able to use the general-purpose code again. Also, be careful about hard-coding values in your code. It may be smarter to declare and initialize a variable or define a term that can be easily changed later.

Think of creative ways to make the computer work for you. Any time you find yourself doing a repetitive task, such as editing artwork, ask yourself, "Could I write a program to automate this task?"

Know when to use other people's code. Sometimes writing code from scratch will actually take less time than deciphering somebody else's code. Third party libraries can be useful, but only if properly used. A low-level library such as Fastgraph will shave months off your development cycle. A GUI or string-handling library may be helpful under some circumstances, but in general you should get in the habit of writing most of your high-level code yourself. If you depend too much on third party libraries, you'll be limited by the functionality of those libraries, and you may not be able to achieve all the special effects you want.

Don't reinvent the wheel. There are only so many ways to write a good set of fast bitmap display routines. If you spend six months optimizing your bitmap function, that's six months you have not spent writing your game. Try to find the proper mix of third party code and your own code to speed up the development cycle without limiting your development options.

Develop good coding habits. Develop a coding style where lines of code are indented consistently. This will make debugging easier. Use comments liberally. Organize and alphabetize your functions. Use header files where appropriate. Pretend that someone like me is going to look at your code. If you give me sloppy code to look at, I can be very critical. I much prefer to look at clean code.

Start small. The first game you write should not be your most ambitious. I don't recommend that people invest two years in their first game. Invest a few months in a less ambitious project, and release it through shareware or low-cost retail channels. Release several simple games before you embark on your masterpiece. Everybody makes mistakes on their path to game development success; you want to make your mistakes on the small investment projects. Once you have a feel for the market, for your tools, and your skills and abilities, you'll be more likely to be successful with your games.

Know where you're going, but be aware that there are multiple paths to get there. Expect your finished product to look somewhat different than your original design. Don't over-design your product, just give yourself general guidelines and then allow room for inspiration as the project progresses. A lot of game programming is done by trial and error. What looks good on paper may not feel right once implemented. Play your game, then let others play your game, and pay attention to their feedback. If a certain part of your game doesn't feel right, abandon it and try something else.

Don't waste time in the design process. Some code requires design documents, but sometimes design documents are a waste of time. Know the difference.

Interact with other game programmers. Nobody functions well in a vacuum. Online forums dedicated to the subject of game development are abundant. Find one you're comfortable with, and then discuss your game and any problems you may be having. Don't be afraid to help other game developers. Don't think of the other developers as your competitors, think of them as your colleagues. Furthering the industry by sharing information benefits everyone. As I said earlier, open communication is the whole premise of this book.

Writing the last 10 percent of a game takes approximately the same amount of time to complete as the first 90 percent. I don't know why, but I've seen this happen over and over. When you think you are 90-percent done, you are probably really about half way. Plan your release date accordingly. Try not to stretch out that last 10 percent. Know when to wrap up your game and call it finished. You can always find *something* to tweak. Acting on this impulse may keep your game at home and not on the market.

Pay attention to the final details. When knitting a sweater, the finishing touches make the difference between a sweater that is "homemade" and one that is "handmade." Similarly, the finishing touches on a game will make the difference between a game that is done by amateurs and one that is done by professionals. Pay attention to everything that is important; the documentation, labeling, packaging, and overall presentation will have a major impact on the salability of your game. Remember, first impressions count.

Take pride in your career as a game developer. Game developers are the brightest and the best of computer programmers. They are the most creative, smartest, most admired, and most marketable. Aspiring to be a game developer is a worthy ambition for any young person, and achieving that goal is the proof of maturity.

Feel good about yourself. You are contributing to the cultural wealth of the human race.

Chapter 3

This chapter explores the heart of the matter, the game editor. This tool incorporates five utilities to help you construct your games.

Using the Game Editor

Many years ago, some time after dinosaurs roamed the Earth and shortly before the discovery of Deluxe Paint II by Electronic Arts, my husband Ted and I put our first bitmaps into a PC game. We accomplished this feat by drawing the images on graph paper with colored pencils, converting the values to hexadecimal numbers by hand, and then typing the numbers into data arrays. This worked well, but it was slow.

Before you start laughing, realize that this was 1987, the early days of game development. Back then, game developers didn't share many secrets. Computer bulletin boards had barely been invented, and shareware games were just beginning to appear. Retail game companies had developed reasonable technologies, but the developers were tight-lipped about what they had discovered. Few books had been published on how to program graphics and the ones that were available didn't cover important topics such as the recently invented EGA cards. The few magazine articles published on this topic only covered the most basic functions, such as how to set the video mode and draw a pixel. No other sources of information for beginning game programmers were readily available. Our only option was to make things up as we went along, and we stumbled onto discoveries that these days seem quite obvious.

One of our first discoveries was that it takes too darn long to enter bitmap data by hand, and it's boring and error-prone besides. After about a week of typing in numbers, we came up with a bitmap editor. It was a keyboard-driven drawing program. Arrow keys moved the cursor around, function keys changed the colors, and the Esc key saved the work to a bitmap file and exited. It was truly primitive.

We could have improved the "quick-and-dirty" bitmap editor and created an early paint program, but we were more interested in writing games. I continue to believe that the proper way to create development tools is to write them quickly and keep them simple. The bitmap editor was a disposable tool. We soon abandoned it for other methods. We would have wasted our time if we had spent months improving the editor.

As the years passed, our needs have changed and we've written a number of editors (or at least we've extended our editor a number of times). The editor presented in this chapter is our latest creation and it includes a number of features to help you automate and fine tune the process of developing games.

Introducing the Game Editor

There are many useful tools on the market for creating and editing artwork. Paint programs like Deluxe Paint II and NeoPaint are well-suited for drawing and editing backgrounds and sprites. Scanners and scanning software are useful for converting paper images to computer images. Image processors, such as John Wagner's Improces, are useful for cleaning up scanned images and manipulating palettes. Image conversion software, like Steve Rimmer's Graphics Workshop, convert files from one format to another. Animation software, such as Autodesk Animator, is useful in perfecting sprite motion. Usually, game programmers use some of these tools, or some of the many other fine tools available through commercial and shareware channels.

But what is missing is a specialized tool that can help you get all of your art in the formats needed for a side-scroller game.

When creating *Tommy's Adventures*, I discovered I needed a sprite editor, level editor, tile editor, tile ripper, and a file manager. I wrote these tools and put them together in a single program, and I called it a game editor. Because I was planning to develop it for other people to use, I wanted it to look a little nicer than is really necessary. I've included some extra features, such as pop-up help, that you wouldn't usually put in an in-house utility. The game editor is provided on the disk, with complete C source code. If you haven't looked at it yet, I suggest you do so now. (Chapter 2 provides a description of each source code file used in the editor.) The rest of this chapter will show you how to use the key features of the game editor. I've included a number of projects to help you use the editor to perform such tasks as editing levels, working with tiles and sprites, and even adding a level. You can also use the chapter as a reference as you begin developing your own game.

Starting the Editor

The editor is called the Fastgraph Game Editor (FGE). To start the program, go to the directory where the editor has been installed on your hard disk and run this command at the DOS prompt:

```
FGE
```

If you plan to use the editor a lot, you should put the name of the program (FGE.EXE) along with its complete path name in your DOS path so that you won't have to move to the directory where the editor is stored each time you run the editor. The game editor takes full advantage of a mouse so make sure that you have a mouse installed on your PC before running the editor. In fact if you don't have a mouse, you won't be able to run the program.

Figure 3.1 shows what the editor looks like after it starts up. Notice that the program provides a display area and a main menu bar with four menus for selecting commands. The display area is set aside for the editing operations, such as sprite, tile, and level editing.

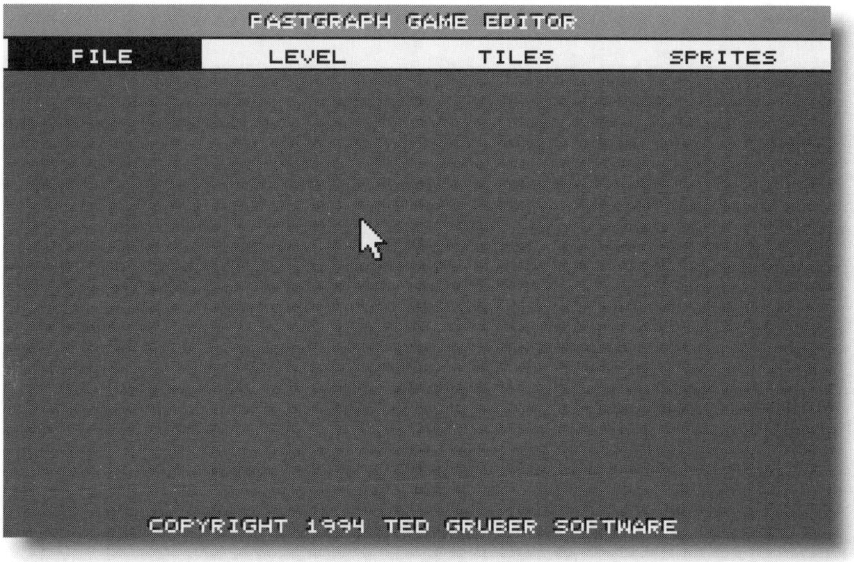

Figure 3.1 *The Fastgraph Game Editor (FGE) ready for action.*

Examining the Game Editor Files

The game editor is distributed on the companion disk in an archived format. You'll find it in the file FGE.ARJ. Use the install program to unarchive the editor, or if you prefer, you may copy it to your hard disk and unarchive it yourself. Robert Jung's program, UNARJ.EXE, has been included on the disk for your convenience. Once the archived distribution is unarchived, you should have the files listed in Table 3.1. These are all of the files needed for the level

Table 3.1 *Files Used with the Game Editor (FGE)*

File	**Description**
FGE.EXE	The FGE program. This is the only file you need to run the game editor. The other files are examples of data files specific to the *Tommy's Adventures* game.
GAME.DAT	An ASCII file containing the number of levels and the filenames for the data files for each level.
EGYPT.LEV	Level data for the Egyptian level. This is a binary file containing the width and height of the level, followed by the background tile indexes and the foreground tile indexes into the EGYPT.PCX file.
EGYPT.PCX	Background tiles for the Egyptian level in a PCX format. This file was generated by the tile ripper. Note, there are no foreground tiles for the Egyptian level.
EGYPT.ATT	Background tile attributes for the Egyptian level. This file was generated by both the level editor and the tile editor.
SPACE.LEV	Level data for the space level.
SPACBACK.PCX	Background and foreground tiles for the space level. (Unlike the Egyptian level, this level contains some foreground tiles.)
SPACBACK.ATT	Background tile attributes for the space level.
SPACFORE.PCX	Foreground tiles for the space level.
SPACFORE.ATT	Foreground tile attributes for the space level.
SPRITE.DAT	The sprite data file. This is an ASCII file containing the filenames of all the sprite list files.
TOMJUMP.LST	Sprite list containing bitmap data for Tommy's jumping frames.
TOMKICK.LST	Sprite list containing bitmap data for Tommy's spin kicking frames.
TOMRUN.LST	Sprite list containing bitmap data for Tommy's running frames.
TOMSCORE.LST	Sprite list containing bitmap data for the scoreboard.
TOMSHOOT.LST	Sprite list containing bitmap data for Tommy's shooting frames.
TOMSTAND.LST	Sprite list containing bitmap data for Tommy's standing frames.
ENEMY.LST	Sprite list containing bitmap data for Tommy's enemies.

data and sprite data that our sample game *Tommy's Adventures* requires. (Remember that the game provides two levels—an Egyptian level and a space platform level—and three types of sprites—Tommy, the scorpion, and the giant grasshopper.) A few of the game files contain graphics information (bitmaps) that can be displayed. For example, Figure 3.2 shows the contents of the three PCX files: EGYPT.PCX, SPACEBACK.PCX, and SPACEFORE.PCX.

Tommy's Tip

Be Careful with Those Files

Keep in mind that the files used by the game editor are the same files used in *Tommy's Adventures.* If you make changes to a file in the editor and save the file, this will effect how the game works. For example, if you edit one of the sprites using the sprite editor, the sprite will appear in the game with your editing changes. I recommend you put the game editor and the game in different subdirectories. That way, if you wipe out a data file, you'll have another copy of it. If you accidentally wipe out both copies of the data file, you can reinstall the game or the game editor from the disk.

Using the Menus

The menu bar in the editor contains the FILE, LEVEL, TILES, and SPRITES menus. Figure 3.3 shows the options available for each of these menus. Let's have a look at the actual menu hierarchy.

Figure 3.2 *Viewing the PCX files used in Tommy's Adventures.*

FILE	LEVEL	TILES	SPRITES
LOAD/SAVE	EDIT	BACKGROUND	EDIT
EXIT	SAVE	FOREGROUND	LOAD
		RIPPER	SAVE

Figure 3.3 *The game editor menu structure.*

Although there are only four menus, they are designed to support the five main parts of the editor (the TILE menu performs double duty):

- The file manager is used for organizing all the files that will be included in the game and selecting the files that should be loaded.
- The level editor is used for editing and saving levels.
- The tile editor is used for generating and modifying foreground and background tiles.
- The tile ripper is used for converting raw level artwork into distinct tiles to create levels.
- The sprite editor is used for saving, loading, organizing, and modifying sprite data.

You select the menu items using the mouse or keyboard. If you use the keyboard, press the arrow keys to navigate through the menus, then press Enter to select a menu item. With the mouse, click on a menu name in the menu bar to open the menu, then move the pointer to the desired menu item and click. Go ahead and experiment with this. As long as you don't save your work, you can try out all the game editor functions without doing any damage.

Using the File Manager

Game files are organized in such a way that they are easy to modify and import into both the game editor and the game. Selecting the LOAD/SAVE option from the game editor FILE menu allows you to view and select the data files. Figure 3.4 shows the information that is displayed when you first select this option. The files that are shown are for our game, *Tommy's Adventures*.

Here you get a complete list of the files used in the game. (The first screen that appears shows the files that are used in the first level. You can view the

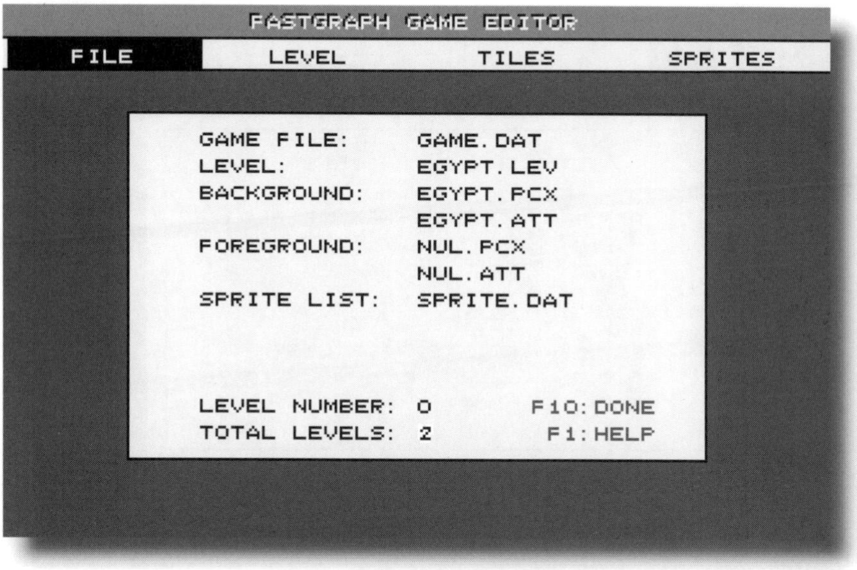

***Figure 3.4** The file status information for Tommy's Adventures.*

files used in the other levels by pressing the PgDn key.) The game file, GAME.DAT, is the primary data file that stores the names of all the other files. We'll explore this file in more detail next. The other files include the level file, the background tile file and its associated attribute file, the foreground tile file and its associated attribute file, and the sprite list file, which specifies the sprites used for this level. Notice that the message box also tells you the current level that is being edited and the number of levels that are used in the game—in this case 2.

In addition to displaying the status information, you can perform a number of operations with the file manager including:

- Selecting a level to edit
- Inserting or deleting a level
- Changing the filenames used in each level (level filename, background tile and attribute filenames, foreground tile and attribute filenames, and sprite list filename)
- Viewing or editing the sprite list used for the selected level
- Loading or saving the GAME.DAT file

The file manager provides hot keys, listed in Figure 3.5, to help you speed along when you are working with a file.

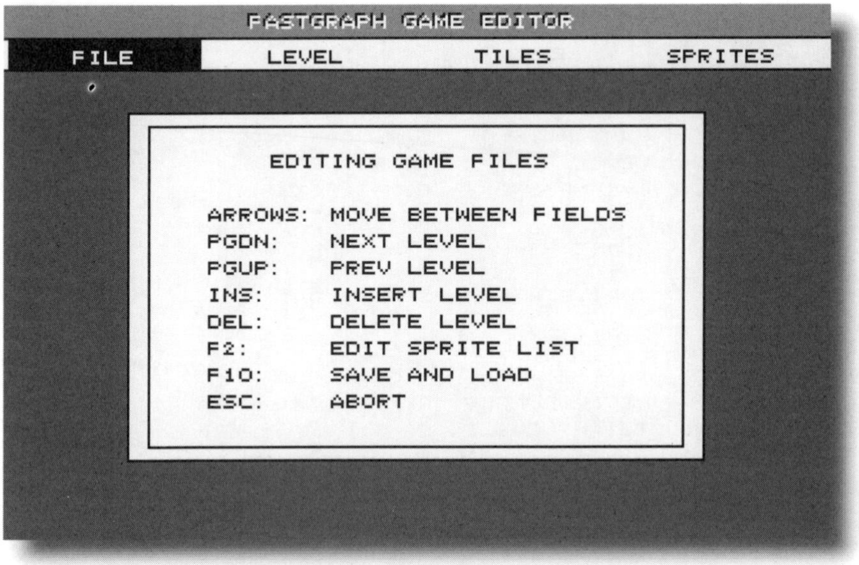

Figure 3.5 *The help screen for the file manager.*

Tommy's Tip

Changing Filenames or Selecting Levels

Whenever you change the names of any of the filenames in the file manager load/save box, or you select a different level by pressing the PgDn or PgUp keys, make sure you press F10 to save your changes and load in the new files into the game editor.

Tommy's Tip

Getting Help on the File Manager

After you've selected the LOAD/SAVE command from the FILE menu, you can get help at any time by pressing F1. Figure 3.5 shows the help screen that is displayed. Here you get a useful summary of all of the hot keys used to control the file manager.

The Game Data File (GAME.DAT)

The file that links everything together in our side-scrolling game is GAME.DAT. This is a text file that you can view and modify with any text editor. You can also use the game editor to modify it. Figure 3.6 shows the organization and contents of the GAME.DAT file for *Tommy's Adventures*.

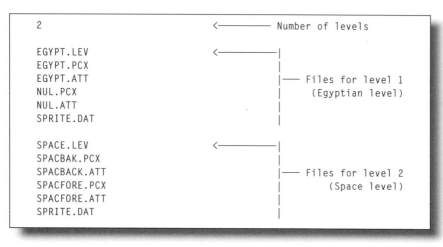

```
2                         <———————— Number of levels

EGYPT.LEV                 <————————|
EGYPT.PCX                          |
EGYPT.ATT                          |—— Files for level 1
NUL.PCX                            |     (Egyptian level)
NUL.ATT                            |
SPRITE.DAT                         |

SPACE.LEV                 <————————|
SPACBAK.PCX                        |
SPACBACK.ATT                       |—— Files for level 2
SPACFORE.PCX                       |        (Space level)
SPACFORE.ATT                       |
SPRITE.DAT                         |
```

Figure 3.6 *The contents of the GAME.DAT file for Tommy's Adventures.*

When a game is started, GAME.DAT is loaded and setup decisions are made based on the contents of the file. This decision making procedure provides you with the ability to make changes to your game, such as modifying or adding a new level, just by changing some of the data files. Of course, most changes also require that you modify your game code. When we look at the source code to our game *Tommy's Adventures* in Chapters 11 through 15, you'll learn how the game data files are loaded and processed in the game.

The integer value on the first line specifies the number of levels used in the game. Since *Tommy's Adventures* provides two levels, this value is set to 2. Following that specification are six filenames for each level. EGYPT.LEV is the level data generated by the level editor for the first level. EGYPT.PCX is the background tiles and EGYPT.ATT is the tile attributes for the background tiles. (You'll learn more about tile and attribute files later in this chapter and in the next chapter.) The next two lines represent the foreground tiles. Since the Egyptian level has no foreground tiles, we've named these files NUL.PCX and NUL.ATT to indicate there are no files for the foreground. The last file for the Egyptian level is SPRITE.DAT. This is the sprite data file that contains the filenames of the sprite lists that are used in the level. We'll explore this file in a moment.

Following the six files for the Egyptian level, are the files for the space level. Again, the pattern is the same. Each time you add a new level, six new entries must be added to the GAME.DAT file.

The Sprite Data File

Like the GAME.DAT file, the sprite data file is a text file that you can edit with any text editor. If you want to edit this file in the game editor, press F2. You'll get a screen with the sprite list filenames, as shown in Figure 3.7. You can edit the filenames on this screen, add new ones, or delete them.

You're now probably wondering how the main sprite data file is organized. Figure 3.8 shows the organization and contents of the SPRITE.DAT file used in *Tommy's Adventures.* Since we are using the same set of sprites for both the Egyptian and space levels, we only need one master sprite data file.

The number on the first line of the sprite data file is the number of the sprite lists used. This number is followed by the filenames containing the

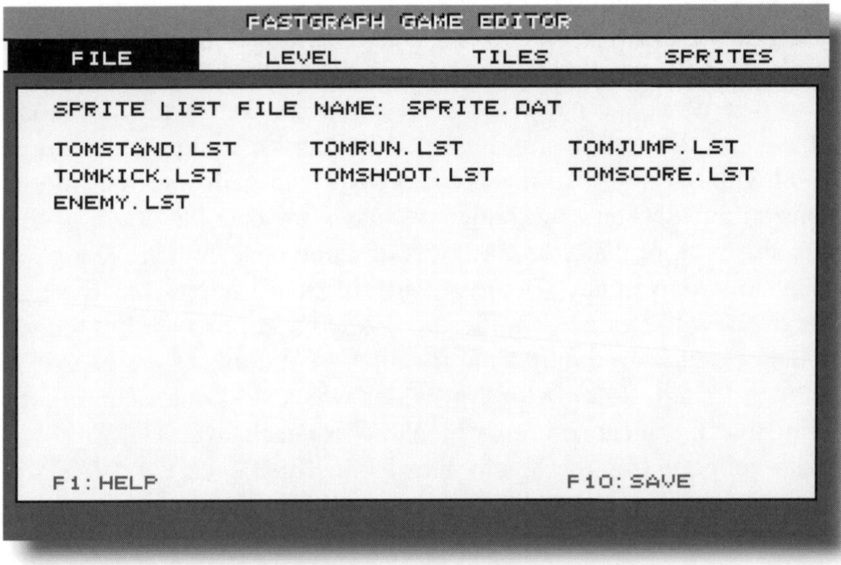

Figure 3.7 *Displaying the sprite list filenames.*

```
7                          <——————— Number of sprite files

TOMSTAND.LST
TOMRUN.LST
TOMJUMP.LST
TOMKICK.LST
TOMSHOOT.LST
TOMSCORE.LST
ENEMY.LST
```

Figure 3.8 *The contents of the SPRITE.DAT file for Tommy's Adventures.*

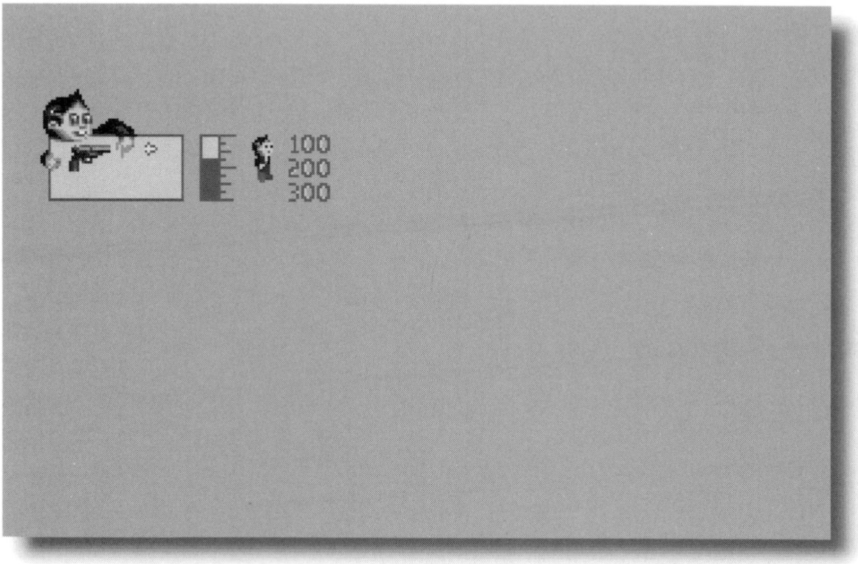

Figure 3.9 The sprite list stored in TOMSCORE.LST.

actual bitmap data for each sprite list. Each sprite list contains data for one or more sprites, and is generated by the sprite editor. For example, Figure 3.9 shows what the bitmap data stored in the TOMSCORE.LST file looks like. This file is considered a sprite list because it contains a sequence of sprites that are stored as a list. Notice that all of the different individual sprites are included in this file to create a score keeper for the game.

When you add new sprites to your game, you'll need to update the sprite data file. In the case of *Tommy's Adventures*, you'll need to add the new sprite LST files to SPRITE.DAT. You also must update the code in your game when you add or delete a sprite.

Viewing Sprites in the Sprite List

Let's use the sprite editing features of the game editor to view the actual sprites stored in one of the sprite list (LST) files. Here are the steps to follow:

1. Run the editor (FGE).
2. Click on the SPRITES menu and select the LOAD option.
3. In the list of files that appear, press the arrow keys to select one of the LST files. (When a file is selected, the blinking cursor will be next to its name.) Select TOMJUMP.LST and press Enter.

4. The sprite editor will appear and you'll see the first sprite in the list, as shown in Figure 3.10. Click on the Next command to view the next sprite in the list. (You can also move backwards by clicking on the Prev command.)
5. When you get to the end of the sprite list, the sprite editor will show a blank sprite. Click on Quit to return to the main game editor menu.

Tips on Managing Your Files

As you can see, it takes a lot of data files to create a game. Together, figures 3.6 and 3.8 list 19 files, and these don't even include music and sound effects. It's easy to see how a game with many levels could require 100 or more files. Since some of the files are very small, we're wasting disk space. DOS allocates disk space in clusters, and cluster size is a multiple of the sectors. As shown in Figure 3.11, sectors are always 512 bytes and clusters vary according to the disk type. A cluster may take from one to eight sectors. That means a 100-byte file would take up 4K on a hard disk with eight sectors per cluster. That's a lot of wasted disk space!

You'll also run into serious file management problems if you plan to release your game (or part of it) as shareware. When a program is zipped for BBS distribution, every file becomes an entry in the ZIP file and requires header

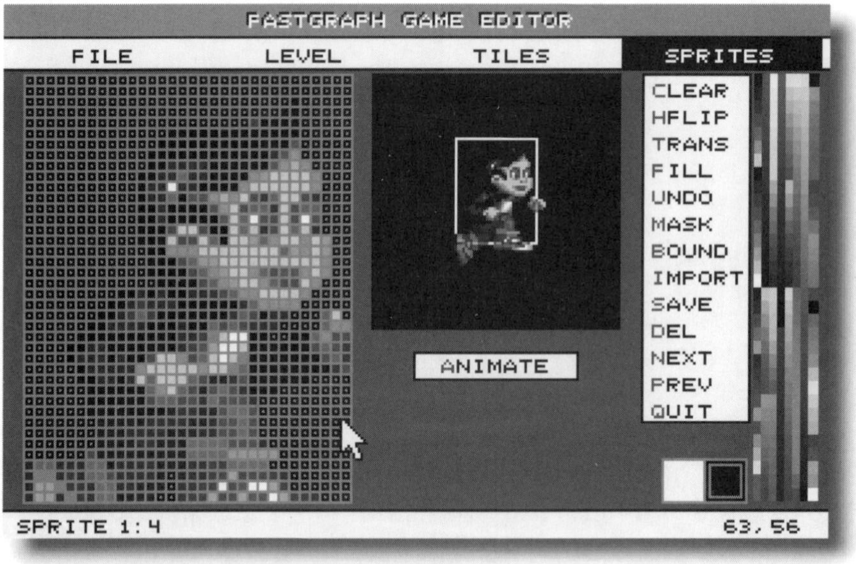

Figure 3.10 *Viewing the sprites in a sprite list file.*

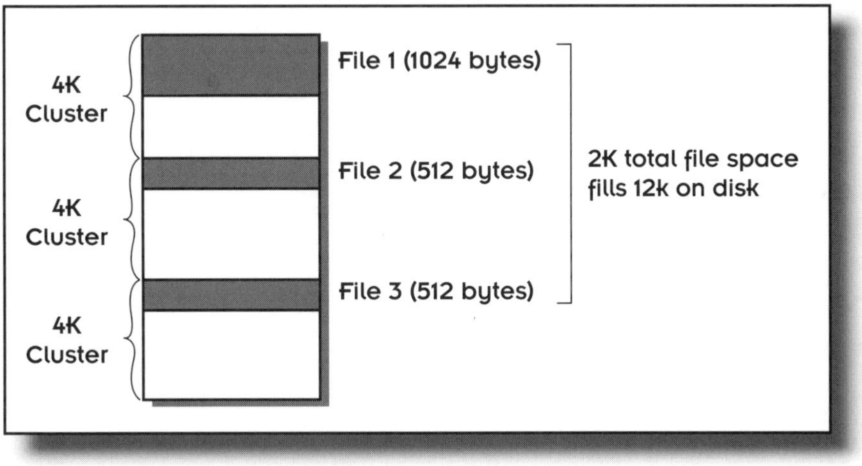

Figure 3.11 *How DOS allocates disk space in clusters.*

information to keep track of it. The more files you have, the larger the ZIP file. Zipping one large file will result in better compression and a smaller ZIP file than zipping multiple small files, even if the file size of the smaller files adds up to the size of the one large file.

With these considerations in mind, I recommend game programmers use a file resource manager such as Fastgraph/Image, to reduce the size of their data files. Fastgraph/Image takes multiple files and stuffs them into a single binary file. You can then distribute a game with several large data files instead of several hundred small ones.

Tommy's Tip

Using a Resource File Manager

A resource file manager allows you to stuff multiple small files into a single large binary file. Several resource file managers are commercially available, including Fastgraph/Image. You may want to add support for resource files at the end of your game development cycle, when your file structure has stabilized. Resource files are efficient in terms of disk space and file download size for ZIP files.

Although you should consider using a file resource manager for your own games that are distributed, we didn't use one in this book. We're primarily interested in dissecting the files and discussing their contents. A resource file makes it a bit more difficult to look at individual files. This is an advantage in a game, but a disadvantage in a book. For now, let's just assume that we'll eventually organize the individual files into a single resource file before our game is released.

Using the Level Editor

The level editor is used to build levels. To activate the level editor, click on EDIT in the LEVEL menu. If everything is working properly, you should see the Egyptian level, which is shown in Figure 3.12. You can scroll around in this level using the arrow keys. The mouse is used to select tiles and move them around. As you slide the mouse, you'll see a black square box that moves around on top of the level art. This box is called the *tile selector* because it is used to select, copy, paste, and delete tiles. To select a tile, position the tile selector on the tile you want to select and click the right mouse button. This performs a copy operation. You can then move the tile selector to a different location and click the left mouse button to place (paste) the tile at this new location.

To pick up a group of tiles at one time, press the right mouse button and drag across the tiles you want to copy. As you drag the mouse, *the size of the tile selector increases.* Release the right mouse button when you've highlighted the desired block of tiles to copy them. To paste those tiles in another part of the level, position the mouse in the upper-left corner of the desired position and click the left mouse button to drop in the entire rectangular block of tiles. Tiles are not pasted off the edge of the screen, so you may have to scroll the screen to paste all of them. This is actually more intuitive than it sounds. After you've worked with the editor for a while, you'll get the hang of it.

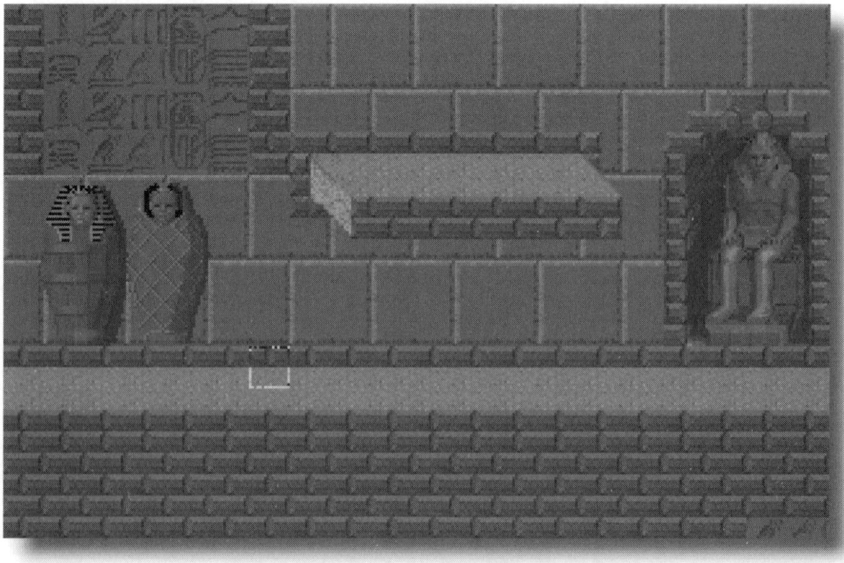

Figure 3.12 *Using the level editor to edit the Egyptian level.*

Moving Tiles around in the Egyptian Level

Let's try out some of the level editing operations by moving tiles around in the Egyptian level. Keep in mind that if you save your work, any changes you make will be stored in the EGYPT.LEV level file. For this project and the remaining projects in this chapter, you should create a project directory and copy the game editor (FGE.EXE) and an extra set of all the files used in the game so that you can change the files in the editor and test them out in the game.

Here are the steps to follow to change the Egyptian level:

1. Load in the Egyptian level into the level editor by selecting EDIT from the LEVEL menu.
2. Position the tile selector in the upper-left corner of the level.
3. Press F2 to display the tile information box. The box will display this information:

   X=0 Y=0 ROW=0 COL=0 TILE=00 10000000

   You use this feature to locate tiles in the level art.
4. Press F2 to remove the information box.
5. Position the tile selector on the head of the Egyptian guy who is sitting down. The information for this tile is:

   X=288 Y=112 ROW=7 COL=18 TILE=67 00000000

   Once you are in position at this location, click the right mouse button to copy the tile.
6. We're ready to copy this guy's head somewhere else. Move the tile selector to a location directly above its current location. Click the left mouse button. Do you see the new head?
7. Now, let's copy and paste one of the standing mummies. Locate the top-left corner of the second mummy from the left edge of the level art. Here is the status information for this tile:

   X=48 Y=128 ROW=8 COL=3 TILE=24 00000000
8. Click and hold down the right mouse button. Drag the tile selector down and to the right until the *tile selector expands to cover the entire mummy.* Release the mouse button to copy the tiles.
9. Move the tile selector to a new location. Try (X=160, Y=32). Click the left mouse button to paste in the mummy.
10. If you'd like to save your changes, press the letter S then the letter Y. To return to the game editor menu bar, press Esc.

Using the Editing Hot Keys

The level editor requires input from both the mouse and the keyboard in order to be used effectively. Our level editor comes with many advanced features that can be accessed using hot keys. These advanced features will help speed up the process of editing levels. Table 3.2 shows a list of the hot keys and what they do. Look over these commands closely because they'll give you an idea of the types of operations you can perform with the level editor.

Loading a Different Level

When you select EDIT from the LEVEL menu, the level editor always loads in the level file for the level previously selected with the file manager. (The first level is always selected by default when the game editor is started.) To load in a different level into the level editor, you must follow these steps:

1. Click on the FILE menu in the game editor and then select LOAD/SAVE to access the file manager.
2. Press the PgDn or PgUp key to select the level you want to view or edit.
3. Press F10.
4. Click on the LEVEL menu and select EDIT.

When you are finished working with a level, press the Esc key to return to the game editor's main menu bar. If you've made changes to the level, you can save your changes before returning to the menu bar by pressing the letter S. You can also save the changes made in the level editor after you return to the main menu bar by selecting SAVE from the LEVEL menu.

Viewing the Space Level

For this project, let's change levels from the first Egyptian level to our second level, the space platform. Here are the steps to follow:

1. View the file manager's list box by selecting LOAD/SAVE from the FILE menu.
2. Press PgDn once. In the category "LEVEL:" you should see the filename SPACE.LEV.
3. Press F10.
4. Select EDIT from the LEVEL menu.

At this point you may want to use the arrow keys to scroll around in the space level. In the next project, we'll make some changes to this level.

Table 3.2 Level Editor Hot Keys

Key	Name	Definition
F1	Help	Lists other hot keys.
F2	Show Coordinates	Displays the row and column coordinates and tile attributes for any tile. Position the tile selector on top of the desired tile and press F2 to display the tile information.
Ins	Insert row or column	Prompts you for your choice of a row or column. Choose which one you want to insert, and the new row or column will appear. The new row or column will be identical to the adjacent row or column.
Del	Delete Row or Column	Prompts you for your choice of a row or column. Choose which one you want to delete.
Space	Get a Tile	Positions your tile selector on the tile page area (the tile library). Use the right mouse button to pick up a tile. Press the Spacebar a second time to position the cursor on the top part of the foreground tile area. Press it a third time to position the cursor on the bottom part of the foreground tile area. The cursor continues to move between tile areas until you either select a tile or press Esc.
Esc	Exit	Quits the level editor. Be sure to save your work before you exit! If you do forget, you'll have another chance. You can select Save from the level editor menu.
A	Show Tile Attributes	Shows the attributes of all currently visible tiles. Tiles that are solid on top will display a *T*. Tiles that are solid on the bottom will display a *B*. Tiles that are solid on the left or right will display an *L* or *R*.
B	Solid on Bottom	Sets a tile attribute to solid on the bottom.
C	Clear Tile Attributes	Clears the left, right, top, and bottom tile attributes for the currently highlighted tile.
D	Delete Foreground Tile	Removes the foreground, leaving the background tile visible.
F	Foreground Tiles	Shows foreground tiles as black rectangles so you can locate them more easily.
K	Show Background Tiles	Makes the foreground tiles disappear so you can see the background tiles behind them.
L	Solid on Left	Sets a tile attribute to solid on the left.
R	Solid on Right	Sets a tile attribute to solid on the right.
S	Save Level	Saves the level from within the editor or from the menu. Be sure to save your work often!
T	Solid on Top	Sets a tile attribute to solid on the top.
U	Undo	Undoes the most recent command performed in the tile editor.

Using Tiles from the Tile Library

One important feature of the level editor that we didn't discuss yet is how the level editor stores and uses tiles for creating levels. The level editor actually builds levels from a library of tiles. The Egyptian and space platform levels that you've seen so far have already been constructed using tiles from tile libraries. You can think of a tile library as if it were a palette of shapes or building blocks that you can choose from. The tiles are stored in offscreen memory. Pressing the Spacebar from within the level editor reveals a full screen of 240 possible background tiles. Pressing the Spacebar a second time reveals a partial screen of 28 possible foreground tiles. (The foreground tiles will be displayed to the right of the screen of background tiles.) Later, we'll look at how the tile editor can be used to make changes to the foreground and background tiles in the library.

Tommy's Tip

Saving Memory by Using Tiles

By creating multiple levels out of the same background tile library, you'll be able to save both valuable disk space and artwork creation expenses.

Figure 3.13 shows the background tile library that is available for editing the Egyptian level. These tiles are the basic building blocks that you must use to

Figure 3.13 *The tile library available for the Egyptian level.*

design your scene. You select a tile from this library (or page) by moving the tile selector on top of the tile and clicking the right mouse button. This effectively copies the tile so that it can be pasted in the level art. After you select a tile, you'll be returned to the actual level so that you can paste in the tile.

Using Tiles from the Tile Library

Let's use the space platform level to copy and paste a tile from the tile library. Here are the steps to follow:

1. Load in the space level into the level editor. (If you need instructions on how to do this, review the previous project.)
2. Press the Spacebar to get to the screen of background tiles. Believe it or not, the complete space level was created using only these tiles and a few foreground tiles.
3. Move the tile selector to the tile in the upper-left corner (this tile looks like part of a circuit board) and click the right mouse button.
4. When you are returned to the level art, find a position for this tile and click the left mouse button. If you don't like how the tile looks in the position you've chosen, press the letter U to undo the paste operation. On the other hand, if you like how the tile looks, you can keep moving the tile selector and clicking the left mouse button to paste in a row or column of these tiles. That's all there is to it!

Inserting and Deleting Rows and Columns

After you play with the level editor for a while, you'll want to know how to make your level bigger or smaller. You can do this by adding or deleting rows and columns of tiles. The largest level you can create is 240 columns by 200 rows. As Figure 3.14 shows, this takes up an area the size of 3,840x3,200 pixels. (Remember, each tile is 16 pixels square.) Since each screen is 320x200 pixels, this provides you with a total level area of 12x16 screens—quite a large scrolling area!

To insert a row or column with the level editor, position the tile selector where you want to insert the row or column and press the Ins key. The editor will then display the simple dialog box shown in Figure 3.15. This dialog box allows you to select either a row or column by pressing either R for row or C for column. The level editor will then insert a row or column of tiles using this simple strategy:

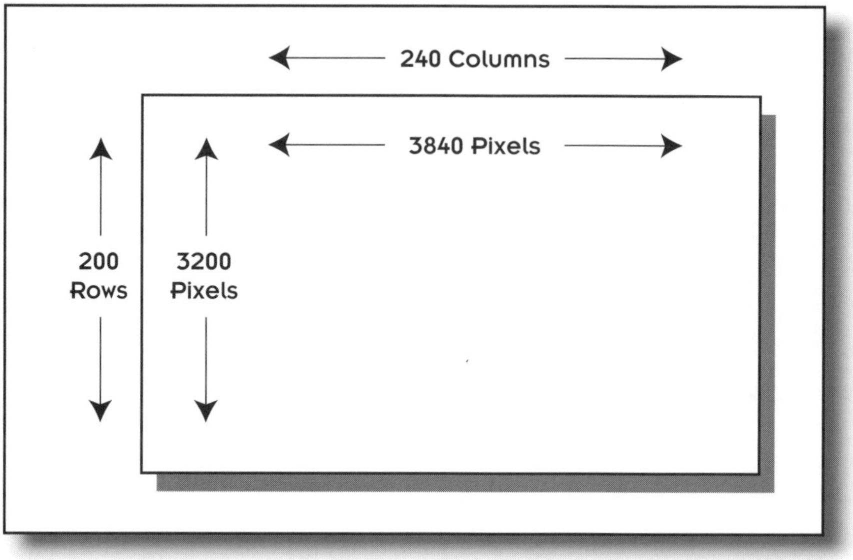

Figure 3.14 *The maximum size of a level.*

- row insertion—the row of tiles located at the current position of the tile selector is copied and inserted below the tile selector
- column insertion—the column of tiles located at the current position of the tile selector is copied and inserted to the right of the tile selector

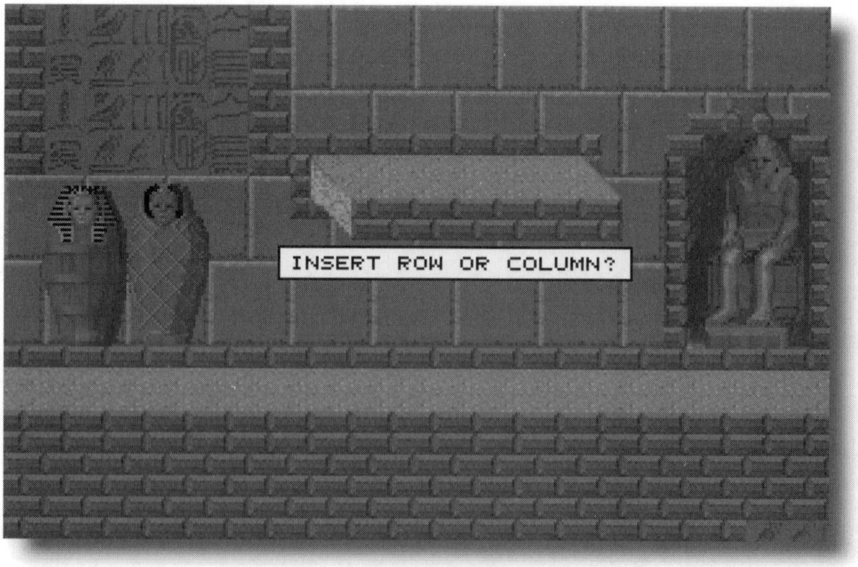

Figure 3.15 *Inserting a row or column of tiles with the level editor.*

To delete a row or column with the level editor, position the tile selector where you want to delete the row or column and press the Del key. The editor will then display the delete dialog box. Press R for row or C for column. The level editor will then delete the row or column of tiles at the current tile selector position.

Modifying the Space Level

In this project, we'll add a new row and a metal door to the space level. After you make these changes, you'll be able to run the *Tommy's Adventures* game to test them out. Remember that we'll be making changes to the game files so you want to make sure that you are working with an extra copy of them in a project directory. Here are the steps to follow:

1. Load in the space level into the level editor.
2. Position the tile selector in the upper-left corner of the level.
3. Press F2 to display the tile information box. The box will display this information:

   X=0 Y=0 ROW=0 COL=0 TILE=10 00000000
4. Press F2 to remove the information box.
5. To insert a new row of tiles, press the Ins key, and then press the letter R.
6. We're ready to insert a new metal door. Position the tile selector at the upper-left corner of the metal door in the level art (see Figure 3.16). If you press F2 at this location, you'll get this status information for the tile:

   X=192 Y=64 ROW=4 COL=12 TILE=107 00000000
7. To copy the door, press and hold the right mouse button and drag the tile selector box down and to the right until it selects the entire door. (The tile selector box will increase in size as you drag it.)
8. Move the tile selector to a position above the current door, and press the left mouse button. Try the location, X=192, Y=0. If you make a mistake, press the letter U to undo your editing change.
9. Press the letter S then the letter Y to save the level. To return to the main game editor menu bar, press Esc.

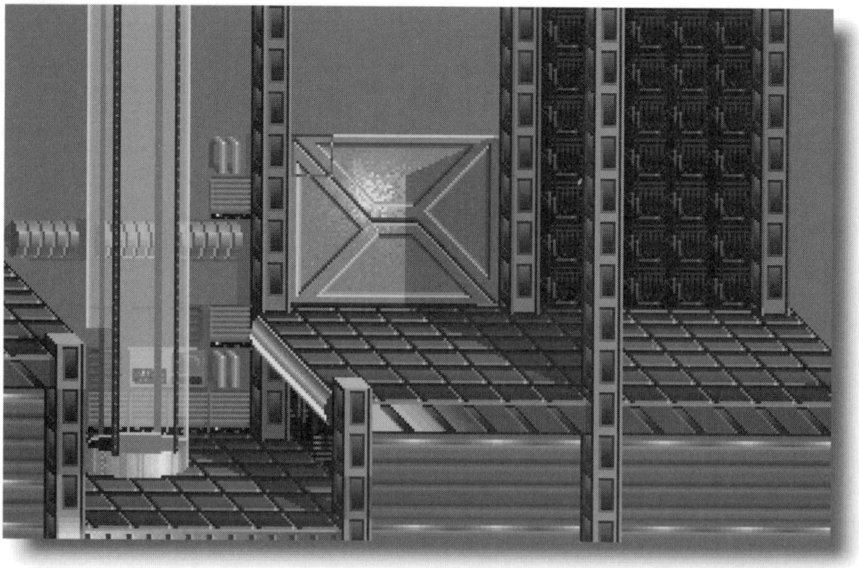

Figure 3.16 Selecting the metal door in the space level.

To test out your changes, make sure that the game data files that you are editing are in a directory with the game program TOMMY.EXE. We'll be using this newly changed level in the next project, so make sure you save it.

Viewing and Setting Basic Tile Attributes

Before we leave the level editor, we need to look at how we can view and set basic tile attributes. The attributes that can be set in the editor control how your sprites interact with your levels. There are four different tile attributes you can set with the level editor: Top, Bottom, Left, and Right. Each attribute specifies which border of the tile should be considered to be a solid area. This is how you can create floors for your sprites to walk on or walls that your sprites can't go through. Floor tiles, for example, are always solid on top. A wall tile could be solid on its right or left border.

To view the solid attributes that have already been set for the tiles used in the current level, press the letter A. As shown in Figure 3.17, the attributes will be indicated with the letters *T, B, L,* or *R.*

To set attributes for a tile, move the tile selector on top of the tile in the level editor and press one of the corresponding letter keys, T, B, L, or R. Keep in mind that when you set an attribute for a tile, all occurrences of that tile in your level will be assigned the attribute. For example, if you select any one of the tiles used for the floor in the Egyptian level and press the letter T, every

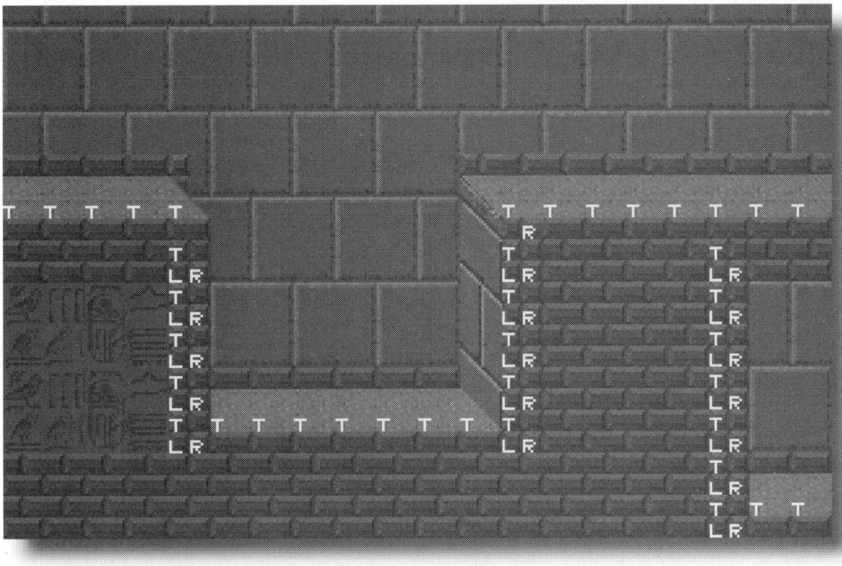

Figure 3.17 Viewing tile attributes with the level editor.

tile used of this type will be assigned the Top attribute. This designation would make these tiles solid on top so that the sprites can walk on them without falling through.

The last attribute-related operation you can perform with the editor is clearing all of the attributes set for a specific tile. To do this, move the tile selector on top of the tile and press the letter C.

Changing Attributes in the Space Level

Let's change a few of the tile attributes in the space level so that you can see how they effect the sprite animation in the game. We'll actually define new attributes so that our main sprite, Tommy, can walk up the space tube. Before you make these attribute changes, you should play with the game for a few minutes (in particular the space level) to get an idea of how the sprites move around. Here are the steps to follow:

1. Load the space level into the level editor.
2. Press the letter A to view the attributes in this level.
3. Notice that a number of attributes have already been defined for the level. Our next step is to add new ones.

4. Move the tile selector to the tile directly below the space tube. The information for this tile is:

   X=128 Y=176 ROW=11 COL=8 TILE=76 1000000
5. Press the letter T then press the letter A to make sure the attribute has been set. Press A again to remove the attribute display.
6. Move up a row (ROW=10, COL = 8) and repeat step 5. Keep moving up rows and setting attributes to create a "channel," as shown in Figure 3.18.
7. Save the level in the editor and test it out in the game.

When you play the game now, you should be able to make Tommy "walk" up the space tube.

Using Foreground Tiles

Although we've introduced foreground tiles, we've primarily been working with background tiles. You'll need to use foreground tiles in your levels whenever you want to create a situation where you want a sprite to move behind a tile instead of in front of the tile. An example of how foreground tiles work can be found in the space level. As you play the game on this level, notice the computer console displayed at the far right. This section of the level is created

Figure 3.18 *Changing attributes in the space level.*

with foreground tiles. When you move the main sprite, Tommy, past the computer console, he is displayed behind it instead of in front of the console.

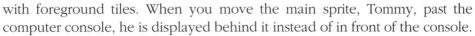

The easiest way to determine where the foreground tiles are in a level is to press the letter F while you are editing the level. All of the foreground tiles will then be displayed as "blocked out" tiles. To delete a foreground tile, select the tile with the tile selector and press the letter D.

Adding Foreground Tiles to the Space Level

This project will show you how to add some level art that the Tommy sprite can move behind. We'll do this by copying the computer console art to another location in the level. This console is actually composed of both foreground and background tiles.

1. First we need to copy the background tiles. Position the tile selector at the left corner of the console (location ROW=7, COL=0). Then, click and hold down the right mouse button and drag the mouse to the bottom-right corner of the console (location ROW=8, COL=3).
2. Now we'll copy the console to the second platform to the right. Position the tile selector at the location ROW=8, COL=14 and click the left mouse button.
3. The next step is to put in the foreground tiles. Press the Spacebar twice, and then select the first two rows of tiles to the right of the background tile page. (See Figure 3.19 for the location of these tiles.) These tiles represent the left half of the computer console.
4. When you return to the level art, position the tile selector at the left corner of the new console (location ROW=8, COL=14) and click the left mouse button.
5. Go back to the background tiles and select the second half of the console.
6. Return to the level art once again and position the tile selector at the second half of the console (location ROW=8, COL=16) and click the left mouse button.

Using the Tile Editor

The techniques we've explored so far only tell half of the story when it comes to creating levels for your games. You can also edit individual tiles using one of the tile editors. There are separate tile editors provided for editing background

Figure 3.19 *Selecting foreground tiles for the computer console.*

and foreground tiles. Select either the BACKGROUND or FOREGROUND option from the TILES menu to activate one of the tile editors. Once you are in the tile editor, you'll see the editing screen shown in Figure 3.20.

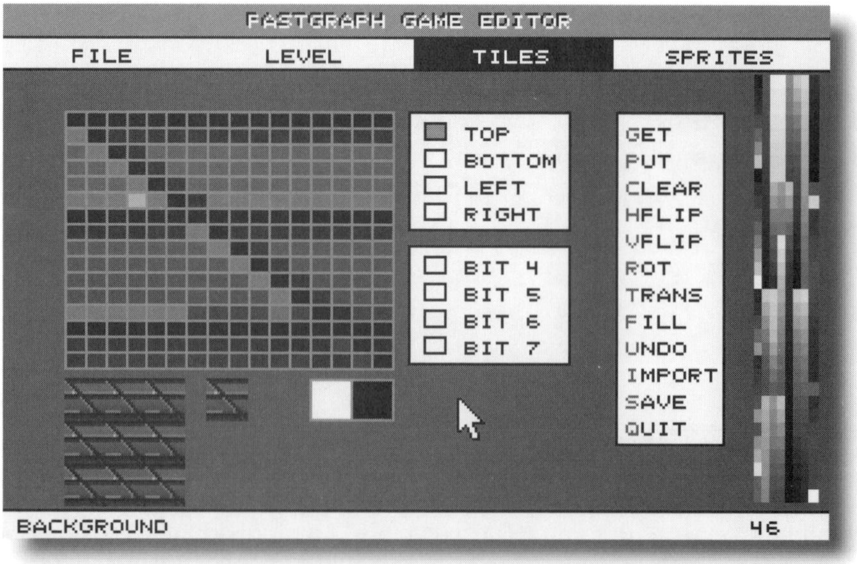

Figure 3.20 *The tile editor screen allows you to tweak your art at the tile level.*

On the left side of the screen is a magnified version of the tile. This is called a *fat bit editor*. You can modify individual pixels in the fat bit editor by clicking on one of the rectangular cells. As the cells change color, the pixels in the tile also change. The tile is displayed in the bottom in both a single version and in a grid of several adjacent tiles. It's important that you be able to see adjacent tiles because tiles are usually designed to fit together in a pattern. For example, it's common to have tiles that look like bricks so that they can be joined together to form a wall.

Next to the tile area are two colored rectangles, representing the background and foreground colors. These colors correspond to left and right mouse button presses that change the tile color when you click in the fat bit grid. You can change these colors with an array of palette colors located on the far right side of the screen. Move the mouse cursor over the desired color in the palette area and click the left mouse button to change the foreground color. Similarly, you can click the right mouse button on a color to change the background color.

If you're editing foreground tiles and you select palette 0, you'll see the color displayed as a black rectangle with a gray box in it; on the fat bit grid you'll see a gray dot on a black rectangle. That image means color 0 is the transparent color. Foreground tiles may have transparent areas where the background shows through. Palette 0 is the designated transparent color for foreground tiles.

At the bottom of the screen is a status line. This line provides feedback, including the number of the tile currently being edited, and whether it's a background tile or a foreground tile. Messages and prompts are also displayed in this area.

Using the Tile Editor Menu

The tile editor menu is located between the tile attribute boxes and the palettes. You can access these with either the mouse or the keyboard. If you're using the keyboard, press the key that is highlighted in blue. Table 3.3 presents the options available in the tile editor menu.

Editing a Space Level Tile

Let's use the tile editor to change one of the background tiles used in the space level. Here are the steps to follow:

1. Make sure that the space level is currently loaded by the file manager.
2. Select BACKGROUND from the TILES menu.
3. When the tile editor appears, click on the Get command.

4. Position the tile selector on the circuit board tile shown in the upper-left corner and click the right mouse button to return to the tile editor.
5. Use the fat bit editor to make changes to the tile. Experiment by adding or deleting a few pixels or changing some of the colors in the tile.
6. When you are finished editing the tile, click on the Put command.
7. To replace the tile, position the tile selector at the upper-left corner of the tile screen and click the left mouse button. (If you wanted to save this tile as a new tile, paste it in a blank location on the tile screen.)

If you now load in the space level into the level editor, you'll see that all of the "circuit board" tiles have changed (assuming that you chose to replace the tile you edited.)

Setting Special Attributes

In the center of the tile editor screen, just to the right of the fat bit editor, are two sets of tile attributes. These are labeled:

Top
Bottom
Left
Right
Bit 4
Bit 5
Bit 6
Bit 7

You can apply these attributes to any tile. You turn a tile attribute on by positioning the mouse cursor over the tile attribute box and clicking the left mouse button. The tile attribute box will be highlighted in gray.

The first four tile attributes designate that the tile will be solid on the top, bottom, left, or right. Recall that this is how walls and floors are constructed. Floor tiles, for example, should always solid on the top, so the sprite won't fall through the tile.

The last four tile attributes are reserved for use by your game code. Essentially, you can specify them to mean anything you want. For example, you may want to specify that a tile is *slippery* (like ice) or a tile may mark a

Table 3.3 The Options Available with the Tile Editor

Option	Description
Get	Gets a tile from the tile library. This option displays either the foreground or the background tile page. Pressing the Spacebar will toggle between the two tile pages. Use the mouse to highlight the tile you want to select. The tile number will be displayed in the upper-right corner of the tile page. Press the right mouse button to get a tile and bring it into the editor.
Put	Puts a tile into the tile library. After you've modified a tile, you'll want to save it. When you select this option, the tile page is displayed. Move the tile selector to the location where you want to store the tile, then press the left mouse button to save the modified tile and its location.
Clear	Clears the tile. This will set all the pixels to the current background color, both in the fat bit editor and in the tile.
Hflip	Flips a tile horizontally. All the pixels are reversed around a vertical axis. That is, the pixels on the left show up on the right, and vice versa. A second horizontal flip puts the pixels back the way they were.
Vflip	Flips a tile vertically. All the pixels are reversed around a horizontal axis. The pixels on the top show up on the bottom, and vice versa. A second vertical flip puts the pixels back the way they were.
Rot	Rotates the image 90 degrees counter-clockwise. Selecting this command four times will put the image back the way it was originally.
Trans	Transposes two colors. Any pixel that is currently the background color will become the foreground color. Be sure to load up the foreground and background palettes with the desired colors before using this function.
Fill	Flood fills an area. Position the mouse cursor on the fat bit editor and press a button. All adjacent pixels of the same color will be changed to either the foreground color if the left mouse button is clicked, or the background color if the right mouse button is clicked.
Undo	Undoes the last change. Each time a change is made to the tile, a copy is saved. You can restore the copy by selecting Undo from the menu. This function acts as a toggle. Selecting it a second time undoes the undo.
Import	Imports tiles from a PCX file. Selecting this option will prompt you for the name of a PCX file on the status line. If the PCX file is found, it will be displayed, along with crosshairs. Use the mouse to move the crosshairs to select the area of the file to import, then click and hold the left mouse button to drag the cursor over the desired tiles. The tile page will be displayed along with an outline of the selected tile area. Move to the desired position on the tile page and click the left mouse button to paste the tiles to the tile page.
Save	Saves the tiles to the specified PCX file, and saves the tile attributes to an associated attribute file. You'll be prompted for the filename on the status line, and warned if you're about to overwrite an existing file.
Quit	Exits the tile editor and returns you to the main menu. If you haven't saved your changes, you'll be prompted to save your work before you exit.

milepost or the end of a level. Having tile attributes available allows you to write code to determine if a sprite's action needs to change when it reaches a certain part of a level. The attribute settings that you define for tiles in the editor can easily be processed by your game program. For example, you can include a **switch** statement in your C code and check for certain attribute settings. When we explore the actual code for *Tommy's Adventures*, you'll see how attributes are processed.

Using the Tile Ripper

In general, tiles are not created in the tile editor, they're created in a paint program and then imported. Usually they're not created as tiles at all; in fact, they're created as full-screen backgrounds, (PCX files) which must then be reduced to tiles.

The tile ripper is a utility that reduces a screen of artwork to tiles, which can then be used by both the tile editor and the level editor. As you've seen, the tiles are the elemental building blocks of the level. Each tile is 16x16 pixels. Since background screens tend to have many duplicate tiles, the tile editor determines which tiles are unique and stores them in the tile library, then it generates an array that represents the original artwork as a list of tiles. The tile list is stored as a binary array in a file with an LEV extension, while the tiles themselves are stored in a PCX file.

Original artwork for a level is generally stored in several PCX files. It's common for several screens of background art to be ripped to form a single screen of tiles. The tile ripper prompts you to enter the name of the input file, the name of the PCX file that will hold the tiles, and the name of the level file, as shown in Figure 3.21.

You should get all your background art ready and rip your tiles before you do any level design. If you rip tiles after you've worked on the level, the position of the tiles may change, and you'll have to throw out the level design work and start over. Similarly, tile attributes should be assigned to tiles *after* they are ripped. Otherwise, the position of the tiles may change in the tile library and you'll have to redo the tile attributes. So the tile ripper function comes first, then the level editor. If you need to make minor changes to the tiles after level editing has started, use the tile editor.

Editing levels is slow, painstaking work even with the help of these powerful tools. Learn to use the tools properly to speed up the editing process, and try to avoid doing redundant editing.

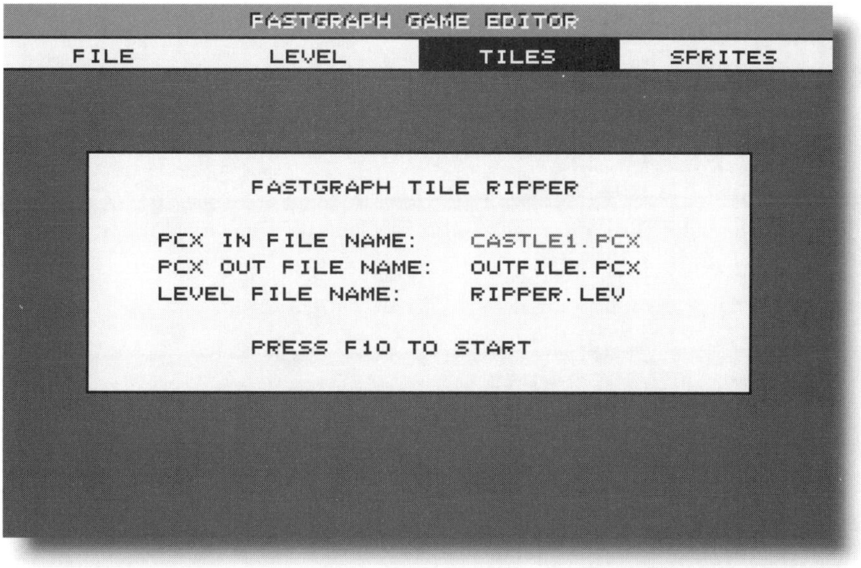

Figure 3.21 *The tile ripper screen.*

Creating a New Level with the Tile Ripper

This project will show you how to add a new level to the *Tommy's Adventures* game. We'll use the tile ripper to "rip" two art files of a castle scene and then we'll add the new castle level after the space level. Once you create the castle level, you can even use the level editor to expand the castle level.

This project requires that you use the art files CASTLE1.PCX and CASTLE2.PCX. Both of these files are provided on the companion disk. Make sure that you copy these files to the directory where the game editor is stored. We'll use these art files to create a new level named CASTLE.LEV. Here are the steps to follow:

1. Select the RIPPER command from the TILES menu and enter the following filenames at the corresponding prompt:

   ```
   PCX IN FILE NAME: CASTLE1.PCX
   PCX OUT FILE NAME: CASTLE.PCX
   LEVEL FILE NAME: CASTLE.LEV
   ```

   The first file is the original level art, the second file is the tile set that will be created, and the third file is the level data.

2. Press F10 to create the tiles.
3. Repeat steps 1 and 2, but this time enter CASTLE2.PCX for the input filename. Leave the other two filenames as they are. Press the Esc key to return to the main menu bar.
4. Select the LOAD/SAVE command from the FILE menu.
5. When the file manager's list box appears, press PgDn to select the space level. Then, press PgDn once more and then the letter Y to insert a new level. Enter the following filenames:

```
GAME FILE:    GAME.DAT
LEVEL:        CASTLE.LEV
BACKGROUND:   CASTLE.PCX
              CASTLE.ATT
FOREGROUND:   NUL.PCX
              NUL.ATT
SPRITE LIST:  SPRITE.DAT
```

6. Press F10 to save and load these files.
7. Select the EDIT command from the LEVEL menu.
8. View the level in the level editor and then press the letter S to save it.

You can also make changes to the castle level, such as adding rows or columns before you save it.

Using the Sprite Editor

The last selection on the main menu bar is the sprite editor. The primary purpose of this tool is to import sprites into the game. Usually, sprites are not drawn in the sprite editor. Instead, they're created in either a paint program such as Deluxe Paint II, or an animation program such as Autodesk Animator. They are then saved with other sprites in a single PCX file. This is a convenient file format for editing sprites, but it's not too convenient for importing them into a game. For one thing, PCX files contain a lot of unnecessary baggage, like the header information and the palettes. We'll be controlling the palettes ourselves in the game, so we don't need redundant copies of the palettes in our data files. Also, we want to strip down the header information to the bare minimum necessary to display the sprite. Finally, the file format of a PCX file isn't convenient for displaying individual sprites. A 256-color bitmap format is better for our game. So we use the sprite editor to strip the image down to the minimum amount of information required to define the sprite, reformat the data, and store it in a format that is most useful to us in the game. It sounds like a tall order, but our sprite editor handles this efficiently and is quite easy to use.

To start the sprite editor, select the EDIT command from the SPRITES menu. The sprite editor screen that appears, shown in Figure 3.22, looks similar to the tile editor screen. Here we have a fat bit editor showing a magnified view of a part of the sprite. There are palettes at the far right side of the screen, and a menu next to the palettes. A sprite area in the middle of the screen shows an actual-size version of the sprite. Foreground and background colors are highlighted in boxes below the menu area, and at the bottom of the screen is a status area displaying relevant information, including the x and y coordinates of the mouse as it moves over the fat bit editor.

You use the mouse to edit pixels on the fat bit editor. Move the mouse over the grid and click the left mouse button to set a grid cell to the foreground color, or the right button to set a grid cell to the background color. As you edit the sprite in the fat bit editor, the changes will appear in the sprite area. Since you can only see a portion of the sprite in the fat bit editor, you may want to move the view around. There's a rectangular box in the sprite area that highlights the part of the sprite currently being edited. You can move that box around by moving the mouse cursor over the box, holding down the left mouse button, and dragging the box to a new location. When you've moved the box to where you want it, release the mouse. The picture in the fat bit editor will change to the part of the sprite you just highlighted. In this way, you can edit a sprite that's larger than the number of cells visible in the fat bit editor.

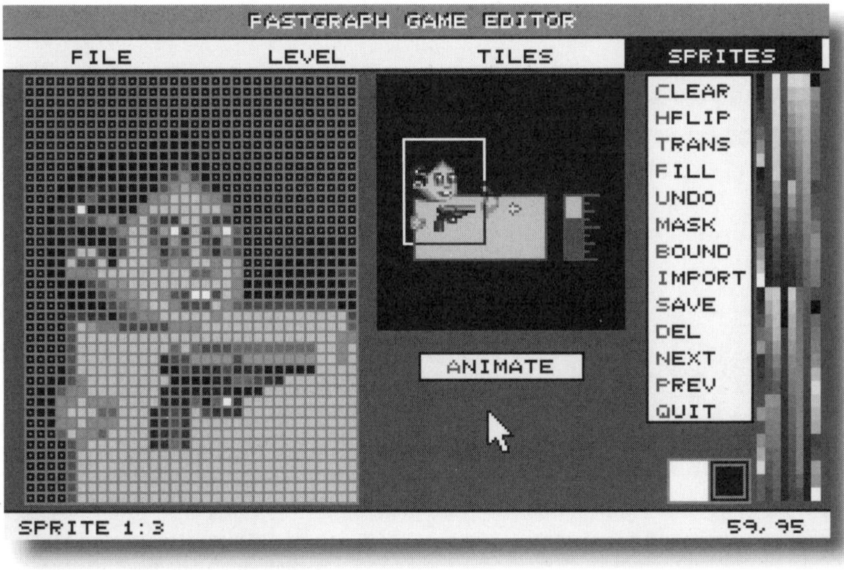

Figure 3.22 *Using the sprite editor.*

As with the tile editor, you can select your foreground and background colors from the palette menu at the left. The default value for the background color is palette 0, which displays as a black cell with a gray dot in it. Palette 0 is the transparent color, which means that when our sprite is displayed on a background, it won't overwrite what was there previously. The background art will show through around Tommy's head, under his arms, between his legs, or wherever there is a transparent pixel.

Using the Sprite Editor Menu

Because sprites are usually edited elsewhere, the most commonly used sprite editor functions are Import and Save. However, I've included a full array of editing functions so that on-the-fly sprite touchups are possible in the sprite editor. As with the tile editor, you can access these menu functions with either the keyboard or the mouse. If you're using the keyboard, you can access the desired menu function by pressing the first character, which is highlighted in blue. Table 3.4 presents the sprite editor menu options.

Loading Sprites

After you have created a sprite by importing art from a PCX file or drawing the sprite in the sprite editor and saving the sprite to a LST file, you can load in the sprite. To do this, select the LOAD option from the SPRITES menu. Figure 3.23 shows the screen that is displayed. Here, the editor lists all of the files

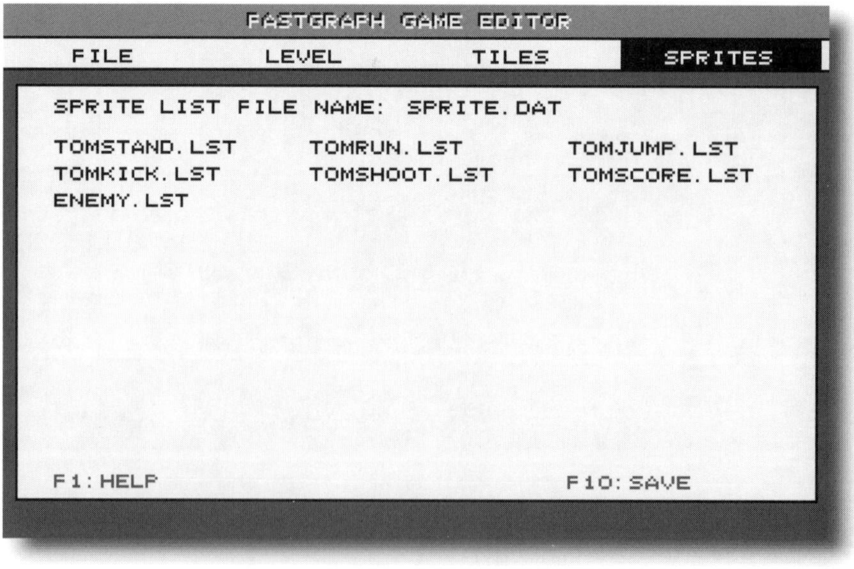

Figure 3.23 *Loading a sprite list file into the sprite editor.*

Table 3.4 The Sprite Editor Menu Options

Option	Description
Clear	Clears the sprite by setting all the pixels in the sprite area and the fat bit editor to the background color.
Hflip	Flips a sprite horizontally. Flips the sprite around a vertical axis, so that all the pixels on the left show up on the right, and vice versa.
Trans	Transposes two colors. All pixels that were the background color become foreground pixels.
Fill	Flood fills an area. Position the mouse cursor on the fat bit editor and click a mouse button. All adjacent pixels of the same color will be changed to either the foreground color if you click the left mouse button, or the background color if you click the right mouse button.
Undo	Undoes the last change.
Mask	Displays the sprite area on a blue background rather than the black background so you can more easily see which pixels are transparent.
Bound	Uses crosshairs to select a bounding box. The bounding box information is stored in the sprite file and is sometimes used in collision detection.
Import	Imports tiles from a PCX file. When you select this option, you're prompted for the name of a PCX file on the status line. If the PCX file is found, it will be displayed along with crosshairs. Use the mouse to move the crosshairs to select an area of the file to import, then click and hold the left mouse button and drag to highlight. The sprite will automatically appear centered in the sprite area, and the appropriate part will be copied to the fat bit editor.
Save	Saves the sprites in the current list to a file with an LST extension. You'll be prompted for the filename and warned if you're about to overwrite an existing file.
Del	Deletes the current sprite. This action will remove the sprite from the sprite list and renumber all the remaining sprites.
Next	Displays the next sprite in the sprite list.
Prev	Displays the previous sprite in the sprite list.
Quit	Exits the sprite editor and returns to the main menu. If you've changed any sprites during the current editing session, you'll be prompted to save your work before you quit.

that are included in the sprite data configuration file SPRITE.DAT. You then use the arrow keys to select a filename. Press Enter to load in the file.

The editor will then load in the list of sprites stored in the file you've selected. You can determine the number of sprites in the list by viewing the status message displayed below the sprite editing grid. For example, the status message

```
SPRITE 1 : 3
```

tells you that the sprite list contains a sequence of three sprites and the first sprite is currently loaded in the editor. To view the next sprite in the list, you click on the Next option.

Changing a Sprite

For this project, we'll change one of the sprites used in the *Tommy's Adventures* game. Here are the steps to follow:

1. Select the LOAD command from the SPRITES menu.
2. Select the file TOMRUN.LST. (Move the cursor until it is on this filename and press Enter.) This is the set of sprites used to make the main character run.
3. Let's put a red key in his left hand. Use the mouse to click on one of the red colors shown in the color palette.
4. Draw a red key in the character's left hand. When you are done, click the Next command to move to the second frame of animation.
5. Repeat step four until you have drawn a key for the first three frames.(Although there are six frames, only the first three show the character's left hand.)
6. When you are finished drawing keys, click the Animate button to test out the animation. (See *Animating Sprites* for more information.)
7. Make any required changes and then click the Save button, press Enter, and the letter Y to save the sprite LST file.

When you play the game now, Tommy will have a red key in his left hand as he is running.

Animating Sprites

One of the more useful features included with the sprite editor is the ability to animate your sprites. This feature allows you to test out the animation sequences you've created before you put the sprites in your game. You can watch the animation and then use the editor to fix any defects that you see.

To animate a sprite, load in the sprite using the SPRITES menu, then click on the Animate button.

Adding New Sprites

In addition to loading and editing sprites, you'll need to know how to add new sprites using the editor. Actually, adding a sprite to a game is a two-fold process. First, you must create the sprite or import the sprite using the sprite editor. Second, you must incorporate the sprite into your game program code so that the sprite can be loaded, displayed, and controlled. In Chapters 12 and 13, you'll learn how to work with sprites at the code level. For now, we'll discuss how new sprites are added using the editor.

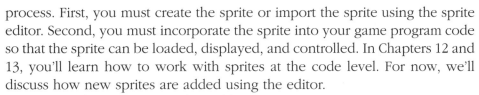

Here are the steps required to add a new sprite:

1. Create a sprite list using the fat bit sprite editor or import a sprite using the fat bit editor. (Only .PCX files can be imported.)
2. Save the set of sprites using the SAVE command. Make sure you use the extension .LST to name the file.
3. Add the new sprite filename you've created to the sprite list data file. (You can access this file by selecting the LOAD command from the SPRITES menu.)

Importing Art to Create a New Sprite List

Let's use the sprite editor to create a new sprite list (PLANE.LST) by importing a few art files. The PCX art files we'll import contain drawings of a plane in different positions. It is included on the companion disk as PLANES.PCX. Here are the steps required to create the new sprite list:

1. Select the LOAD command from the SPRITES menu.
2. Press the Ins key. A new .LST filename will appear named UNTITLED.LST.
3. Type in the new name PLANES.LST and press Enter. The fat bit editor will appear with a blank editing screen.
4. Click on the IMPORT command.
5. Enter the filename PLANES.PCX and press Enter.
6. Locate the crosshairs that appear. Move the crosshairs to the upper-left corner of the plane, click and hold down the left mouse button, and drag the box that appears to cover the complete plane. Try to select only the fish and not the black background. When you release the mouse button, you'll be returned to the fat bit editor. If the object does not come in correctly, click on the CLEAR command and try importing the file again.
7. Let's create a second frame. Click on the NEXT command to view the frame that has the label "SPRITE 2:2."
8. Click on the IMPORT command and load in the file PLANES.PCX.

9. Select this plane art using the techniques presented in step 6.
10. Let's import one more sprite (a third frame). Click the NEXT command to view the frame "SPRITE 3:3." Then, follow steps 4 through 6 to import the art in the file PLANES.PCX again. This time, however, select some of the black background above the plane. This will make the sprite swim in a down motion when the sprite is animated.
11. Click the ANIMATE button to test out your new animated sprite.
12. When you are done, click the SAVE command to save the new sprite list file.

Note: *If you were planning to use a sprite like the plane in a game, you'll need to remove all of the background color that surrounds the object and set this color to the sprite editor's background color. You can easily do this by using the FILL command. If you have trouble determining the color of the background in the sprite viewing area, click on the MASK command.*

Tips on Drawing and Importing Sprites

As we've mentioned, sprites are typically created by an external painting program and then imported into the sprite editor to build the sprite list. When creating sprites to be imported into the sprite editor, don't make your sprites too large. A main sprite such as Tommy, is only about 32 pixels wide and 50 pixels tall. A enemy sprite, such as the scorpion is only about 30 pixels tall, although it is wider than the main character. Before you get carried away and create too many sprites with a painting program, you might want to import a few of them to test their size. Here are some additional tips to help you create your sprites:

Working with large sprites. If the sprite art you import is too large for the fat bit editor, you can access other areas of the sprite by sliding around the sprite border displayed in the sprite viewing area.

Handling color matching problems. In order for your sprites to look good with your level art, the color palettes of the sprite and level art may need to be adjusted. Chapter 9 presents a useful color palette utility to help you fix any color palette problems that may occur.

Creating smooth animation. Sprite animation, like programming, is a trial and error practice. Don't give up if your sprites aren't as professionally looking as you might want them to be. When you create your sprites, try to draw the different frames side-by-side so that you can better visualize the animation. Remember that the maximum number of frames you can use in a sprite list is 12.

Quitting the Game Editor

When you're finished editing your sprites, tiles, and levels, you'll want to save all your work and exit the game editor. Pressing the Esc key exits you to DOS, as will selecting the QUIT function from the FILE menu.

Remember, the file management files, GAME.DAT and the various SPRITE.DAT files, are text files that you can modify with your text editor. If you want to rearrange levels, you may find it easier to simply edit these files in your programmer's editor. You'll no doubt develop your own habits with practice.

That covers the features of the game editor. You'll become intimately familiar with this program as you develop your game. If you find something you don't like about the level editor, the tile editor, the tile ripper, the sprite editor, or the file manager, change the program to suit your needs. The complete source code for the game editor is included on the companion disk, and it's documented in the next few chapters. Again, I encourage you to modify and customize the game editor, and find unique ways to use this program to generate original games. The more original ideas you can put into your game, the better, and original games require original tools. As you read the next few chapters, think in terms of modifying the code to create images and special effects that nobody has thought of yet. In this way, your game will be unique and special, and will stand out from the other side-scroller games in the market.

Are you ready to write some code? Then turn off the phone, roll up, your sleeves, and let's get started!

Chapter 4

Find out how you can transform an artist's rendition of a scene to re-usable tiles for creating great visual effects.

The Art of Creating Levels

Now that you've seen the Fastgraph game editor and have learned about the different components needed to create a side-scrolling arcade game, you're probably eager to jump in and start writing your own game. But before you begin the coding process, you'll need a way to create your level art.

In this chapter, we'll have a look at a valuable utility—the tile ripper. This powerful tool can help you automate the process of creating your game levels by breaking up your art into distinct tiles. This tile ripper is the same one that is included in the game editor introduced in the previous chapter. For simplicity, it is presented here as a standalone program.

Creating Level Art for Your Games

One of the first steps in writing a game is to acquire the level art for the game. I have always found this step to be fraught with problems. I can only think of two ways to get art—you either draw it yourself or you get somebody else to draw it for you. Either way, acquiring good level art will be a challenge.

Remember that the level art that you create for your games needs to be designed so that it can be represented as distinct tiles. As an example, Figure 4.1 shows how one of the levels in *Tommy's Adventures* is divided into tiles.

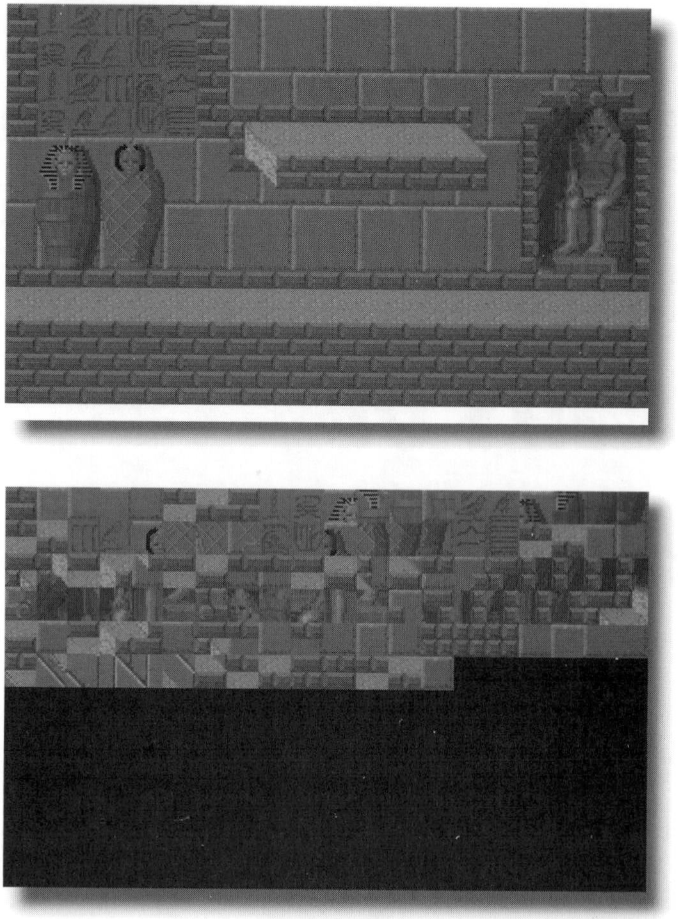

Figure 4.1 *Representing your level art as distinct tiles.*

The tiles in the level have been selected from the tile library. Recall that each tile is 16×16 pixels in size. Designing art like this poses quite a challenge, especially if you don't have any experience creating art in this fashion. Should you just draw each tile by hand and then piece them together to create your levels? Or, should you hire an artist to draw your levels as a complete scene and then divide the art into distinct tiles?

There's no perfect solution.

Making One Tile at a Time

Because programmers are typically pragmatic, technical, and tend to see in things in patterns, they tend to make inferior tile artists. If you take the "programmer approach" to drawing tiles, your levels would probably look like a checkerboard. Figure 4.2 shows an example of a game level that was created by drawing tiles one at a time. The tiles look distinctly rectangular and symmetric, and the background does not look very natural. Rectangular tiles are appropriate for games like Scrabble, Mahjongg, and Dominoes. In side scrollers, we need to create our levels so that they don't look like they are made of tiles. Ideally, we should be able to use our tiles to create asymmetrical objects like trees, gardens, clouds, and space ships. Unless you have natural artistic ability (a rare talent in a programmer), you will get better results if you hire an artist to draw your backgrounds.

Working with an Artist

An experienced side-scrolling game artist will create levels that can be reduced to a set of unique tiles. Unfortunately, most artists seem to have trouble with the concept of reducing artwork to tiles. They tend to give you screens of art that look wonderful, but from which you can not extract any duplicate tiles. This poses a problem because tile duplication is essential to building large levels. You want to be able to build levels containing patterns of tiles that offer variety as well as repetition. Describing this to an artist is very difficult. Suppose, for example, you tell your artist you want some trees and bushes. He understands that you must use the same branches over and over,

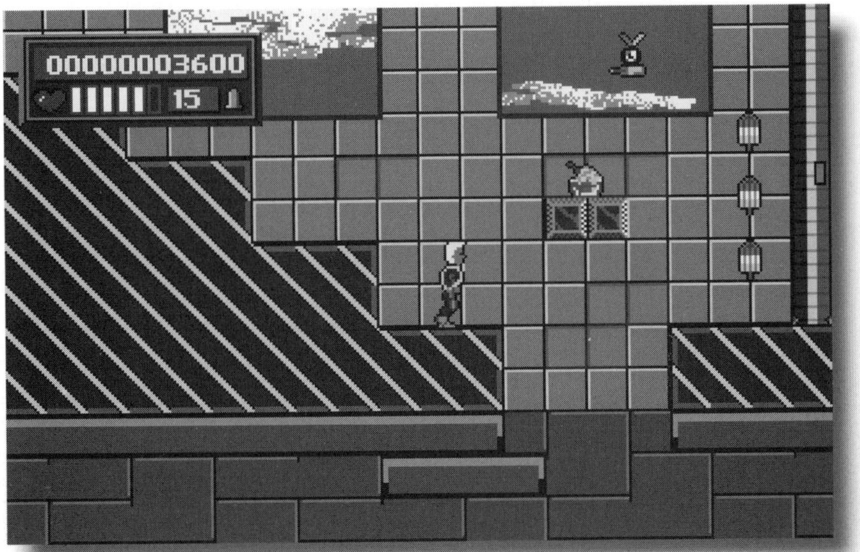

***Figure 4.2** Tiles drawn individually—like these to create Jason Storm in Space Chase (Safari Software)—tend to look choppy.*

so he draws you a background with many copies of the same greenery in it. The problem is that the duplicates do not appear at evenly spaced 16-pixel intervals. A perfectly beautiful branch may be repeated 15 or 17 pixels away. When the art is reduced to tiles, both branches show up in unique tiles, rather than the desired multiple copies of the same tile as shown in Figure 4.3.

Creating Ideal Art

We want a special kind of background artwork for our games. The artwork must be repetitive without looking blocky, and it must lend itself to building the kind of world we want our characters to inhabit. In particular, we need something for our sprites to stand on—a path or a floor. To compliment that, we will need background scenery, either indoors or outdoors. Some of this scenery will be strictly decorative, but we will also expect our sprites to respond to and interact with parts of the background. That means we will need things like doors, windows, ledges, and tunnels. We need to stretch a small amount of art to cover a very large level.

The tiling technique gives us the technology we need to make a small amount of artwork look like a lot of artwork. To make the tiling technique work, the artwork must be designed to lend itself to creating re-usable tiles.

Because we can only work with 240 tiles, we need to get as much mileage as possible out of each tile. The tiles need to be carefully constructed so that

Figure 4.3 *Creating art that can be turned into distinct tiles.*

we can get repeating patterns that don't look identical. For example, one set of tiles could be used to create both a tall tree and a short tree by simply reusing a few tiles to extend the trunk. Similarly, you can create a very long stretch of floor by repeatedly displaying three or four tiles. Of course, the tiles must also be drawn to fit together perfectly. The left side of one floor tile must match up with the right side of the next floor tile, and that tile must match the next tile, which happens to be identical to the previous tile—because it is the same tile. This sounds complicated, but it is actually quite simple. Figure 4.4 shows an example of how floor tiles should match.

Building an Actual Level

To understand how you go about building an actual level, take a look at the following steps, which summarize the process:

1. Create art that can be arranged into tiles.
2. Divide the art into distinct 16x16 pixel tiles.
3. Construct the level from the set of tiles.

To draw the level correctly, you must keep track of where each tile goes. As Figure 4.5 shows, a two-dimensional array holds byte values that represent tiles. The entire level is built by examining the array, and placing the appropriate tile at each location. Our job is to break down the artwork into tiles, and generate the array so that we can reconstruct the level.

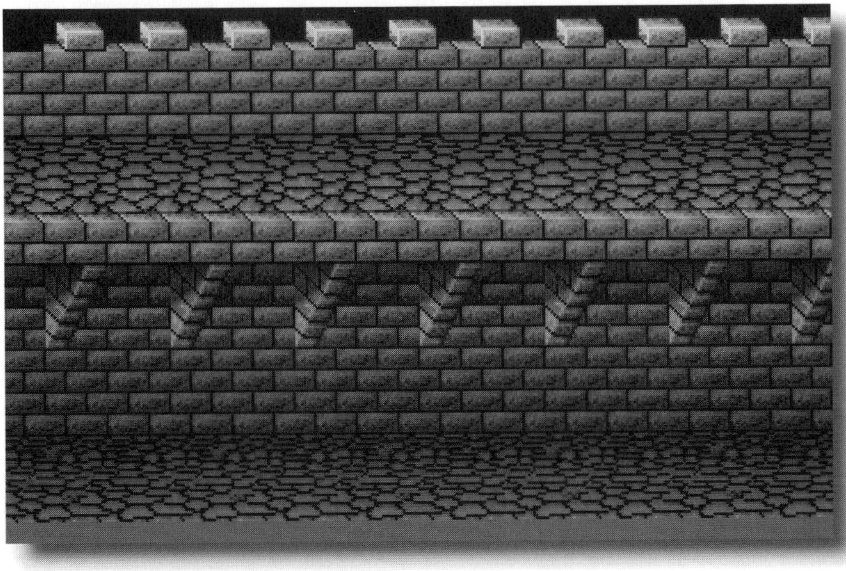

Figure 4.4 *A long section of floor may be made from only four tiles.*

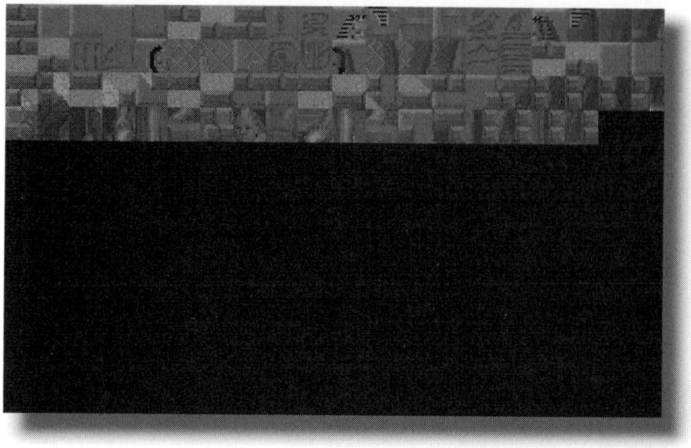

0	8	14	22	28	34	0	38	1	3	1	3	1	3	1	3	1	3	1	3
0	9	15	23	29	35	0	39	2	4	2	4	2	4	2	4	2	4	2	4
0	8	14	22	28	34	0	1	3	1	3	1	3	1	3	1	54	60	66	72
0	9	15	23	29	35	0	40	42	45	45	45	45	49	51	2	55	61	67	73
1	10	16	24	30	3	1	41	43	46	46	46	46	50	52	3	56	62	68	74
2	11	17	25	31	4	2	4	44	47	48	47	48	47	53	4	57	63	69	75
3	12	18	26	32	1	3	1	3	1	3	1	3	1	3	1	58	64	70	76
4	13	19	27	33	2	4	2	4	2	4	2	4	2	4	2	59	65	71	77
5	5	20	20	20	36	20	20	20	36	20	20	20	36	20	20	36	5	5	5
6	6	21	21	21	37	21	21	21	37	21	21	21	37	21	21	37	6	6	6
7	7	7	7	7	7	7	7	7	7	7	7	7	7	7	7	7	7	7	7
7	7	7	7	7	7	7	7	7	7	7	7	7	7	7	7	7	7	7	7

Figure 4.5 *Building a level with tiles.*

The 16×16 tile size gives us a good balance between speed and versatility. Smaller tiles, such as 8×8, would give us more variety, but would also create more data to work with, slowing us down. Larger tiles, say 32×16 or 32×32, would allow us to redraw the screen faster, but we would be constrained to working with fewer tiles. The 16×16 tile size is standard for side scrollers, and it is the tile size we will use throughout this book.

Paying for Your Art

If you use an artist, you can pay him or her on an hourly basis, a royalty basis, or a per-tile basis. My best artist charges a fixed rate per tile and gives me great tiles. When he creates background screens that can't easily be reduced to fewer than 240 tiles—the maximum number of tiles that can fit on a screen—I reject them. The bottom line is that when you pay for art, make sure you get your money's worth. If you find an artist who can create dazzling level art and can make duplicate tiles line up on 16 pixel boundaries, reward him or her well.

How do you determine how many tiles your artist has drawn? One easy way is to use a tile ripper to reduce the screen to tiles, and then count the tiles. I'll give you the code for this tile ripper soon. By exploring this simple program, you'll learn about the basic graphics programming concepts that we'll use in the later chapters.

The tile ripper is useful for more than counting tiles. It also is the first step in preprocessing background artwork to import into our game. As we will see, preparing artwork is one of the biggest jobs we will face in game development. Having tools to help us with this job will make the development process faster and infinitely more pleasant.

Let 'er Rip!—Introducing the Tile Ripper

Our tile ripper takes raw artwork stored in PCX files and reduces the art to its elemental tiles. The unique tiles that the ripper locates are then stored in a *tile library*. Later, you can use the tiles in the tile library to add or replace tiles in your level art. The addition and/or replacement of tiles is done by using the level editor presented in the previous chapter. You can also edit the individual tiles in the tile library using the tile editor presented in the previous chapter.

Tommy's Tip

The Tile Library

Background artwork is made up of unique tiles stored in a *tile library*. Our tile library consists of 240 unique tiles, These are stored on disk in a PCX file and are displayed in offscreen video memory during level editing and game play.

Here's how the tile ripper works: It loads in a PCX file and then displays the art on the screen. Next, the ripper starts at the upper-left corner, picks up a tile as a 16×16 bitmap, and stores it in RAM and in offscreen video memory. Then, the ripper moves down the first column and picks up a second tile bitmap and compares it to the first copy in RAM (see Figure 4.6). If it finds a match, it throws out the second tile, and updates an array called the **level_map**. If a match isn't found, the new tile is stored on the hidden page, and the tile library is increased by one. Each subsequent tile is compared to the first tile and any other tiles that are found to be unique. Eventually, the tile page contains only unique tiles, and the picture is stored as an array of indices into the tile library.

As the tile ripper progresses, it "blacks out" the duplicate tiles, leaving only the unique tiles visible. After the ripper has reduced the picture to its elemental tiles, it writes out the level to a binary file and creates a PCX file containing the tile library. Finally, the ripper checks its work by reconstructing the original picture from the tiles and the tile array, and displays it on the visual page. Figure 4.7 shows how the tile ripper processes a sample level art.

Using the Tile Ripper Program

You can use the tile ripper program stored on the companion disk by running the program from the DOS command line:

```
RIPPER infile1 <infile2> ... <infile6>
```

Notice that you can specify up to six input files. Each of these must be a PCX file. If you don't include at least one PCX file to rip, you'll get the following error message:

```
Command syntax is: RIPPER infile1 <infile2>...
```

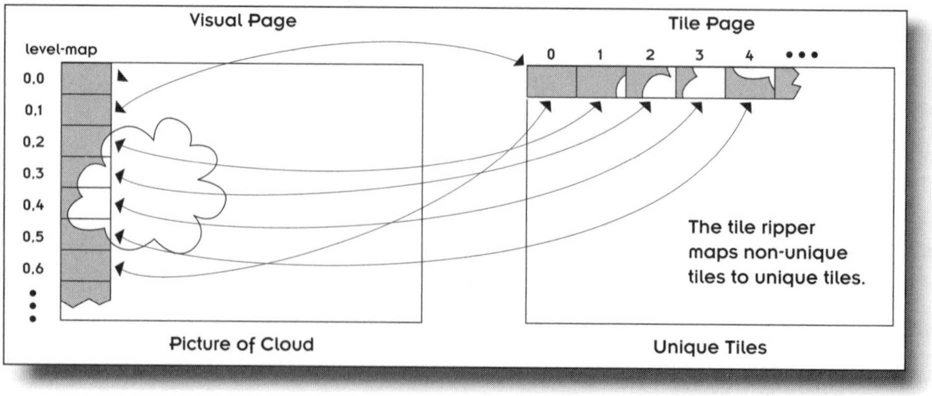

Figure 4.6 *How the tile ripper creates tiles.*

Figure 4.7a

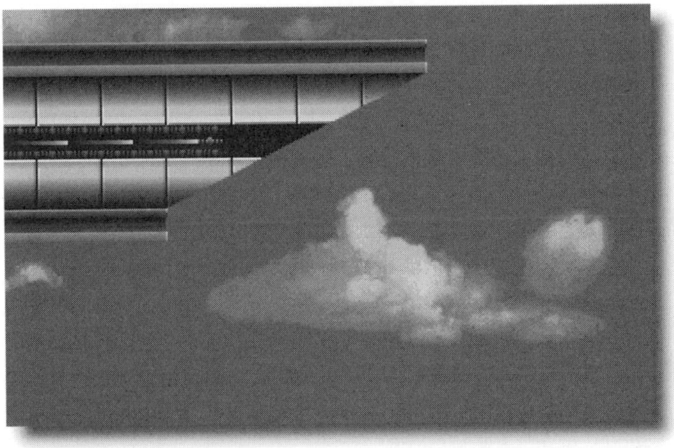

Figure 4.7b

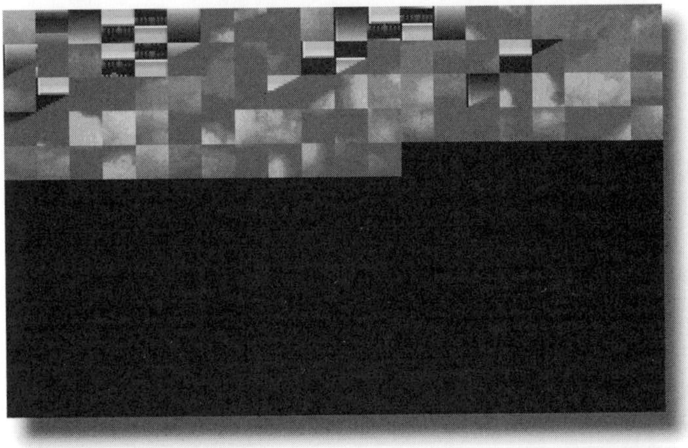

Figure 4.7c

Figure 4.7 *(a) The original level art; (b) the tile library created by ripping the level art; (c) and the background reduced to unique tiles.*

To simplify running the tile ripper, I have included a batch file, GO.BAT, with some suggested PCX filenames in it.

The tile ripper program will process all of the PCX files you include and will create two output files: TILES.PCX and RIPPER.LEV. The file, TILES.PCX, contains a bitmap image of all the distinct tiles that are created by the ripper. The RIPPER.LEV file contains the information needed to construct levels from the tile library that is created by ripping your art.

On Disk *The tile ripper program is stored on the companion disk as RIPPER.EXE in the directory \FG\UTIL\. If you compile the RIPPER.C source file yourself, make sure that you have either the Fastgraph or Fastgraph/Light library available to link the program.*

The Complete Tile Ripper Program

It's time to look at the tile ripper code. Although the code shown here is for a standalone program, when you are working on your game, you will probably want to use the more complete tile ripper that is incorporated into the game editor. The program is called from a menu when the computer is already in graphics mode, and filenames are passed to it according to user input.

For our standalone version, we'll need to include the basic code to read in PCX art files and set the proper video modes for processing the art work that is read in. Here is the complete RIPPER.C program:

```
/******************************************************************\
  ripper.c — tile ripper for preprocessing background tiles
             by Diana Gruber

  compile using large memory model
  requires Fastgraph(tm) or Fastgraph/Light(tm) to link

\******************************************************************/

#include <fastgraf.h>    /* Fastgraph header file */
#include <stdio.h>       /* standard include files */
#include <stdlib.h>
#ifdef __TURBOC__
   #include <mem.h>      /* header file for Borland C and Turbo C */
#else
   #include <memory.h>      /* header file for Microsoft C */
#endif

int rip(char *filename); /* function declarations */
void write_level(void);
void display_level(int col);
```

```
FILE *stream;              /* level output data file */

#define TILESIZE  256      /* tiles are 16 pixels x 16 pixels */
#define TILELIMIT 240      /* only 240 unique tiles */
#define MAXROWS   12       /* 12 rows per page */
#define MAXCOLS   120      /* up to 6 screens of art = 120 columns */

/* the ripper_tiles array is used to store the unique tiles as
   bitmaps RAM in for easy tile comparisons */

unsigned char far ripper_tiles[TILELIMIT][TILESIZE];

/* the level_map array stores the information needed to rebuild
   the level from tiles */

unsigned char far level_map[MAXCOLS][MAXROWS];

int tile_index;            /* keep track of current tile */
int level_index;           /* keep track of level position */
int ncols;                 /* total columns in level map */
int col;                   /* keep track of current tile position */

/****************************************************************/

void main(int argc, char *argv[])
{
   register int i;

   /* check that an input file was specified */
   if (argc < 2)
   {
      printf("Command syntax is: RIPPER infile1 <infile2>...\n");
      exit(1);
   }

   /* initialize the video mode to Mode X: 320x200x256 */
   fg_setmode(20);

   /* initialize some globals */
   tile_index = 0;
   level_index = 0;
   ncols = 0;
   col = 0;

   /* set all the tiles in the level map to 255 */
   memset(level_map,255,MAXCOLS*MAXROWS);

   /* rip all the files specified on the command line */
   for (i = 1; i <= argc; i++)
     rip(argv[i]);

   /* write the level data and tiles out to disk */
   write_level();
```

```
   /* check your work — reconstruct the picture from the tiles */
   for (i = 0; i < ncols; i+=20)
      display_level(i);

   /* restore the text video mode and exit */
   fg_setmode(3);
   fg_reset();
   exit(0);
}

/******************************************************************/

int rip(char *filename)
{
   register int i,n;
   unsigned char new_tile[TILESIZE];
   int x,y,x1,y1;
   int status;
   int row;

   /* if you already have a full screen tiles, return an error */
   if (tile_index >= TILELIMIT)
      return(-1);

   /* display the PCX file on the visual page */
   fg_setpage(0);
   fg_setvpage(0);
   fg_move(0,0);
   status = fg_showpcx(filename,0);

   /* return an error code if the PCX file is bad or missing */
   if (status > 0)
      return(status);

   /* loop on the PCX file, starting at upper-left corner, moving
      down the columns in sequence */

   row = 0;
   for (n = 0; n < TILELIMIT; n++)
   {
      x = (n/12)*16;
      y = (n%12)*16 + 15;

      /* get the new tile bitmap */
      fg_move(x,y);
      fg_getimage(new_tile,16,16);

      /* compare the new tile to all the ripper tiles */
      for (i = 0; i < tile_index; i++)
      {
         if (memcmp(new_tile,ripper_tiles[i],TILESIZE) == 0)
         {
            /* a duplicate tile is found, update the level map */
            level_map[col][row] = (unsigned char)i;
```

```
            /* black out the duplicate tile */
            fg_setcolor(0);
            fg_rect(x,x+15,y-15,y);
            break;
         }
      }

      /* no match was found, therefore the tile must be unique */
      if (level_map[col][row] == 255)
      {
         /* copy the new tile to the hidden page */
         x1 = (tile_index%20)*16;
         y1 = (tile_index/20)*16 + 23;
         fg_transfer(x,x+15,y-15,y,x1,y1,0,3);

         /* build the level map with the tile index */
         level_map[col][row] = (unsigned char)tile_index;

         /* hold the array in RAM for later comparisons */
         memcpy(ripper_tiles[tile_index],new_tile,TILESIZE);

         /* we can't have more than 240 unique tiles */
         tile_index++;
         if (tile_index >= TILELIMIT)
            break;
      }

      /* increment the row and column count */
      row++;
      if (row >= 12)
      {
         row = 0;
         col++;
      }
   }

   /* total number of columns */
   ncols = col;
}

/******************************************************************/

void write_level(void)
{
   register int i,j;

   /* make a PCX file out of the tile page */
   fg_setpage(3);
   fg_setvpage(3);
   fg_makepcx(0,319,8,199,"tiles.pcx");

   /* open a binary file for the level array */
   stream = fopen("ripper.lev","wb");
```

```
   /* write out all the columns, 12 tiles per column */
   j = 0;
   for (i = 0; i < ncols; i++)
   {
      fwrite(&level_map[i][0],sizeof(char),12,stream);
      j+=12;
   }
   fclose(stream);
}

/******************************************************************/

void display_level(int col)
{
   register int i,j;
   int x,y,x1,y1;
   int tile;

   /* set the visual page to page 0 and erase whatever is on it */
   fg_setpage(0);
   fg_setvpage(0);
   fg_erase();

   /* display the tiles starting at the top of the first column */
   for (i = 0; i < 20; i++)
   {
      for (j = 0; j < 12; j++)
      {
         tile = (int)level_map[col+i][j];
         x = (tile%20)*16;
         y = (tile/20)*16 + 23;

         x1 = i*16;
         y1 = j*16 + 15;

         fg_transfer(x,x+15,y-15,y,x1,y1,3,0);
      }
   }

   /* wait a bit so you can see what you did */
   fg_waitfor(20);
}
```

Table 4.1 *The Functions Used in RIPPER.C*

Function	Description
main()	Opens the PCX art files, sets the video modes, and calls the other functions to create the tiles
rip()	Performs the work of ripping tiles and building the tile library
write_level()	Creates a PCX file to store the tiles and a binary file to store the level data
display_level()	Reconstructs a screen of art from the tiles and level data

Exploring the Tile Ripper Code

Let's go through the program and discuss what each section does. As Table 4.1 shows, the tile ripper program only requires four functions.

Including FASTGRAF.H

Starting at the top, we see the usual include files for an ANSI C program, plus a special one:

```
#include <fastgraf.h>    /* Fastgraph header file */
```

This is the header file required for Fastgraph. You should include this file in any program that calls any Fastgraph functions. The first few lines of the FASTGRAF.H file look like this:

```
/*********************************************************************\
*  FASTGRAF.H
*  This file contains the C and C++ function prototypes for Fastgraph v3.05  *
*  and Fastgraph/Light v3.05.
*  Copyright (c) 1991-1993 Ted Gruber Software. All rights reserved.
\*********************************************************************/

#ifdef __cplusplus
extern "C" {
#endif

int    fg_allocate (int);
int    fg_alloccms (int);
int    fg_allocems (int);
int    fg_allocxms (int);
int    fg_automode (void);

int    fg_bestmode (int, int, int);
void   fg_box (int, int, int, int);
void   fg_boxdepth (int, int);
void   fg_boxw (double, double, double, double);
void   fg_boxx (int, int, int, int);
void   fg_boxxw (double, double, double, double);
int    fg_button (int);

int    fg_capslock (void);
void   fg_chgattr (int);
void   fg_chgtext (char *, int);
void   fg_circle (int);
void   fg_circlef (int);
void   fg_circlefw (double);
void   fg_circlew (double);
void   fg_clipmask (char *, int, int);
void   fg_clpimage (char *, int, int);
```

```
void    fg_clprect (int, int, int, int);
void    fg_clprectw (double, double, double, double);
void    fg_copypage (int, int);
void    fg_cursor (int);

void    fg_dash (int, int, int);
void    fg_dashrel (int, int, int);
void    fg_dashrw (double, double, int);
void    fg_dashw (double, double, int);
void    fg_defcolor (int, int);
void    fg_defpages (int, int);
void    fg_dispfile (char *, int, int);
void    fg_display (char *, int, int);
void    fg_displayp (char *, int, int);
void    fg_draw (int, int);
void    fg_drawmap (char *, int, int);
void    fg_drawmask (char *, int, int);
void    fg_drawrel (int, int);
void    fg_drawrelx (int, int);
void    fg_drawrw (double, double);
void    fg_drawrxw (double, double);
void    fg_draww (double, double);
void    fg_drawx (int, int);
void    fg_drawxw (double, double);
void    fg_drect (int, int, int, int, char *);
void    fg_drectw (double, double, double, double, char *);
void    fg_drwimage (char *, int, int);
```

As you can see, the header file only contains function declarations for the Fastgraph functions. No variables or structures are declared, no constants or macros are defined, and no additional header files are embedded in the Fastgraph header file. It is really a very benign file, and we don't need to worry about it further.

Tommy's Tip

Looking Up a Function

If you need more information about a Fastgraph function (these functions all have the prefix **fg_**), use the online manual provided with the companion disk. You can view the manual by reading the text file REF.DOC.

Adding the Definitions

In accordance with commonly accepted C programming practices, we use the C preprocessor directive, **#define**, to assign logical names to some fixed values. These definitions are included at the top of RIPPER.C:

```
#define TILESIZE  256
#define TILELIMIT 240
#define MAXROWS   12
#define MAXCOLS   120
```

These values will be useful to us in allocating space for our tiles and managing the tile library:

- **TILESIZE** is the size of a single tile. Since each tile is 16 pixels wide and 16 pixels high, a tile will take up 256 bytes (16x16 = 256). When we allocate space in RAM for a tile, this is how much space we'll need.
- **TILELIMIT** is the number of tiles we can have. We are limiting ourselves to 240 tiles, which is the number of tiles that can be displayed on a single screen of graphics. As shown in Figure 4.8, our screen is 320x200 pixels, so we can fit 20 tiles horizontally and 12 tiles vertically.

```
 20 columns of tiles
x12 rows of tiles
—
240 total tiles on one page
```

Tommy's Tip

Why Limit Your Tiles?

We could conceivably fit more than 240 tiles in video memory, but we choose not to. Our upper limit on tiles is 256 because we want

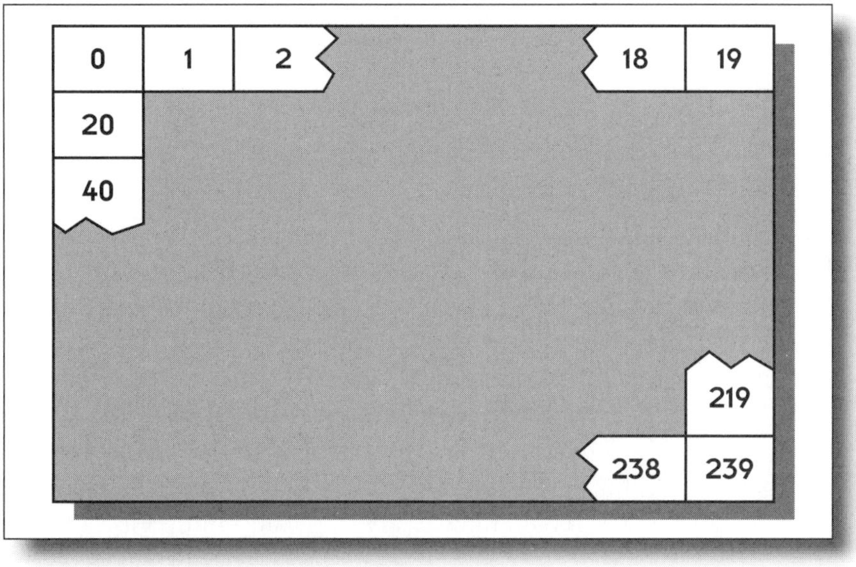

Figure 4.8 *How tiles are arranged on a screen.*

to address them as unsigned bytes. If we have more than 256 tiles, we will have to use integer indices to access the tile array. This is not particularly desirable because our tile arrays are going to be large, and we are going to be facing RAM limitations later on. Byte arrays take up half as much room in RAM as integer arrays. Remember, as game programmers we need to always think in terms of conserving RAM. As our game develops, we'll use every last byte of RAM for things like sprites and sound effects, and the more room we have, the more exciting stuff we can put into our game.

- **MAXROWS** is the number of rows of tiles. We use 12 rows of tiles per screen:

```
 200 lines of pixels in the vertical direction
÷ 16 pixels per tile
------------------------------------------------
  12 rows of tiles, plus 8 lines of pixels left over
```

  Since the screen resolution is 200 lines, we cannot evenly divide it into tiles. We have eight lines of pixels left over. We will ignore those extra eight lines for now, but we'll find a use for that space later. In the tile editor, we will use the extra room for labeling the pages and the tile numbers. In our game, we'll use every bit of video memory we can get our hands on, but in the tile ripper, we don't really need that little bit of extra space, so we'll just ignore it.

- **MAXCOLS** is the total number of columns. There are 20 columns of tiles per screen, and up to six screens of tiles can be ripped at one time:

```
 320 pixels horizontally
÷ 16 pixels per tile
---------------------------------
  20 tiles per screen (horizontally)
x  6 screens of artwork
---------------------------------
 120 total columns
```

  It's unusual to rip more than six screens of tiles at a time. Usually we'll only rip two or three, as in Figure 4.9. But you can rip more screens if you want to, depending on what your art looks like. If you have a lot of screens that contain lots of duplicate tiles, you can increase the number of **MAXCOLS**. Eventually, though, you will run out of RAM. Also, since there can only be a maximum of 240 unique tiles, you usually reach that number in fewer than six screens of art. If you have more than six screens of art, you probably have unnecessary duplication in your artwork, and

Figure 4.9 *Three screens of background art for ripping.*

you can reduce the number of screens by combining similar pictures into one picture.

Adding the Declarations

The goal of the tile ripper is to reduce several screens of artwork to a single screen of unique tiles, but let's remember we'll also want to reconstruct the original pictures from the tiles. To do that, we'll construct an array to hold the tile data as it relates to the original pictures. Since we'll want to access this array often and from many different functions, it is most convenient to make it a global array, which we declare like this:

```
unsigned char far level_map[MAXCOLS][MAXROWS];
```

Every element of **level_map** is a number between 0 and 239, representing the 240 unique tiles. We use this array to construct a level out of the tiles. The tile ripper generates this array, and later we'll use a level editor to add rows and columns, rearrange blocks of tiles, and so on. We declare the **level_map** as a far array to get it out of the default data segment. It will be a fairly large array, and we only have 64K in the default data segment. Even when using the large memory model, we always declare large arrays as **far** whenever possible to avoid overflowing the near data segment. That's why we also declare the **ripper_tiles** array to be far:

```
unsigned char far ripper_tiles[TILELIMIT][TILESIZE];
```

The **ripper_tiles** array keeps copies of the unique tile bitmaps in RAM for fast comparisons.

Next, we'll need to declare some global variables.

```
int tile_index;          /* keep track of current tile */
int level_index;         /* keep track of level position */
int ncols;               /* total columns in level map */
int col;                 /* keep track of current tile position */
```

The **tile_index** and **level_index** variables will be useful as we work our way through the **rip()** function. The **ncols** variable is the total number of columns we will rip. The final global variable we declare is **col**. Since we are going to rip the tiles one column at a time, we need to keep track of which column we are currently working on. This value does not need to be global; we could declare it in function **main()** and pass it to **rip()**. Some people frown on using global variables, but as a game programmer, I am in the habit of using them. Gamers must think in terms of optimizing everything, including stack space. If you have functions nested several levels deep, and you pass a variable all the way down and all the way back up again, it's not as efficient as having a value immediately available as a global.

On the other hand, you need to be careful with global variables. You don't want to overdo it. Globals take up room in the default data segment (unless declared **far**), and when working in real mode, gamers are constantly facing a shortage of near memory. Try to use globals appropriately, but sparingly.

Getting to main()

The tile ripper program begins with the **main()** function. The first thing **main()** does is examine the command-line parameters and make sure at least one input file is specified. If not, it notifies the user and politely exits. (We could have better error-checking at this point, such as checking the suffix to make sure a PCX file is specified. For a program designed for public consumption, this would be a requirement. But since we are designing this program for in-house use, we can be a little more relaxed about error-checking and just give ourselves enough of an error message to remind ourselves how the program works.)

The mystery function call in the next line of code is:

```
fg_setmode(20);
```

This code has far-reaching consequences. It is, perhaps, the most important thing we have done to this point. This single line of code assumes control of the VGA card and sets the video mode to Mode X.

Fastgraph Tip

fg_setmode()

The **fg_setmode()** function establishes a video mode and initializes Fastgraph's internal parameters for that mode. It must be called before any Fastgraph function that performs video output. A program can call **fg_setmode()** as many times as needed to switch among different video modes.

```
void fg_setmode(int mode_number);
```

- *mode_number* is the video mode number, between 0 and 29. These video modes are explained in detail in the *Fastgraph Users Manual* stored on the companion disk.

Tommy's Tip

Introducing Mode X

Mode X is a VGA mode that is available on all VGA cards with 256K of memory. Fastgraph calls this mode Mode 20. This particular incarnation of Mode X has a visible resolution of 320x200 and allows you to display 256 simultaneous colors out of a selection of 262,143. Mode 20 is a planar mode, meaning that data is moved in four groups called planes, as opposed to a linear mode where all data is moved sequentially. Don't worry about that right now. Fastgraph will handle the data moves for us. I would prefer not to get sidetracked into a discussion of bit twiddling, because if we do, we may never get our program written. The inner workings of Mode X are documented in many other places. Exactly how Mode X works is not nearly so interesting as what you can do with it. For now, let's just accept that this is the best video mode to use, and move on to some of the wondrous things we can do in this fabulous video mode.

The original Mode X, as defined by Michael Abrash, called for a 320x240 resolution. Our video mode has a smaller vertical resolution but retains the other properties of Mode X, including the planar memory organization. Originally, Mode X was known by gamers as the "secret mode."

Initializing Variables

Our next step in the tile ripper program is to initialize the global variables. The indexes and column count all start at 0, and all the elements of the level map are set to 255. Because there are only 240 tiles, 255 is an invalid value for a tile in the level map. We don't want to initialize the level map to all 0s, because 0 is a valid tile number. Later, we'll see how this value is used to check an array position to see if a tile has been assigned to it yet. To initialize the level map, we use the C function **memset()**:

```
memset(level_map,255,MAXCOLS*MAXROWS);
```

Processing PCX Files

Now that we have declared and initialized everything and set the video mode, we are ready to rip. For each PCX file specified on the command line, we'll call the **rip()** function to rip each file in sequence.

```
for (i = 1; i <= argc; i++)
   rip(argv[i]);
```

The first step in ripping a PCX file is displaying it in video memory. We use Fastgraph's **fg_showpcx()** function to accomplish this with a minimum of fanfare:

```
status = fg_showpcx(filename,0);
```

Fastgraph Tip

fg_showpcx()

The **fg_showpcx()** function displays an image stored in a PCX file. By default, the image will be positioned as specified in the PCX header…

```
int fg_showpcx(char *filename, int flags);
```

- *filename* is the name of the PCX file. A device and path name may be included as part of the filename. The filename must be terminated by a null character (that is, a zero byte).
- *flags* is a bit mask that controls how the image is displayed:

  Bit 0
  0 = use palette values stored in the PCX file
  1 = use the current palette settings
  Bit 1
  0 = display image at position indicated in PCX header

1 = display image at current graphics position
Bit 2
0 = display image from disk to video memory
1 = display image from an array in RAM to video memory
Bits 3-15 are reserved for future use and should be 0

Supporting Multiple Pages

One of the marvelous things about Mode X is that we have more than one page to work with. That means we can display graphics to any one of four pages, and we can also look at any of those pages. We don't necessarily have to be looking at the same page we are writing to, and it is a common trick to write graphics to offscreen video memory. But in the case of the PCX file, we want to display it on the visual page, which is page 0, and we also want to make sure we are looking at page 0 when we display it. The following two Fastgraph function calls accomplish this:

```
fg_setpage(0);
fg_setvpage(0);
```

The **fg_setpage()** function and the **fg_setvpage()** function set the active and visual page, respectively. That means the PCX file will be displayed on page 0, and page 0 will be visible when the PCX file is displayed.

Fastgraph Tip

fg_setpage()

The **fg_setpage()** function establishes the active video page. It may be a physical or virtual video page. The **fg_setmode()** function designates video page 0 as the active page.

```
void fg_setpage(int page_number);
```

- *page_number* is the active video page number, between 0 and 63.

Fastgraph Tip

fg_setvpage()

The **fg_setvpage()** function establishes the visual video page. It may be a physical or virtual video page, but not a logical page. The **fg_setmode()** function designates video page 0 as the visual page.

```
void fg_setpage(int page_number);
```

- *page_number* is the active video page number, between 0 and 63.

Into the Heart of the rip() Function

Now comes the heart of the **rip()** function. We loop continuously, stopping either when we have ripped the whole picture, or when we have reached our limit of 240 unique tiles. We start by grabbing tiles and comparing them to each other, beginning with the tile in the upper-left corner of the picture and moving down the columns. The x and y screen coordinates for the lower-left corner of the tile are calculated based on the loop index, n, and then the **fg_move()** function is used to move the graphics cursor to the desired location. Then, we use Fastgraph's **fg_getimage()** function to grab the bitmap from video memory and put it in RAM:

```
x = (n/12)*16;
y = (n%12)*16 + 15;
fg_move(x,y);
fg_getimage(new_tile,16,16);
```

Fastgraph Tip

fg_move()

The **fg_move()** function establishes the graphics cursor position at an absolute screen space point.

```
void fg_move(int ix, int iy);
```

- *ix* is the screen space x coordinate of the graphics cursor's new position.
- *iy* is the screen space y coordinate of the graphics cursor's new position.

Tommy's Tip

Introducing Fastgraph's Graphics Cursor

The *graphics cursor* is Fastgraph's internal method of keeping track of an x and y position on the screen. Many Fastgraph functions that "happen" at the graphics cursor include **fg_getimage()**, **fg_drwimage()**, **fg_display()**, and **fg_draw()**. The graphics cursor is not a real cursor, just a set of (x,y) coordinates referencing a position in video memory.

Fastgraph Tip

fg_getimage()

The **fg_getimage()** function retrieves an image as a mode-specific bitmap. The graphics cursor position (the text cursor position in text video modes) defines the lower-left corner of the image to retrieve.

```
void fg_getimage(char *map_array, int width, int height);
```

- *map_array* is the arbitrary-length array in which to retrieve the bitmap.
- *width* is the width in bytes of the bitmap.
- *height* is the height in bytes (pixel rows) of the bitmap.

The bitmap array, **new_tile**, is declared to hold 256 elements. Our tile is 16x16, so it fits nicely in this array. Since this is our first tile, we know it is going to be unique and will obviously fail the comparison test.

Processing Unique Tiles

When a tile fails the comparison loop, several things happen. First, the tile is copied to a hidden page (page 3 in this case). This is where the tile library is stored.

```
x1 = (tile_index%20)*16;
y1 = (tile_index/20)*16 + 23;
fg_transfer(x,x+15,y-15,y,x1,y1,0,3);
```

The x and y coordinates of the tile library destination are calculated in terms of the tile index. If it is the first tile, it will be copied to x = 0, y = 23. The second tile will be placed to the right of the first tile, and so on. Tiles are lined up in rows of 20 on the hidden page, as shown in Figure 4.10.

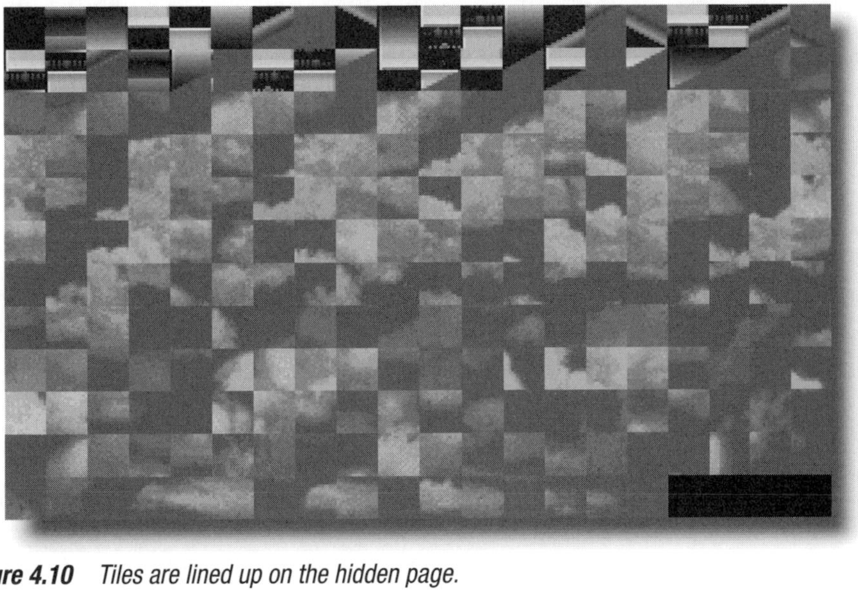

Figure 4.10 *Tiles are lined up on the hidden page.*

A direct video-to-video blit is used to copy the tile from page 0, the visual page, to page 3, the tile library page. Fastgraph's **fg_transfer()** function handles the video-to-video blit for us.

Tommy's Tip

Introducing Blits

A *blit*, also known as a *blt* or *bitblt*, is a block image transfer. It is a shorthand term, commonly used by gamers to describe applying an image to video memory, usually a rectangular shape, and originating either in RAM or in another part of video memory. It's usually used as a verb ("to blit a tile"), and is also used as slang among gamers ("I'm getting an awesome blit rate in Mode X").

Fastgraph Tip

fg_transfer()

The **fg_transfer()** function copies a rectangular region from any position on any video page to any position on any video page.

```
void fg_transfer (int minx, int maxx, int miny, int maxy, int newx,
int newy, int source_page, int dest_page);
```

- *minx* is the x coordinate of the source region's left edge. In some graphics modes, such as the 16-color modes, its value is reduced to a byte boundary if necessary.
- *maxx* is the x coordinate of the source region's right edge. It must be greater than or equal to the value of *minx*. Its value is extended to a byte boundary if necessary.
- *miny* is the y coordinate of the source region's top edge.
- *maxy* is the y coordinate of the source region's bottom edge. It must be greater than or equal to the value of *miny*.
- *newx* is the x coordinate of the destination region's left edge. Its value is reduced to a byte boundary if necessary.
- *newy* is the y coordinate of the destination region's bottom edge.
- *source_page* is the video page number containing the source region.
- *dest_page* is the video page number for the destination region.

The first y coordinate is 23 instead of 15 because of those extra eight lines of video memory we mentioned earlier. We will leave those eight lines empty at the top of the screen as shown in Figure 4.11. Later, we'll use that area for labels and status messages in the tile editor.

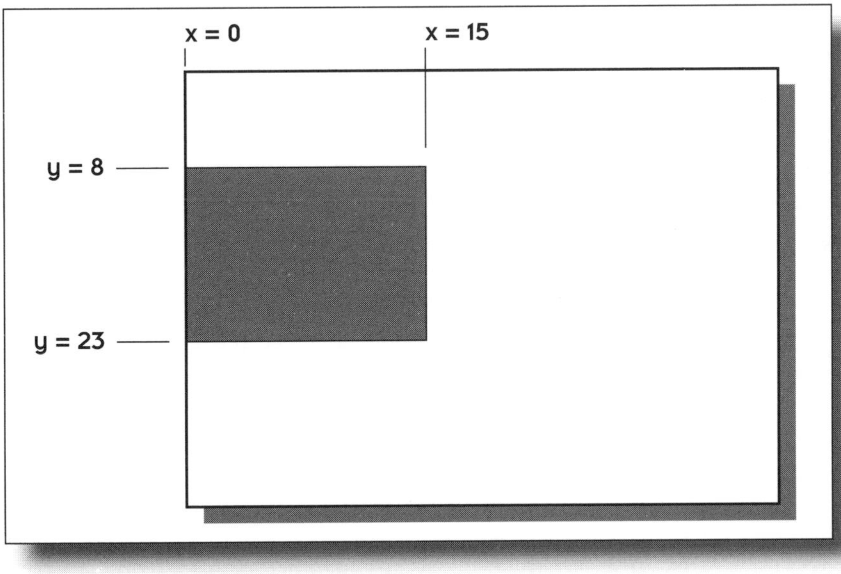

Figure 4.11 *Accessing the first y coordinate.*

The next step is for the tile ripper to add the tile to the **level_map array**:

```
level_map[col][row] = (unsigned char)tile_index;
```

As we move down the column of tiles in the PCX file, we'll add to this array. This array contains the indexes into the tile library and will be used later to reconstruct the original picture. We also want to keep a copy of the tile in RAM for comparisons to other tiles. We copy it to the **ripper_tiles** array using C's **memcpy()** function, like this:

```
memcpy(ripper_tiles[tile_index],new_tile,TILESIZE);
```

Tommy's Tip

Repeated String Instructions

Whenever possible, we use C's string functions like **memcmp()**, **memcpy()**, and **memset()** to manipulate arrays. These functions are much faster than writing our own code to compare, copy, and initialize arrays because they take advantage of the microprocessor's repeated string instructions. The code to copy the tile array could be written like this:

```
for (i = 0; i < tilesize; i++)
   ripper_tiles[tile_index][i] = new_tile[i];
```

But it would be slower than using the **memcpy()** function.

Then, we increment the tile index, checking to make sure we haven't exceeded the limit of 240 tiles:

```
tile_index++;
if (tile_index >= TILELIMIT)
   break;
```

Finally, we increment the row index, and if we are at the end of a row, we increment the column index as well:

```
row++;
if (row >= 12)
{
   row = 0;
   col++;
}
```

Processing Duplicate Tiles

The code in the previous section handles the case of the unique tile, but what about the non-unique tiles? Suppose the second tile is exactly the same as the first tile, a not-so-unusual situation if you are dealing with a wall or a blue sky, for example. To find duplicate tiles, you need to compare the current tile to all the other tiles in a loop, using the C **memcmp()** function:

```
if (memcmp(new_tile,ripper_tiles[i],TILESIZE) == 0)
```

If a match is found, we don't need to copy the tile to the hidden page or update the **ripper_tile** array. All we need to do is add the tile to **level_map**:

```
level_map[col][row] = (unsigned char)i;
```

For good measure, we draw a black rectangle over the tile, indicating it is a duplicate tile, as shown here:

```
/* black out the duplicate tiles */
fg_setcolor(0);
fg_rect(x, x+5,y-15,y);
```

It is not really necessary to black out the duplicate tiles, but it is helpful when watching the program to get a feel for how many tiles are unique and where they are. It is also helpful in debugging the program. You can tell if the tile ripper is doing something or just sitting there thinking.

Fastgraph Tip

fg_setcolor()

The **fg_setcolor()** function establishes the current color index (which may be a virtual color index) in graphics modes. In text modes, **fg_setcolor()** provides an alternate method of defining the current text attribute.

```
void fg_setcolor(int color);
```

- *color* defines the current color index (in graphics modes) or text attribute (in text modes). Its value must be between 0 and 255.

Fastgraph Tip

fg_rect()

The **fg_rect()** function draws a solid (filled) rectangle in screen space or character space, without regard to the clipping region.

```
void fg_rect (int minx, maxx, int miny, int maxy);
```

- *minx* is the x coordinate of the rectangle's left edge.
- *maxx* is the x coordinate of the rectangle's right edge. It must be greater than or equal to the value of *minx*.
- *miny* is the y coordinate of the rectangle's top edge.
- *maxy* is the y coordinate of the rectangle's bottom edge. It must be greater than or equal to the value of *miny*.

If no match is found, the **level_map** array remains at its original value of 255. After we exit the comparison loop, we look at the level map and see if it has been assigned a value:

```
if (level_map[col][row] == 255)
```

If the level map is 255, then we know no match was found and the current tile is unique.

Saving the Level Information

The tile ripper progresses through the screen, grabbing tiles, comparing them to previous unique tiles, throwing out the duplicates, and adding unique tiles to the tile library, until it runs out of artwork or hits the 240-tile limit. It rips all the PCX files specified on the command line, and in this way the tile ripper reduces several screens of art to one screen of tiles. As it rips, it generates an array containing the information necessary to rebuild the artwork from the tiles. After all the tiles are ripped, the function **write_level()** is called and the level information is written to disk. A PCX file is created to store the tiles, and a binary file is created to hold the level data so that the level art can be reconstructed later. The PCX file, TILES.PCX, is created using these three Fastgraph calls:

```
/* make a PCX file out of the tile page */
fg_setpage(3);
fg_setvpage(3);
fg_makepcx(0,319,8,199,"tiles.pcx");
```

Fastgraph Tip

fg_makepcx()

The **fg_makepcx()** function creates a PCX file from the specified rectangular region of the active video page. The region's extremes are expressed in screen space units.

```
int fg_makepcx(int minx, int maxx, int miny, int maxy, char *filename);
```

- *minx* is the x coordinate of the region's left edge.
- *maxx* is the x coordinate of the region's right edge. It must be greater than or equal to the value of *minx.*
- *miny* is the y coordinate of the region's top edge.
- *maxy* is the y coordinate of the region's bottom edge. It must be greater than or equal to the value of *miny.*
- *filename* is the name of the PCX file to create.

The actual level data is stored in RIPPER.LEV. Once this file is created with the **fopen()** function, a simple loop is used to send the level data stored in the **level_map** array to the file:

```
for (i = 0; i < ncols; i++)
   {
      fwrite(&level_map[i][0],sizeof(char),12,stream);
      j+=12;
   }
```

Finishing Up

Once the level information has been saved, a final function, **display_level()**, is called to double-check our work. If **display_level()** is able to reconstruct the screens of art from the tiles and the level array, we can assume the rip was successful. Each reconstructed screen of art is left on the screen for just over a second, long enough to see the results, but not so long that it becomes boring. We use Fastgraph's **fg_waitfor()** function to control the delay:

```
fg_waitfor(20);
```

Fastgraph Tip

fg_waitfor()

The **fg_waitfor()** function delays a program's execution for a given number of clock ticks. There are 18.2 clock ticks per second, regardless of the system's processor speed.

```
void fg_waitfor(int ticks);
```

- *ticks* is the number of clock ticks to wait.

Returning to DOS

Like all well-behaved programs, our tile ripper will put everything back the way it was before it exits. Most importantly, we will set the video mode back to mode 3, which is the default text mode that computers operate in when they are not doing something funny, like running Windows. We will also call **fg_reset()** to clear the screen and reset the screen attributes, if any.

```
fg_setmode(3);
fg_reset();
```

The **fg_reset()** function may require a little more explanation. It is not immediately obvious why it is called. If you are used to looking at white text on a black screen, or if you do not have the ANSI.SYS device driver loaded, then resetting the screen attributes will not affect you. Some of us prefer a more colorful screen at the DOS prompt. For example, I like to look at white letters on a blue screen. I use the Norton Control Center program (from Norton Utilities) to set the default state of my computer to the desired colors. When I exit some programs, I see a partially black screen with a blue and white DOS prompt up in the corner. I think it is more attractive to see a program exit to a fully blue screen with white letters on it. That's what **fg_reset()** does, it clears the screen to whatever screen attributes were set with ANSI.SYS.

Fastgraph Tip

fg_reset()

When the ANSI.SYS driver is not loaded, the **fg_reset()** function erases the screen. When ANSI.SYS is loaded, **fg_reset()** also restores any previously set screen attributes. It is generally the last Fastgraph function called in a program.

```
void fg_reset(void);
```

More about Fastgraph

In this chapter we have introduced many of the Fastgraph functions that we will be using in the later chapters. For a complete listing of Fastgraph functions, you can refer to the Fastgraph Reference Manual which is included on the companion disk. You may print out the entire manual, if you want, but be warned — it's pretty big! If you print out both the *Fastgraph User's Guide* and the *Fastgraph Reference Manual*, it will total about 700 pages. That will keep your printer busy for a while. You can also read the manuals online (they are in a straight ASCII format), or you can get a hard copy version. Information about ordering Fastgraph is in the back of this book. Meanwhile, you can always refer back to this chapter for information about the Fastgraph functions we have discussed so far.

Chapter 5

Take a look at this chapter to see how reshaping video memory allows for lightning-fast, but smooth scrolling.

The Magic of Side Scrolling

When my husband Ted first suggested we buy a personal computer for our home, I was skeptical. Men can be so impractical! I was not thrilled with the idea of throwing away money on another toy. Why spend money on a computer when we could use the money for more important things like clothes or a vacation? Ted finally convinced me be saying he would use it to write programs and make money to pay for it all. We picked out an AT and within a few weeks I was nagging him to do something useful with it.

Ted's first attempt at graphics programming in BASIC was silly—he mastered launching pixel projectiles in a CGA mode. I wanted nothing to do with it. After all, I had outgrown BASIC months earlier and was now programming in FORTRAN. Ted's next attempt was a bit more dignified. He used assembly language to set an EGA video mode and draw a pixel. His pixel quickly became a line and then a rectangle. Within a few weeks, he had functions for supporting text, bitmaps, and keyboard control. Now I was getting interested.

"You should write a video poker game," Ted said, and I did. A programming partnership was born. Ted continued to supply me with low-level graphics functions, and I continued to write games to test them out. Sometimes I would get ahead of him and ask for more functions, like video-to-video blits. Other times, Ted passed me by and then I would be hard-pressed to think up a new game to use his discoveries.

One day, Ted discovered how to resize video memory in Mode X. This was pure power. I didn't know how to use this feature at first even though it was certainly something to brag about. That's the problem with great inventions. Unless you can find a practical application, it is just another quirk in the system, interesting only to computer nerds. Eventually, though, I found an application for Ted's discovery. As other gamers before me had learned, it is just the perfect thing to use in a tile-based scrolling game. We are about to examine the theory behind the scrolling, and the basis of this technique is Ted's resizeable video memory in Mode X.

The Importance of Scrolling

Scrolling is a fundamental part of the game we'll be working on in the later chapters. I'm introducing it now because we'll also be using it in the game editor. The next development tool we'll discuss is the level editor. We'll use the level editor to build and modify levels. Of course, the level editor must be able to scroll the entire level if it's going to be useful to us. To understand the level editor, we must first understand the theory behind tile-based scrolling. The scrolling code that I'll be presenting in this chapter is from the LEVEL.C source file used to build the game editor. Although we'll be exploring this file in detail in the next chapter, we'll look at some of the scrolling code in this chapter so that you can see how the scrolling concepts are implemented. If some of the material confuses you a little, don't worry, it will become clearer as we dissect the level editor in the next chapter.

The type of scrolling used in the level editor is slightly less complicated than the scrolling used in the game itself. For example, we don't need to perform diagonal scrolling. We also don't need to scroll in one-pixel increments, although we can. All we'll need for the level editor is simple two-directional scrolling. So this is a good place to start. When we are ready to do the game scrolling in Chapter 11, we'll add more features to the scrolling technique we are introducing now.

Preparing to Scroll

The first thing we need to do to scroll our level art is initialize the video mode. This is the same wonderful Mode X video mode we discussed in the previous chapter. But now we are going to do something new with it. We are going to *resize* it. Mode X allows for four pages of video memory on any VGA card, only don't think of it in that way. Rather than four pages of video memory, try to think of it as one continuous block of video memory. We'll take control of this video memory and reshape it to suit our needs. The way we do this is by initializing video memory and calling two Fastgraph functions:

```
fg_setmode(20);
fg_resize(352,744);
```

Notice that we first set the video mode to Mode X by calling the Fastgraph **fg_setmode()** function that we introduced in Chapter 4. Then we call **fg_resize()**.

Fastgraph Tip

fg_resize()

The **fg_resize()** function changes the dimensions of a video page in EGA, VGA, and SVGA graphics modes.

```
void fg_resize(int width, int height);
```

- *width* specifies the new video page width in pixels.
- *height* specifies the new video page height in pixels.

The call to **fg_resize()** creates a big block of video memory that is 352 pixels wide and 744 pixels high, as shown in Figure 5.1. Video memory has now been resized to a single large rectangle. Inside is the part of video memory that represents the screen—a smaller (320×200 pixels) visible rectangle, also shown in Figure 5.1. The visible rectangle can be located anywhere within the larger rectangle.

Shaping Video Memory

We can divide up video memory any way we want, and how we use this video memory is going to be critical to both our game editor and the actual game we develop later in this book. Let's examine the thought process that goes into designing the use of video memory.

Think of yourself as a mathematician or an engineer. Get out a piece of graph paper, a ruler, and a calculator. Now ask yourself, *"What is the optimal use of this big chunk of video memory?"*

Let's start by assigning an area for the visible screen to reside. We need to find a good place to put it, and leave enough room for it so that nothing else

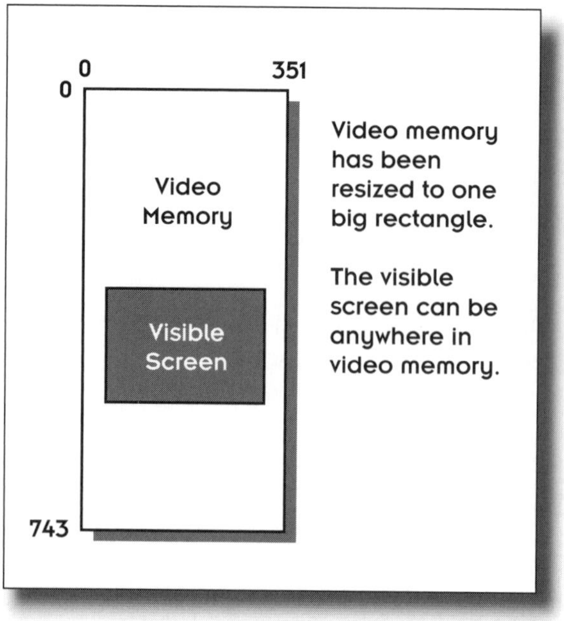

***Figure 5.1** Resizing video memory.*

gets in its way. We have already decided we are going to need tiles in our game. Experience has shown 16×16 tiles are a good size. On a regular 320×200 screen, you have enough room to fit 20 of them in the horizontal direction, and 12-1/2 in the vertical direction. Hmmm...12-1/2? That is going to present a problem. We are going to have some overlap in the vertical direction. Better plan a space on your paper that is at least half a tile longer than 200 lines. So the height of our page needs to be at least 208 lines. But is this enough? What if we want to scroll up and down in one-pixel increments? We better leave enough room for a tile at the top and a tile at the bottom. So our page height is going to be 15 tiles high, with 12-1/2 tiles visible at any one time. We'll also have a couple of extra rows of tiles to give us some room to scroll around in. The formula works out like this:

```
  12.5 rows of tiles always visible, round up to          13
+ an extra row of tiles at the top to scroll up          + 1
+ an extra row of tiles at the bottom to scroll down     + 1
                                                         ----
  total rows of tiles:                                    15
  sixteen rows of pixels per tile                       x 16
                                                         ----
  total height of our page in pixels                     240
```

Therefore, the size of the page we will have to rebuild each frame is 240 pixels; we'll reserve an area this size at the top of our rectangle of video memory and call it page 0, as shown in Figure 5.2.

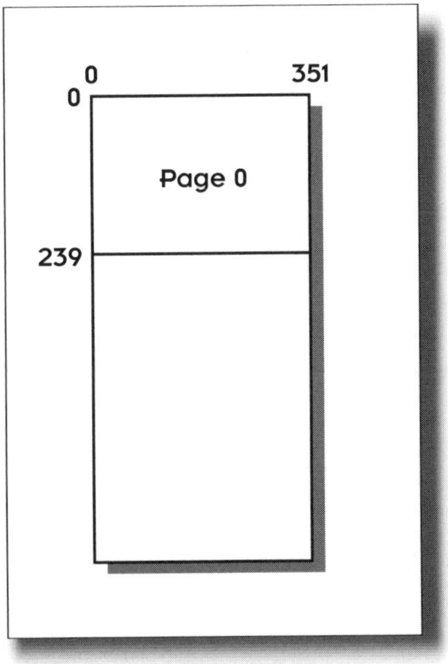

Figure 5.2 *240 rows of pixels reserved in video memory.*

The top area will always be a page. We won't use that part of video memory for anything else. The actual visible screen will fit somewhere in this page and will float around as required by the scrolling. We will begin by putting the visible screen right in the middle, at x = 16, y = 16, as shown in Figure 5.3.

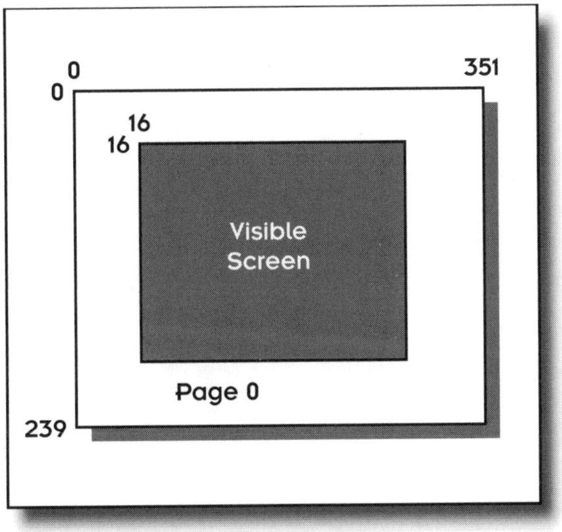

Figure 5.3 *The visible screen is located in page 0.*

The visible screen is 320×200 pixels and can be located anywhere inside of page 0. It floats easily in this area. All we need is a single call to Fastgraph's **fg_pan()** function:

```
fg_pan(screen_orgx, screen_orgy);
```

Fastgraph Tip

fg_pan()

The **fg_pan()** function changes the screen origin (the upper-left corner of the screen) to the specified screen space coordinates.

```
void fg_pan(int ix, int iy);
```

- *ix* is the new screen space x coordinate for the screen origin.
- *iy* is the new screen space y coordinate for the screen origin.

We've introduced two variables here called **screen_orgx** and **screen_orgy**. These variables represent the (x,y) coordinates of the origin of the screen in video memory. Since we'll need to refer to them often, we'll make them global variables and declare them like this:

```
int screen_orgx, screen_orgy;
```

We begin with **screen_orgx** = 16 and **screen_orgy** = 16, as shown in Figure 5.3. Throughout our discussion, we'll assume that **screen_orgx** and **screen_orgy** are constrained to the following values:

```
0 <= screen_orgx < 32
0 <= screen_orgy < 40
```

If **screen_orgx** is greater than 31, or **screen_orgy** is greater than 39, our visible screen will overflow the space we allocated for the page, and we'll see garbage around the edges of the screen. You don't want that to happen! Allowing the visible screen to overflow the edges of the page is like taking a trip into the Twilight Zone. You never quite know what will appear over the horizon. It is an experience best avoided. So we will limit the origin of our visible page to a small area, called the *panning area*, as shown in Figure 5.4.

Notice that **screen_orgx** and **screen_orgy** must be less than 32 and 40, respectively. That is, they can have a maximum value of 31 and 39. The reason is obvious: We start counting pixels at 0, so the range from 0 to 31 is 32 pixels, or exactly two tiles.

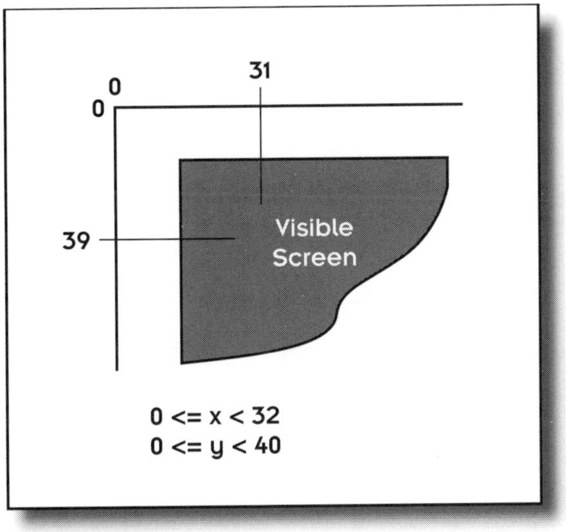

Figure 5.4 *Page 0 panning limits.*

By now, it should also be obvious why we chose the value 352 as the width of our video memory rectangle. The visible screen is 320 pixels across, which is 20 tiles. We need to leave room for one tile on the left for scrolling left, and another tile on the right for scrolling to the right, so our page needs to be 22 tiles wide; 22 tiles multiplied by 16 pixels per tile equals 352.

Moving Beyond the Limits of Video Memory

Is one tile all around the edge of the screen all the scrolling room we need? Most scrolling games allow us to move more than 16 pixels in any direction. But what is going to happen to us when we try to move the screen out of the panning area? The answer is, we will need to redraw the screen with new tiles on it. For best results, we'll want to draw the new screen in offscreen video memory. This is going to take some more room. In fact, we're going to need another whole page. Let's put it underneath the first page, and call it *page 1*, as shown in Figure 5.5.

Notice that page 1 is exactly the same size and shape as page 0. Now that we have two pages, we can alternate between them, in a technique known as *page flipping*. Our version of page flipping might be a little different than the page flipping you may be familiar with. Physically, video memory is all the same page. All we are doing is moving from one area of video memory to another using **fg_pan()**. But at this low level, there is really no difference between our technique and conventional page flipping. Both involve changing

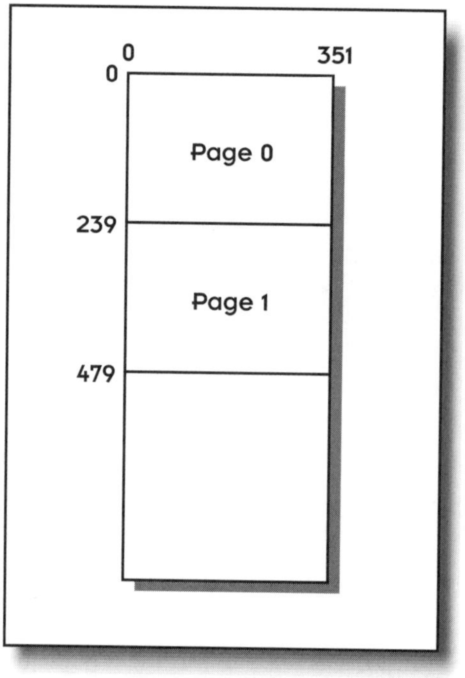

Figure 5.5 *Page 1, located beneath page 0.*

the starting address of display memory. Resizing video memory to one page simply gives us a little more control over the process. In addition to flipping from one page to the other, we can also control just where on the page we flip to.

Page 1 gives us the panning area shown in Figure 5.6.

If the visible screen is at (16,16) on page 0, the same screen will be at (16,256) on page 1. In other words, page 1 is just page 0 with 240 added to the y coordinate.

To simplify things, we will define a variable called **yoffset**. This variable will be equal to either 0 or 240 depending on whether we are currently displaying page 0 or page 1. Every time we flip pages, all we have to do is change the value of **yoffset**, as shown in Figure 5.7.

In our game, we will flip pages quite often—usually between 10-25 frames per second. In fact, we will define one *frame of animation* to mean a sequence ending in a page flip. Every time we flip pages, we will move the visible screen from page 0 to page 1, or vice versa. We will do this by updating the value of **yoffset**, and then calling **fg_pan()**:

```
yoffset = 240 - yoffset;
fg_pan(screen_orgx,screen_orgy+yoffset);
```

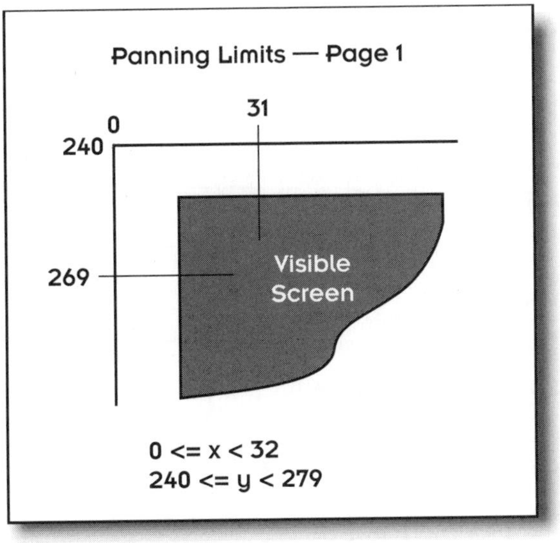

Figure 5.6 Page 1 panning limits.

This function performs a very fast update of the screen (approximately as fast as the rate of the vertical refresh).

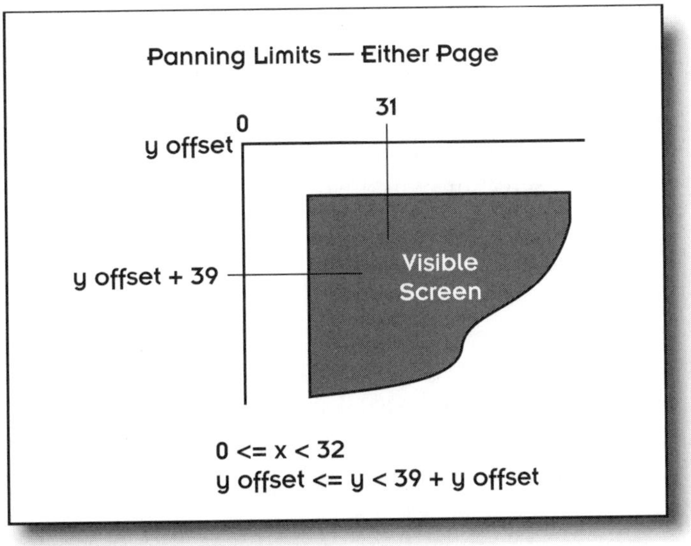

Figure 5.7 Change the value of yoffset when flipping pages.

Tommy's Tip

Toggling a Variable

To toggle a variable between two numbers, subtract the current value of the variable from the sum of the numbers. For example, if you want to toggle x between 0 and 1, you could write this code

```
if (x == 0)
   x = 1;
else
   x = 0;
```

which has exactly the same effect as this much shorter bit of code:

```
x = 1-x;
```

Using Hidden and Visual Pages

At this point, let's introduce the concept of the *hidden* and *visual* pages. The page that is currently hosting the screen is called the visual page. The other page is the hidden page. In our game, page 0 and page 1 will be constantly alternating roles (10-25 times per second, as I said earlier). Screen updates are always done to the hidden page, then the pages are flipped, and the hidden page becomes the visual page. We then immediately update the new hidden page in anticipation of the next page flip. These updates and page flips continue as long as the program is running. Even when the program appears to be doing nothing (for example, when all our sprites are standing perfectly still), we are still flipping pages at approximately 25 frames per second.

In the level editor, scrolling works slightly different. We do not need to animate at the same high speed as in the game, so we will not be constantly flipping pages; we only need to flip a page when the level has scrolled out of the viewing area.

As we work through the scrolling code, we will find it convenient to keep track of a little more information. The **swap()** function updates all the variables that define the hidden and visual pages. The **vpo** (visual page offset) variable is the same as **yoffset**. Knowing the bottom of the visual page, as well as the top and the bottom of the hidden page, will be useful to us later. We could always calculate these values "on the fly," but since we will be using them several times per frame and we are interested in saving time, we will compute them once in the **swap()** function and store them in globals. Then we can have access to them when we need them:

```
void swap()
{
   vpo = 240 - vpo; /* visual page offset */
   vpb = vpo + 239; /* visual page bottom */
   hpo = 240 - hpo; /* hidden page offset */
   hpb = hpo + 239; /* hidden page bottom */

   /* set the origin to the visual page */
   fg_pan(screen_orgx,screen_orgy+vpo);
}
```

After the **swap()** function updates the variables, it calls **fg_pan()** to do the page flip.

Horizontal Scrolling

Page 0 and page 1 will almost always be very similar. Most of the time, they will contain the same tiles. There are 15 rows of 22 tiles on page 0, and the same 15 rows of 22 tiles on page 1. The only time when the two pages do not match is when one of the coordinates scrolls outside of the panning limits.

Let's imagine our character is walking east. We want to scroll the screen to the right, continuously and slowly. We will increment the x coordinate one pixel each frame:

```
screen_orgx = 16;
screen_orgy = 16;
do
{
   fg_pan(screen_orgx,screen_orgy+vpo)
   screen_orgx++;
}

while (screen_orgx < 32);
```

We are now at the limit of our panning area. We can't continue on like this. We have to do something! But what?

What we need to do is rebuild the hidden page with all the tiles shifted to the left by one column, and then recalculate the x coordinate to match the new set of tiles.

Suppose we number our columns from 0 to 21, as shown in Figure 5.8. To scroll the picture to the right, we simply need to shift all the tiles of columns to the left. It's that easy. All we need to do is copy the tiles from the last 21 columns of the visual page to the first 21 columns of the hidden page, like this:

```
fg_transfer(16,251,vpo,vpb, 0,hpb, 0,0);
```

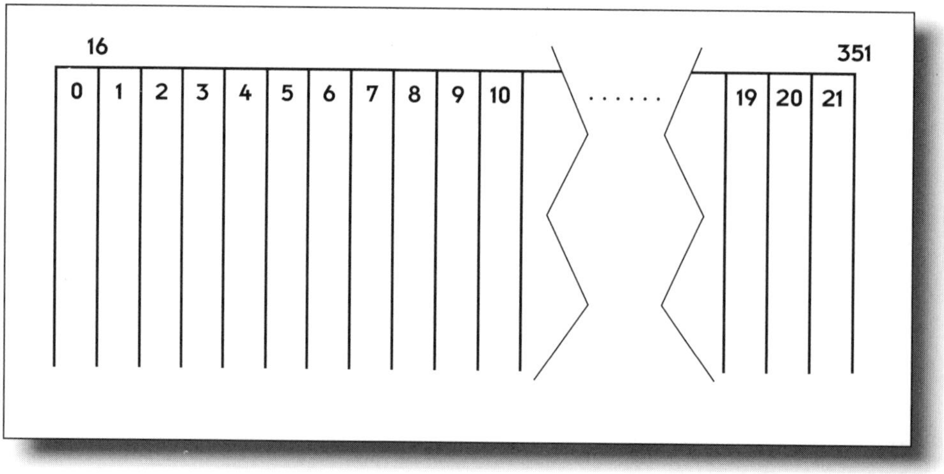

Figure 5.8 *Columns numbered from 0 to 21.*

After the transfer, the columns on the hidden page look like Figure 5.9.

The large rectangular area from 16 to 351 on the visual page has been copied to the area from 0 to 336 on the hidden page. Column 0 is gone; it's been covered up by column 1, and all the other columns have been shifted to the left. Column 21 is duplicated. We don't really need two copies of column 21 on the hidden page; what we need is the next column of tiles (column 22). We call the appropriate function to blit the tiles to column 22.

Now our hidden page looks like Figure 5.10.

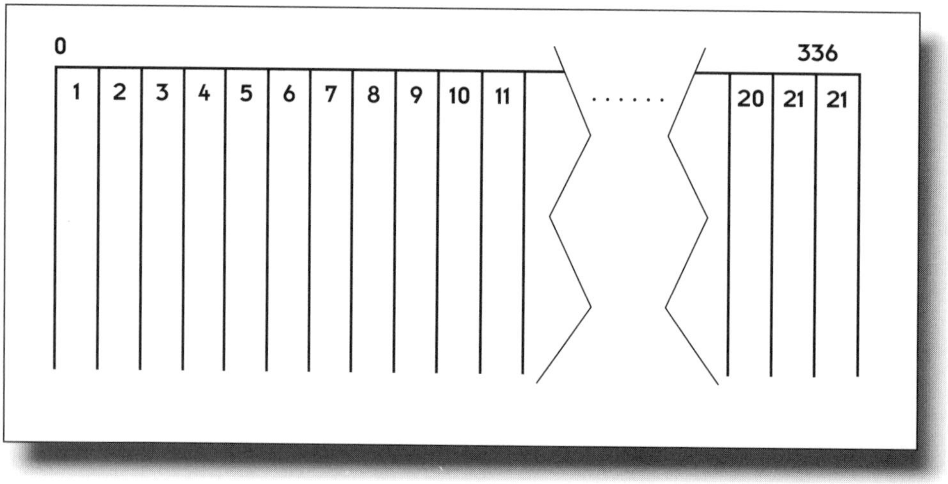

Figure 5.9 *Columns are shifted left during the scroll.*

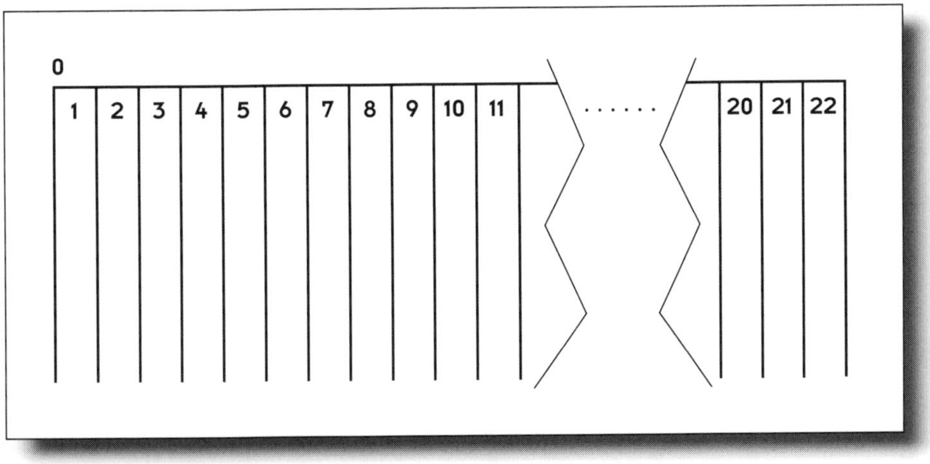

Figure 5.10 *Updating the hidden page.*

This is exactly what we wanted. But we are not quite ready to complete the frame yet. We need to adjust the x coordinate before we do the page flip. Since all the visual elements of the screen have effectively been moved 16 pixels to the left, we need to decrement the x coordinate by 16 as well:

```
screen_orgx -= 16;
fg_pan(screen_orgx,screen_orgy+yoffset);
```

The frame is complete. We have moved one more pixel to the right; now we can keep scrolling right and we won't have to do redraw the screen again for 15 more pixels.

The scrolling technique will be most useful if we write a function to handle various cases. The **scroll_right()** function in the level editor source file, LEVEL.C, looks like this:

```
int scroll_right(int npixels)
{
   register int i;

   /* no tiles need to be redrawn */
   if (screen_orgx <= 32-npixels)
   {
      screen_orgx+=npixels;
      fg_pan(screen_orgx,screen_orgy);
   }

   /* redraw one column of tiles and do a page swap */
   else if (tile_orgx < ncols - 22)
   {
```

```
      tile_orgx++;
      screen_orgx-=(16-npixels);
      fg_transfer(16,351,vpo,vpo+239,0,hpo+239,0,0);
      swap();
      for(i = 0; i< 15; i++)
         put_tile(21,i);
   }

   /* can't scroll right */
   else
      return(ERR);

   return(OK);
}
```

The **scroll_right()** function allows us to pass a variable number of pixels and handles these three cases:

- The new screen origin is within the panning limits.
- The screen origin is outside the panning limits, but the tile origin is still within the limits of tile space.
- Both the screen origin and the tile origin have moved as far in this direction as they can.

Tile Space

Usually, our scrolling background is going to have more than 22 columns and 15 rows. In fact, it will have many, many more. We need to start thinking in *tile space.* Tile space is a coordinate system based on rows and columns of tiles. Since each tile is 16×16 pixels, conversions from tile space to pixels usually involve subtracting the origin and multiplying by 16. Similarly, converting from pixels coordinates in video memory to tile space will require dividing by 16 and adding the origin.

Just as the visible screen floats in the visual page, the visual page floats within the tile space. This concept is illustrated in Figure 5.11.

Tile space is a huge map, stretching 240 tiles long and 200 tiles high. The visual page can be located anywhere in this tile space, occupying only 22 columns and 15 rows at a time. The shaded part in the Figure 5.11 represents the visual page. Remember, the screen is smaller than the visual page by about two tiles in the x and y directions. So as the screen floats freely in the visual page, and the visual page floats in the tile space, and the illusion of scrolling is accomplished.

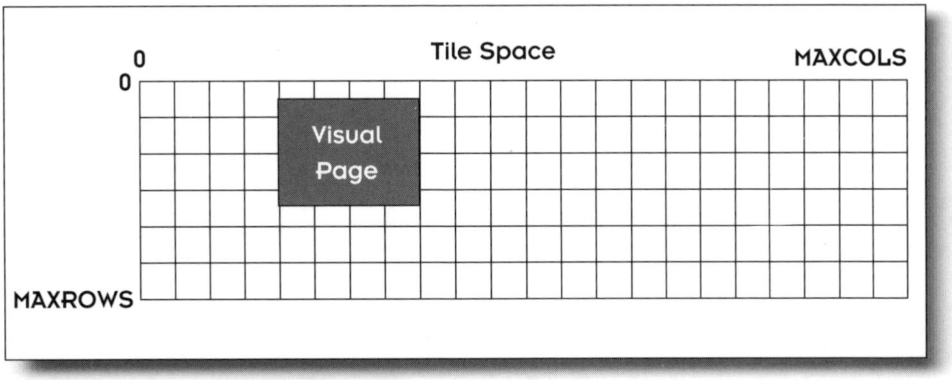

Figure 5.11 *A closer look at the tile area.*

Just as the origin of the screen must stay within the panning limits, the origin of the visual page must stay within some limits too. We cannot let the visual page scroll off the edge of the tile map in any direction. The smallest value for **tile_orgx** is 0, and the largest value is **MAXCOLS - 22**. Similarly, the smallest value for **tile_orgy** is 0 and the largest value is **MAXROWS - 15**. We will test for these limits in our scrolling function. If we meet or exceed the tile limits, then we have reached the end of the world and are unable to scroll any further.

The Tile Area

Now let's look at how we built those columns of tiles. Each column has 16 tiles. But where do the tiles come from? The best place to store tiles is in some area of video memory where nothing else is happening. Since we have already defined areas for page 0 and page 1, let's look at Figure 5.12 to see what we have left.

The shaded area is as good a place as any to put the tiles. We'll allocate an area 320×200 pixels for this function. Let's call this the *tile area*; we'll plan on not using this for anything else.

Let's take a closer look at the tile area. As you can see in Figure 5.13, there are 240 unique tiles, numbered from 0 to 239: Their location in the tile area determines their number. Tile number 0 is in the upper-left corner, tile number 239 is in the lower-right corner, and all the other tiles are in between.

All the backgrounds in our game are constructed from some combination of these tiles. The tiles are simply copied from the tile area to the hidden page using a straight video memory-to-video memory blit. The function to copy the tile from the tile area to the hidden page looks like this:

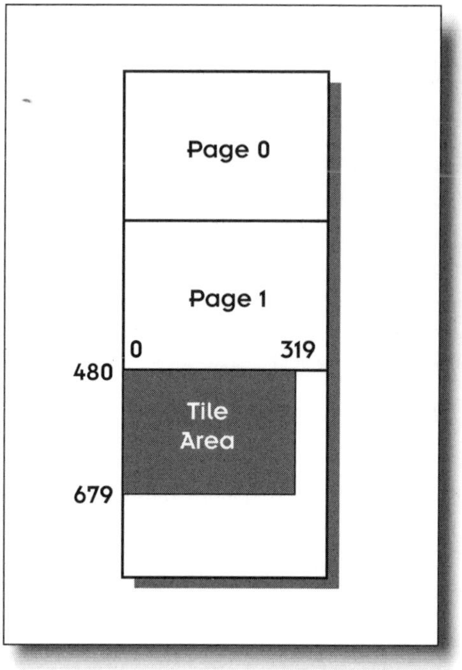

Figure 5.12 *The visible page floats within the available tile space.*

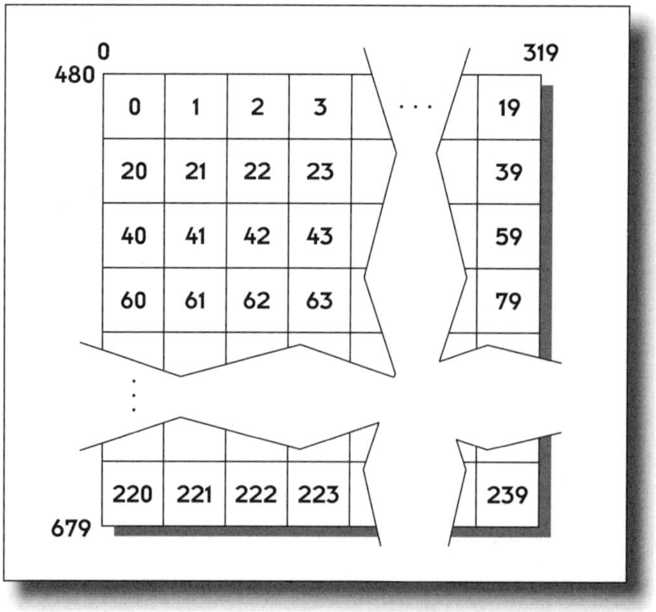

Figure 5.13 *Video memory.*

```
void put_tile(int column, int row)
{
   int tile_num;
   int x,y;
   int x1,x2,y1,y2;

   /* get the tile information from the tile map */
   tile_num = (int)level_map[column+tile_orgx][row+tile_orgy];

   /* calculate the destination coordinates */
   x = column * 16;
   y = row * 16 + 15 + hpo;

   /* calculate the source coordinates */
   x1 = (tile_num%20)*16;
   x2 = x1+15;
   y1 = (tile_num/20)*16 + tpo;
   y2 = y1+15;

   /* copy the tile */
   fg_transfer(x1,x2,y1,y2,x,y,0,0);
}
```

This function calculates the tile number based on the row and column destination, then it finds the location of the tile number in the tile area. It also calculates the destination in pixels. Finally, the rectangular area is copied from the tile area to the correct position on the hidden page.

This function also introduces some new global variables, and before we go any further, let's define them. First, **tile_orgx** is the x origin in tile space. That is, it is the number of the first column. In our previous example, before the screen scrolled, **tile_orgx** was 0. After the scroll, it was 1. Similarly, **tile_orgy** defines the row coordinate at the top of the page, also called the *y origin.*

The **put_tile()** function makes it very easy to define another useful function, **redraw_screen()**. The **redraw_screen()** function builds a whole screen, one tile at a time:

```
void redraw_screen (void)
{
   register int i, j;

   for (i=0; i<22; i++)
   {
      for (j=0; j<15; j++)
      {
         put_tile (i,j);
      }
   }
}
```

The Level Map

The tile information that defines the background is stored in the array **level_map**. This is a two dimensional array defined like this:

```
unsigned char far level_map[MAXCOLS][MAXROWS];
```

We can use this array to define some very large levels. Suppose we want our level map to be 240 tiles wide and 240 tiles high. This will give us a total of 48,000 tiles, as shown here:

```
  240 columns
 x 200 rows
------------
48,000 tiles
```

It is easy to see why we use a char (byte) array instead of an integer array. If this was an integer array instead, we would quickly overflow a 64K segment boundary. However, defining this as an unsigned char array means each tile must have a value less than or equal to 254. This isn't a problem because, as illustrated earlier, we have exactly 240 unique tiles. That was certainly good planning! Isn't it nice how this works out?

240 columns and 200 rows actually defines a huge area. Remember, each tile has 256 pixels (16×16). Or in other words:

```
  240 columns      x 16 = 3840 pixels horizontally
 x 200 rows        x 16 = 3200 pixels vertically
------------      ---------------------------------
48,000 tiles       x256 = 12,288,000 pixels total
```

That's over 12 million pixels! Yet, amazingly, we're keeping all this information in one 48K array, as well as within the tile area in video memory.

The way we can do this, of course, is by duplicating a lot of information. If our game calls for 20 windows, what we'll actually have is one window repeated 20 times. Small trees and big trees are composed of the same branches organized in different ways. One blue tile can be repeated infinitely for an apparently endless sky. Think of your level map as the whole world. The rows and columns are the coordinate system that keep track of it, and the tiles themselves define what it looks like.

Vertical Scrolling

Vertical scrolling is accomplished in approximately the same way as horizontal scrolling. The y coordinate is incremented (or decremented) until it is outside the panning limits. Then a large area, missing a row either from the top or the bottom, is copied from the visual page to the hidden page. The missing row is added at the top or bottom as needed, and the page flip completes the frame. Here is the function for the scrolling part of the frame:

```
int scroll_up(int npixels)
{
   register int i;

   /* no tiles need to be redrawn */

   if (screen_orgy >= npixels)
   {
      screen_orgy-=npixels;
      fg_pan(screen_orgx,screen_orgy);
   }
   /* redraw one row of tiles and do a page swap */

   else if (tile_orgy > 0)
   {
      tile_orgy--;
      screen_orgy+=(16-npixels);
      fg_transfer(0,351,vpo,223+vpo,0,hpo+239,0,0);
      for(i = 0; i< 22; i++)
         put_tile(i,0);
      swap();
   }

   else   /* can't scroll up */
      return(-1);
return(OK);
}
```

Getting a Clear Picture

You should now have a good grasp of how scrolling works. Once you can visualize the various coordinate systems and the page flipping and scrolling techniques, the other functions will fall easily into place. Be sure you have a clear understanding of the concepts discussed in this chapter before continuing. As we said before, this chapter is the foundation for the rest of our game engine, and is at the very heart of the side-scrolling arcade game technology.

In case you were wondering about whether I am currently ahead of Ted in finding uses for the technology he develops, I am afraid I am not. He is most decidedly ahead of me. He has developed Fastgraph to run in 32-bit flat model protected mode and he wants me to write code to make use of virtual bitmaps many megabytes in size. Talk about raw power! I haven't the foggiest idea what to do with all this new stuff. But something will come to me...eventually.

Chapter 6

Learn how to fine-tune your levels to elevate the status of your games from good to professional-quality.

Inside the Level Editor

Years ago I did contract work for several major commercial game publishing and development houses. These are the big boys in the industry who sell games on the shelves in attractive boxes for $50 or more.

I wrote some of those games, but not from scratch. My job was coding up somebody else's specs, so I can't claim any responsibility for their content. I merely followed instructions and stayed away from the game design issues. I remember on one project my producer gave me some of the worst advice I had ever received. He told me, "Don't write games you like to play, write games that sell!"

Then he and I wrote a boxing game. I have never been a fan of contact sports or sports simulations, so I had no knowledge or "feel" for a boxing game. The game itself seemed pointless to me—two men punched each other in the face until they were both bruised and bloody. The player (or computer player) who inflicted the most damage on his opponent was declared the winner.

My producer assured me this would sell. It didn't. Fortunately, I was paid for my time and not how well the game sold. Why am I telling you this now?

I want to warn you not to fall into the same trap. Don't write games that don't inspire you, even if you are offered money to do it. Write games that you personally get a thrill out of playing. That way your games will be much better.

If you share my enthusiasm for side-scrolling arcade games, you've probably played many levels of many games and you have some idea of how a level should be designed. They must be fun, challenging, and they must feel just right. You'll have a much better chance of designing good levels if you're an avid player.

Which brings us to the ultimate question: how are levels designed? You can design them in your head or you can design them on paper, but eventually you will need to commit your design to data files. For this, you will need another tool and I have just the one for the job—a level editor.

Introducing the Level Editor

The level editor is the tool that helps you refine your levels. You can think of this as the second stage of processing your level art. After the tile ripper has done its job, you will have from one to several screens of art and a library of tiles. These need to be further processed to build levels. The general idea is to start adding rows and columns to the screens you already have. Then you can use block moves to copy tiles from one area to another. In this manner, you can build walls, doors, platforms, tunnels, scenery, and whatever else appeals to your imagination.

Editing the level consists of using the keyboard and the mouse to insert or delete rows and columns, selecting tiles from the level itself or from the tile library, and copying tiles onto the level. These functions are the bare minimum needed to build game levels. Additional features will make the level editor easier and faster to use. If you recall from Chapter 3, the level editor can scroll your art. The scrolling technique we discussed in Chapter 5 will be put to practical use in this chapter. You can use the arrow keys on your keyboard to scroll the level up, down, left, or right, so that any part of it can be viewed and edited. The technique used to scroll the editor is similar to the technique to scroll the game, but it is a little bit simpler. The primary difference is the number of page flips. In the game, we will flip pages constantly. In the level editor, we only flip pages when we need to redraw the screen during a scroll. Also, scrolling in the level editor is done in 16-pixel increments in only four directions. The game can scroll any number of pixels in any direction. So game scrolling is more complicated than level editor scrolling, but as we will see, the underlying technique of resizing video memory and rebuilding screens by moving columns and rows of tiles is the same.

Running the Level Editor Program

You can use the level editor stored on the companion disk by running this program from the DOS command line:

```
LEVEL
```

You'll then see the program shown in Figure 6.1.

Make sure that you have a mouse installed before trying to run the program. Otherwise, you'll get the error message

```
Mouse not found!
```

and the program will exit.

Notice that you don't need to specify any input files or command-line arguments. The level editor uses the two files created by the tile ripper program presented in Chapter 4, TILES.PCX and RIPPER.LEV. Thus, before you use the level editor you should follow these steps:

1. Create your level art as PCX files.
2. Run the tile ripper program (RIPPER.EXE) and convert your art into tiles.

Figure 6.1 *The standalone level editor program.*

When you quit the level editor, it updates the file RIPPER.LEV. Recall that this file stores your level data in a binary format (so, don't try to read it with your word processor!).

On Disk *The level editor program is stored on the companion disk as LEVEL.EXE in the directory \FG\UTIL. If you compile the LEVEL.C source file yourself, make sure that you have either the Fastgraph or Fastgraph/Light library available to link the program.*

The Complete Level Editor Program

The source code for the level editor shown next can be compiled into a standalone program. It has been simplified for our discussion. A more complete level editor, along with the source code, is included as part of the game editor on the companion disk.

When reading this code, you may want to take note of how the code is structured and the programming style used. For example, notice how the functions are listed in roughly alphabetical order after the **main()** function—one of my personal style preferences. Other style preferences include placing declarations and definitions at the top of the file, using capital letters for defined constants, *not* using capital letters in function names or variable names, placing curly brackets on a line by themselves, and using the /* */ comment style. You may have your own preferences; that's fine, but I urge you to be consistent in your coding style so that you can debug and maintain your code. Also, gamers often share code among themselves. Clean, commented, and consistently styled code will make you popular among your peers, who will trade valuable information with you.

Some game programmers prefer to code in C++ these days, although the majority of gamers still code in straight C. C is still my language of preference as well. Again, in the interest of sharing code, it is a good idea to use the languages other game programmers are coding in. Both C and C++ have advantages and disadvantages, and the debate about which is better is likely to continue. Since most game code is "event-driven" and "object-oriented" by nature, you shouldn't have too much trouble turning C code into C++. Here is the complete program for the level editor:

```
/******************************************************************\
 level.c -- level editor code for side-scrolling games by
          Diana Gruber

 compile using large model
```

```
 requires Fastgraph(tm) or Fastgraph/Light(tm) to link

\*******************************************************************/

#include <fastgraf.h>     /* header for the Fastgraph lib */
#include <stdio.h>
#include <stdlib.h>

/* standard defines */
#define OFF   0
#define ON    1
#define OK    1
#define FALSE 0
#define TRUE  1

/* define keys */
#define ESC         27
#define SPACE       32
#define UP_ARROW    72
#define LEFT_ARROW  75
#define RIGHT_ARROW 77
#define DOWN_ARROW  80
#define INSERT      82
#define DELETE      83

/* define colors */
#define WHITE       255
#define BLACK         0

/* mouse variable declarations */
int xmouse,ymouse;         /* mouse position  */
int buttons;               /* state of mouse buttons */
int tile_xmouse;           /* mouse position on the tile page */
int tile_ymouse;

/* tile variable declarations */
int tile_orgx;             /* tile coords of upper-left corner */
int tile_orgy;
int screen_orgx;           /* screen coords of upper-left corner */
int screen_orgy;

/* screen coordinates for scrolling */
int vpo;                   /* visual page offset (0 or 240) */
int hpo;                   /* hidden page offset (240 or 0) */
int tpo;                   /* tile page offset (always 480) */

/* level map declarations
#define MAXROWS 200        /* maximum number of tile rows in level */
#define MAXCOLS 240        /* maximum number of tile cols in level */

/* large array containing all the tile information for the level */
unsigned char far level_map[MAXCOLS][MAXROWS];
```

```
int nrows;                /* actual number of rows in the level */
int ncols;                /* actual number of columns in level */

FILE *stream;             /* file handle for level data */

/**** function declarations */
void  main(void);
void  edit_level(void);             /* main editor loop */
int   get_tile(void);               /* get tile from tile page */
void  put_tile(int x,int y);        /* put a tile */
void  delete_tiles(void);           /* delete row or column */
void  insert_tiles(void);           /* insert row or column */
void  load_level(void);             /* read level from file */
void  redraw_screen(void);          /* put all tiles on screen */
void  save_level(void);             /* save level to file */
int   scroll_left(int npixels);     /* scrolling functions */
int   scroll_right(int npixels);
int   scroll_down(int npixels);
int   scroll_up(int npixels);
void  swap(void);                   /* flip pages */

/*****************************************************************/

void main()
{
   /* set the video mode to Mode X 320x200x256 */
   fg_setmode(20);

   /* resize video memory */
   fg_resize(352,727);

   /* initialize the Mode X mouse handler */
   if (fg_mouseini() <= 0)
   {
      fg_setmode(3);
      fg_reset();
      printf("Mouse not found!\n");
      exit(0);
   }

   /* the mouse cursor is invisible throughout the program */
   fg_mousevis(0);

   /* load the level data from a file */
   load_level();

   /* edit the level */
   edit_level();

   /* save the level */
   save_level();

   /* release the Mode X mouse handler */
   fg_mousefin();
```

```
   /* reset the video mode and exit */
   fg_setmode(3);
   fg_reset();
   exit(0);
}

/**********************************************************************/

void delete_tiles()
{
   register int i,j;
   unsigned char key,aux;
   int tile;

   /* pop up a message: what do you want to delete? */
   fg_setcolor(WHITE);
   fg_rect(screen_orgx+60,screen_orgx+260,
           screen_orgy+90+vpo,screen_orgy+110+vpo);
   fg_setcolor(BLACK);
   fg_move(screen_orgx+80,screen_orgy+105+vpo);
   fg_print("Delete Row or Column?",21);

   /* wait for a key press */
   fg_getkey(&key,&aux);

   /* delete a column at the current mouse position */
   if ((key|32) == 'c' && ncols > 22)
   {
      /* calculate the current tile column */
      tile = tile_orgx + xmouse/16;

      /* shift all the tiles left by one column */
      for (j = 0; j < nrows; j++)
         for (i = tile; i < ncols-1; i++)
            level_map[i][j] = level_map[i+1][j];

      /* zero out the last column */
      i = ncols-1;
      for (j = 0; j < nrows; j++)
         level_map[i][j] = 0;

      /* decrement the number of columns */
      ncols--;
   }

   /* delete a row at the current mouse position */
   else if ((key|32) == 'r' && nrows > 15)
   {
      /* calculate the current tile row */
      tile = tile_orgy + (ymouse-vpo)/16;

      /* shift all the tiles up by one row */
      for (j = tile; j < nrows-1; j++)
```

```
         for (i = 0; i < ncols; i++)
            level_map[i][j] = level_map[i][j+1];

      /* zero out the last row */
      j = nrows-1;
      for (i = 0; i < ncols; i++)
          level_map[i][j] = 0;

      /* decrement the number of rows */
      nrows--;
   }

   /* fix the screen by redrawing all the tiles */
   redraw_screen();
   return;
}

/******************************************************************/

void edit_level()
{
   register int i,j;
   unsigned char key,aux;
   int xbox,ybox,oldx,oldy;       /* mouse coordinates */
   int cursor_flag;               /* flag for mouse cursor */
   int tile;                      /* tile to get or put */

   /* start with the mouse at the center of the visual screen */
   fg_mousemov(160,100+vpo);
   fg_mousepos(&xmouse,&ymouse,&buttons);

   /* normalize the x and y coordinates to a tile boundary */
   xbox = xmouse&0xfff0;
   ybox = ymouse&0xfff0;

   /* update oldx and oldy */
   oldx = xbox;
   oldy = ybox;

   /* draw the cursor */
   fg_setcolor(WHITE);
   fg_boxx(xbox,xbox+15,ybox, ybox+15);
   cursor_flag = ON;
   tile = 0;

   /* loop continuously and handle events as they are detected */
   for(;;)
   {
      fg_intkey(&key,&aux);

      /* no key press detected, take care of mouse functions */
      if (key+aux == 0)
      {
         /* get the current mouse status */
```

```
fg_mousepos(&xmouse,&ymouse,&buttons);

/* normalize for tile space */
xbox = xmouse&0xfff0;
ybox = ymouse&0xfff0;

/* mouse has moved to a new tile position */
if (xbox != oldx || ybox != oldy)
{
   /* xor the old cursor box to get rid of it */
   fg_setcolor(WHITE);
   if (cursor_flag)
      fg_boxx(oldx,oldx+15,oldy,oldy+15);

   /* draw the cursor box at new position */
   fg_boxx(xbox,xbox+15,ybox,ybox+15);

   /* update the cursor flag */
   cursor_flag = ON;

   /* the new coordinates become the old coordinates */
   oldx = xbox;
   oldy = ybox;
}

/* if the mouse cursor is off, turn it on */
else if (!cursor_flag)
{
   fg_setcolor(WHITE);
   fg_boxx(xbox,xbox+15,ybox,ybox+15);
   cursor_flag = ON;
}

/* the left mouse button puts down a tile */
if (buttons == 1)
{
   /* first turn off the mouse cursor */
   fg_setcolor(WHITE);
   fg_boxx(xbox,xbox+15,ybox,ybox+15);

   /* set the cursor flag to OFF */
   cursor_flag = OFF;

   /* calculate the level array indices */
   i = xbox/16;
   j = (ybox-vpo)/16;

   /* update the level array */
   level_map[i+tile_orgx][j+tile_orgy]=(unsigned char)tile;

   /* draw the tile */
   put_tile(i,j);
}
```

```
         /* right button picks up a tile */
         else if (buttons == 2)
         {
            /* calculate the level array indices */
            i = tile_orgx + xmouse/16;
            j = tile_orgy + (ymouse-vpo)/16;

            /* find the tile in the tile map */
            tile = level_map[i][j];
         }
      }

      /* keypress detected -- process the key */
      else
      {
         /* turn off the mouse cursor and set the flag to OFF */
         if (cursor_flag)
         {
            fg_setcolor(WHITE);
            fg_boxx(xbox,xbox+15,ybox,ybox+15);
            cursor_flag = OFF;
         }

         /* Escape key was pressed, we are finished */
         if (key == ESC)
            return;

         /* arrow keys were pressed -- scroll around */
         else if (aux == LEFT_ARROW)
            scroll_left(16);
         else if (aux == RIGHT_ARROW)
            scroll_right(16);
         else if (aux == UP_ARROW)
            scroll_up(16);
         else if (aux == DOWN_ARROW)
            scroll_down(16);

         /* Spacebar gets at tile from the tile page */
         else if (key == SPACE)
            tile = get_tile();

         /* delete a row or column of tiles */
         else if (aux == DELETE)
            delete_tiles();

         /* insert a row or column of tiles */
         else if (aux == INSERT)
            insert_tiles();
      }
   }
}

/**********************************************************************/
```

```
int get_tile()
{
   int xbox,ybox;
   int oldx,oldy;
   int old_xmouse, old_ymouse;
   int tile_num;
   unsigned char key, aux;

   /* keep track of the current mouse position */
   old_xmouse = xmouse;
   old_ymouse = ymouse;

   /* pan to the tile page area */
   fg_pan(0,tpo);

   /* change the mouse limits and move the mouse */
   fg_mouselim(0,319,tpo,tpo+176);
   fg_mousemov(tile_xmouse,tile_ymouse);

   /* calculate the mouse cursor position */
   xbox = tile_xmouse&0xfff0;
   ybox = tile_ymouse&0xfff0;
   oldx = xbox;
   oldy = ybox;

   /* draw the mouse cursor */
   fg_setcolor(WHITE);
   fg_boxx(xbox,xbox+15,ybox,ybox+15);

   for(;;)
   {
      fg_intkey(&key,&aux);
      if (key == ESC)
         break;

      /* check the mouse position and normalize for tile space */
      fg_mousepos(&xmouse,&ymouse,&buttons);
      xbox = xmouse&0xfff0;
      ybox = ymouse&0xfff0;

      /* mouse has moved, redraw the mouse cursor */
      if (xbox != oldx || ybox != oldy)
      {
         /* clear the old cursor */
         fg_boxx(oldx,oldx+15,oldy,oldy+15);

         /* draw the new cursor */
         fg_boxx(xbox,xbox+15,ybox,ybox+15);

         /* update the old x and y values */
         oldx = xbox;
         oldy = ybox;
      }
```

```
      /* button_press detected, we have chosen our tile */
      if (buttons == 1)
         break;
   }

   /* calculate the tile number from the mouse position */
   tile_num = ((ybox-tpo)/16) * 20 + (xbox/16);

   /* clear the mouse cursor */
   fg_boxx(xbox,xbox+15,ybox,ybox+15);

   /* keep track of the position for the next time */
   tile_xmouse = xbox;
   tile_ymouse = ybox;

   /* pan back to the visual page */
   fg_pan(screen_orgx,screen_orgy+vpo);

   /* reset mouse limits and move the mouse back where it was */
   fg_mouselim(0,336,vpo,vpo+224);
   fg_mousemov(old_xmouse,old_ymouse);

   /* give yourself enough time to get your finger off the button */
   fg_waitfor(5);
   return(tile_num);
}

/******************************************************************/

void insert_tiles()
{
   register int i,j;
   unsigned char key,aux;
   int tile;

   /* pop up a message: what do you want to insert? */
   fg_setcolor(WHITE);
   fg_rect(screen_orgx+60,screen_orgx+260,
           screen_orgy+90+vpo,screen_orgy+110+vpo);
   fg_setcolor(BLACK);
   fg_move(screen_orgx+80,screen_orgy+105+vpo);
   fg_print("Insert Row or Column?",21);

   /* wait for a keypress */
   fg_getkey(&key,&aux);

   /* insert a column at the current mouse position */
   if ((key|32) == 'c' && ncols < MAXCOLS)
   {
      /* increment the number of columns */
      ncols++;

      /* calculate the current column */
      tile = tile_orgx + xmouse/16;
```

```
      /* shift all the columns right by one */
      for (j = 0; j < nrows; j++)
         for (i = ncols-1; i > tile; i--)
            level_map[i][j] = level_map[i-1][j];
   }

   /* insert a row at the current mouse position */
   else if ((key|32) == 'r' && nrows < MAXROWS)
   {
      /* increment the number of rows */
      nrows++;

      /* calculate the current row */
      tile = tile_orgy + (ymouse-vpo)/16;

      /* shift all the rows down by one */
      for (j = nrows-1; j > tile; j--)
         for (i = 0; i < ncols; i++)
            level_map[i][j] = level_map[i][j-1];
   }

   /* fix the screen by redrawing all the tiles */
   redraw_screen();
   return;
}

/******************************************************************/

void load_level()
{
   register int i,j;

   /* initialize some global variables */
   tile_orgx = 0;
   tile_orgy = 0;
   screen_orgx = 0;
   screen_orgy = 0;
   vpo = 0;
   hpo = 240;
   tpo = 480;
   tile_xmouse = 0;
   tile_ymouse = 480;

   /* set the mouse limits */
   fg_mouselim(0,336,vpo,vpo+224);

   /* display the tiles in the tile area */
   fg_move(0,tpo);
   fg_showpcx("tiles.pcx",2);

   /* open the level file and read the level information */
   if ((stream = fopen("ripper.lev","rb")) != NULL)
   {
```

```
      fread(&ncols,sizeof(int),1,stream);
      fread(&nrows,sizeof(int),1,stream);

      for (i = 0; i < ncols; i++)
         fread(&level_map[i][0],sizeof(char),nrows,stream);
      fclose(stream);
   }

   /* if you didn't find the file, just initialize the tiles to 0 */
   else
   {
      ncols = 22;
      nrows = 15;
      for (i = 0; i < ncols; i++)
         for (j = 0; j < nrows; j++)
            level_map[i][j] = 0;
   }

   /* fix the screen by redrawing all the tiles */
   redraw_screen();
}

/******************************************************************/

void put_tile(int xtile, int ytile)
{
   int tile_num;
   int x,y;
   int x1,x2,y1,y2;

   /* get the tile information from the tile map */
   tile_num = (int)level_map[xtile+tile_orgx][ytile+tile_orgy];

   /* calculate the destination coordinates */
   x = xtile * 16;
   y = ytile * 16 + 15 + vpo;

   /* calculate the source coordinates */
   x1 = (tile_num%20)*16;
   x2 = x1+15;
   y1 = (tile_num/20)*16 + tpo;
   y2 = y1+15;

   /* copy the tile */
   fg_transfer(x1,x2,y1,y2,x,y,0,0);
}

/******************************************************************/

void redraw_screen()
{
   register int i,j;
```

```
   /* copy all the tiles to the visual page */
   for (i = 0; i < 22; i++)
      for (j = 0; j < 15; j++)
         put_tile(i,j);
}

/************************** save_level ****************************/

void save_level()
{
   register int i;

   /* open a binary file for writing */
   if ((stream = fopen("ripper.lev","wb")) != NULL)
   {
      /* write out the number of columns and rows */

      fwrite(&ncols,sizeof(int),1,stream);
      fwrite(&nrows,sizeof(int),1,stream);

      /* write each column, in sequence */

      for (i = 0; i < ncols; i++)
         fwrite(&level_map[i][0],sizeof(char),nrows,stream);
      fclose(stream);
   }
}

/******************************************************************/

int scroll_down(int npixels)
{
   register int i;

   /* no tiles need to be redrawn */
   if (screen_orgy <= 40-npixels)
   {
      screen_orgy+=npixels;
      fg_pan(screen_orgx,screen_orgy);
   }

   /* redraw one row of tiles and do a page swap */
   else if (tile_orgy < nrows - 15)
   {
      tile_orgy++;
      screen_orgy-=(16-npixels);
      fg_transfer(0,351,16+vpo,vpo+239,0,223+hpo,0,0);
      swap();
      for(i = 0; i< 22; i++)
         put_tile(i,14);
   }

   /* can't scroll down */
   else
```

```
      return(-1);

   return(OK);
}

/****************************************************************/

int scroll_left(int npixels)
{
   register int i;

   /* no tiles need to be redrawn */
   if (screen_orgx >= npixels)
   {
      screen_orgx-=npixels;
      fg_pan(screen_orgx,screen_orgy);
   }

   /* redraw one column of tiles and do a page swap */
   else if (tile_orgx > 0)
   {
      tile_orgx--;
      screen_orgx+=(16-npixels);
      fg_transfer(0,335,vpo,vpo+239,16,hpo+239,0,0);
      swap();
      for(i = 0; i< 15; i++)
         put_tile(0,i);
   }

   /* can't scroll left */
   else
      return(ERR);

   return(OK);
}

/****************************************************************/

int scroll_right(int npixels)
{
   register int i;

   /* no tiles need to be redrawn */
   if (screen_orgx <= 32-npixels)
   {
      screen_orgx+=npixels;
      fg_pan(screen_orgx,screen_orgy);
   }

   /* redraw one column of tiles and do a page swap */
   else if (tile_orgx < ncols - 22)
   {
      tile_orgx++;
      screen_orgx-=(16-npixels);
```

```
      fg_transfer(16,351,vpo,vpo+239,0,hpo+239,0,0);
      swap();
      for(i = 0; i< 15; i++)
         put_tile(21,i);
   }

   /* can't scroll right */
   else
      return(ERR);

   return(OK);
}

/******************************************************************/

int scroll_up(int npixels)
{
   register int i;

   /* no tiles need to be redrawn */
   if (screen_orgy >= npixels)
   {
      screen_orgy-=npixels;
      fg_pan(screen_orgx,screen_orgy);
   }
   /* redraw one row of tiles and do a page flip */
   else if (tile_orgy > 0)
   {
      tile_orgy--;
      screen_orgy+=(16-npixels);
      fg_transfer(0,351,vpo,223+vpo,0,hpo+239,0,0);
      swap();
      for(i = 0; i< 22; i++)
         put_tile(i,0);
   }

   /* can't scroll up */
   else
      return(ERR);

   return(OK);
}

/******************************************************************/

void swap()
{
   /* reverse the hidden page and visual page offsets */
   vpo = 240 - vpo;
   hpo = 240 - hpo;

   /* set the origin to the visual page */
   fg_pan(screen_orgx,screen_orgy+vpo);
```

```
    /* calculate the new mouse position */
    ymouse -= hpo;
    ymouse += vpo;

    /* reset the mouse limits and move the mouse */
    fg_mouselim(0,336,vpo,vpo+224);
    fg_mousemov(xmouse,ymouse);
}
```

Exploring the Level Editor Code

Although the level editor might seem like a big complex program to you, it is actually very easy to follow. Let's take a quick look at all of the functions that are defined and then we'll move in a little closer and examine some of the important details. Table 6.1 shows all of the functions listed in order of their appearance.

Declarations, Definitions, and Preprocessor Directives

As with the tile ripper code, we begin by including the standard C header files and the Fastgraph header file containing the Fastgraph function declarations. Then, we define some constant values, including integer values for keystroke characters and colors. Giving commonly used constants a logical name is a standard practice for writing clean, readable C code.

Table 6.1 *Functions Used in LEVEL.C*

Function	Description
main()	Initializes the graphics environment and mouse, and launches the editing function
delete_tiles()	Deletes a row or column of tiles
edit_level()	Handles mouse and keyboard events
get_tile()	Selects a tile from the tile library
insert_tiles()	Inserts a row or column of tiles
load_level()	Loads tile library and level data from disk
put_tile()	Copies a tile from the tile library to the level
redraw_screen()	Rebuilds the entire screen by copying all the necessary tiles
save_level()	Writes the level data to disk
scroll_down()	Scrolls the screen down
scroll_left()	Scrolls the screen left
scroll_right()	Scrolls the screen right
scroll_up()	Scrolls the screen up
swap()	Toggles visible page between 0 and 1 (do a page flip)

We declare a number of global variables, starting with the variables used to keep track of the mouse status. The level editor makes heavy use of the mouse, and keeping track of the mouse cursor in a resized Mode X video mode is tricky. Global variables keep track of the mouse position on both the level and the tile page, and, as we swap between those two areas, we will reposition the mouse to where it was previously.

We can use the same global variables introduced in Chapter 5 to keep track of tile and screen coordinates::

```
int tile_orgx;          /* tile coords of upper-left corner */
int tile_orgy;
int screen_orgx;        /* screen coords of upper-left corner */
int screen_orgy;
```

The **tile_orgx** and **tile_orgy** variables represent the screen origin in terms of tile space. That is, if the 22 horizontal tiles currently in video memory range from column 10 to column 31, then **tile_orgx** will be 10. Similarly, if the horizontal tiles range from row 100 to row 114, then **tile_orgy** will be 100, as shown in Figure 6.2.

The **screen_orgx** and **screen_orgy** variables are the coordinates in physical video memory of the origin of the screen. They will range in value from 0 to 31 for **screen_orgx** and 0 to 39 for **screen_orgy**, as shown in Figure 6.3.

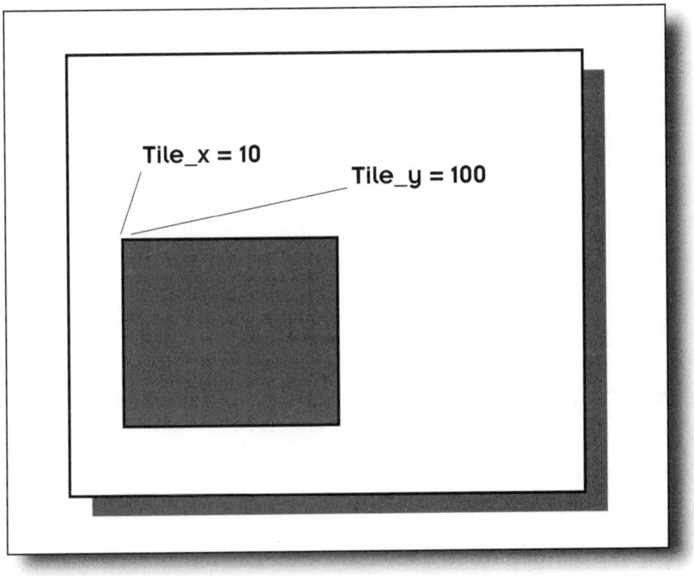

***Figure 6.2** The tile origin designates the position of the screen in tile space.*

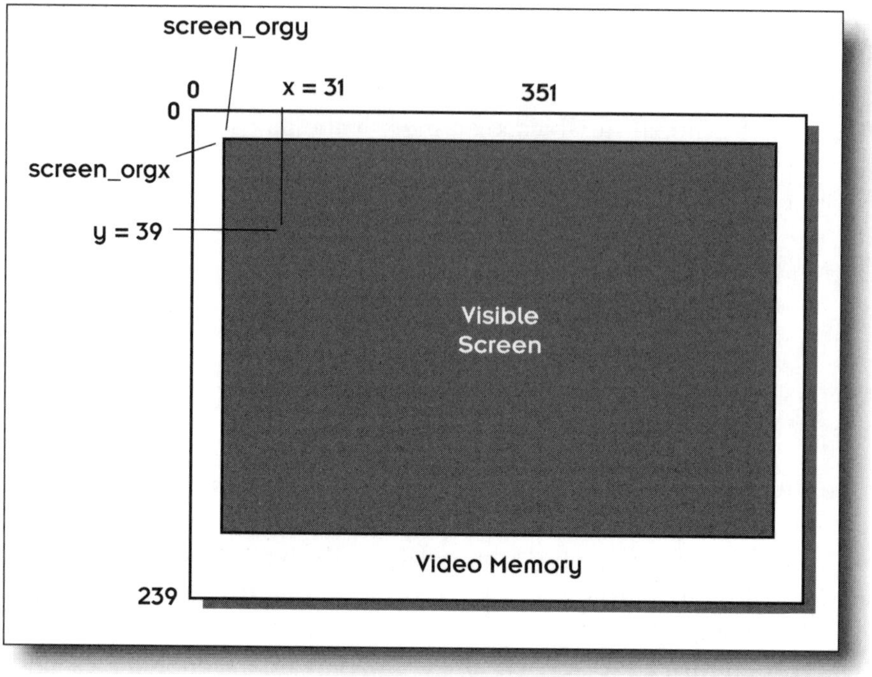

Figure 6.3 *The screen floats in video memory.*

Three global offset variables are declared, **vpo**, **hpo**, and **tpo**. The **vpo** variable (discussed briefly in Chapter 5) is the *visual page offset.* It is the y coordinate of the top of the visual page. It will always be either 0 or 240. In general, we'll add the value **vpo** to **screen_orgy** every time we do a page flip. Similarly, **hpo** is the *hidden page offset.* It is the y coordinate of the top of the hidden page. We will add this value to a tile's y coordinate whenever we want to draw the tile on the hidden page. The **tpo** variable is the *tile page offset*; it is located at y = 480. This is the top y coordinate of the area where the tiles are located in video memory. The mappings for these global variables are shown in Figure 6.4.

The **level_map** array is used to hold the tile information for the level. This is the same array we used in the tile ripper, but it is declared with a bigger size this time. **MAXROWS** is defined to be 200 and **MAXCOLS** is defined to be 240. That gives us a nice large rectangular level. You can change these values if you want; for example, you may want to design a level that is very tall but not too wide. Remember, these values represent the maximum values for the rows and columns. In general, the size of our level will be somewhat smaller than this.

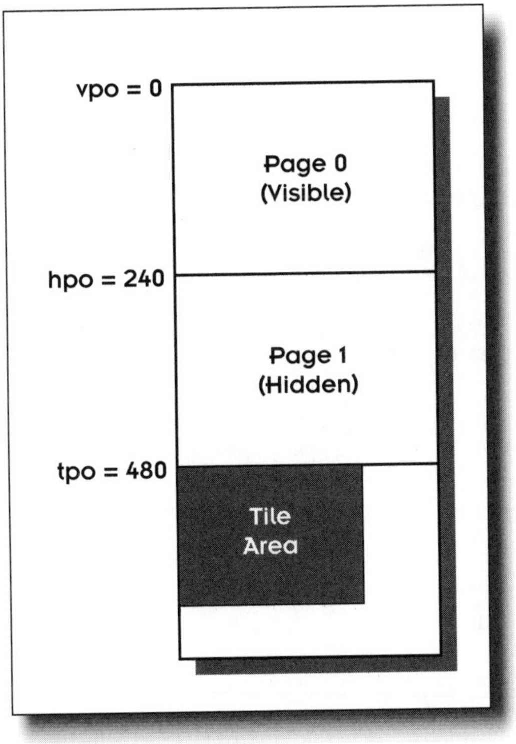

Figure 6.4 *Mappings for the global variables used in the level editor.*

Here's main()

LEVEL.C begins with function **main()**, which starts by initializing the video mode and resizing video memory (as discussed in Chapter 5). Then the mouse is initialized.

Using the mouse in Mode X is tricky. Since most commercial mouse drivers are unaware of Mode X (in fact, I'm not aware of one that is), we use Fastgraph to handle the mouse functions. Fastgraph controls the mouse cursor in Mode X by hooking its own mouse handler to the mouse driver. It accomplishes this through function 12 of interrupt 33 hex. The Fastgraph call to initialize the mouse is **fg_mouseini()**. Here's the code in **main()** that performs this task:

```
/* initialize the Mode X mouse handler */
   if (fg_mouseini() <= 0)
   {
      fg_setmode(3);
      fg_reset();
```

```
        printf("Mouse not found!\n");
        exit(0);
    }
```

Note that if Fastgraph is unable to initialize the mouse, the level editor exits with an error message. The mouse *is required* to run the level editor.

Fastgraph Tip

fg_mouseini()

The **fg_mouseini()** function initializes the mouse and must be called before any of Fastgraph's other mouse support functions.

```
int fg_mouseini(void);
```

Fastgraph's mouse handler remains in effect until it is explicitly disabled, so it's important to unhook the handler before your program exits, which is the purpose of Fastgraph's **fg_mousefin()** function. You'll find a call to this function at the end of **main()**.

Fastgraph Tip

fg_mousefin()

The **fg_mousefin()** function unhooks Fastgraph's XVGA or SVGA mouse handler from the mouse driver. This function should be used just before reverting to a text mode in programs that have called **fg_mouseini()** in XVGA or SVGA graphics mode.

```
void fg_mousefin(void);
```

After the mouse is initialized by loading Fastgraph's mouse handler, we need to turn off the mouse cursor. This is accomplished by calling **fg_mousevis()**, as shown here:

```
/* the mouse cursor is invisible throughout the program */
fg_mousevis(0);
```

Fastgraph Tip

fg_mousevis()

The **fg_mousevis()** function makes the mouse cursor visible or invisible. After calling **fg_mouseini()**, the mouse cursor is invisible.

```
void fg_mousevis(int state)
```

- *state* defines the mouse cursor visibility. If state is 0, the mouse cursor is made invisible. If it is 1, the mouse cursor is made visible.

Loading the Level Data

Once all of the initialization tasks are completed, it's time to call the **load_level()** function to load the level data from the disk. This includes the tiles that are stored in the PCX file, TILES.PCX, and the level array, which is stored in a binary data file, RIPPER.LEV. The PCX file is displayed in the tile area that we defined in Chapter 5, as shown in Figure 6.5. This is accomplished with just a few function calls:

```
/* display the tiles in the tile area */
fg_move(0,tpo);
fg_showpcx("tiles.pcx",2);
```

Notice that the **load_level()** function also sets up the mouse limits.

```
/* set the mouse limits */
fg_mouselim(0,336,vpo,vpo+224);
```

The mouse limits will need to be changed often. Since we have resized video memory to one large page, it is quite easy to move the mouse cursor off the edge of the screen. Because the mouse cursor is only useful when we can see it, we want to keep it visible. The **fg_mouselim()** function constrains the movement of the mouse to a rectangular area. We will use this function to keep the mouse cursor within the visible part of video memory. Since the visible screen floats in video memory, we will need to recalculate and change the mouse limits every time we change the screen origin.

Figure 6.5 *Background tiles are stored in video memory.*

Fastgraph Tip

fg_mouselim()

The **fg_mouselim()** function defines the rectangular area in which the mouse cursor may move. In graphics modes, the area is defined in screen space coordinates. In text mode, it is defined in rows and columns.

```
void fg_mouselim(int minx, int maxx, int miny, int maxy);
```

- *minx* is the x coordinate of the area's left edge.
- *maxx* is the x coordinate of the area's right edge. This value must be greater than or equal to the value of *minx*.
- *miny* is the y coordinate of the area's top edge.
- *maxy* is the y coordinate of the area's bottom edge. This value must be greater than or equal to the value of *miny*.

Next, we need to read the level data from the RIPPER.LEV file. Here's the code that opens the file and reads the data into the **level_map** array:

```
/* open the level file and read the level information */
if ((stream = fopen("ripper.lev","rb")) != NULL)
{
   fread(&ncols,sizeof(int),1,stream);
   fread(&nrows,sizeof(int),1,stream);

   for (i = 0; i < ncols; i++)
      fread(&level_map[i][0],sizeof(char),nrows,stream);
   fclose(stream);
}
```

If the RIPPER.LEV file is not found, this code is skipped and the **load_level()** function initializes the level for editing. It begins by setting the level size to the size of one page—22 columns by 15 rows—and then sets that part of the **level_map** array to all zeros:

```
/* if you didn't find the file, just initialize the tiles to 0 */
else
{
   ncols = 22;
   nrows = 15;
   for (i = 0; i < ncols; i++)
      for (j = 0; j < nrows; j++)
         level_map[i][j] = 0;
}
```

Finally, **load_level()** calls **redraw_screen()**, which simply draws the screen by copying all the tiles from the tile area to the visual page.

After initializing the video mode and the mouse, and loading the level data, it's time to start editing the level. This is handled in the **edit_level()** function.

Editing a Level

The first thing the **edit_level()** function does is move the mouse to the center of the visual page and then read the position of the mouse using two useful Fastgraph functions:

```
/* start with the mouse at the center of the visual screen */
fg_mousemov(160,100+vpo);
fg_mousepos(&xmouse,&ymouse,&buttons);
```

Fastgraph Tip

fg_mousemov()

The **fg_mousemov()** function moves the mouse cursor to the specified position.

```
fg_mousemov(int ix, int iy);
```

- *ix* is the x coordinate of the new mouse cursor position.
- *iy* is the y coordinate of the new mouse cursor position.

Fastgraph Tip

fg_mousepos()

The **fg_mousepos()** function returns the current mouse position and button status. In graphics modes, the position is defined in screen space coordinates. In text modes, it is defined in rows and columns.

```
void fg_mousepos(int *ix, int *iy, int *buttons);
```

- *ix* receives the x coordinate of the mouse cursor position.
- *iy* receives the y coordinate of the mouse cursor position.
- *buttons* receives a bit mask representing the button status, where each bit is set if the corresponding button is pressed. Bit 0 corresponds to the left button, bit 1 to the right button, and bit 2 to the middle button.

The Mouse Cursor

One of the level editor's tricks is keeping track of the mouse cursor. Even though the cursor is only 16×16 pixels and we could let Fastgraph's default mouse cursor handle it, we are choosing to draw the cursor ourselves. There are several reasons for this, the obvious being we want to highlight tiles in 16-pixel increments. Instead of trying to figure out how to move the mouse in 16-pixel jumps, it is easier to just move the mouse smoothly and redraw the cursor after the mouse has moved 16 pixels. As we add features to our editor, we'll want to increase the size of the mouse cursor. Picking up tiles one at a time works only for the most rudimentary level editing. To really whip out levels in a hurry, we want to pick up entire blocks of tiles—whole doors or platforms, for example. If we pick up blocks of 10 or 20 tiles, we'll need a bigger mouse cursor to highlight them. Also, sometimes we don't want a cursor at all. When importing graphics, for example, we may want to use the mouse to move crosshairs. Since we know we are going to have to eventually take control of the mouse cursor, let's do it from the beginning when it's easy.

The algorithm is simple, but requires a bit of bookkeeping. We need to keep track of not only where the mouse is now, but where it was the last time a cursor was drawn. We don't want to redraw the cursor every frame, because that would cause an unacceptable level of flickering. The only time the cursor is redrawn is when the mouse has moved at least 16 pixels so that it is sitting on a different tile. Then the old tile is unhighlighted and the new tile is highlighted.

The **xmouse** and **ymouse** variables are the current mouse coordinates, as returned by the function **fg_mousepos()**. These need to be normalized to tile space. We use this code to normalize the mouse coordinates:

```
xbox = xmouse&0xfff0;
ybox = ymouse&0xfff0;
```

This code has the effect of reducing **xmouse** and **ymouse** to multiples of 16. As long as the mouse moves around in the same tile, **xbox** and **ybox** will remain the same. If **xbox** or **ybox** change, then the mouse has moved outside a tile and we need to draw a new cursor. To do the comparison, we'll need some variables to store the old mouse values. We'll call them **oldx** and **oldy**.

```
oldx = xbox;
oldy = ybox;
```

To draw the mouse cursor, we display a box in *exclusive or* (xor) mode to outline the current tile. First we call the **fg_setcolor()** function to set the current color to white, then we call the **fg_boxx()** function to draw the xor box.

```
/* draw the cursor */
fg_setcolor(WHITE);
fg_boxx(xbox,xbox+15,ybox, ybox+15);
```

Fastgraph Tip

fg_boxx()

The **fg_boxx()** function draws a hollow rectangle in *exclusive or* (xor) mode.

```
void fg_boxx(int minx, int maxx, int miny, int maxy);
```

- *minx* is the x coordinate of the rectangle's left edge.
- *maxx* is the x coordinate of the rectangle's right edge. The value must be greater than or equal to the value of *minx*.
- *miny* is the y coordinate of the rectangle's top edge.
- *maxy* is the y coordinate of the rectangle's bottom edge. The value must be greater than or equal to the value of *miny*.

The box we have just drawn outlines the tile the mouse is currently positioned over. We will consider this outline box to be the mouse cursor, and we will say the mouse is currently *pointing to* the tile that is highlighted. Since the cursor consists of an xor box, we need to keep track of whether the cursor is on or off. If it's off, drawing an xor box turns it on. If it's on, drawing an xor box turns it off. If you try to turn it on or off twice in a row, you are going to have problems. You may get cursor remnants on the screen, or you may lose your current cursor. The easiest way to keep track of the cursor status is to set a flag to ON every time the cursor is turned on, and set it to OFF every time the cursor is turned off. Then you only turn the cursor on if it is currently off, and vice versa. We'll call this flag **cursor_flag**, and declare it to be a local variable. After drawing the box, we'll set the cursor flag to ON:

```
cursor_flag = ON;
```

Moving the Mouse Cursor

To move the mouse cursor around in the editor, we need to poll the mouse continuously and compare it to the previous position. As I said before, we don't want to redraw the mouse cursor every iteration because that would cause blinking, so we just need to draw it when it changes position. We handle this by including the following code in a continuous loop:

```
/* loop continuously and handle events as they are detected */
for(;;)
{
   fg_intkey(&key,&aux);

   /* no key press detected, take care of mouse functions */
   if (key+aux == 0)
   {

    /* get the current mouse status */
    fg_mousepos(&xmouse,&ymouse,&buttons);

    /* normalize position for tile space */
    xbox = xmouse&0xfff0;
    ybox = ymouse&0xfff0;

    /* mouse has moved to a new tile position */
    if (xbox != oldx || ybox != oldy)
    {
       /* xor the old cursor box to get rid of it */
       fg_setcolor(WHITE);
       if (cursor_flag)
           fg_boxx(oldx,oldx+15,oldy,oldy+15);

       /* draw the cursor box at new position */
       fg_boxx(xbox,xbox+15,ybox,ybox+15);

       /* update the cursor flag */
       cursor_flag = ON;

       /* the new coordinates become the old coordinates */
       oldx = xbox;
       oldy = ybox;
    }
```

Executing this code in a loop allows us to move the mouse cursor around the screen smoothly, outlining tiles as the mouse passes over them.

Handling Keyboard and Mouse Events

The **edit_level()** function accepts input from both the mouse and the keyboard, and processes the input, or *events*, as it encounters them. Keyboard input and mouse status are polled in the same loop. The keyboard is checked first, using Fastgraph's key intercept function, **fg_intkey()**.

Fastgraph Tip

fg_intkey()

The **fg_intkey()** function reads the next entry from the BIOS keyboard buffer (without echo) and returns the keystroke's standard or extended keyboard code. It is similar to **fg_getkey()**, but it does not wait for a keystroke if the keyboard buffer is empty.

```
void fg_intkey(unsigned char *key, unsigned char *aux);
```

- *key* receives the keystroke's standard keyboard code if it represents a standard character. If the keystroke represents an extended character, *key* will be set to zero.
- *aux* receives the keystroke's extended keyboard code if it represents an extended character. If the keystroke represents a standard character, *aux* will be set to zero.

If no keypress is detected, the mouse code is executed. However, if a keypress is detected, the mouse is temporarily ignored while the key is processed. Since most of the keyboard functions require the mouse cursor to be turned off, we immediately turn it off as soon as a keypress is detected.

```
/* turn off the mouse cursor and set the flag to OFF */
if (cursor_flag)
{
     fg_setcolor(WHITE);
     fg_boxx(xbox,xbox+15,ybox,ybox+15);
     cursor_flag = OFF;
}
```

This code turns off the mouse cursor by xoring the cursor box, then it sets the cursor flag to OFF. We then need to decide what to do with the key we just detected. The following code handles the keystrokes in the **edit_level()** event loop:

```
if (key == ESC)
    return;

   /* arrow keys were pressed -- scroll around */
   else if (aux == LEFT_ARROW)
      scroll_left(16);
   else if (aux == RIGHT_ARROW)
      scroll_right(16);
   else if (aux == UP_ARROW)
      scroll_up(16);
```

```
   else if (aux == DOWN_ARROW)
      scroll_down(16);

   /* Spacebar gets at tile from the tile page */
   else if (key == SPACE)
      tile = get_tile();

   /* insert a row or column of tiles */
   else if (aux == INSERT)
      insert_tiles();

   /* delete a row or column of tiles */
   else if (aux == DELETE)
      delete_tiles();
}
```

Selecting Tiles

There are two ways to get a tile. The first—and most common—way is to use the right mouse button to grab a tile from the level. This is very simple to do, and it is handled in the event loop in the **edit_level()** function, as follows:

```
/* right button picks up a tile */
else if (buttons == 2)
{
    /* calculate the level array indices */
    i = tile_orgx + xmouse/16;
    j = tile_orgy + (ymouse-vpo)/16;

    /* find the tile in the tile map */
    tile = level_map[i][j];
}
```

The level indices, **i** and **j**, are calculated based on the mouse coordinates and the tile origin. The tile is "marked" by storing it in a byte-sized variable called *tile*. This variable represents a value that is found in the **level_map** array at the **[i][j]** position.

A second way to select a tile is to use the keyboard to make the tile library visible, and then use the mouse to select a tile from the tile library. The event loop handles this task by calling the **get_tile()** function whenever the Spacebar has been pressed. The **get_tile()** function similarly loads a byte value from the **level_map** into the byte variable **tile**.

Copying Tiles

The tile value that is stored in the **tile** variable may be placed anywhere on the level by pointing at a tile location with the mouse and pressing the left mouse button. Since this is also a simple matter, the code is handled in the **edit_level()** event loop, the same way we handled selecting a tile with the mouse:

```
/* the left mouse button puts down a tile */
if (buttons == 1)
{
    /* first turn off the mouse cursor */
    fg_setcolor(WHITE);
    fg_boxx(xbox,xbox+15,ybox,ybox+15);

    /* set the cursor flag to OFF*/
    cursor_flag = OFF;

    /* calculate the level array indices */
    i = xbox/16;
    j = (ybox-vpo)/16;

    /* update the level array */
    level_map[i+tile_orgx][j+tile_orgy]=(unsigned char)tile;

    /* draw the tile */
    put_tile(i,j);
}
```

The first thing that happens is the mouse cursor is turned off and the flag is set to OFF. Then the tile coordinates are determined based on the position of the mouse. The level map is updated to show the new tile at that location and the tile is drawn on the screen.

Functions Called in the Editing Event Loop

The **edit_level()** event loop gives the keyboard precedence over the mouse. Thus, when a keystroke is detected, it is processed first, despite anything that may be going on with the mouse. Usually when a keystroke is detected, a function is called to handle the event. Unlike the mouse events (moving, selecting a tile, copying a tile), the keyboard events are more complex and are best handled in function calls. The keystrokes presented in the following sections are detected by **edit_level()** and result in function calls.

Arrow Keys

The functions **scroll_left(), scroll_right(), scroll_up()** and **scroll_down()** are called when the arrow keys are pressed. These functions are described in Chapter 4.

Spacebar

When the Spacebar is pressed, the **get_tile()** function is called. This function repositions the visible part of video memory to the tile area and allows you to select a tile from the tile library using the mouse. Most of this code is fairly straightforward; there are only a few tricks. For example, you must change the mouse limits when the screen changes:

```
/* change the mouse limits and move the mouse */
fg_mouselim(0,319,tpo,tpo+176);
fg_mousemov(tile_xmouse,tile_ymouse);
```

The mouse coordinates are stored in two global variables, **tile_xmouse** and **tile_ymouse**. We keep track of these so that the next time we flip to the tile page, we'll be highlighting the same tile as the last time. The logic to move the mouse cursor around is the same as in the **edit_level()** function. When a button press is detected, we break out of the loop. The tile we have chosen is calculated based on the x and y position of the mouse. We have the option of exiting the function without getting a tile by pressing the Esc key.

When we exit the **get_tile()** function, we pause for five clock ticks. This is important; we don't want to exit back to the **edit_level()** function with our finger still on the mouse button. If we do that, we'll place a tile on the level immediately upon returning to **edit_level()**, which is undesirable. It's a nonfatal error, but an aggravating one nonetheless. Usually, we want to move the mouse around a little before we drop a new tile.

Delete Key

When the Delete key is pressed, the **delete_tiles()** function is called. This function will delete either a row or column of tiles. The first thing that happens is the Row/Column dialog box is displayed, as shown in Figure 6.6, prompting you to delete a row or column. You then press R for row, C for column, or Esc to exit the deletion operation.

The code that displays the Row/Column dialog box consists of a few Fastgraph functions:

```
/* pop up a message: what do you want to delete? */
fg_setcolor(WHITE);
fg_rect(screen_orgx+60,screen_orgx+260,
        screen_orgy+90+vpo,screen_orgy+110+vpo);
fg_setcolor(BLACK);
fg_move(screen_orgx+80,screen_orgy+105+vpo);
fg_print("Delete Row or Column?",21);
```

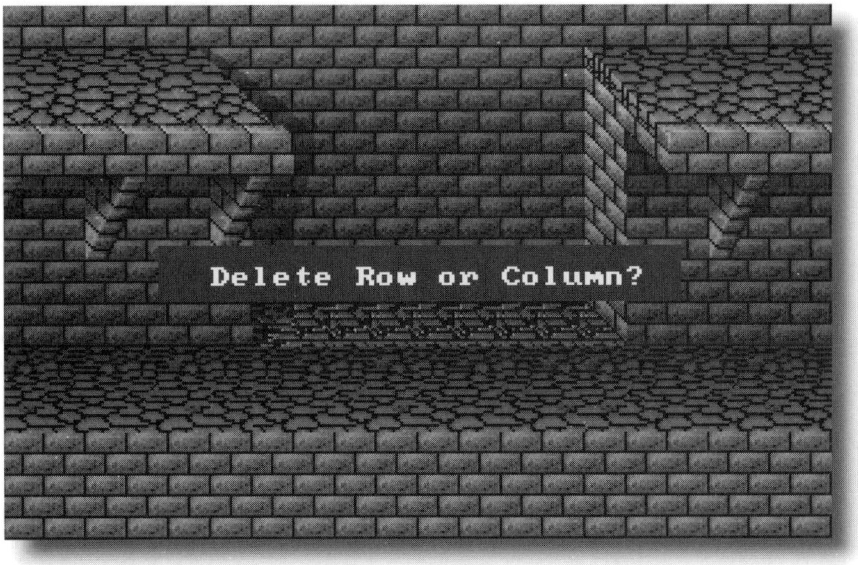

Figure 6.6 *The Row/Column dialog box allows you to specify column or row deletion.*

```
/* wait for a key press */
fg_getkey(&key,&aux);
```

A column is deleted by shifting all the columns to the left and decrementing the column count. The code to delete a column looks like this:

```
/* delete a column at the current mouse position */
if ((key|32) == 'c' && ncols > 22)
{
   /* calculate the current tile column */
   tile = tile_orgx + xmouse/16;

   /* shift all the tiles left by one column */
   for (j = 0; j < nrows; j++)
      for (i = tile; i < ncols-1; i++)
         level_map[i][j] = level_map[i+1][j];

   /* zero out the last column */
   i = ncols-1;
   for (j = 0; j < nrows; j++)
      level_map[i][j] = 0;

   /* decrement the number of columns */
   ncols--;
}
```

As Figure 6.7 shows, all of the columns in the level map are shifted to the left by one column. The last column is set to all zeros. The value **ncols**, which

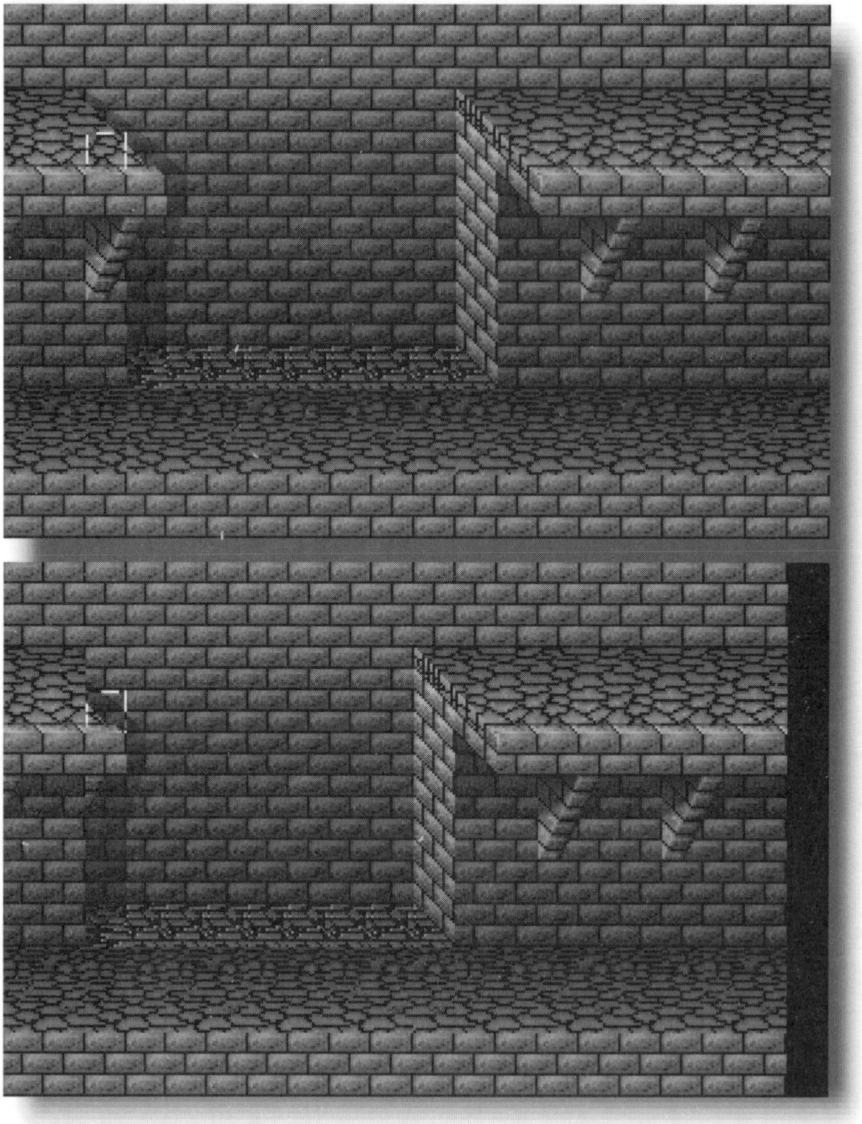

Figure 6.7 Deleting a column from a level.

is the number of columns, is decremented. At the end of the function, we call **redraw_screen()** to redraw all the tiles.

Deleting a row is similar to deleting a column. When the user selects R to delete a row, the row at the current mouse position is removed. This is accomplished by first calculating the current tile row

```
tile = tile_orgy + (ymouse-vpo)/16;
```

and then shifting all of the tiles up by one row. To complete the row deletion, the last row in the **level_map** array is set to all zeros.

Insert Key

When the Insert key is pressed, the **insert_tiles()** function is called. This function will insert either a row or column of tiles. The first thing that happens is the Row/Column dialog box is displayed prompting you to insert either a row or column. You press R to select row, C for column, or the Esc key to exit the insertion operation.

If you look closely at the code in **insert_tiles()** you'll see that it looks very similar to the code found in **delete_tiles()**. For example, when a column of tiles is inserted, the steps are the same as those used to remove a column except all the tiles are shifted to the right, duplicating one column of tiles instead of shifting to the left to remove a column.

Exiting the Program

Only one other keypress is processed in the **edit_level()** event loop—the Esc key. This event does not cause a function to be called, rather it causes the **edit_level()** function to return control to **main()**. The **main()** function then calls the **save_level()** function, which writes the level data to the binary file, RIPPER.LEV. As the code shows, this function first stores the number of columns and rows in the level file:

```
/* write out the number of columns and rows */
fwrite(&ncols,sizeof(int),1,stream);
fwrite(&nrows,sizeof(int),1,stream);
```

Then, it spins through a loop and writes each column to the file:

```
/* write each column, in sequence */
for (i = 0; i < ncols; i++)
   fwrite(&level_map[i][0],sizeof(char),nrows,stream);
fclose(stream);
```

Finally, the **main()** function finishes up and exits, taking care to disable the mouse handler and reset the video mode on its way out.

Finishing Up

As mentioned before, the level editor code has been simplified for this chapter, and there is a more complete level editor on disk. Some of the advanced features on the disk include the ability to pick up more than one tile at a time, undo your mistakes, and view tile coordinates, tile numbers, and tile attributes. The additional functionality is important, because you need all the help you can get to design excellent levels. In today's competitive market, good level design is essential to making a game playable and marketable. Level design is an important part of the game design process and should be given priority attention.

Chapter 7

What would a game be without sprites? Here's your chance to learn how to use the sprite editor to create them quickly.

Inside the Sprite Editor

As I was reading Michael Abrash's new book, *Zen of Code Optimization*, it occurred to me that there are times when some of his optimization suggestions could be ignored by game programmers. The game market has changed considerably over the past few years. These days, games are bigger, expectations are higher, and the game developer's job is harder than it ever was. We find ourselves writing thousands of lines of code. We can't afford to focus too much attention on code optimization. A greater concern to us is *development* optimization. By that I mean, we need to think in terms of shortening the amount of time it takes to develop a game.

So save your pedal-to-the-metal optimizations for where they count—in the game itself. Design your utilities to be simple, functional, easy to code, and easy to maintain. So let's have a look at how a nice, clean, functional sprite editor can be written.

Introducing the Sprite Editor

The sprite editor we'll be exploring in this chapter is the same one that is incorporated into the game editor introduced in Chapter 3. The actual code file used to implement the sprite editor is SPRITE.C. The global definitions that the editor needs are found in EDITDEFS.H. The sprite editor is the biggest coding project that I've introduced so far. Table 7.1 provides a description of the main functions used to help you navigate through the source file.

Table 7.1 *Functions Used in SPRITE.C*

Function	Description
activate_sprite_editor()	Main event loop for sprite editor
animate_sprite_list()	Displays all sprites in sequence
array_to_sprite()	Copies from array to working variables
bitmap_to_grid()	Copies a sprite from RAM to the fat bit grid
bounding_box()	Sets bounding box limits
calculate_sprite_size()	Eliminates blank rows and columns
check_sprite_suffixes()	Checks for ".PCX" on import files
clear_sprite()	Sets all pixels to background color
delete_sprite()	Removes a sprite from the list
draw_sprite_editor()	Draws the screen
edit_sprites(void)	Main calling function
flip_sprite(void)	Rotates the sprite around a vertical axis
flood_fill_sprite(void)	Flood fills an area
get_minimal_sprite()	Trims empty rows and columns
get_sprite()	Copies a sprite from video memory to RAM
import_sprite(void)	Imports a sprite from a PCX file
init_sprite()	Initializes sprite editor
init_this_spritelist()	Loads from disk
load_edit_sprites(void)	Loads a new sprite list, then calls edit_sprites
load_sprites(void)	Initializes and loads sprites from disk
mask_sprite()	Removes transparent (black) background
move_grid_boundary()	Moves the grid boundary around
next_sprite()	Views/edits the next sprite in the list

continued

Table 7.1 Functions Used in SPRITE.C (Continued)

Function	Description
previous_sprite()	Views/edits the previous sprite in the list
put_spritenum()	Displays number of current sprite on status line
restore_this_sprite()	Copies a sprite from RAM to the fat bit grid
save_sprite()	Saves the sprite list to disk
set_grid_boundary()	Turns grid boundary on or off
set_sprite_background_color()	Selects a background color
set_sprite_foreground_color()	Selects a foreground color
set_sprite_grid()	Draws a small rectangle on the fat bit grid
set_sprite_point()	Draws a point on sprite area
show_sprite_coords()	Displays coordinates in status area
sprite_to_array()	Copies from working variables to array
transpose_sprite_colors()	Sets all background color pixels to foreground color
undo_sprite()	Undoes last edit (works as a toggle)
update_sprite_old()	Updates undo information
xor_horiz_line()	Creates horizontal xor line for crosshairs
xor_vert_line()	Creates vertical xor line for crosshairs

Designing the Sprite Editor

The first task of designing any usable utility like the sprite editor is drawing the screen. The screen should be attractive and functional, but not too fancy. Keeping in mind that our sprite editor takes precedence over form, we'll draw the editor as cleanly and simply as possible. As shown in Figure 7.1, the sprite editor has six main parts. Let's look at how each of these parts is created.

Drawing the Fat Bit Grid

If you recall from Chapter 3, the fat bit grid is the rectangular area that shows a magnified version of part of the sprite. Here, a pixel in the sprite is represented by a small rectangle in the fat bit grid, as shown in Figure 7.2. The sprite is edited by clicking on rectangles in the fat bit grid. The general idea is that it's easier to see magnified parts of the sprite, and it's easier to guide the mouse to a rectangle, which is a bigger target than a single pixel.

The fat bit grid is built by drawing a single large black rectangle, then using crisscrossing gray rectangles to create a grid. The width of the fat bit grid is

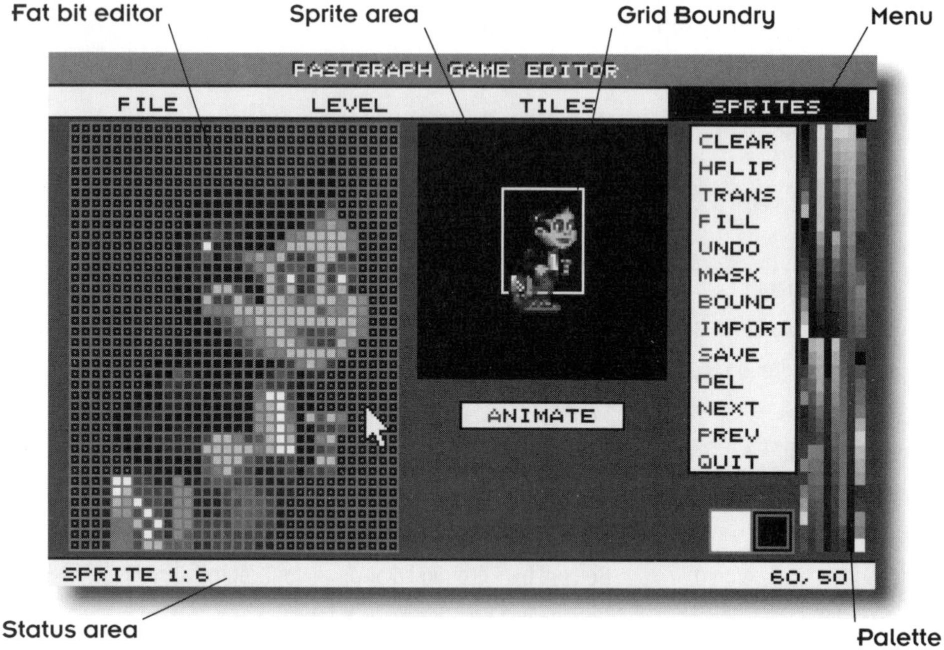

Figure 7.1 *The main parts of the sprite editor.*

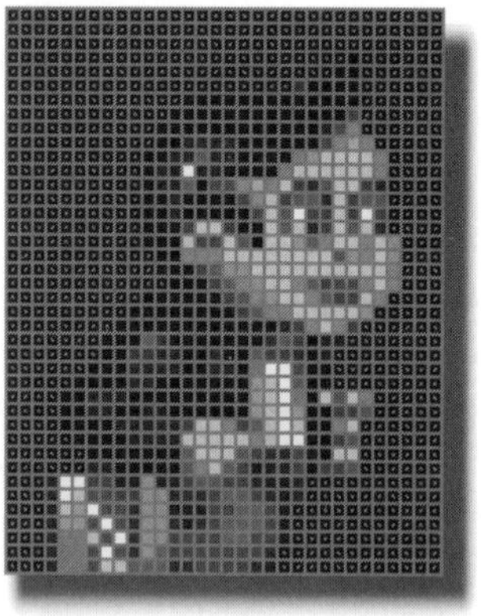

Figure 7.2 *Using the fat bit grid to edit sprites.*

128 pixels. This value is divided by lines at 4-pixel increments, creating a total of 32 grid boxes in the horizontal direction. Similarly, the 40 grid boxes in the vertical direction take 160 pixels. The code to create the grid is located in the function **draw_sprite_editor()**:

```
/* draw the background for the fat bit grid */
fg_setcolor(black);
fg_rect(8,136,26,186);
```

```
/* use vertical bars to divide into 32 horizontal grid boxes */
x = 8;
fg_setcolor(gray);
for (i = 0; i <= 32; i++)
{
   fg_rect(x,x,26,186);
   x += 4;
}

/* use horizontal bars to divide into 40 vertical grid boxes */
y = 26;
for (j = 0; j <= 40; j++)
{
   fg_rect(8,136,y,y);
   y += 4;
}

/* fill the squares with gray dots */
for(i = 0; i < 32; i++)
{
   for(j = 0; j < 40; j++)
   {
      x = (i * 4) + 10;
      y = (j * 4) + 28;
      fg_setcolor(gray);
      fg_point(x,y);
   }
}
```

Each box in the fat bit grid is initially set to black with a gray dot in the middle of it. This indicates the sprite has a zero pixel at this location. Color zero is the transparent color, so a black box with a gray dot represents a transparent pixel.

Fastgraph Tip

fg_point()

The **fg_point()** function draws a point.

```
void fg_point(int ix, int iy);
```

- *ix* is the point's x coordinate.
- *iy* is the point's y coordinate.

Drawing the Sprite Area

The fat bit grid shows only a part of the whole sprite. For example, it may show our sprite Tommy's legs, waist, and shoulders, but not his head. We also want to look at the whole sprite while it's being edited, so we allocate an area of the screen for this purpose. The *sprite area* is located to the right of the fat bit grid. It consists of a rectangle 96 pixels wide and 96 pixels tall, which should be plenty large enough for most of our sprites. Certain sprites, such as a big enemy, could be larger than 96×96 pixels, and would have to be handled as a special case. But we're not designing the sprite editor for special cases, we're designing it to handle large quantities of ordinary sprites. After all, our primary concern is streamlining the process of importing artwork into the game. A smaller sprite area will allow us to handle more sprites in RAM at one time, so the 96×96 pixel size seems to be about right.

Creating the Grid Boundary

Since the sprite area shows more of the sprite than the fat bit grid, we need some way of highlighting which part of the sprite is currently being edited. The *grid boundary* is a hollow box 32 pixels wide by 40 pixels tall. It outlines the part of the sprite that is currently visible in the fat bit grid. You can use your mouse to move the grid boundary around, which will cause different parts of the sprite to appear in the fat bit grid. The grid boundary is drawn using an xor method, so that drawing the box in the same location twice will make it disappear. The code to make the grid boundary appear and disappear is in the **set_grid_boundary()** function:

```
void set_grid_boundary(int status)
{
   /* turn the grid boundary on if it is off */
   if (status == ON && grid_boundary == OFF)
   {
      fg_mousevis(OFF);
      fg_setcolor(white);

      /* use an xor box to draw the grid boundary */
      fg_boxx(144+x_offset,144+x_limit,26+y_offset,26+y_limit);
      grid_boundary = ON;
   }

   /* turn the grid boundary off if it is on */
   else if (status == OFF && grid_boundary == ON)
   {
      fg_mousevis(OFF);
      fg_setcolor(white);

      /* use an xor box to erase the grid boundary */
      fg_boxx(144+x_offset,144+x_limit,26+y_offset,26+y_limit);
      grid_boundary = OFF;
   }
}
```

Creating Palettes

We have 256 palettes available to us. These are displayed at the far right side of the screen. In general, I try to use only the first 32 palettes in any sprite, and reserve the other 224 palettes for the background. Palette 0 is usually black, and will be transparent in a sprite. Menus are drawn in 32 rows of eight rectangles each. This is done conveniently in a loop in the **draw_sprite_editor()** function as follows:

```
/* palettes */
y = 26;
for (i = 0; i < 32; i++)
{
   fg_setcolor(i);
   fg_rect(291,293,y,y+4);

   fg_setcolor(i+32);
   fg_rect(294,296,y,y+4);

   fg_setcolor(i+64);
   fg_rect(297,299,y,y+4);

   fg_setcolor(i+96);
   fg_rect(300,302,y,y+4);

   fg_setcolor(i+128);
   fg_rect(303,305,y,y+4);

   fg_setcolor(i+160);
   fg_rect(306,308,y,y+4);

   fg_setcolor(i+192);
   fg_rect(309,311,y,y+4);

   fg_setcolor(i+224);
   fg_rect(312,315,y,y+4);

   y += 5;
}
```

The foreground and background colors are highlighted in two larger rectangles at the bottom of the screen. The foreground color is the color used when the left mouse button is pressed. The background color is used when the right mouse button is pressed.

Creating Menus

The user can select a sprite editor command by using the mouse to choose an item from a *menu*. The menu is displayed on the right side of the screen next to the palettes. Each menu item has its first letter highlighted in blue, which allows us to select a menu item either by clicking on it, or typing the highlighted letter. To highlight the first letter, we need to make a temporary string containing only the first letter of the menu item and null terminator. Then we overwrite the menu string with the temporary string:

```
char *string[] = {
   "Clear",
   "Hflip",
   "Trans",
   "Fill",
   "Undo",
   "Mask",
   "Bound",
   "Import",
   "Save",
   "Del",
   "Next",
   "Prev",
   "Quit"
};

/* draw the menu area in white and outline it in black */
fg_setcolor(white);
fg_rect(248,289,26,156);
fg_setcolor(black);
fg_box(248,289,26,156);

/* null terminate the temporary string, which will hold the
   first letter of each menu item */

temp_string= '\0';

x = 252;
y = 34;
for (i = 0; i < 13; i++)
{
   /* draw the menu item */
   fg_setcolor(black);
   put_bstring(string[i],x,y);

   /* highlight the first letter of the menu item in blue */
   temp_string[0] = string[i][0];
   fg_setcolor(blue);
   put_bstring(temp_string,x,y);
   y+=10;
}
```

Creating the Status Area

Two-way communication is necessary for any worthwhile utility. A program needs to tell us what its current status is, and what it expects from us. We, in turn, need an area to give information to the program.

The *status area* in the sprite editor is a white rectangular bar at the bottom of the screen. It asks us questions like "Save the sprite file Yes/No?" We may also type in a filename in this area.

Other information about the editing process is displayed in this area, including the current x and y position of the mouse cursor on the fat bit grid, the current sprite number in the list, and whether we are currently performing a flood fill.

The status area is drawn in white with a black bar above it as shown here:

```
/* bottom status area */

fg_setcolor(white);
fg_rect(0,319,190,199);
fg_setcolor(black);
fg_rect(0,319,189,189);
```

Loading the Sprites

After drawing the components of the sprite editor, we load and initialize the sprites. Recall from Chapter 3 that sprites are saved in files with an LST extension. Each file can contain a maximum of 10 sprites, which is about all the sprites that will fit into RAM at one time in the sprite editor. A sequence of sprites is called a *sprite list*, and each LST file contains one sprite list. I find it convenient to store similar sprites in a single sprite list; for example, all the walking sprites go in one sprite list, and all the shooting sprites go in another sprite list. Only one sprite list can be loaded into the sprite editor at a time.

Sprites are stored in structures, and the sprite list is stored in RAM as an array of structures. The sprite structures are declared at the top of the SPRITE.C file as follows:

```
typedef struct _sprite      /* sprite structure */
{
   char far *bitmap;
   int width;
   int height;
   int xorg;
   int yorg;
   int bound_x;
   int bound_y;
   int bound_width;
   int bound_height;
}  SPRITE;

SPRITE sprite[10];          /* sprite list array */
```

Since the sprites are rather large—9,216 bytes each—only a limited number of them can be stored in RAM at one time. We allow room for 10 sprites in the array. If you have more than 10 sprites, put them in two sprite lists—which means two separate files.

The code to read sprites from a file is in the **init_sprites()** function and looks like this:

```
/* open the file */
if ((tstream = fopen(spritelist_fname,"rb")) != NULL)
{
   /* how many sprites are there? */
   fread(&nsprites,sizeof(int),1,tstream);

   /* read one sprite at a time */
   for (i = 0; i < nsprites; i++)
   {
      fread(&sprite_width,sizeof(int),1,tstream);
      fread(&sprite_height,sizeof(int),1,tstream);
      if (sprite_width <= 0) sprite_width = 1;
      if (sprite_height <= 0) sprite_height = 1;
      nbytes = sprite_width*sprite_height;

      fread(&sprite_xorg,sizeof(int),1,tstream);
      fread(&sprite_yorg,sizeof(int),1,tstream);

      fread(&sprite_boundx,sizeof(int),1,tstream);
      fread(&sprite_boundy,sizeof(int),1,tstream);
      fread(&sprite_boundwidth,sizeof(int),1,tstream);
      fread(&sprite_boundheight,sizeof(int),1,tstream);

      fread(bitmap,sizeof(char),nbytes,tstream);

      /* is there room for another sprite in RAM? */
      if ((sprite[i].bitmap = malloc(9216)) != NULL)
      {
         /* store the sprite in a RAM array */
         sprite_to_array(i);
      }

      /* out of room -- that was the last sprite! */
      else
      {
         nsprites = i+1;
         break;
      }
   }
   fclose(tstream);

   /* current sprite is sprite 0 */
   current_sprite = 0;
   array_to_sprite(current_sprite);
}
```

```
/* no file open */
else
{
   memset(bitmap,0,9216);
   sprite_xorg = 144;
   sprite_yorg = 121;
   sprite_width = 96;
   sprite_height = 96;

   sprite_boundx = 0;
   sprite_boundy = 0;
   sprite_boundwidth = 96;
   sprite_boundheight = 96;

   current_sprite = 0;
   sprite[current_sprite].bitmap = malloc(9216);
}
```

The first integer value in the file is the number of sprites in the current sprite list. Following that is the data for each sprite. Each sprite has a width and height, an x and y origin, bounding box information, and bitmap data. If the sprite editor cannot open the file, it initializes the sprite by assigning some default values to the sprite structure members. The x and y origin are assumed to be 144 and 121, respectively. The width and height are assigned the values 96, and the bounding box is assigned an area as large as the largest possible sprite.

The sprite is stored in RAM twice, once as a temporary working copy of the sprite we are currently editing, and once as a more permanent copy stored in the sprite array. When we want to edit a different sprite—for example the "next" or "previous" sprite—we copy the current sprite into the sprite array, then we copy the desired sprite out of the sprite array into the temporary working variables. This is accomplished in the functions **sprite_to_array()** and **array_to_sprite()**, as follows:

```
void sprite_to_array(int n)
{
   int nbytes;

   sprite[n].width        = sprite_width;
   sprite[n].height       = sprite_height;
   sprite[n].xorg         = sprite_xorg;
   sprite[n].yorg         = sprite_yorg;
   sprite[n].bound_x      = sprite_boundx;
   sprite[n].bound_y      = sprite_boundy;
   sprite[n].bound_width  = sprite_boundwidth;
   sprite[n].bound_height = sprite_boundheight;
```

```
   nbytes = sprite_width*sprite_height;
   memcpy(sprite[n].bitmap,bitmap,nbytes);
}

void array_to_sprite(int n)
{
   int nbytes;

   sprite_width       = sprite[n].width;
   sprite_height      = sprite[n].height;
   sprite_xorg        = sprite[n].xorg;
   sprite_yorg        = sprite[n].yorg;
   sprite_boundx      = sprite[n].bound_x;
   sprite_boundy      = sprite[n].bound_y;
   sprite_boundwidth  = sprite[n].bound_width;
   sprite_boundheight = sprite[n].bound_height;

   if (sprite_width <= 0) sprite_width = 1;
   if (sprite_height <= 0) sprite_height = 1;

   nbytes = sprite_width*sprite_height;
   memcpy(bitmap,sprite[n].bitmap,nbytes);
}
```

Once the sprite data is in the temporary working variables, it can then be manipulated in RAM and blitted to the screen as needed.

The Sprite Data File

An ASCII file, called the *sprite data file*, contains the names of all the sprite lists. Usually I like to call this file SPRITE.DAT, or if there is more than one, I will call them SPRITE0.DAT, SPRITE1.DAT, and so on. The idea is that you'll have different sprites in different levels, but there will be some overlap between levels. While some sprites will appear in more than one level, you don't want to store the sprite data more than once, you just want to keep track of the filenames in each level. So you have a sprite list file for each level that specifies which sprites need to be loaded for that level. Currently, the sprite editor is designed to handle 13 sprite lists of 10 sprites each, which means you can have 130 unique sprites per level. I don't know if you really need that many sprites in a level; it seems like a generous number. If you have more sprites than that, you will definitely face memory problems. On the other hand, if your game has many small sprites, and you need room for more than 130 sprites, you can either increase the size of the sprite data file or use two sprite data files.

Viewing the Sprite

After we have loaded the sprites, we'll need to view them. We'll use Fastgraph's **fg_drwimage()** function to display the sprite in the sprite area:

```
fg_move(sprite_xorg,sprite_yorg);
fg_drwimage(bitmap,sprite_width,sprite_height);
```

This code is used frequently to display sprites. For example, in the **previous_sprite()** function, the last sprite in the list is displayed, as shown here:

```
void previous_sprite()
{
   /* display the previous sprite */

   if (current_sprite > 0)
   {
      update_sprite_old();
      set_grid_boundary(OFF);
      get_minimal_sprite();

      sprite_to_array(current_sprite);
      current_sprite--;
      array_to_sprite(current_sprite);

      fg_mousevis(OFF);
      fg_setcolor(0);
      fg_rect(144,239,26,121);
      fg_move(sprite_xorg,sprite_yorg);
      fg_drwimage(bitmap,sprite_width,sprite_height);
      get_sprite();
      bitmap_to_grid();
      put_spritenum();
   }
}
```

Fastgraph Tip

fg_drwimage()

The **fg_drwimage()** function displays an image stored as a mode-specific bitmap. The image will be positioned so that its lower-left corner is at the graphics cursor position (or the text cursor position in text video modes).

```
void fg_drwimage (char *map_array, int width, int height);
```

- *map_array* is the arbitrary-length array containing the bitmap.
- *width* is the width in bytes of the bitmap.
- *height* is the height in bytes (pixel rows) of the bitmap.

We don't want to edit the sprite at its default size. That would be too difficult to see and control. We want to do our editing on the fat bit grid. To copy the tiny sprite to the fat bit grid, we need to draw a series of small rectangles. The function **bitmap_to_grid()** accomplishes this task:

```
void bitmap_to_grid()
{
   register int i,j;
   int color;
   int x,y;
   int byte_ptr;

   fg_mousevis(OFF);
   get_sprite();

   /* copy to fat bit grid */
   byte_ptr = 0;
   for (j = 95; j >= 0; j--)
   {
      for (i = 0; i < 96; i++)
         this_sprite[i][j] = bitmap[byte_ptr++];
   }

   /* set the points in the fat bit, if they have changed */
   for (i = 0; i < 32; i++)
   {
      for (j = 0; j < 40; j++)
      {
         x = x_offset+i;
         y = y_offset+j;

         if (this_sprite[x][y] != old_sprite[x][y])
         {
            color = (int)this_sprite[x][y];
            set_sprite_grid(i,j,color);
         }
      }
   }
}
```

We've introduced another global array here. This is a two-dimensional array called **this_sprite**. I find it convenient to edit pixels in an array that has the same width and height as the sprite being edited. The **this_sprite** array contains the same data as the bitmap array, but is organized a little differently.

Since Fastgraph displays bitmaps from bottom to top, and we're addressing pixels from top to bottom, we have to do a little conversion here.

Tommy's Tip

Bottom-Up Sprites

I'm sometimes asked why Fastgraph displays bitmaps from the bottom to the top, when memory is usually addressed from the top to the bottom. There are a couple of good reasons for this, and one not-very-good reason. The good reasons are, we're usually more concerned with the bottom of a sprite than the top of a sprite. We're interested in the location of Tommy's feet, but we don't much care where the top of his head is. Similarly with fonts, we're more concerned about where the bottom of a letter is than the top. We want our letters to line up on a given line even if they're different heights. For these reasons, when we first developed Fastgraph it seemed like the proper way to address a bitmap was from the lower-left corner.

We made that decision many years ago. But since then, we've wondered if we made the right decision. These days it's standard to address a bitmap from the upper-left corner. The problem is, if we change Fastgraph now, we'll break everybody's code. People hate it when you do that. For now, Fastgraph will continue to address bitmaps from the lower-left corner, but we may provide an option in the future to change the location of a bitmap origin. If you have a strong opinion about this, I suggest you let Ted know how you feel about it. If enough people ask him to change the code, he'll probably do it.

Another array is introduced in the **bitmap_to_grid()** function: the **old_sprite** array. This array holds the *undo* information for the sprite editor. Whenever a sprite is changed, the old sprite is stored. If you make an undesirable change, you can go back to the earlier sprite by selecting the undo option. As we update the fat bit grid, we compare the current sprite to the old sprite. If the byte has not changed, there is no reason to redraw the rectangle. This saves a significant amount of time in redrawing the fat bit editor.

Each rectangle in the fat bit editor is updated by using the function **set_sprite_grid()**. This function simply calculates the position and draws the rectangle as follows:

```
void set_sprite_grid(int i,int j,int color)
{
   /* draw a little rectangle on the fat bit editor */
   int x,y;
```

```
      fg_mousevis(OFF);
      x = (i * 4) + 9;
      y = (j * 4) + 27;

      this_sprite[i+x_offset][j+y_offset] = (char)color;
      fg_setcolor(color);
      fg_rect(x,x+2,y,y+2);

      if (color == 0)
      {
         fg_setcolor(gray);
         fg_point(x+1,y+1);
      }
}
```

Notice that if the current color is zero (the transparent color), a small gray dot is displayed in the box to show that it's a transparent pixel.

The fat bit grid is updated by clicking on the squares. These squares then change color, depending on what the current color is and which mouse button was pressed. As the fat bit grid is updated, the sprite itself must also be updated. We do this by drawing a point in the sprite area, using the **set_sprite_point()** function:

```
void set_sprite_point(int x,int y,int color)
{
   /* just set a point to the current color */

   fg_mousevis(OFF);
   fg_setcolor(color);
   fg_point(x,y);
}
```

When the sprite is modified in RAM, it must then be copied back to video memory, as with some of the editing functions. The **restore_this_sprite()** function updates both the sprite area and the fat bit grid:

```
void restore_this_sprite()
{
   register int i,j;
   int color;
   int x,y;

   for (i = 0; i < 32; i++)
   {
      for (j = 0; j < 40; j++)
      {
         x = x_offset+i;
         y = y_offset+j;
```

```
            if (this_sprite[x][y] != old_sprite[x][y])
            {
               color = (int)this_sprite[x][y];
               set_sprite_grid(i,j,color);
            }
         }
      }

      set_grid_boundary(OFF);
      fg_mousevis(OFF);
      for(i = 0; i < 96; i++)
      {
         for(j = 0; j < 96; j++)
         {
            if (this_sprite[i][j] != old_sprite[i][j])
            {
               color = (int)this_sprite[i][j];
               fg_setcolor(color);
               fg_point(144+i,26+j);
            }
         }
      }
      set_grid_boundary(ON);
   }
```

Copying the sprite from video memory back into RAM is accomplished using the **get_sprite()** function. This is done to update the bitmap array, which may then be copied to the sprite list array or written to a file:

```
void get_sprite()
{
   /* get the sprite from the sprite area, store in a RAM bitmap */

   sprite_width = 96;
   sprite_height = 96;

   sprite_xorg = 144;
   sprite_yorg = 121;

   fg_move(sprite_xorg,sprite_yorg);
   fg_getimage(bitmap,sprite_width,sprite_height);
}
```

This collection of functions moves the sprite data around between RAM and video memory. As mentioned earlier, there may be more optimal ways to accomplish this, but these functions seem to do the job well enough. Now that we have pretty good control over our sprite data, we can start to do things with it. The first thing we want to do is be able to move the data around in the fat bit grid.

The Grid Boundary

Since the fat bit grid displays a magnified version of the sprite, it can only display a part of the sprite at any one time. For example, if we are currently looking at Tommy's head and we want to modify his feet, we'll need to move the visible area down a few pixels, as shown in Figure 7.3. We do this by dragging the grid boundary around.

We start by defining a global variable called **grid_boundary**:

```
int grid_boundary;          /* flag - is boundary box on or off? */
```

The **grid_boundary** variable is a global Boolean integer value. It will be set to either ON or OFF. The grid boundary will be drawn as an xor box, so if it is on, drawing it again will turn it off, and vice versa.

Four other global variables define the extents of the grid boundary. These are changed as the grid boundary is dragged around:

```
int x_offset;               /* x location of the grid boundary box */
int x_limit;                /* width of the grid boundary box */
int y_offset;               /* y location of the grid boundary box */
int y_limit;                /* height of the grid boundary box */
```

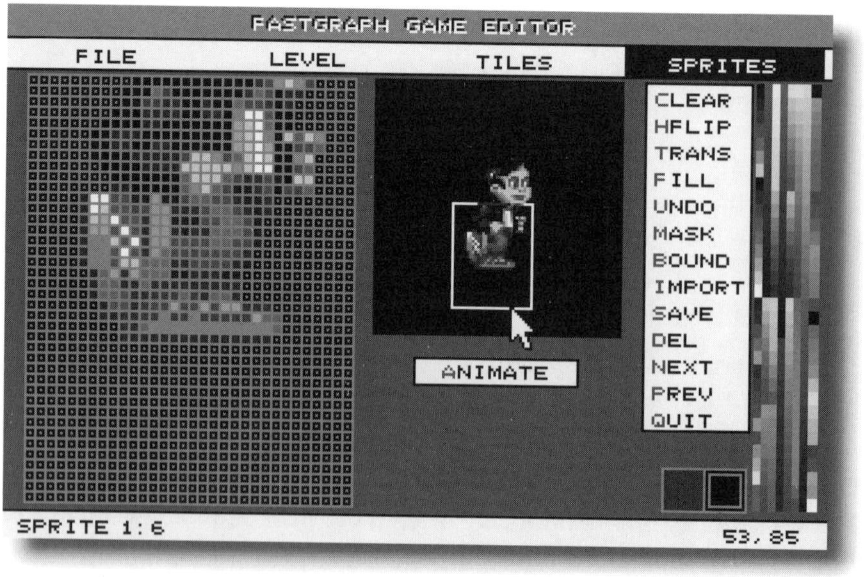

Figure 7.3 *Moving the visible area down to view another portion of a sprite.*

Every time the bitmap is copied to or from the sprite area, the grid boundary must be turned off, then turned back on when the operation is complete. The code to turn the grid boundary off and on looks like this:

```
void set_grid_boundary(int status)
{
   /* turn the grid boundary on if it is off */
   if (status == ON && grid_boundary == OFF)
   {
      fg_mousevis(OFF);
      fg_setcolor(white);

      /* use an xor box to draw the grid boundary */
      fg_boxx(144+x_offset,144+x_limit,26+y_offset,26+y_limit);
      grid_boundary = ON;
   }

   /* turn the grid boundary off if it is on */
   else if (status == OFF && grid_boundary == ON)
   {
      fg_mousevis(OFF);
      fg_setcolor(white);

      /* use an xor box to erase the grid boundary */
      fg_boxx(144+x_offset,144+x_limit,26+y_offset,26+y_limit);
      grid_boundary = OFF;
   }
}
```

Similarly, the grid boundary is dragged by repeatedly turning it off and on as the mouse is moved. After the grid boundary is moved to a new location, the fat bit editor is redrawn to show the desired part of the sprite.

Importing Sprites

Although the sprite editor contains many powerful editing features, in general, sprites are not usually created in the sprite editor. It is most common to create sprites in a paint program and import the sprite images into the sprite editor. There are several reasons for this approach. Most artists are more comfortable using their favorite paint program, and they'll be more productive using familiar tools. Also, there is simply more functionality in a paint program. You can look at many sprites simultaneously, for example, and you can superimpose sprites on top of each other to gauge animated movements. Also, sprites saved in PCX files can be imported into a number of popular programs, including animation programs where sprite movement can be prototyped.

The **import_sprite()** function assumes that you have created sprites elsewhere and stored them in a PCX file. The PCX file should be in a 320×200×256 resolution, which will be compatible with the video mode we are using. This shouldn't be any problem. If your PCX file was created at some other resolution, it is easy enough to find a commercial or shareware program to convert it. The **import_sprite()** function is used often, so it was designed to be reasonably user friendly. Here's the function code:

```
void import_sprite()
{
   /* import a PCX file */

   unsigned char key,aux;
   char fname[13];
   int error;
   char *strptr;
   int index;
   int buttons,count;
   int old_xmouse,old_ymouse;
   int corner_x,corner_y;
   int dx,dy;
   int skip;
   int x,y,x2,y2;

   skip = FALSE;
   fg_mousevis(OFF);
   fg_setcolor(black);
   put_bstring("PCX file name:",80,197);
   put_bstring(sprite_pcxname,170,197);

   /* try to read in a filename */
   fg_getkey(&key,&aux);
   if (key == CR)
      strcpy(fname,sprite_pcxname);
   else
      get_bstring(fname,170,197,12,key,0);

   error = FALSE;
   strptr = strchr(fname,'.');

   /* period in string */
   if (strptr > 0)
   {
      index = (int)(strptr - fname);
      if (index > 8)
         error = TRUE;
      else if ((strcmpi(&fname[index],".pcx") == 0)
                || fname[index+1] == '\0')
         error = FALSE;
      if (!error && fname[index+1] == '\0')
         strcat(fname,"pcx");
   }
```

```
/* no period in string */
else
{
   if (strlen(fname) > 8)
      error = TRUE;
   if (!error)
      strcat(fname,".pcx");
}

if (!error)
{
   if (!file_exists(fname))
      error = TRUE;
}

if (error)
{
   fg_setcolor(white);
   fg_rect(80,289,190,199);
   fg_setcolor(black);
   put_bstring("File not found.",80,197);
   wait_for_keystroke();
}
else
{
   set_grid_boundary(OFF);
   strcpy(sprite_pcxname,fname);

   /* display the PCX file on page 1 */
   fg_setpage(1);
   fg_move(0,0);
   fg_showpcx(fname,1);
   fg_setvpage(1);

   fg_mousepos(&xmouse,&ymouse,&buttons);
   old_xmouse = xmouse;
   old_ymouse = ymouse;

   /* draw crosshairs */
   fg_setcolor(white);
   xor_horiz_line(0,319,ymouse);
   xor_vert_line(xmouse,0,199);

   /* move the crosshairs around until the left button is pressed */
   while(buttons == 0)
   {
      fg_waitfor(1);
      fg_mousepos(&xmouse,&ymouse,&buttons);

      if (xmouse != old_xmouse || ymouse != old_ymouse)
      {
         xor_horiz_line(0,319,old_ymouse);
         xor_vert_line(old_xmouse,0,199);
```

```
         xor_horiz_line(0,319,ymouse);
         xor_vert_line(xmouse,0,199);

         old_xmouse = xmouse;
         old_ymouse = ymouse;
      }

      /* check for the Esc key */
      fg_intkey(&key,&aux);
      if (key == ESC)
      {
         skip = TRUE;
         break;
      }
   }

   /* clear the crosshairs */
   xor_horiz_line(0,319,ymouse);
   xor_vert_line(xmouse,0,199);

   /* return to sprite editor if Esc was pressed */
   if (skip)
   {
      fg_setpage(0);
      fg_setvpage(0);

      fg_mouselim(0,319,0,199);
      fg_setcolor(white);
      fg_rect(80,289,190,199);

      fg_waitfor(3);
      fg_mousebut(1,&count,&xmouse,&ymouse);
      fg_mousebut(2,&count,&xmouse,&ymouse);
      return;
   }

   /* no more crosshairs, now draw a box around the sprite */
   corner_x = xmouse;
   corner_y = ymouse;

   y2 = MIN(199,ymouse+95);
   x2 = MIN(319,xmouse+95);
   fg_mouselim(xmouse+2,x2,ymouse+2,y2);

   /* move the box around until a button is pressed */
   while(buttons > 0)
   {
      fg_waitfor(1);
      fg_mousepos(&xmouse,&ymouse,&buttons);

      if (xmouse != old_xmouse || ymouse != old_ymouse)
      {
         fg_boxx(corner_x,old_xmouse,corner_y,old_ymouse);
         fg_boxx(corner_x,xmouse,corner_y,ymouse);
```

```
      old_xmouse = xmouse;
      old_ymouse = ymouse;
   }

   /* check for the Esc key interrupt */
   fg_intkey(&key,&aux);
   if (key == ESC)
   {
      skip = TRUE;
      break;
   }
}

/* clear the box */
fg_boxx(corner_x,xmouse,corner_y,ymouse);

/* make sure it is a non-zero sprite */
if (corner_x >= xmouse || corner_y >= ymouse)
   skip = TRUE;

/* sprite not imported */
if (skip)
{
   fg_setpage(0);
   fg_setvpage(0);

   fg_mouselim(0,319,0,199);
   fg_setcolor(white);
   fg_rect(80,289,190,199);

   fg_waitfor(3);
   fg_mousebut(1,&count,&xmouse,&ymouse);
   fg_mousebut(2,&count,&xmouse,&ymouse);
   return;
}

/* sprite imported; calculate width and height */
dx = xmouse - corner_x;
dy = ymouse - corner_y;

/* get the sprite */
fg_move(corner_x,ymouse);
fg_getimage(bitmap,dx,dy);

/* back to sprite editor */
fg_setpage(0);
fg_setvpage(0);

/* clear the old sprite */
fg_setcolor(0);
fg_rect(144,239,26,121);

x = 144 + (96 - dx)/2;
```

```
        y = 122 - (96 - dy)/2;
        fg_move(x,y);

        /* draw the new sprite */
        fg_drwimage(bitmap,dx,dy);

        update_sprite_old();
        bitmap_to_grid();
    }

    /* fix the mouse limits */
    fg_mouselim(0,319,0,199);

    /* clear the status bar */
    fg_setcolor(white);
    fg_rect(80,289,190,199);

    /* clear the mouse buttons */
    fg_waitfor(3);
    fg_mousebut(1,&count,&xmouse,&ymouse);
    fg_mousebut(2,&count,&xmouse,&ymouse);

    sprite_changed = TRUE;
}
```

The first thing the **import_sprite()** function does, after declaring local variables, is prompt for a filename by displaying a message on the status line. The function even provides a default filename (the name of the last PCX file imported). A carriage return accepts the default, any other key triggers a call to the **get_bstring()** function, which accepts bitmapped character input and stores the result in the **fname** string. The **fname** string is then put through a series of tests. First, we check for a period in the string. If it is there, we check that the period and the characters following the period match the string ".pcx." We use the C **strcmpi()** function to do the comparison without regard to upper- and lowercase letters. If we find a period with no characters after it, we append the PCX file extension.

Similarly, if we don't find period in the string, and if the string is less than eight characters, we append the file extension. This allows us to type in filenames in a hurry, without worrying about typing in the file extension. We then check that the file exists. If it does not exist, or if there was any other error in typing in the filename, we display an error message, "file not found," and wait for a keystroke.

If we get past the filename error checking, we can proceed with the import. First, though, we turn off the grid boundary, in preparation for writing to the sprite area. Then we copy the PCX filename into the global string **pcxname** so we can use this name as the default on the next import.

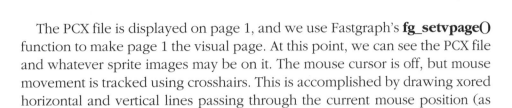

The PCX file is displayed on page 1, and we use Fastgraph's **fg_setvpage()** function to make page 1 the visual page. At this point, we can see the PCX file and whatever sprite images may be on it. The mouse cursor is off, but mouse movement is tracked using crosshairs. This is accomplished by drawing xored horizontal and vertical lines passing through the current mouse position (as returned by **fg_mousepos()**). The crosshairs allow us to move around freely in a loop until either the left mouse button is pressed, or the Esc key is pressed.

Images are selected in the PCX file by positioning the crosshairs on the upper-left corner, and then holding the left mouse button down and dragging the mouse to the lower-right corner of the image. As the button is held down, the crosshairs are replaced by an xor box, similar to the one used in the grid boundary. The box shrinks and grows as the mouse moves. We ensure that the mouse can only move down and to the right by using the **fg_mouselim()** function to constrain the mouse to the part of the screen below and to the right of the upper-left corner of the image. If we decide that the upper-left corner is in the wrong place, no problem—the Esc key allows us to break out of this function at any time and start over.

After the sprite is outlined with the xor box, we are ready to import it into the sprite editor. First we turn off the xor box so we have a clean image on page 1. Then we calculate the width and height of the image and use Fastgraph's **fg_getimage()** function to grab the sprite and store it in the **bitmap** array. The sprite editor screen is made visible again, and the bitmap is blitted to the sprite area using Fastgraph's **fg_drwimage()** function. The destination position is calculated on the fly—the sprite will be roughly centered in the sprite area. The fat bit grid is updated by calling the **bitmap_to_grid()** function. Finally, the screen is restored to what it was before. The status area is cleared, the mouse limits are reset to the whole screen, and the mouse buttons are "cleared" in preparation for the next action. The sprite import is complete.

Sprite Editing Functions

As I mentioned before, sprites are generally not created in the sprite editor. They are created in a paint program, such as Deluxe Paint or NeoPaint, and imported into the sprite editor. Once in the sprite editor, the editing functions are used to do minor touch-ups, or to change the orientation of a sprite. I'm not going to document all of the sprite editing functions here, because they are simply not that interesting, but I'll show you a few of them and describe how they work. If you want to see the others, take a look at the code in the SPRITE.C file.

clear_sprite()

The **clear_sprite()** function turns all the pixels in the bitmap to the background color. It does this by modifying the **this_sprite** array, then updating the fat bit grid. It also clears the sprite area by drawing a rectangle over it. Notice how the grid boundary is turned off before the sprite area is modified, then turned back on:

```
void clear_sprite()
{
   register int i,j;

   /* clear the sprite to the background color */
   update_sprite_old();
   for(i = 0; i < 96; i++)
   {
      for(j = 0; j < 96; j++)
      {
         this_sprite[i][j] = (char)background_color;
      }
   }

   /* also set the fat bit grid */
   for (i = 0; i < 32; i++)
   {
      for (j = 0; j < 40; j++)
      {
         set_sprite_grid(i,j,background_color);
      }
   }

   set_grid_boundary(OFF);
   fg_setcolor(background_color);
   fg_rect(144,239,26,121);
   set_grid_boundary(ON);

   sprite_changed = TRUE;
}
```

Notice that the **clear_sprite()** function introduces another global variable: **sprite_changed**. This global variable is a flag that tells us whether or not a sprite has been modified. Before we exit the sprite editor, we'll have a look at this flag. If we notice that a sprite has been changed, we'll prompt ourselves to save the new sprite data to disk.

flip_sprite()

The **flip_sprite()** function can be very useful. If the sprite is drawn in the wrong orientation, for example facing left when you want it to face right, it's sometimes convenient to import it as is and just flip it once you get it in the sprite editor. The **flip_sprite()** function modifies the **this_sprite** array by copying it to a temporary array in reverse, and then copying the temporary array back into the main array, as shown in Figure 7.4. However, before it does that, **flip_sprite()** saves the sprite data in the **old_sprite** array. The **restore_this_sprite()** function is then called to copy the new sprite to the sprite area and the fat bit grid.

```
void flip_sprite()
{
   /* rotate by 180 degrees */

   char temp_grid[96];
   register int i,j;

   for(j = 0; j < 96; j++)
   {
      for(i = 0; i < 96; i++)
      {
         old_sprite[i][j] = this_sprite[i][j];
         temp_grid[i] = this_sprite[95-i][j];
      }
      for(i = 0; i < 96; i++)
         this_sprite[i][j] = temp_grid[i];
   }
   restore_this_sprite();
   sprite_changed = TRUE;
}
```

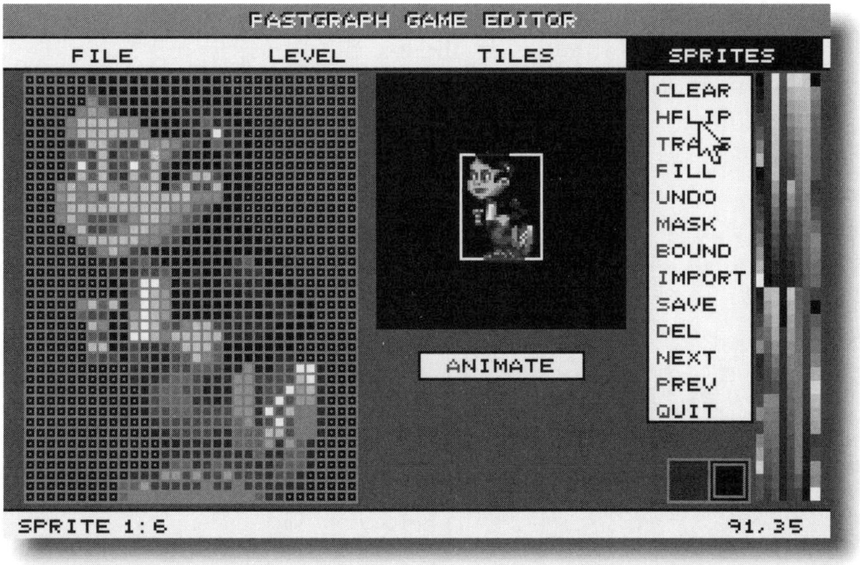

Figure 7.4 *Reversing the this_sprite array.*

transpose_sprite_colors()

The **transpose_sprite_colors()** function changes all pixels of one color to another color. If the current background color is green, and the foreground color is red, all the green pixels will be changed to red. Once again, the modifications are done in RAM by modifying the **this_sprite** array, and the changes are copied to video memory using the **restore_this_sprite()** function.

```
void transpose_sprite_colors()
{
   /* set everything that is the background color to the foreground
      color */

   register int i,j;

   for(i = 0; i < 96; i++)
   {
      for(j = 0; j < 96; j++)
      {
         old_sprite[i][j] = this_sprite[i][j];
         if (this_sprite[i][j] == (char)background_color)
            this_sprite[i][j] = (char)foreground_color;
      }
   }

   restore_this_sprite();
   sprite_changed = TRUE;
}
```

Minimizing Sprites

Throughout this discussion, we've talked about sprites as full 96×96 bitmaps. It's convenient to edit fixed-sized sprites, but we would not want to put them in our game that way. A 96×96 bitmap takes almost 9K of storage! It would be very wasteful to put a sprite that size in our game. We need to trim the sprite down to the smallest size, then record the width and height. The **calculate_sprite_size()** function determines the sprite origin, width, and height by eliminating all the transparent pixels on the top, bottom, left, and right:

```
void calculate_sprite_size()
{
   /*  figures out the smallest rectangle containing the entire sprite */
   int x,y;
   int bottom,top,left,right;
   unsigned char *sprite;

   bottom = 95; top = 0;  /* impossible values for the edges */
   left = 95; right = 0;
```

```
   sprite = bitmap;
   for (y = 0; y < 96; y++)
      for (x = 0; x < 96; x++)
         if (*sprite++)   /* found a non-transparent pixel! */
         {
            if (x<left) left = x;     /* if (further left) new left edge */
            if (x>right) right = x;   /* if (further right) new right edge */
            if (y<bottom) bottom = y; /* if (further down) new bottom edge */
            if (y>top) top = y;       /* if (further up) new top edge */
         }

   if (left == 95) /* if (left edge still impossible) sprite must be empty */
   {
      sprite_width = 1;  /* give empty sprites a 1-pixel size for grins */
      sprite_height = 1;
      sprite_xorg = 144;
      sprite_yorg = 122;
   }
   else
   {
      sprite_width = right - left + 1;
      sprite_height = top - bottom + 1;
      sprite_xorg = 144 + left;
      sprite_yorg = 122 - bottom - 1;
   }

}
```

This function looks complicated but it really isn't. It handles four cases: the bottom, top, left, and right. It figures out the smallest rectangle containing the entire sprite by setting the left edge to something impossibly large like the rightmost edge of the bitmap, x=95. It walks through the sprite, and if it sees a pixel that's nearer the left edge, it pulls the left edge over to where that pixel is. The same sort of thing happens for the right, top, and bottom edges.

We end up with four values: right, left, bottom, and top. The width of the sprite is calculated by subtracting the left from the right and adding one. Similarly, the height of the sprite is calculated by subtracting the bottom from the top and adding one. The x and y origins are calculated in terms of the sprite area on the sprite editor screen. These values are not used in the game itself.

The case of a blank sprite is handled by giving it a width and height of one pixel. This prevents problems in trying to read null data from a file. In general, it's best to not store empty sprites, but in case you accidentally do, it's nice to write code that can handle it.

Anytime you can write code that will handle a tedious task for you, you are ahead of the game. Game programmers should get in the habit of looking for solutions like this. Even though you can solve the sprite reduction problem by hand (simply by editing the sprite in a paint program) you don't want to do that. It's too boring. Writing code to solve a problem is always less boring than solving the problem by brute force.

Chapter 8

Creative use of color will bring your game to life, but beware! Matching colors can be more trouble than matching socks.

Color Considerations

Just a few years ago, programmers had to write games to run on Hercules, CGA, and EGA systems. That meant our games had to support 2, 4, and 16 colors. We organized our code and artwork accordingly. Then one day, the marketing gurus decided the time had come to support 256 colors. The hardware changed, along with the buying habits of game players, and VGA became a viable option. It was wonderful. It was like Dorothy stepping out of her dull gray farm house into the land of Oz. Everything looked so much better in 256 colors!

Managing 256 colors is a bit more difficult than managing 16 colors, mainly because there is much more data to deal with. But the results are worth the extra work. In this chapter, we'll look at some of the tricks that make managing colors easier.

The Magic of Color Palettes

The game editor and the actual game that we'll be creating both make heavy use of color palettes. If you know how to use color palettes effectively, you can perform a number of amazing animation and visual effects, such as *fade-ins*, *fade-outs*, and *palette scrolling*. Fortunately, palettes are easy to work with in the VGA's 256-color mode. Let's take a look at how palettes are used without going into too much technical detail.

In 256-color mode, the VGA provides you with 256 separate color registers, each of which can be assigned three color values to create a unique color. As shown in Figure 8.1, each color in a palette is made up of a red, green, and blue (RGB) component. In this respect, you get to choose which color is assigned to each of the 256 color registers by "mixing" the three base colors together.

Once color values have been assigned to the color palettes, you can use them in your programs. Fortunately, Fastgraph provides us with some powerful functions, such as **fg_setdacs()**, **fg_palette()**, **fg_palettes()**, **fg_setrgb()**, **fg_getdacs()** and **fg_getrgb()**, for working with palettes. Let's take a look at how color values are assigned to a palette and then used.

Assigning Colors to a Palette

Colors are assigned to a palette by modifying the *video DAC register* values, or DACs, that the VGA provides. As you might guess from our previous discussion, each DAC has a red, green, and blue component. The color components range from 0 to 63, with higher values representing more intense colors. The RGB values determine which color is displayed. Table 8.1 shows some examples of colors that can be set in the palette.

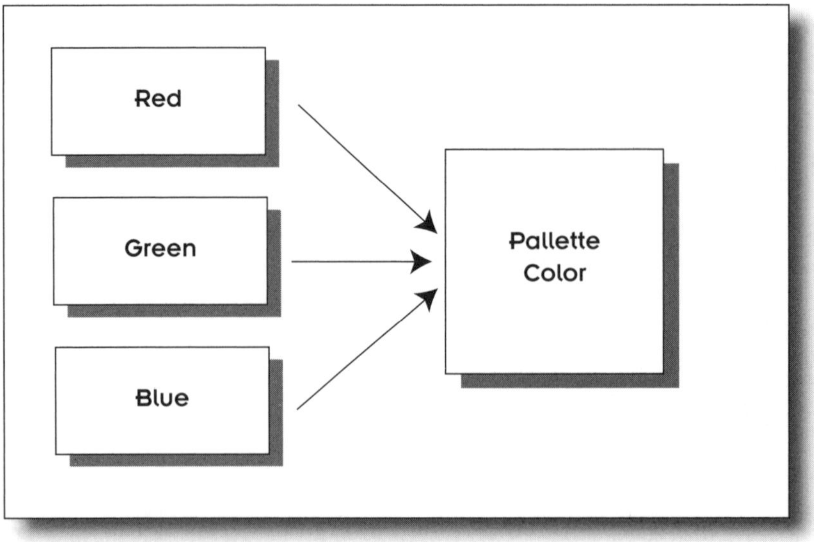

Figure 8.1 *How the 256-color palette is arranged.*

Table 8.1 *Some Example Palette Colors Used in Tommy's Adventures*

Color Register	Red	Green	Blue	Color
0	0	0	0	black
16	0	0	63	blue
22	63	0	0	red
25	56	44	47	flesh tone
255	63	63	63	white

Tommy's Tip

What Is a DAC?

DAC stands for Digital to Analog Converter. The VGA monitor is an analog device, and the RGB components are digital values. The digital to analog converter takes the digital values from the DAC registers, converts them to an analog signal, and sends the signal to the VGA monitor.

When the video mode is initialized, Fastgraph sets the color registers to the default palette set as defined in the VGA video modes. We usually want to change the color registers to our own choice of colors. If you change the value of a color register, every pixel on the screen assigned to that color register will change color simultaneously. In general you don't want the user to see this happen, unless it's part of a special effect, such as a fade-in, fade-out, or a palette scroll.

Creating Color Effects

A palette *fade-in* is accomplished by setting all the DAC values to 0, then gradually incrementing them in sequence until they reach their target values. In this way, a screen will start out black, then gradually be colorized. A variation of this is a *fade-out*, in which you start with a color screen and have it gradually turn black as the DAC values are decremented to 0. These visual effects can be used nicely in games in transition areas such as when a title screen is displayed or when the player quits the game.

Palette Fading

The code to create palette fade effect is shown here. This code was donated by Eric Lund:

```
/******************************************************************\
*                                                                  *
*  Fade.C -- palette fade program                                  *
*                                                                  *
*  Written by Eric W. Lund (CIS:74041,1147) with thanks to Ted     *
*  Gruber and Randy Dryburgh. Copyright (C) 1994 by Eric "Please   *
*  use and share this code" Lund.                                  *
*                                                                  *
\******************************************************************/

#include <fastgraf.h>
#ifdef __TURBOC__
  #include <mem.h>
#else
  #include <memory.h>
#endif

#define FADE_COLORS   256 /* number of screen colors    */
#define FADE_CHANNELS 768 /* colors x 3 (for R, G, & B) */

/* global variables */
char fade_pal[FADE_CHANNELS];
char fade_keyhalt=0;
int fade_steps=32;
int fade_delay=0;
void fade (int dir, int start, int count);
void fade_blackout (void);

/* macros */
#define fade_init()            fg_getdacs (0, FADE_COLORS, fade_pal);
#define fade_in_all()          fade(1,0,FADE_COLORS)
#define fade_out_all()         fade(0,0,FADE_COLORS)
#define fade_in(start,count)   fade(1,start,count);
#define fade_out(start,count)  fade(0,start,count);
/******************************************************************/
void main (void)
{
   int x;
   char pal[768];

   fg_setmode(20);            /* set mode to 320x200 Mode X */
   fg_setvpage(1);            /* look at a blank screen */

   /* adjust the palettes */
   for (x=0; x<256; x++)
   {
       pal[x*3]  =x/16;       /* set reds */
       pal[x*3+1]=x%64;       /* set greens */
       pal[x*3+2]=(255-x)/4;  /* set blues */
   }
   pal[0]=0; pal[1]=0; pal[2]=0; /* color 0 is background, keep it black */
   fg_setdacs (0,256,pal);
```

```
   /* Draw colorful shapes on hidden page */
   for (x=0; x<256; x++)
   {
       fg_setcolor(x);
       fg_move(319-x,199);
       fg_draw (x,0);
   }

   /* Illustrate fading routines: */
   fade_keyhalt=1;      /* allow a keypress to abort fading */
   fade_init();         /* make copy of screen palette to RAM */
   fade_blackout();     /* blackout screen palette */
   fg_setvpage(0);      /* look at page with graphic (now blacked out) */

   fade_steps=128;      /* very smooth, slow fade */
   fade_in_all();       /* fade in screen palette to match RAM copy */
   fade_out_all();      /* fade out screen palette to blackout */

   fade_steps=64;       /* slow fade */
   fade_in_all();       /* fade in screen palette to match RAM copy */
   fade_out_all();      /* fade out screen palette to blackout */

   fade_steps=32;       /* restore normal fading speed */
   fade_in(64,64);      /* fade in selected portion of palette */
   fade_in(128,64);     /* fade in selected portion of palette */
   fade_in(0,64);       /* fade in selected portion of palette */
   fade_in(192,64);     /* fade in selected portion of palette */

   fade_steps=16;       /* very fast fade */
   fade_out(128,64);    /* fade out selected portion of palette */
   fade_out(64,64);     /* fade out selected portion of palette */
   fade_out(192,64);    /* fade out selected portion of palette */
   fade_out(0,64);      /* fade out selected portion of palette */

   fg_setmode(3);       /* back to our regular DOS video mode! */
   fg_reset();          /* reset any ANSI attributes */
}
/*****************************************************************/
void fade (int dir,int start,int count)
{
   register int k,n;
   int i,j;                         /* loop variables */
   char fade_pal_new [FADE_CHANNELS]; /* modified (faded) palette */
   unsigned char key1,key2;         /* used for for keycheck */

   /* loop through all gradations of the fade */
   for (i=dir?1:fade_steps-1; dir?i<=fade_steps:i>=0; dir?i++:i--)
   {
      if (fade_keyhalt) /* default is do not halt on keyhit */
      {
         fg_intkey (&key1, &key2);
         if (key1+key2>0)
         {
```

```
            fade_keyhalt++; /* let user detect aborted fade */
            break;          /* halt fade on keypress */
         }
      }
      /* create new (faded) palette */
      for (k=0, n=start*3, j=0; j<count; j++)
      {
         fade_pal_new[k++] = (char)(((int)fade_pal[n++] * i)/fade_steps);
         fade_pal_new[k++] = (char)(((int)fade_pal[n++] * i)/fade_steps);
         fade_pal_new[k++] = (char)(((int)fade_pal[n++] * i)/fade_steps);
      }
      fg_setdacs(start,count,fade_pal_new); /* install new palette */
      if (fade_delay)
         fg_waitfor (fade_delay);           /* pause if needed */
   }
}
/*****************************************************************/
void fade_blackout(void)
{
   /* empty palette for quick clearing */
   char empty_palette[FADE_CHANNELS];

   /* set all palette entries to 0 */
   memset (empty_palette,0,FADE_CHANNELS);

   /* set dacs to zero */
   fg_setdacs(0,FADE_COLORS,empty_palette);
}
```

You will find this program in the file FADE.C in your \FG\UTIL subdirectory. I suggest you run the program to see how it works. First it draws an attractive rectangular pattern, then it gradually fades the colors in and out several times. This is accomplished by repeated calls to **fg_setdacs()**. The result is an attractive, smooth fade.

Fastgraph Tip

fg_setdacs()

The **fg_setdacs()** function defines the values of a block of consecutive video DAC registers by specifying their red, green, and blue color components.

```
void fg_setdacs (int start, int count, char *values);
```

- *start* is the starting video DAC register number, between 0 and 255.
- *count* is the number of consecutive DAC registers to define, between 1 and 256. If the sum of *start* and *count* exceeds 256, the register numbers wrap around and resumes with register number 0.

- *values* is the array containing the color components. The first three bytes of this array must contain the red, green, and blue components for DAC register *start*, the next three bytes contain the components for register *start+1*, and so on. The size of the *values* array must be at least *3*count* bytes.

Palette Scrolling

The *palette scrolling* technique is often used with streams and waterfalls. Palette colors representing the water are assigned several shades of blue, which constantly change to give the impression of moving water. When using the palette scrolling technique, you need to be careful to reserve those palettes for use in the water only. If you use the same blue pixels somewhere else on the screen, they'll change color, too. For example, you don't want the pupils of Tommy's eyes changing shades of blue as he jumps over a waterfall.

The Quickfire launch chute uses the palette scrolling effect to create the illusion of motion. This effect was suggested by Les Pardew of Cygnus Multimedia, who also drew the launch chute and the rest of the beautiful Quickfire artwork.

Choosing Colors

Palettes can present us with some problems. We have 256 palette entries, and each one can be assigned to our choice of 262,144 colors (64×64×64 = 262,144). We could simplify our code by using the same colors throughout an entire game, but I don't recommend that approach. Games are best when they have rich and beautiful artwork, and that means the extravagant use of color. Since most side scrollers will have many levels, we can change colors between levels for dramatic effect. For example, a desert background will require earth tones, a jungle background will require tropical colors, and a space ship background will need dramatic, metallic colors.

There are some colors, such as sprite colors, that we will not want to change. We'll see the same sprites on many levels, and we want them to look the same each time. This especially applies to our main sprite Tommy. While it may be acceptable for him to have a green shirt on level one and a blue shirt on level two, for example, we most certainly do not want him to have a purple face on level three. So we need to have certain color registers that are constant throughout the game.

In my case, I found it convenient to have 33 fixed colors and 223 variable colors. As shown in Table 8.2, I assigned colors 1 through 31 to the sprite

Table 8.2 Use of Color Registers in Tommy's Adventures

Color Register	Usage
0	Transparent sprite color (usually black)
1-31	Sprite colors
32-254	Background colors
255	Background color (usually white)

color values; color registers 32 through 254 are changeable; and color 0 is a transparent sprite color, which can be used in background tiles, and is usually set to black. Color 255 is usually set to white for reasons we will see in a minute.

Once you have designed your color strategy, you can give instructions to your artist to change some colors and keep other colors consistent. Your artist will probably have trouble understanding this. If your artist modifies the wrong palette set, don't panic. Just write code to fix the artwork so you can use it.

Remapping Colors

If your artist gives you artwork with the colors set up improperly, you will need to change them. Since this is such a common problem, I have written a program to handle palette reduction, merging, and matching, which we will explore in a minute. I've also included a function in the Fastgraph game editor that will reassign the sprite colors and find the closest match to the menu colors. We're going to look at that function first because it's a little simpler. You will find the **fix_palettes()** function in the COMMON.C source code file:

```
void fix_palettes(int status)
{
   static char sprite_palette[] = {
       0, 0, 0, 18, 7, 0, 27,13, 3, 36,21,10, 45,31,19, 54,42,32,
      63,55,47,  0, 0, 0, 14,14,14, 21,21,21, 28,28,28, 35,35,35,
      42,42,42, 49,49,49, 56,56,56, 63,63,63,  0, 0,42,  8, 8,52,
      21,21,63, 21,37,61, 21,53,60, 36, 0, 0, 45, 0, 0, 54, 0, 0,
      63, 0, 0, 56,44,47,  0,35, 0,  0,57, 0, 21,63, 0, 63,63, 0,
      63, 0,63, 63, 0,63};

   register int i;
   int color;
   int white_value, black_value;
   int blue_value, gray_value;
```

```
int distance;
static char game_palette[768];

/* set the palettes for the first 32 colors (sprite colors) */
if (status == 1)
   fg_setdacs(0,32,sprite_palette);

/* get the current palette values */
fg_getdacs(0,256,game_palette);

/* find the closest colors to white, black, blue and gray for menus */
white_value = 0;
black_value = 189;
white = 15;
black = 0;
blue_value = 63*63*3;
gray_value = 63*63*3;

for (i = 0; i < 255*3; i+=3)
{
   color = game_palette[i]+game_palette[i+1]+game_palette[i+2];

   /* biggest total color value is closest to white */
   if (color > white_value)
   {
      white = i/3;
      white_value = color;
   }

   /* black color is closest to 0 */
   if (color < black_value)
   {
      black = i/3;
      black_value = color;
   }

   /* find closest blue color using least squares method */
   distance =
      (63 - game_palette[i+2]) * (63 - game_palette[i+2]) +
      (21 - game_palette[i+1]) * (21 - game_palette[i+1]) +
      (21 - game_palette[i]) * (21 - game_palette[i]);

   if (distance < blue_value)
   {
      blue = i/3;
      blue_value = distance;
   }

   /* find closest gray color using least squares method */
   distance =
      (42 - game_palette[i+2]) * (42 - game_palette[i+2]) +
      (42 - game_palette[i+1]) * (42 - game_palette[i+1]) +
      (42 - game_palette[i]) * (42 - game_palette[i]);
```

```
        if (distance < gray_value)
        {
           gray = i/3;
           gray_value = distance;
        }
     }
  }
```

This code does two things: First, it sets the first 32 colors to the RGB values defined in the **game_palette** array, using Fastgraph's **fg_setdacs()** function:

```
fg_setdacs(0,32,game_palette);
```

Second, the code scans the palettes to find the closest colors to black, white, blue, and gray. The reason I chose these colors is because my game editor uses them for the menus. When a new PCX file is loaded and the palettes are changed, I "fix" the menu colors by finding the closest match to black, white, blue, and gray. Of course, since the first 32 palettes are fixed, I don't really need to keep calculating the black, white, blue, and gray values, because they will be the same the next time. But in the development process, the first 32 palettes are not fixed. Sometimes we change our mind about a sprite. Perhaps the sprite started with a blue shirt, but ended up with a red shirt. Instead of hard-coding the value for blue into our code, we calculate it on the fly, which speeds up our development process and saves us the aggravation of recalculating blue, changing it in the header file, and then recompiling all the modules.

You'll find this color-matching algorithm useful in other places in your game as well. You may decide at some point that you must have a dark magenta for a menu item, for example. Instead of manually editing your artwork to find the closest color to magenta, which will change every time your artwork changes (as it constantly does), just write code to find the color you want.

Using the Least Squares Method

To actually perform the work of color matching, we use a strategy called the *least squares method.* Here is how it works: Think of a color as a point in space. The RGB coordinates represent distances on three axes. The problem is then reduced to finding the shortest distance between two points in three-dimensional space, as shown in Figure 8.2.

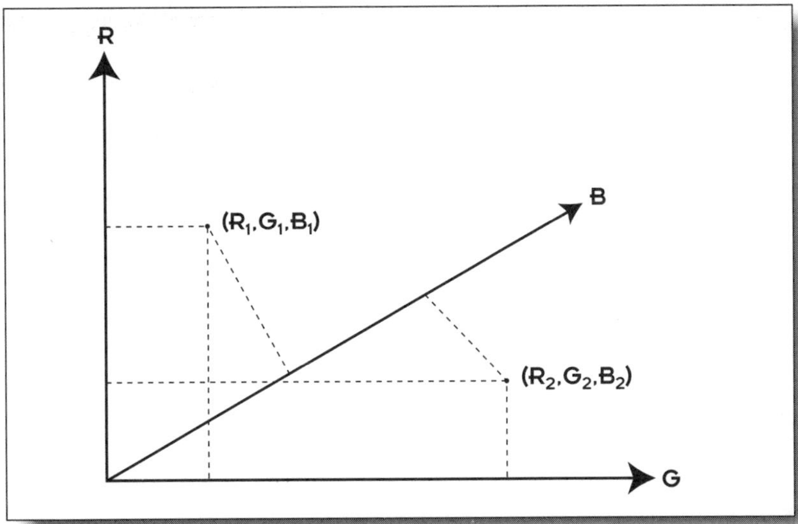

Figure 8.2 *Colors represented as points in space.*

In the **fix_palettes()** function, we are interested in matching the following four colors:

	R	G	B
white	63	63	63
black	0	0	0
gray	42	42	42
blue	21	21	63

There are lots of points in color space, and we want to find the ones closest to our desired points. We find them by calculating the distance between all the points and choosing the point with the shortest distance.

The distance between two points is determined by taking the square root of the sum of the squares of the distances in three directions, corresponding to the three axes in Cartesian coordinates. (If you need a brush up on this, check your high school geometry book). The formula is shown here:

$$\sqrt{(x2-x1)^2 + (y2-y1)^2 + (z2-z1)^2}$$

Similarly, the distance between two points in color space is:

$$\sqrt{(R2-R1)^2 + (G2-G1)^2 + (B2-B1)^2}$$

All we need to do is find the distance between our desired color and all the other colors, then choose the shortest distance. We do this by looping from i = 0 to i < 255*3, in groups of three. This gives us an index for traversing the **game_palette[]** array. The **game_palette[]** array stores the red, green, and blue components of the color, so we must increment by three bytes for each color:

```
/* find closest blue color using least squares method */
distance =
   (63 - game_palette[i+2]) * (63 - game_palette[i+2]) +
   (21 - game_palette[i+1]) * (21 - game_palette[i+1]) +
   (21 - game_palette[i]) * (21 - game_palette[i]);
```

For simplicity (and efficiency), we don't take the square root. We are not concerned with the actual distance between points, just the relative distances, which will be consistent in the squares. We compare the distance to the previous value for blue (which was initialized to a high value):

```
if (distance < blue_value)
{
   blue = i/3;
   blue_value = distance;
}
```

If the distance is the lowest, the color blue is assigned to the current palette, and the **blue_value** variable is assigned the shortest distance. This continues in a loop until all 255 colors are examined.

It is possible to have no blue value in the selected palettes. When this happens, the algorithm will choose a shade of gray or cyan, or whatever color is closest to blue. If you need a shade of blue that isn't in the palette, then you will need to adjust your palettes manually. To do this, I recommend a good paint program such as Deluxe Paint, NeoPaint, or Improces.

Changing a Single Color

Occasionally you will want to change a single color instead of a whole range of colors. In particular, I notice that I often want palette 255 to be white. That is especially true in programs that use the mouse, such as a game editor. Fastgraph's default mouse cursor uses palette 255 for the white arrow, and palette 0 for the black outline. Once again, you have to tell your artist to keep his or her hands off of that palette, and once again there is a good likelihood he or she will ignore you. To change color 255 back to white, use Fastgraph's **fg_setrgb()** function:

```
fg_setrgb(255,63,63,63);
```

This function call sets the red, blue, and green components of the DAC register to the highest intensity (in other words, white).

Fastgraph Tip

fg_setrgb()

The **fg_setrgb()** function defines the value of a video DAC register by specifying its red, green, and blue color components.

```
void fg_setrgb(int number, int red, int green, int blue);
```

- *number* is the palette or video DAC number.
- *red, green,* and *blue* respectively specify the red, green and blue component of the specified palette or video DAC register.

Fixing Palettes with PALETTE.EXE

During the process of writing this book, I had several people beta test my code by trying to import their artwork into my game. I discovered they always had problems with palettes. Common problems included a sprite file changing a background palette, two sprite files using different palettes, and background files using too many colors and overflowing into the sprite palette set. All of these problems are fixable, but the fix was time consuming and is difficult to explain. In an effort to remedy this situation, I wrote a quick-and-dirty palette-management program called PALETTE.EXE, which is included on the disk. The purpose of this program is to give you control over the colors in your artwork so that it can be easily imported into the game. The PALETTE.EXE program allows you to reduce a file to either 32 sprite colors or 224 background colors, match a file to 32 sprite colors or 224 background colors, or merge the color palettes from two files, combining the first 32 colors from one file with the last 224 colors of another file. Here's how it works.

Running PALETTE.EXE

If you installed the software properly with the default directories, you will find the palette program in the subdirectory \FG\UTIL. When you launch the program by typing PALETTE, you will see the screen in Figure 8.3.

The palette program has a simple interface. You may move between the fields using the arrow keys. You can enter the filenames and choose file

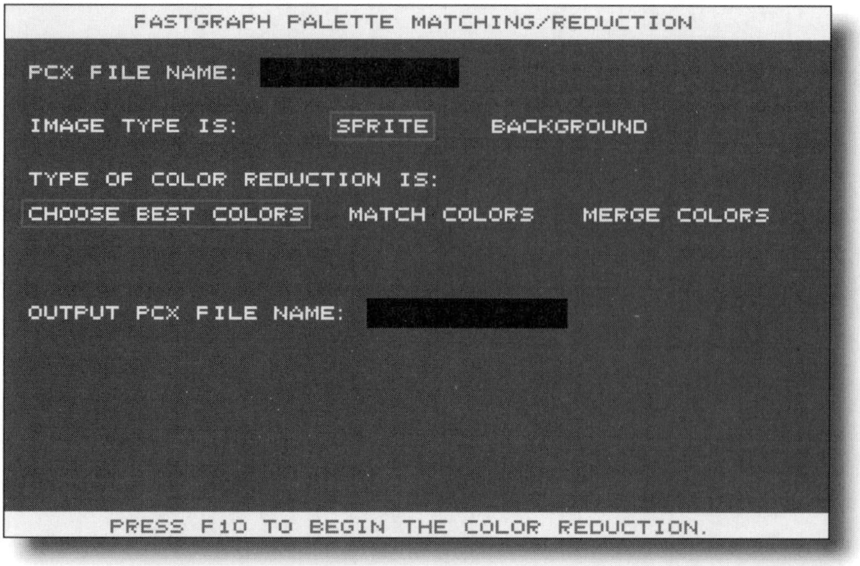

Figure 8.3 *The input screen for PALETTE.EXE.*

types, match files, and operations, and you will get an output file with the new colors. The possible combinations are listed in Table 8.3.

Table 8.3 *Palette Operations*

Input File Type	Operation	Match File	Result
Background	Reduce	None	Output file contains 224 colors that are the closest match to the original 256 colors
Background	Match	Background	Output file contains 224 colors that match the last 224 colors in the match file
Background	Merge	Sprite	Output file contains 256 colors that match the last 224 colors in the background file and the first 32 colors in the sprite file
Sprite	Reduce	None	Output file contains 32 colors that are the closest match to the original 256 colors
Sprite	Match	Sprite	Output file contains 32 colors that match the first 32 colors in the match file
Sprite	Merge	Background	Output file contains 256 colors that match the first 32 colors in the sprite file and the last 224 colors in the background file

Reducing Background Colors

Background files contain tiles. The colors are assumed to be different than the sprite colors. The reason for this assumption is that sprite colors are consistent throughout the game, but background colors may be different on different levels. If your background file was drawn using more than 224 colors, you will want to reduce it to 224:

Load the file TOMMY.PCX. Specify the file type as background. Select the choose best colors operation. Enter TEMP.PCX as the output filename. The screen should look like Figure 8.4. Press F10 to begin the reduction. The Palette program will reduce the file to 224 colors. It will set the first 32 colors to black and redraw the picture so that only the last 224 colors are used. The modified picture will be written to the file TEMP.PCX. If you want to view the TEMP.PCX file, you may use any paint program or file viewer, or for convenience I have included a simple file viewer on the disk called PCX.EXE. To view the output file, exit the palette manager program and type this:

```
PCX TEMP.PCX
```

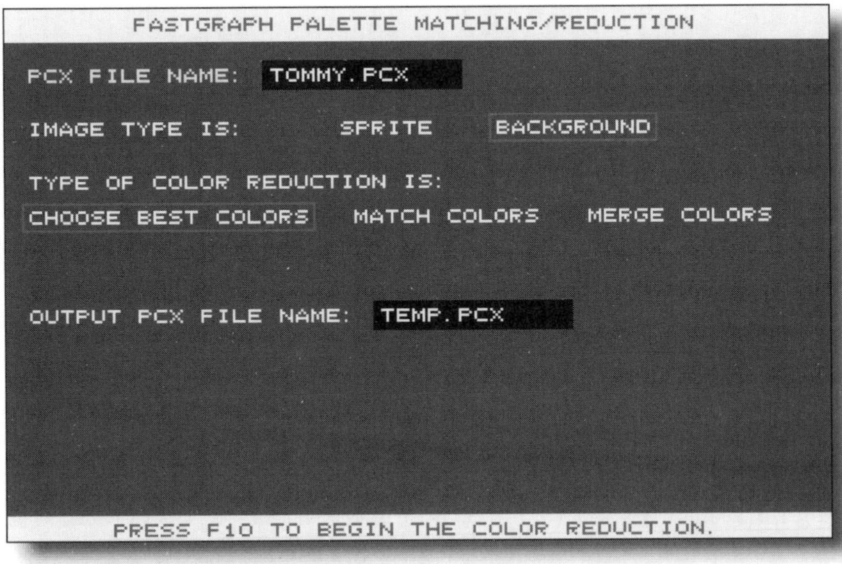

Figure 8.4 *Reducing background colors.*

Reducing Sprite Colors

Sprite files are assumed to have 31 visible colors and one transparent color (color 0). Often your artist will give you an art file using many random palettes. To reduce this to 31 colors, let the Palette program choose the best colors for you.

> Load the file SCORPION.PCX. Specify the file type as sprite. Select the choose best colors operation. Enter TEMP.PCX as the output filename. The program will reduce the number of colors in SCORPION.PCX to 31 and put them in palettes 1 through 31. Palette 0 and palettes 32 through 255 will be set to black.

Matching Background Colors

Occasionally an artist may draw two backgrounds, or two parts of the same background, that are intended to be used together in the same level. If the palettes don't match, you can make them match. This option will match all the colors in the input file to the last 224 colors in the match file.

> Load the file JUNGLE.PCX on the first line. Specify the file type as background. Select the match operation. Enter TOMMY.PCX in the match file field. Enter TEMP.PCX in the output file field. The program will match all the colors in JUNGLE.PCX to the last 224 colors in TOMMY.PCX.
>
> Now reverse the process. Enter TOMMY.PCX as the input file and match all the colors in JUNGLE.PCX. Notice that you get better results matching colors in this direction. The reason is that some files have better color selection than other files. The JUNGLE.PCX file has a nice spectrum of colors. The TOMMY.PCX file is a product of a ray-trace program, and has too many pastel colors. It is easier to map a pastel palette to a general purpose palette than vice versa.

Matching Sprite Colors

Most often, you will want to match a sprite file to a file you already have. For example, if your artist draws a scorpion in the colors of his choice, you will want to modify the picture to match Tommy's colors.

Load the file SCORPION.PCX. Specify the file type as sprite. Select the match operation. Enter TOMRUN.PCX in the match file field. Enter TEMP.PCX in the output file field. The palette program will reduce the scorpion art to the 31 colors that match Tommy's colors. Color 0, the transparent color, will be set to black.

Merging Colors

After your sprite files and background files have been reduced, you may want to merge them together. The reason is that if you display a background file and the first 32 colors are all 0, you will wipe out your foreground palettes. Similarly, when you display your sprites you will wipe out your background colors. The easiest way to solve this is to include the sprite palette information in the background files.

Load the file JUNGLE.PCX. Specify the file type as background. Select the merge operation. Merge with the file TOMRUN.PCX. Call the output file TEMP.PCX. The result will be a file containing background art and both background and foreground colors.

Be sure to specify JUNGLE.PCX as a background file; otherwise, the program will match the first 32 colors from JUNGLE.PCX and the last 224 colors from TOMRUN.PCX. This results in all the colors being set to bright magenta—definitely not the desired result!

To reverse the process and merge the sprite colors and background colors in the sprite file, enter TOMRUN.PCX as the input file and specify that is of file type sprite. Select the merge operation and enter JUNGLE.PCX as the match file. The output will be the sprite file artwork with the first 32 colors the same, and the last 224 colors set to the colors in JUNGLE.PCX.

Examining the Palette Source Code

The source code for the palette program is found in the \FG\UTIL subdirectory. The files required to build PALETTE are listed in Table 8.4.

We'll discuss the CHAR.C file in Chapter 9. The functions of interest are in the PALETTE.C file and are listed in Table 8.5.

Table 8.4 Source Code Files Required to Rebuild PALETTE

Filename	Description
PALDEFS.H	Definitions and global declarations
CHAR.C	Character string functions
PALETTE.C	Palette merging, matching, and reduction; controlling functions

Table 8.5 Functions in PALETTE.C

Function	Description
main()	Main function
activate_screen()	Activates the user interface
do_reduction()	Selects type of palette reduction/matching
error_message()	Displays an error message
file_exists()	Checks for an existing file
fix_suffix()	Adds ".PCX" to a filename
match()	Palette matching function
merge()	Palette merging function
quit_graphics()	Resets the video mode and returns to DOS
redraw_screen()	Draws the user-interface screen
reduce()	Palette reduction function
show_match_string()	Displays the match string

The source code to manage the user interface is long and boring, and I am not going to list it here. The three functions that do the work of managing palettes are **match()**, **merge()**, and **reduce()**. Let's take a closer look at those, beginning with **match()**.

```
void match(int ncolors)
{
    unsigned long target,distance;
    int color,match;
    unsigned int i,j;
    unsigned int start,end;

    fg_setpage(1);
    fg_showpcx(matchfile,0);
    fg_setpage(0);
    fg_move(0,199);
    fg_getimage(buffer1,320,200);
```

```
   if (ncolors == 32)
   {
      start = 0;
      end = 32*3;
   }
   else
   {
      start = 32*3;
      end = 256*3;
   }

   fg_getdacs(0,256,match_colors);
   for (i = 0; i < 256*3; i+= 3)
   {
     target = 63L*63L*63L;
     for (j = start; j < end; j+= 3)
     {
        distance =
        (input_colors[i+2] - match_colors[j+2]) *
        (input_colors[i+2] - match_colors[j+2])
        +
        (input_colors[i+1] - match_colors[j+1]) *
        (input_colors[i+1] - match_colors[j+1])
        +
        (input_colors[i] - match_colors[j]) *
        (input_colors[i] - match_colors[j]);

        if (distance < target)
        {
           match = j/3;
           target = distance;
        }
     }
     match_palette[i/3] = (unsigned char)match;
   }
   for (i = 0; i < 320*200; i++)
      buffer2[i] = match_palette[buffer1[i]];

   fg_move(0,199);
   fg_putimage(buffer2,320,200);
   return;
}
```

The **match()** function uses the same least squares method we saw earlier in the **fix_palette()** function. A variable called **ncolors**, containing a value of either 32 or 224 is passed to **match()**, indicating whether we want to match the first 32 colors or the last 224 colors. Similarly, **ncolors** is passed to the **merge()** function, indicating which type of merge we need to do:

```
int merge(int ncolors)
{
   register int i;
```

```
    if (!file_exists(matchfile))
       return(ERR);

    fg_setpage(1);
    fg_showpcx(matchfile,0);
    fg_setpage(0);
    fg_getdacs(0,256,match_colors);

    if (ncolors == 32)
    {
       for (i = 0; i < 32*3; i+=3)
       {
         output_colors[i] =   match_colors[i];
         output_colors[i+1] = match_colors[i+1];
         output_colors[i+2] = match_colors[i+2];
       }
       for (i = 32*3; i < 256*3; i+=3)
       {
         output_colors[i] =   input_colors[i];
         output_colors[i+1] = input_colors[i+1];
         output_colors[i+2] = input_colors[i+2];
       }
    }
    else
    {
       for (i = 0; i < 32*3; i+=3)
       {
         output_colors[i] =   input_colors[i];
         output_colors[i+1] = input_colors[i+1];
         output_colors[i+2] = input_colors[i+2];
       }
       for (i = 32*3; i < 256*3; i+=3)
       {
         output_colors[i] =   match_colors[i];
         output_colors[i+1] = match_colors[i+1];
         output_colors[i+2] = match_colors[i+2];
       }
    }
    fg_setdacs(0,256,output_colors);
    return(OK);
}
```

The **merge()** function is actually quite simple. It generates values for the **output_colors** array based on what it finds in two other arrays: **input colors** and **match colors**. By comparison, the **reduce()** function is quite complicated:

```
void reduce(int ncolors)
{
   unsigned long target,distance;
   unsigned long max_target;
   int color,match;
   unsigned int i,j,k;
```

```
int empty;
int nmatches;
int nzeros;

if (ncolors == 224)
   nmatches = 32;
else
   nmatches = 225;

fg_move(0,199);
fg_getimage(buffer1,320,200);

for (i = 0; i < 256; i++)
{
   pixel_count[i] = 0L;

   /* start with everything matching itself */
   match_palette[i] = (unsigned char)i;
}

/* count how many of each color */
for (i = 0; i < 320*200; i++)
   pixel_count[buffer1[i]]++;

empty = 0;
for (i = 0; i < 256; i++)
   if (pixel_count[i] == 0L) empty++;

/* find two colors that are close to each other */
for (max_target = 1; max_target < 63L*63L*63L; max_target*=2)
{
   /* compare every color to every color greater than it */
   for (i = 0; i < 256*3; i+=3)
   {
      if (pixel_count[i/3] != 0)
      {
         target = 63L*63L*63L;
         for (j = i+3; j < 256*3; j+= 3)
         {
            if (pixel_count[j/3] != 0L)
            {
               distance =
               (input_colors[i+2] - input_colors[j+2]) *
               (input_colors[i+2] - input_colors[j+2])
               +
               (input_colors[i+1] - input_colors[j+1]) *
               (input_colors[i+1] - input_colors[j+1])
               +
               (input_colors[i] - input_colors[j]) *
               (input_colors[i] - input_colors[j]);

               if (distance < target)  /* closest match so far */
               {
                  match = j/3;
```

```
                  target = distance;   /* how close is it? */
               }
            }
         }
         if (target < max_target)      /* within tolerance */
         {

            /* set all i colors to whichever j color matched */
            pixel_count[i/3] = 0L;
            match_palette[i/3] = (unsigned char)match;

            /* if any colors matched i, match them to j */
            for (k = 0; k < j/3; k++)
            {
               if (match_palette[k] == (unsigned char)(i/3))
                  match_palette[k] = (unsigned char)match;
            }
            empty++;
            if (empty >= nmatches) break;
         }
      }
   }

   /* update the image for this pass */
   for (i = 0; i < 64000; i++)
      buffer2[i] = match_palette[buffer1[i]];
   memcpy (buffer1,buffer2,(unsigned int)64000);
   fg_move(0,199);
   fg_putimage(buffer1,320,200);

   /* tally the pixels again */
   for (i = 0; i < 256; i++)
   {
      pixel_count[i] = 0L;

      /* each color matches itself again */
      match_palette[i] = (unsigned char)i;
   }

   /* count how many of each color */
   for (i = 0; i < 320*200; i++)
      pixel_count[buffer1[i]]++;

   /* we have reached our target--enough empty palettes */
   if (empty >= nmatches) break;
}

if (ncolors == 224)
{
   /* move all the colors to the last 224 */
   j = 32;
   for (i = 0; i < 256; i++)
   {
      if (pixel_count[i] > 0L)
```

```
            {
               match_palette[i] = (unsigned char)j;

               fg_setrgb(j,input_colors[i*3],
                           input_colors[i*3+1],
                        input_colors[i*3+2]);
               j++;
            }
         }
         /* set the first 32 colors to 0 */
         for (i = 0; i < 32; i++)
             fg_setrgb(i,0,0,0);
      }
      else
      {
         /* move all the colors to the first 32 */
         j = 1;
         for (i = 0; i < 256; i++)
         {
            if (pixel_count[i] > 0L)
            {
               match_palette[i] = (unsigned char)j;

               fg_setrgb(j,input_colors[i*3],
                           input_colors[i*3+1],
                           input_colors[i*3+2]);
               j++;
            }
         }
         /* set the first 224 colors to 0 */
         for (i = 32; i < 256; i++)
             fg_setrgb(i,0,0,0);
      }

      /* update the image one last time */
      for (i = 0; i < 64000; i++)
         buffer2[i] = match_palette[buffer1[i]];
      memcpy (buffer1,buffer2,(unsigned int)64000);
      fg_move(0,199);

      /* display the new image */
      fg_putimage(buffer1,320,200);
      return;
   }
```

The **reduce()** function reduces colors in a picture by moving pixels from one color register to another color register. When it is determined two colors are close (within a given tolerance), the function assigns pixels of both colors to just one of the color registers. It does this by updating an array called **match_palette**. Each pass through the reduction loop, pixels are assigned to either their original color or their match color. The number of empty colors is then counted. Eventually, the number of colors has been reduced to the target value, either 224 or 32.

This function is a bit complicated, and understanding it is not really necessary to understanding the rest of the game-engine code. If you are having trouble with it, I suggest you skip it and move on to the next chapter.

Some Good Advice

That covers the palette problems we face while constructing our game and game editor. We will close this chapter with a bit of good advice from Tommy:

Tommy's Tip

Planning Your Palettes

Plan your palettes carefully and try to choose your colors early in the development cycle. Last minute changes in your colors can cause expensive and time-consuming changes in your code and artwork.

Chapter 9

Last stop on the game editor tour. You'll learn about the file manager and the tile editor in preparation for our dive into the actual game code.

Wrapping Up the Game Editor

We've now explored a number of the features of the game editor, including the tile ripper in Chapter 4, the level editor in Chapter 6, and the sprite editor in Chapter 7. We also looked at the powerful scrolling technique used in the game editor. But if you are keeping count, you probably remember that the game editor provides a few additional features, including the file manager and the tile editor. So, before we leave the game editor and move on to the fun of creating our game, *Tommy's Adventures*, we need to finish up our programming tour of the game editor.

We'll begin by taking a closer look at the game editor's interface. Then, we'll look at some of the main code highlights for the file manager and the tile editor. You'll want to know something about these components if you ever decide to add new features to the editor. We'll also take a quick look at how the character font is displayed, and introduce an interesting concept—a utility program that generates source code that is then used by another utility program.

Creating the Game Editor Interface

As we discovered in Chapter 3, the game editor provides an easy-to-use menu bar that allows you to select different operations. Table 9.1 shows the functions in the file MENU.C that control the menu bar and the pull-down menus.

The menu code is really quite simple. There are two kinds of menus. The horizontal menu (menu bar) launches the vertical (pull-down) menus, as shown in Figure 9.1.

Table 9.1 The Main Functions Used to Support the Interface

Function	Description
highlight_option()	Highlights a menu option (reverses colors)
horizontal_menu()	Displays and selects an option from the horizontal menu
submenu1()	Calls vertical_menu with FILE options
submenu2()	Calls vertical_menu with LEVEL options
submenu3()	Calls vertical_menu with TILE options
submenu4()	Calls vertical_menu with SPRITE options
vertical_menu()	Displays and selects an option from the vertical menu
wait_for_keystroke()	Waits for keyboard input
wait_for_mouse_buttons()	Waits for mouse input
exit_program()	Menu selection to exit to DOS

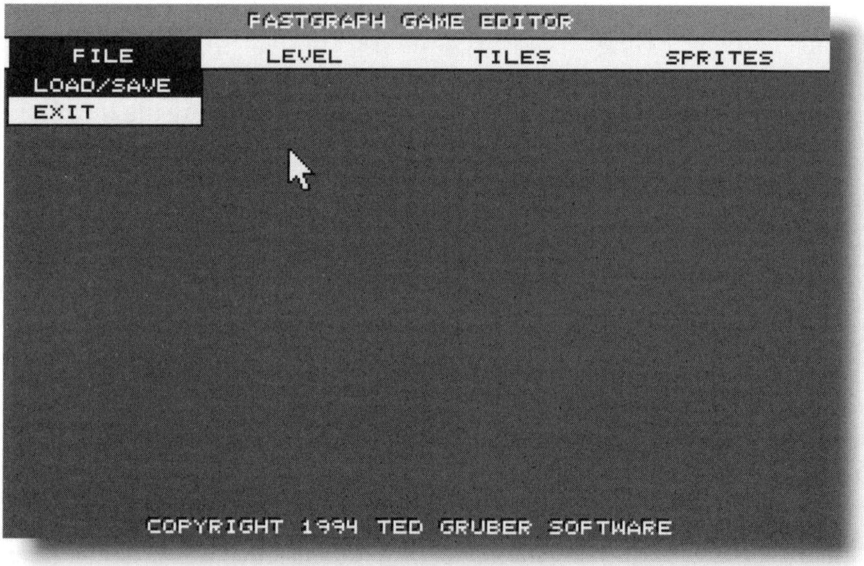

Figure 9.1 Horizontal and vertical menus of the game editor.

Designing the Menus

The vertical menus launch the other functions, such as **edit_level()** or **edit_sprite()**. The data structures are very helpful in simplifying the job of launching functions from the menus. We include a pointer to an integer function as a structure member in the menu structure. This pointer, called **PFI** in remembrance of our roots (that's what Brian Kernigan and Dennis Richie called it in their classic language definition, *The C Programming Language*), points to the integer function we wish to launch. Similarly, the menu command structures are defined as type **CMD** in remembrance of the good old days when three letter structure labels were considered descriptive. In the **horizontal_menu()** function, the **PFI** points to one of the submenus. In the **vertical_menu()** function, the **PFI** points to the level editor, sprite editor, and so on. Here is how the **PFI**, the **CMD** structure, and the **main_menu** structure array are declared:

```
typedef int (*PFI)();    /* pointer to an integer function */
#define ITEMS 4          /* number of items on main menu */

/* command structure */
typedef struct cmd
{
   PFI menu_func;        /* function to carry out the command */
   char *menu_item;      /* the menu item as written on the screen */
   int x1;               /* coordinates of location of menu_item */
   int x2;
}  CMD;

extern CMD main_menu[ITEMS];
extern int mouse_limits[ITEMS+1];
DECLARE int main_option;
```

These declarations are found in the file EDITDEFS.H, which is included in all the C files. The declarations are global because they will need to be seen by more than one function. In particular, the **main_menu** array will need to be seen by the **edit_menu()** function, which is in the file FGE.C. We'll get to that in a minute.

Managing the Menus

The menu data structures greatly simplify the job of building and executing menus. Each menu is put together by defining an array of structures of type **CMD**. A pointer to the **CMD** array is passed to the **horizontal_menu()** or **vertical_menu()** function. Changing the menus is as easy as changing the declarations and the function call. The menus are defined in the file MENU.C, and the code for handling the menus is in that file as well. The contents of the file MENU.C is shown here:

```
/******************************************************************\
*  menu.c -- game editor source code                                *
*  copyright 1994 Diana Gruber                                      *
*  compile using large model, link with Fastgraph (tm)              *
\******************************************************************/

#include "editdefs.h"

int (*menu_func)(void);
int selection = 0;
CMD main_menu[] =
{
   submenu1, "FILE",       2,  76,
   submenu2, "LEVEL",     80, 156,
   submenu3, "TILES",    160, 236,
   submenu4, "SPRITES",  240, 316
};

CMD menu1[] =
{
 load_game_file,  "load/save", 2,  76,
   exit_program,  "Exit",      2,  76
};

CMD menu2[] =
{
      edit_level, "edit",    80, 156,
 save_level_name, "save",    80, 156
};

CMD menu3[] =
{
   do_background, "background",160,236,
   do_foreground, "foreground",160,236,
       do_ripper, "ripper",    160,236
};

CMD menu4[] =
{
   edit_sprites,      "edit ",   240, 316,
   load_edit_sprites, "load",    240, 316,
   load_sprites,      "save",    240, 316
};

int mouse_limits[] = {2,80,160,240,320};
/*****************************************************************/
horizontal_menu(CMD *cmdtab,int n,int current)
{
   register int i;
   int c;
```

```
   int new;
   int ymin, ymax;

   if (current >= abs(n))
      return(ERR);

   ymin = menu_top;
   ymax = ymin + 10;

   fg_mousevis(OFF);
   fg_setpage(0);

   /* set up the list of options */
   if (n < 0)
   {
      for (i = 0; i < abs(n); i++)
      {
         fg_setcolor(white);
         fg_rect(cmdtab[i].x1,cmdtab[i].x2,ymin,ymax);
         fg_setcolor(black);
         center_string(cmdtab[i].menu_item,
                       cmdtab[i].x1,cmdtab[i].x2,ymax-2);
      }
      fg_save(0,319,menu_top,menu_bottom);
   }

   /* highlight the current option */
   i = current;

   fg_setcolor(black);
   fg_rect(cmdtab[i].x1,cmdtab[i].x2,ymin,ymax);
   fg_setcolor(white);
   center_string(cmdtab[i].menu_item,
                 cmdtab[i].x1,cmdtab[i].x2,ymax-2);

   /* if we're just displaying the menu options, return */
   if (n < 0) return(OK);

   flushkey();

   /* choose an option */
   new = current;
   fg_mousevis(ON);
   for(;;)
   {
      /* activate the corresponding vertical menu */
      main_option = i;

#ifdef __TURBOC__
      c = cmdtab[i].menu_func();
#else
      *menu_func = *cmdtab[i].menu_func;
      c = menu_func();
#endif
```

```
      /* cycle through the choices */
      if (c == LEFT_ARROW || c == BS)
      {
         selection = 0;
         new = i-1;
         if (new < 0) new = n-1;
      }
      else if (c == RIGHT_ARROW || c == SPACEBAR)
      {
         selection = 0;
         new = i+1;
         if (new >= n) new = 0;
      }

      /* Esc exits to DOS */
      else if (c == ESC)
      {
         exit_program();
         return(i);
      }

      else
      {
         main_option = i;
         selection = 0;
         return(i);
      }

      if (i != new)
      {
         /* unmark previous option */
         fg_mousevis(OFF);
         fg_setcolor(white);
         fg_rect(cmdtab[i].x1,cmdtab[i].x2,ymin,ymax);
         fg_setcolor(black);
         center_string(cmdtab[i].menu_item,
                        cmdtab[i].x1,cmdtab[i].x2,ymax-2);

         /* mark new option */
         i = new;
         fg_setcolor(black);
         fg_rect(cmdtab[i].x1,cmdtab[i].x2,ymin,ymax);
         fg_setcolor(white);
         center_string(cmdtab[i].menu_item,
                        cmdtab[i].x1,cmdtab[i].x2,ymax-2);
         fg_mousevis(ON);
      }
   }
}
/*****************************************************************/
int submenu1()
{
   return(vertical_menu(menu1,0,2));
}
```

```
int submenu2()
{
   return(vertical_menu(menu2,1,2));
}
int submenu3()
{
   return(vertical_menu(menu3,2,3));
}
int submenu4()
{
   return(vertical_menu(menu4,3,3));
}
/******************************************************************/
vertical_menu(CMD *cmdtab,int index,int n)
{
   register int i, j;
   int new;
   int height;
   int left, right;
   int string_x;
   int x1, x2, y1, y2;
   int ymin, ymax;
   int count;
   char key, aux;

   /* height in pixels of an individual menu item */
   height = 10;

   /* the first menu item determines the x coordinate for the other items */
   string_x = get_center(cmdtab[0].menu_item,cmdtab[0].x1,cmdtab[0].x2);

   /* define the menu extremes */
   x1 = cmdtab[0].x1 - 1;
   x2 = cmdtab[0].x2 + 3;
   y1 = menu_bottom+1;
   y2 = menu_bottom + n*height + 1;

   /* define the associated horizontal mouse limits */
   left  = mouse_limits[index];
   right = mouse_limits[index+1] - 2;

   /* display the vertical menu if necessary */
   fg_setpage(hidden);

   /* draw the menu outline and the shadow around it */
   fg_mousevis(OFF);
   fg_setcolor(white);
   fg_box(x1,x2-2,y1,y2-1);

   fg_setcolor(black);
   fg_box(x1,x2-2,y1,y2);

   /* set up list of options */
   ymax = menu_bottom;
```

```
for (i = 0; i < n; i++)
{
   ymin = ymax + 1;
   ymax = ymin + height-1;
   fg_setcolor(white);
   fg_rect(cmdtab[i].x1,cmdtab[i].x2,ymin,ymax);
   fg_setcolor(black);
   put_string(cmdtab[i].menu_item,string_x,ymax-2);
}

/* highlight first or previously selected option */
i = selection;
if (i >= n) i = 0;
ymin = menu_bottom + i*height;
ymax = ymin + height;
fg_setcolor(black);
fg_rect(cmdtab[i].x1,cmdtab[i].x2,ymin,ymax);
fg_setcolor(white);
put_string(cmdtab[i].menu_item,string_x,ymax-2);

/* restore the menu to the visual page */
fg_setpage(visual);
fg_restore(x1,x2,y1,y2+2);
fg_setpage(hidden);

/* clear the hidden page under the menu */
fg_setcolor(blue);
fg_rect(x1,x2,y1,y2+2);

fg_setpage(visual);
fg_mousevis(ON);

/* choose an option */
new = i;
fg_setnum(OFF);
flushkey();

for(;;)
{
   /* read a keystroke */
   fg_mousevis(ON);
   fg_waitfor(1);
   fg_intkey(&key,&aux);

   /* if using a mouse, check its position */
   if (key+aux == 0)
   {
      fg_mousebut(1,&count,&xmouse,&ymouse);

      if (count > 0)
      {
         if (BETWEEN(xmouse,x1,x2) && BETWEEN(ymouse,y1,y2-2))
         {
            new = (ymouse - y1) / height;
```

```
          /* check if this is the second click of a double-click */
          if (i == new)
             key = CR;
       }
       else if (!BETWEEN(xmouse,left,right)
                && BETWEEN(ymouse,menu_top,y1-1))
       {
          fg_mousevis(OFF);
          fg_restore(0,xlimit,menu_bottom,ylimit);
          selection = 0;
          for (j = 0; j <= ITEMS; j++)
          {
            if (BETWEEN(xmouse,mouse_limits[j],mouse_limits[j+1]))
               return(j);
          }
       }
       else
       {
          fg_mousevis(OFF);
          fg_restore(0,xlimit,menu_bottom,ylimit);
          selection = 0;
          return(ERR);
       }
    }
}

/* cycle through choices */
if (aux == UP_ARROW || key == BS)
{
   new = i-1;
   if (new < 0) new = n-1;
}
else if (aux == DOWN_ARROW || key == SPACEBAR)
{
   new = i+1;
   if (new >= n) new = 0;
}
else if (aux == HOME || aux == PGUP)
   new = 0;

else if (aux == END || aux == PGDN)
   new = n - 1;

else if (aux == LEFT_ARROW || aux == RIGHT_ARROW)
{
   fg_mousevis(OFF);
   fg_restore(0,xlimit,menu_bottom,ylimit);
   selection = 0;
   return((int)aux);
}

/* pick one choice */
else if (key == CR)
{
```

```
#ifdef __TURBOC__
         cmdtab[i].menu_func();
#else
         (*menu_func) = *cmdtab[i].menu_func;
         menu_func();
#endif
         wait_for_mouse_buttons();
         selection = i;
         return(index);
      }
      else if (key == ESC)
      {
         selection = 0;
         return(ESC);
      }
      else if (key+aux > 0) /* any other key */
      {
         return(ERR);
      }
      if (i != new)
      {
         /* unmark previous option */
         ymin = menu_bottom + i*height;
         ymax = ymin + height;
         fg_mousevis(OFF);
         fg_setcolor(white);
         fg_rect(cmdtab[i].x1,cmdtab[i].x2,ymin,ymax);
         fg_setcolor(black);
         put_string(cmdtab[i].menu_item,string_x,ymax-2);

         /* mark new option */
         i = new;
         ymin = menu_bottom + i*height;
         ymax = ymin + height;
         fg_setcolor(black);
         fg_rect(cmdtab[i].x1,cmdtab[i].x2,ymin,ymax);
         fg_setcolor(white);
         put_string(cmdtab[i].menu_item,string_x,ymax-2);

         /* move mouse cursor to the new option */
         fg_mousepos(&xmouse,&ymouse,&buttons);
         if (BETWEEN(xmouse,x1,x2)) fg_mousemov(xmouse,(ymin+ymax)/2);
         fg_mousevis(ON);
      }
   }
}
/*******************************************************************/
void wait_for_keystroke()
{
   int buttons;
   int count;
   int x, y;
   unsigned char key, aux;
```

```
   flushkey();
   fg_mousebut(1,&count,&x,&y);
   fg_mousebut(2,&count,&x,&y);

   /* if the mouse is loaded, must loop and wait for button or keystroke */
   fg_mousevis(ON);
   for(;;)
   {
      fg_waitfor(1);
      fg_intkey(&key,&aux);
      if (key+aux > 0) break;
      fg_mousebut(1,&count,&x,&y);
      if (count > 0) break;
      fg_mousebut(2,&count,&x,&y);
      if (count > 0) break;
   }
   do
      fg_mousepos(&x,&y,&buttons);
   while (buttons&3);
   fg_mousevis(OFF);
}
/******************************************************************/
void wait_for_mouse_buttons()
{
   int buttons;
   int x, y;

   do
      fg_mousepos(&x,&y,&buttons);
   while (buttons&3);
}
/******************************************************************/
int exit_program()
{
   /* Called from menu. This would be a good place to prompt for
      "save before quitting?" */

   quit_graphics();
   return(0);
}
```

The menu functions wait for keyboard and mouse input, highlight options, and launch functions in a very straightforward manner. The only tricky part is calling the **PFI**, which doesn't seem to work the same way in the Microsoft and Borland compilers—at least the compiler versions I have. To make the compilers happy, we launch the functions differently according to which compiler we are currently using:

```
#ifdef __TURBOC__
         cmdtab[i].menu_func();
#else
```

```
        (*menu_func) = *cmdtab[i].menu_func;
        menu_func();
#endif
```

I am not completely satisfied with this approach; I would prefer to write portable ANSI C code. (And since the **PFI**'s are defined in Kernigan and Richie, if they are not ANSI C, they should be.) I don't know why Microsoft and Borland don't agree on how to declare and execute a **PFI**. All you can do in a situation like this is find a way to work around the compilers to get a clean compile. If this presents a problem, I suggest you call the Borland and Microsoft technical support lines and bombard them with questions and suggestions.

Tommy's Tip

Preprocessor Directives

When writing code for multiple compilers, you can use the **__TURBOC__** symbolic name to direct the compiler to only compile a part of the code. The Borland C/C++ and Turbo C/C++ compilers recognize this symbolic constant, and the other C compilers do not. We usually try to avoid doing this, but sometimes we can't help it.

A Look at the File Manager Code

The file manager lets you organize your data files and store them in a convenient data file, called GAME.DAT. It also loads the tiles, sprites, and level files as required for the current level. The file manager is pictured in Figure 9.2.

Most of the file-management code is handled in the **load_game_file()** function in the MAIN.C file. The functions in FGE.C are listed in Table 9.2.

Like the menu code, the file-manager code is very straightforward. It lets the user move between fields and enter filenames using the **get_string()** function described in Chapter 8. The **load_game_file()** function is a bit long, but it is not at all tricky. The code is listed here:

```
load_game_file()
{
   register int i,j;
   int k;
   char fname[13];
   unsigned char key,aux;
   int error;
   char string[50];
   static char *stringlist[] =
   {
      game_fname,
```

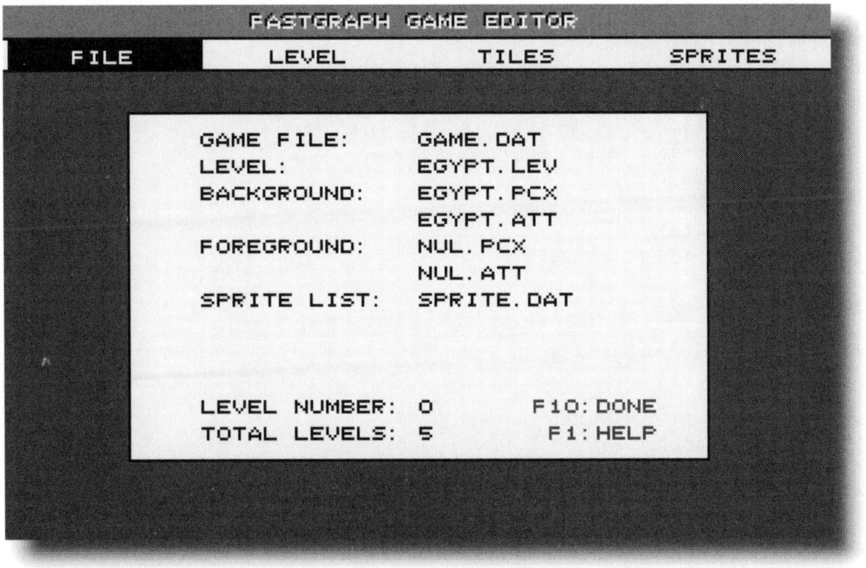

Figure 9.2 *The file manager helps us to organize data files.*

```
   level_fname,
   background_fname,
   foreground_fname,
   spritelist_fname
};

static int y[] = {52,62,72, 92,112,132};

/* copy the level information from the semi-permanent array to the
   temporary working copy */
```

Table 9.2 *Functions Used in the FGE.C File*

Function	Description
main()	It all starts here
edit_menu()	Main controlling event loop; calls horizontal_menu()
draw_screen()	Draws the game editor screen
load_game_file()	Loads GAME.DAT and intializes variables
check_suffixes()	Checks filenames for PCX, LEV, and so on
file_help_screen()	Displays online help
level_to_array()	Copies current level to a structure array
array_to_level()	Copies data from structure array to working variables
show_level_names()	Displays filenames on file manager screen

```
array_to_level(current_level);
strcpy(fname,game_fname);

/* draw some rectangles */
fg_mousevis(OFF);
fg_setcolor(blue);
fg_rect(0,319,25,199);

fg_setcolor(white);
fg_rect(48,271,40,170);

fg_setcolor(black);
fg_rect(0,319,24,24);
fg_box(48,271,40,170);

/* display the information */
fg_setcolor(black);
put_string("Game file:",76,52);
put_string("level:",76,62);
put_string("background:",76,72);
put_string("foreground:",76, 92);
put_string("sprite list:",76,112);

fg_setcolor(blue);
put_string("F10:DONE",204,152);
put_string("F1:HELP",210,162);

/* display the current filenames */
show_level_names();

/* change the filenames */
i = 0;
error = FALSE;
for(;;)
{
   strcpy(string,stringlist[i]);
   fg_setcolor(blue);
   j = get_string(string,160,y[i],12,0,0);

   /* abandon file editing */
   if (j == ESC)
   {
      error = TRUE;
      break;
   }

   /* done */
   else if (j == F10)
      break;

   /* press F1 for help */
   else if (j == F1)
      file_help_screen();
```

```
else if (j == DOWN_ARROW || j == UP_ARROW || j == ENTER)
{
   /* load a different game file */
   if (i == GAMEFILE  && strcmpi(string,game_fname)!=0)
   {
      strcpy(game_fname,string);
      if ((tstream = fopen(game_fname,"rt")) != NULL)
      {
         fscanf(tstream,"%d",&nlevels);
         for (k = 0; k < nlevels; k++)
         {
            fscanf(tstream,"%s",level_fname);
            fscanf(tstream,"%s",background_fname);
            fscanf(tstream,"%s",backattr_fname);
            fscanf(tstream,"%s",foreground_fname);
            fscanf(tstream,"%s",foreattr_fname);
            fscanf(tstream,"%s",spritelist_fname);
            level_to_array(k);
         }
         fclose(tstream);
         current_level = 0;
      }
   }
   else
   {
      check_suffixes(string,i);
      level_to_array(current_level);
   }
   show_level_names();
}

/* edit the sprite list */
if (j == F2)
{
   fg_copypage(0,1);
   load_sprites();
   fg_copypage(1,0);
   fg_setpage(0);
   fg_setcolor(white);
   fg_rect(160,270,y[4]-8,y[4]);
   fg_setcolor(black);
   put_string(stringlist[4],160,y[4]);
}

/* next field */
else if (j == DOWN_ARROW || j == TAB)
{
   i++;
   if (i > 4) i = 0;
}

/* previous field */
else if (j == UP_ARROW)
```

```
{
   i--;
   if (i < 0) i = 4;
}

/* next level */
else if (j == PGDN && current_level < MAXLEVELS-1)
{
   level_to_array(current_level);
   current_level++;
   if (current_level >= nlevels)
   {
      fg_setcolor(white);
      fg_rect(48,271,180,192);
      fg_setcolor(black);
      fg_box(48,271,180,192);
      sprintf(string,"add level %d?",current_level);
      center_string(string,48,271,188);
      fg_getkey(&key,&aux);
      fg_setcolor(blue);
      fg_rect(48,271,180,192);

      if ((key|32) == 'y')
         nlevels++;
      else
         current_level--;
   }
   show_level_names();
}

/* previous level */
else if (j == PGUP && current_level > 0)
{
   level_to_array(current_level);
   current_level--;
   show_level_names();
}

/* insert a new level */
else if (j == INSERT && current_level < MAXLEVELS-1)
{
   fg_setcolor(white);
   fg_rect(48,271,180,192);
   fg_setcolor(black);
   fg_box(48,271,180,192);
   sprintf(string,"insert level %d?",current_level);
   center_string(string,48,271,188);

   fg_getkey(&key,&aux);
   fg_setcolor(blue);
   fg_rect(48,271,180,192);

   if ((key|32) == 'y')
      nlevels++;
```

```
      else
         continue;

      for (k = nlevels-1; k > current_level+1; k--)
      {
         array_to_level(k-1);
         level_to_array(k);
      }
      show_level_names();
   }

   /* delete the current level */
   else if (j == DELETE && nlevels > 1)
   {
      fg_setcolor(white);
      fg_rect(48,271,180,192);
      fg_setcolor(black);
      fg_box(48,271,180,192);
      sprintf(string,"delete level %d?",current_level);
      center_string(string,48,271,188);

      fg_getkey(&key,&aux);
      fg_setcolor(blue);
      fg_rect(48,271,180,192);

      if ((key|32) == 'y')
         nlevels--;
      else
         continue;

      if (current_level >= nlevels)
         current_level--;
      else
      {
         for (k = current_level; k < nlevels; k++)
         {
            array_to_level(k+1);
            level_to_array(k);
         }
      }
      show_level_names();
   }
}

/* if we have changed the filenames, save the information */
if (!error)
{
   /* update the array */
   level_to_array(current_level);

   /* display new background and foreground tiles */
   init_tiles();
```

```
      /* write the game data out to a file */
      tstream = fopen(game_fname,"wt");
      if (tstream != NULL)
      {
         fprintf(tstream,"%d\n",nlevels);
         for (i = 0; i< nlevels; i++)
         {
            array_to_level(i);
            fprintf(tstream,"%s\n",level_fname);
            fprintf(tstream,"%s\n",background_fname);
            fprintf(tstream,"%s\n",backattr_fname);
            fprintf(tstream,"%s\n",foreground_fname);
            fprintf(tstream,"%s\n",foreattr_fname);
            fprintf(tstream,"%s\n",spritelist_fname);
         }
         fclose(tstream);
      }
   }

   /* now, put the current level back */
   array_to_level(current_level);

   /* clear the dialog box and return */
   fg_setpage(0);
   fg_setcolor(blue);
   fg_rect(0,319,25,199);
   return(0);
}
```

In general, I prefer to write shorter functions than this. I shortened this function considerably by extracting the filename display functions and putting them in a separate function, **show_level_names()**, but it is still a very long function.

Storing Level Data

Level data is stored in an array of structures. The current level is stored in temporary working variables, which are moved in and out of the structure array as needed. For example, when we use the PgUp key to select the previous level, the current level is copied into the **level** array, and the previous level is retrieved from the **level** array, like this:

```
/* previous level */
else if (j == PgUp && current_level > 0)
{
   level_to_array(current_level);
   current_level--;
   show_level_names();
}
```

The **current_level** variable is an integer value that tells us what level we are currently editing. Level numbers start at 0, so if the current level is 0 you obviously can't edit the previous one. The **levdef** structure and the **level** array are declared as globals in the EDITDEFS.H file, and look like this:

```
/* max 6 levels per episode */
#define MAXLEVELS 6

typedef struct levdef
{
   char level_fname[13];
   char background_fname[13];
   char backattr_fname[13];
   char foreground_fname[13];
   char foreattr_fname[13];
   char sprite_fname[13];
}  LEVDEF;

DECLARE LEVDEF far level[MAXLEVELS];
```

If you need more than six levels in your game, you can change the value of MAXLEVELS. The code to copy the level data from the level array into the temporary working variables looks like this:

```
void array_to_level(int n)
{
   /* copy from the array into the temporary working variables */

   strcpy(level_fname,      level[n].level_fname);
   strcpy(background_fname,level[n].background_fname);
   strcpy(backattr_fname,  level[n].backattr_fname);
   strcpy(foreground_fname,level[n].foreground_fname);
   strcpy(foreattr_fname,  level[n].foreattr_fname);
   strcpy(sprite_fname,level[n].spritelist_fname);
}
```

Similarly, the code to copy the current level data from temporary working variables into the **level** array looks like this:

```
void level_to_array(int n)
{
   /* level information is stored in a semi-permanent RAM array,
      and copied to some temporary working variables. This function
      copies from the variables to the array. */

   strcpy(level[n].level_fname,      level_fname);
   strcpy(level[n].background_fname,background_fname);
   strcpy(level[n].backattr_fname,  backattr_fname);
```

```
   strcpy(level[n].foreground_fname,foreground_fname);
   strcpy(level[n].foreattr_fname,  foreattr_fname);
   strcpy(level[n].sprite_fname,spritelist_fname);
}
```

The only reason we use temporary working variables in this context is to keep the code small and easy to read. For example, we will use the variable **level_fname** in many places throughout the game editor. I find it much easier to type and read a simple variable name than an element of a structure array. In other words, I find

```
level_fname
```

easier to deal with than:

```
level[current_level].level_fname
```

This form reflects of my personal preference, and as with other style preferences, you may change it if you wish.

Supporting the Tile Editor

Because the tile editor is similar to the sprite editor, a lot of our work has already been completed. As you can see from Figure 9.3, the tile editor has the same elements as the sprite editor:

- A fat bit grid
- A tile area
- A palette selection area
- A menu area
- A status area
- Foreground and background colors

In addition, the tile editor has a multiple tile area below the fat bit grid. This is so we can see how several tiles look when they fit together. This is especially useful when we are drawing floor tiles, walls, or bricks.

I am not going to describe tile editor functions in detail because they are so similar to the sprite editor functions. I will list them in Table 9.3, though, so you can see in general what the tile editor does.

Notice the same functions are used to edit both the foreground and background tiles. To differentiate between the two tile types, we define a global

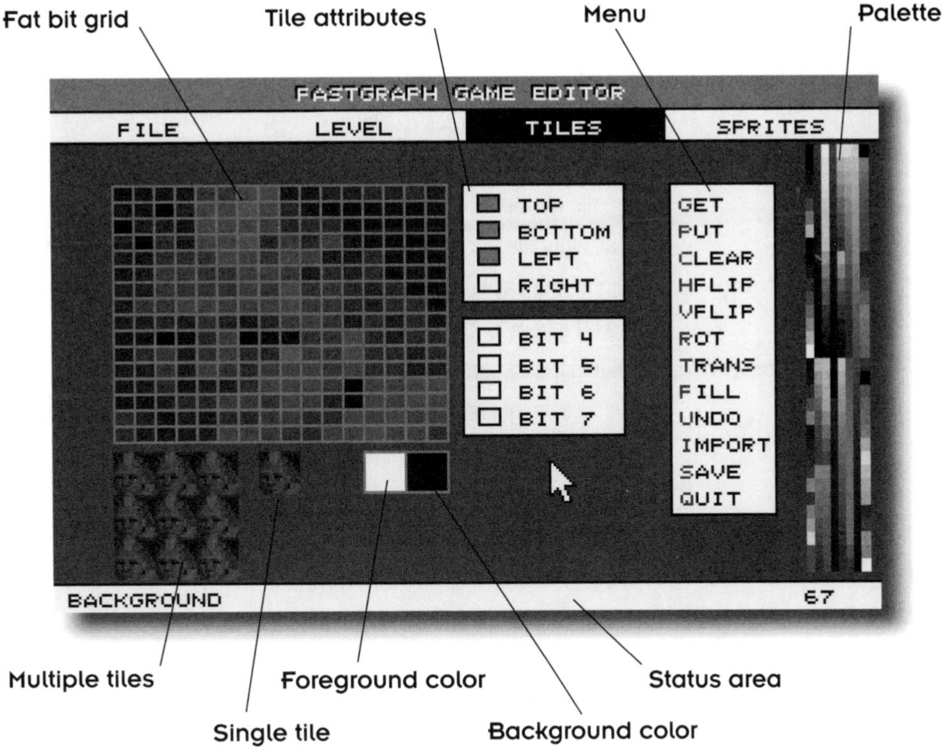

Figure 9.3 *Elements of the tile editor.*

Table 9.3 *Functions Used for the Tile Editor*

Function	Description
activate_tile_editor()	Main controlling event loop for tile editor
clear_tile()	Sets all tile pixels to background color
do_background()	Launches tile editor for background tiles
do_foreground()	Launches tile editor for foreground tiles
draw_this_tile()	Copies tiles to tile area and fat bit grid
draw_tile_editor()	Draws the tile editor screen
fill_tile()	Flood fills an area on the tile
get_attributes()	Retrieves the tile attributes from the array
get_tile()	Gets a tile from the tile library
horizontal_flip()	Flips the tile around a vertical axis
import_tiles()	Imports one or more tiles from a PCX file
init_tiles()	Initializes the variables and arrays

continued

Table 9.3 Functions Used for the Tile Editor (Continued)

Function	Description
rotate_tile()	Rotates a tile 90 degrees clockwise
save_tiles()	Writes the tile library and attributes to disk
set_attribute()	Sets a tile attribute
set_attributes()	Sets all eight tile attributes
set_background_color()	Highlights the background color
set_bit()	Sets a bit in a byte (for tile attributes)
set_foreground_color()	Highlights the foreground color
set_grid()	Draws a rectangle on the fat bit grid
test_bit()	Gets a bit from a byte (for tile attributes)
tile_put()	Puts a tile in the tile library
transpose_tile_colors()	Sets all the background color pixels to foreground color
undo_tiles()	Undoes the last editing command (toggle)
update_attributes()	Copies the tile attributes to the array
update_old()	Updates the undo information
update_tiles()	Displays multiple tiles below fat bit grid
vertical_flip()	Flips the tile around a horizontal axis

integer variable called **tile_type** that can be defined as either FOREGROUND or BACKGROUND. This variable acts as a flag and is referred to frequently in the tile editor code. For example, in the **get_tile()** function

```
if (tile_type == FOREGROUND)
   page_no = 2;
else
   page_no = 3;
```

the foreground tiles are stored on page 2, the background tiles are stored on page 3, and the **tile_type** flag tells us which page is the proper one to flip to.

How Foreground Tiles Are Stored

Foreground tiles were designed to squeeze in around the edges of video memory, as we will see in Chapter 10. In order to make them fit, we must display them as two columns of fourteen tiles each, as shown in Figure 9.4.

However, to edit foreground tiles in the tile editor, it is more convenient to display them in four columns of seven tiles each, as shown in Figure 9.5.

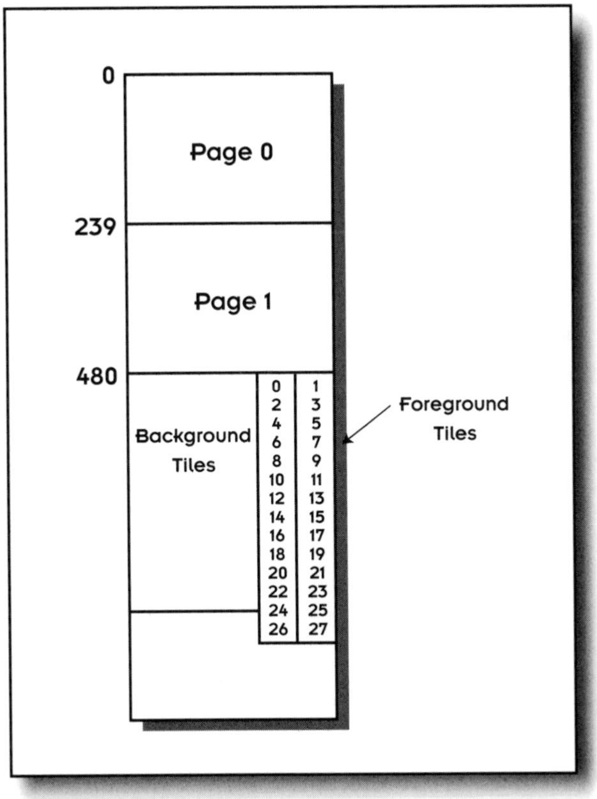

Figure 9.4 *How foreground tiles are stored in the game.*

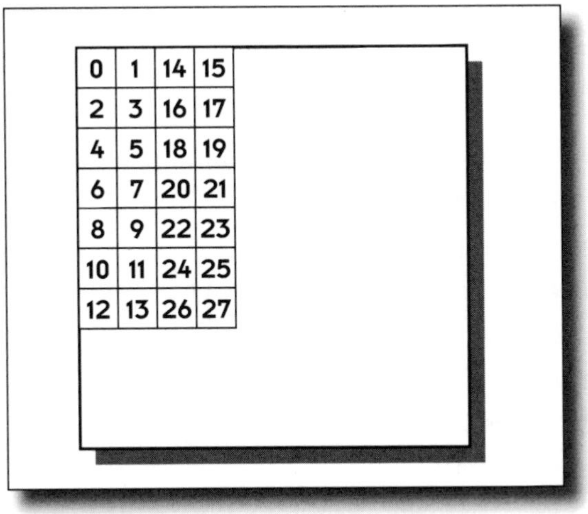

Figure 9.5 *How foreground tiles are stored in the tile editor.*

Supporting Bitmapped Characters

There are many ways to incorporate a bitmapped character font into a game or utility. One convenient method is to use *Fastgraph/Fonts*, which provides 40 bitmapped fonts and the code to display them quickly. I found it convenient to generate my own font for the game editor, however. Our font needs are simple, and a small, simple font can easily be generated and compiled into a program like this.

All the code for displaying characters and strings is in the file CHAR.C, shown here. Table 9.4 lists the functions in CHAR.C.

```
/******************************************************************\
*  char.c -- game editor source code                               *
*  copyright 1994 Diana Gruber                                     *
*  compile using large model, link with Fastgraph (tm)             *
\******************************************************************/

#include "editdefs.h"
#include "font5.h"   /* bitmap data for 5x5 font */
/******************************************************************/
void center_string(char *string,int x1,int x2,int y)
{
   /* center a string between x1 and x2 */

   register int nchar,x;

   nchar = strlen(string);
   x = ((x1 + x2) / 2) - nchar*3;
   put_string(string,x,y);
}
/******************************************************************/
void erase_char(int x,int y)
{
```

Table 9.4 *Functions Used in CHAR.C*

Function	Description
center_string()	Displays a string centered around a point
erase_char()	Erases a character
get_center()	Calculates the center position of a string
put_char()	Displays one character
put_cursor()	Displays a cursor
get_string()	Gets user input in string format
put_string()	Displays a character string

```
   /* erase a character (when doing character input) */
   register int color;

   color = fg_getcolor();
   fg_setcolor(white);
   fg_rect(x,x+5,y-5,y);
   fg_setcolor(color);
}
/**********************************************************************/
get_center(char *string,int x1,int x2)
{
   return(((x1 + x2) / 2) - strlen(string)*3);
}
/******************************************************************/
void put_char(unsigned char key,int x,int y)
{
   /* just put one character */

   int index;

   index = (char)(key-33) * 5;
   fg_move(x,y);
   fg_drawmap(&font5[index],1,5);
}
/******************************************************************/
void put_cursor(int x,int y,int cursor_color)
{
   /* the text cursor is just a little rectangle */
   register int color;

   color = fg_getcolor();
   fg_setcolor(cursor_color);
   fg_rect(x,x+5,y,y);
   fg_setcolor(color);
}
/******************************************************************/
get_string(char *string,int x,int y,int max_length,
         unsigned char key,unsigned char aux)
{
   register int i;
   int color;
   int cursor_timer;
   int foreground;
   int background;
   int xmax, ymin;
   int first;

   first = TRUE;

   foreground = fg_getcolor();
   background = white;

   xmax = x + 6*max_length;
   ymin = y - 6;
```

```
   i = 0;
   cursor_timer = 16;
   color = foreground;
   fg_setcolor(foreground);

   for (;;)
   {
      cursor_timer--;
      if (cursor_timer == 8)
         color = background;
      else if (cursor_timer == 0)
      {
         cursor_timer = 16;
         color = foreground;
      }
      if (i < max_length) put_cursor(x,y+1,color);
      if (key+aux > 0)
         if (i < max_length) put_cursor(x,y+1,background);

      if (i == 0 && islower(key)) key ^= 32;

      /* printable character or Spacebar */
      if ((isalnum(key) || key == SPACE || ispunct(key)) && i < max_length)
      {
         if (first)
         {
            string[i] = '\0';
            fg_setcolor(background);
            fg_rect(x-2,xmax+1,ymin,y+1);
            first = FALSE;
            fg_setcolor(foreground);
         }

         put_cursor(x,y+1,background);
         put_char(key,x,y);
         x += 6;
         string[i++] = key;
         string[i] = '\0';
      }

      /* Backspace deletes previous character */
      else if (key == BS && i > 0)
      {
         if (i < max_length) put_cursor(x,y+1,background);
         x -= 6;
         erase_char(x,y);
         i--;
         string[i] = '\0';
      }

      /* done entering string */
      else if (key == ESC || key == ENTER || key == TAB || aux > 0)
      {
         if (i < max_length) put_cursor(x,y+1,background);
```

```
            return(key+aux);
        }

        fg_waitfor(1);
        fg_intkey(&key,&aux);
    }
}
/********************************************************************/
void put_string(unsigned char *string,int ix,int iy)
{
    /* draw the letters one at a time as bitmaps */
    register int i;
    int index, nchar;
    char ch;

    nchar = strlen(string);

    for (i = 0; i < nchar; i++)
    {
        ch = (char)(string[i]-33);
        if (ch >= 0)
        {
            index = ch*5;

            /* move to the x,y location */
            fg_move(ix,iy);

            /* display one letter */
            fg_drawmap(&font5[index],1,5);
        }
        ix += 6;
    }
}
```

The code to display a single character or a string of characters is fairly straightforward. A character is stored in a mode-independent bitmap, and Fastgraph's **fg_drawmap()** function is used to display the bitmap.

fg_drawmap()

The **fg_drawmap()** function displays an image stored as a mode-independent bitmap. The image will be positioned so that its lower-left corner is at the graphics cursor position.

```
fg_drawmap(char *map_array, int width, int height);
```

- *map_array* is the arbitrary length array containing the bitmap. Each byte of *map_array* represents eight pixels. Bits that are set to 1 result in the corresponding pixel being displayed in the current color. Bits that are set to 0 leave the corresponding pixel unchanged.

- *width* is the width in bytes of the bitmap.
- *height* is the height in bytes (pixel rows) of the bitmap.

Tommy's Tip

The Proper Bitmap Image for Fonts

The mode-independent bitmap format is well suited for character fonts because images can be displayed in any color, and look about the same in any video mode. Bits in each byte are either *on* (displayed in current color) or *off* (transparent), which is the usually the way we want a font to work.

The data for the 5×5 bitmapped font is included in a header file, FONT5.H, and compiled into the executable program. This way, the font data is not read from a separate file at runtime.

The MAKEFONT Program

You may be wondering where the FONT5.H file came from originally. Here is the answer: I drew the font in a paint program, stored the image in a PCX file, and then wrote a utility program to capture the font. This is an interesting process—writing a utility program to generate source code that is used in another utility program that is used to process artwork used in a game. We are getting several layers deep into utilities now.

In case you are interested, here is the code I wrote to display the PCX file and capture the font:

```
/******************************************************************\
*  MAKEFONT.C -- source code to turn a PCX file into a header file *
*                containing 5x5 font data.                         *
*  copyright 1994 Diana Gruber                                     *
*  compile using large model, link with Fastgraph (tm)             *
\******************************************************************/

#include <stdio.h>
#include <stdlib.h>
#include <Fastgraf.h>

FILE *stream;
unsigned char font5[480];
```

```
void main()
{
   unsigned char i,j;
   int x,y;
   int index;

   /* set the video mode to 320x200x256 VGA */
   fg_setmode(19);

   /* display the PCX file */
   fg_showpcx("font5.pcx",0);

   /* open the header file */
   stream = fopen("font5.h","wt");

   /* write the array declaration in the header file */
   fprintf(stream,"static unsigned char font5[] = {\n");

   /* get the characters */
   fg_setcolor(15);
   index = 0;
   x = 16;
   y = 16;

   /* move down the columns */
   for (i = 33; i <= 126; i++)
   {
      fg_move(x,y);
      fg_getmap(&font5[index],1,5);
      for (j = 0; j<5; j++)
      {
        fprintf(stream," 0x%4.4X,",font5[index++]);
      }
      fprintf(stream,"  /* %c */",i);
      fprintf(stream,"\n");
      y+= 16;

      /* end of column, go to next column */
      if (y > 199)
      {
         y = 16;
         x += 16;
      }
   }

   fprintf(stream,"};\n\n");
   fclose(stream);

   fg_waitkey();
   fg_setmode(3);
   fg_reset();
   exit(0);
}
```

The MAKEFONT program created the FONT5.H file, which looks like this:

```
static unsigned char font5[] = {
 0x0020, 0x0000, 0x0020, 0x0020, 0x0020,   /* ! */
 0x0000, 0x0000, 0x0000, 0x0050, 0x0050,   /* " */
 0x0050, 0x00F8, 0x0050, 0x00F8, 0x0050,   /* # */
 0x0020, 0x0070, 0x0020, 0x0070, 0x0020,   /* $ */
 0x0088, 0x0040, 0x0020, 0x0010, 0x0088,   /* % */
 0x0030, 0x0058, 0x0020, 0x0050, 0x0020,   /* & */
 0x0000, 0x0000, 0x0000, 0x0020, 0x0020,   /* ' */
 0x0020, 0x0040, 0x0040, 0x0040, 0x0020,   /* ( */
 0x0020, 0x0010, 0x0010, 0x0010, 0x0020,   /* ) */
 0x0088, 0x0050, 0x00A8, 0x0050, 0x0088,   /* * */
 0x0020, 0x0020, 0x00F8, 0x0020, 0x0020,   /* + */
 0x0080, 0x0040, 0x0000, 0x0000, 0x0000,   /* , */
 0x0000, 0x0000, 0x0070, 0x0000, 0x0000,   /* - */
 0x0040, 0x0000, 0x0000, 0x0000, 0x0000,   /* . */
 0x0080, 0x0040, 0x0020, 0x0010, 0x0008,   /* / */
 0x0070, 0x0088, 0x0088, 0x0088, 0x0070,   /* 0 */
 0x0070, 0x0020, 0x0020, 0x0060, 0x0020,   /* 1 */
 0x00F0, 0x0040, 0x0020, 0x0090, 0x0060,   /* 2 */
 0x00E0, 0x0010, 0x0060, 0x0010, 0x00E0,   /* 3 */
 0x0010, 0x0010, 0x00F0, 0x0090, 0x0090,   /* 4 */
 0x0070, 0x0008, 0x00F0, 0x0080, 0x00F8,   /* 5 */
 0x0070, 0x0088, 0x00F0, 0x0080, 0x0070,   /* 6 */
 0x0040, 0x0040, 0x0020, 0x0010, 0x00F8,   /* 7 */
 0x0070, 0x0088, 0x0070, 0x0088, 0x0070,   /* 8 */
 0x0010, 0x0008, 0x0078, 0x0088, 0x0070,   /* 9 */
 0x0040, 0x0000, 0x0000, 0x0040, 0x0000,   /* : */
 0x0040, 0x0020, 0x0000, 0x0020, 0x0000,   /* ; */
 0x0010, 0x0020, 0x0040, 0x0020, 0x0010,   /* < */
 0x0000, 0x0070, 0x0000, 0x0070, 0x0000,   /* = */
 0x0040, 0x0020, 0x0010, 0x0020, 0x0040,   /* > */
 0x0010, 0x0000, 0x0010, 0x0048, 0x0030,   /* ? */
 0x0070, 0x0080, 0x00B0, 0x00B0, 0x0060,   /* @ */
 0x0088, 0x00F8, 0x0088, 0x0050, 0x0020,   /* A */
 0x00F0, 0x0088, 0x00F0, 0x0088, 0x00F0,   /* B */
 0x0078, 0x0080, 0x0080, 0x0080, 0x0078,   /* C */
 0x00F0, 0x0088, 0x0088, 0x0088, 0x00F0,   /* D */
 0x00F8, 0x0080, 0x00F0, 0x0080, 0x00F8,   /* E */
 0x0080, 0x0080, 0x00F0, 0x0080, 0x00F0,   /* F */
 0x0070, 0x0088, 0x0098, 0x0080, 0x0078,   /* G */
 0x0088, 0x0088, 0x00F8, 0x0088, 0x0088,   /* H */
 0x0070, 0x0020, 0x0020, 0x0020, 0x0070,   /* I */
 0x0060, 0x0090, 0x0010, 0x0010, 0x0038,   /* J */
 0x0088, 0x0090, 0x00E0, 0x0090, 0x0088,   /* K */
 0x00F8, 0x0080, 0x0080, 0x0080, 0x0080,   /* L */
 0x0088, 0x00A8, 0x00A8, 0x00D8, 0x0088,   /* M */
 0x0088, 0x0098, 0x00A8, 0x00C8, 0x0088,   /* N */
 0x0070, 0x0088, 0x0088, 0x0088, 0x0070,   /* O */
 0x0080, 0x0080, 0x00F0, 0x0088, 0x00F0,   /* P */
 0x0078, 0x00A8, 0x0088, 0x0088, 0x0070,   /* Q */
```

```
0x0090, 0x00A0, 0x00F0, 0x0088, 0x00F0,  /* R */
0x00F0, 0x0008, 0x0070, 0x0080, 0x0078,  /* S */
0x0020, 0x0020, 0x0020, 0x0020, 0x00F8,  /* T */
0x0070, 0x0088, 0x0088, 0x0088, 0x0088,  /* U */
0x0020, 0x0050, 0x0088, 0x0088, 0x0088,  /* V */
0x0088, 0x00D8, 0x00A8, 0x00A8, 0x0088,  /* W */
0x0088, 0x0050, 0x0020, 0x0050, 0x0088,  /* X */
0x0020, 0x0020, 0x0020, 0x0050, 0x0088,  /* Y */
0x00F8, 0x0040, 0x0020, 0x0010, 0x00F8,  /* Z */
0x0070, 0x0040, 0x0040, 0x0040, 0x0070,  /* [ */
0x0008, 0x0010, 0x0020, 0x0040, 0x0080,  /* \ */
0x0070, 0x0010, 0x0010, 0x0010, 0x0070,  /* ] */
0x0000, 0x0000, 0x0088, 0x0050, 0x0020,  /* ^ */
0x00F8, 0x0000, 0x0000, 0x0000, 0x0000,  /* _ */
0x0000, 0x0000, 0x0000, 0x0020, 0x0020,  /* ' */
0x0088, 0x00F8, 0x0088, 0x0050, 0x0020,  /* a */
0x00F0, 0x0088, 0x00F0, 0x0088, 0x00F0,  /* b */
0x0078, 0x0080, 0x0080, 0x0080, 0x0078,  /* c */
0x00F0, 0x0088, 0x0088, 0x0088, 0x00F0,  /* d */
0x00F8, 0x0080, 0x00F0, 0x0080, 0x00F8,  /* e */
0x0080, 0x0080, 0x00F0, 0x0080, 0x00F0,  /* f */
0x0070, 0x0088, 0x0098, 0x0080, 0x0078,  /* g */
0x0088, 0x0088, 0x00F8, 0x0088, 0x0088,  /* h */
0x0070, 0x0020, 0x0020, 0x0020, 0x0070,  /* i */
0x0060, 0x0090, 0x0010, 0x0010, 0x0038,  /* j */
0x0088, 0x0090, 0x00E0, 0x0090, 0x0088,  /* k */
0x00F8, 0x0080, 0x0080, 0x0080, 0x0080,  /* l */
0x0088, 0x00A8, 0x00A8, 0x00D8, 0x0088,  /* m */
0x0088, 0x0098, 0x00A8, 0x00C8, 0x0088,  /* n */
0x0070, 0x0088, 0x0088, 0x0088, 0x0070,  /* o */
0x0080, 0x0080, 0x00F0, 0x0088, 0x00F0,  /* p */
0x0078, 0x00A8, 0x0088, 0x0088, 0x0070,  /* q */
0x0090, 0x00A0, 0x00F0, 0x0088, 0x00F0,  /* r */
0x00F0, 0x0008, 0x0070, 0x0080, 0x0078,  /* s */
0x0020, 0x0020, 0x0020, 0x0020, 0x00F8,  /* t */
0x0070, 0x0088, 0x0088, 0x0088, 0x0088,  /* u */
0x0020, 0x0050, 0x0088, 0x0088, 0x0088,  /* v */
0x0088, 0x00D8, 0x00A8, 0x00A8, 0x0088,  /* w */
0x0088, 0x0050, 0x0020, 0x0050, 0x0088,  /* x */
0x0020, 0x0020, 0x0020, 0x0050, 0x0088,  /* y */
0x00F8, 0x0040, 0x0020, 0x0010, 0x00F8,  /* z */
0x0030, 0x0020, 0x0060, 0x0020, 0x0030,  /* { */
0x0020, 0x0020, 0x0000, 0x0020, 0x0020,  /* | */
0x0060, 0x0020, 0x0030, 0x0020, 0x0060,  /* } */
0x0000, 0x0000, 0x0090, 0x0068, 0x0000,  /* ~ */
};
```

As you can see, the MAKEFONT program generated nicely formatted and commented source code, just the way we want it.

This concludes our discussion of the game editor program and the various utilities we use in game design, and the strategies we used to create those utilities. By now you should have a good understanding of how to program in a Mode X graphics mode using Fastgraph, and the types of data and images we'll be working with. In the next chapter, we'll get to the good stuff—we'll take our first look at the source code for the *Tommy's Adventures* game.

Chapter 10

We have the tools, we put in the time, and we have the enthusiasm. Let's make a game!

Birth of a Computer Game

We have spent enough time talking about development tools, and it's time to start building our game. In the next six chapters, we will see how a side-scrolling game is constructed from the bottom up. In this chapter, we'll discuss how the source code is organized, and we'll look at the defining features of the items we'll be manipulating in the game: tiles, levels, sprites, and objects. Then in Chapter 11, we'll take a closer look at scrolling the tile-based levels. This scrolling technique is based on the scrolling theory we discussed in Chapter 5, but the code has been modified slightly to achieve a higher frame rate. In Chapter 12, we'll take a close look at the sprite and object data structures. These data structures are a bit complicated, but they are important because they speed up the animation *and* reduce the amount of necessary code. The code that controls the motion of the objects is organized into *action functions,* and we'll examine several action functions in detail in Chapter 13. In Chapter 14, we will see how all the components can be put together to create smooth, fast animation. Last but not least, we'll add our special effects in Chapter 15.

Components of a Side-Scroller Game

I've included Table 10.1 to help you sort out the different components that are used in our side-scroller game, *Tommy's Adventures.*

If the relationship between sprites and objects is giving you trouble, read on. In previous chapters, we always referred to Tommy as a sprite. Now we are going to begin talking about Tommy as an object. The reason is this: a sprite is defined to be a graphical representation of only one position of an object. That is, a sprite can be one walking frame or one shooting frame of Tommy. Tommy, in fact, consists of 37 different sprites, any of which can be viewed and modified in the sprite editor. But he is still just Tommy, one character in our game. In casual speech, we will still refer to Tommy as a sprite, but for the purposes of code we must define Tommy more precisely. Tommy is an object, and each of his various manifestations: a walking frame, a jumping frame, a shooting frame, and so on, is a sprite. This will become clearer as we examine the data structures in Chapter 12.

Introducing *Tommy's Adventures* Source Code

The source code for *Tommy's Adventures* is organized into seven source code files and two header files. If you have installed the software using the INSTALL program on the companion disk and the default directories, you will find these source code files in the \FG\TOMMY subdirectory. Each of the files is listed and discussed in the next few chapters. Here is a list of the source code files, in the order in which they are discussed:

- **GAMEDEFS.H** - This header file is included in all the source code files, and contains definitions and global declarations. It will be presented later in this chapter.

Table 10.1 *Components of a Side-Scroller Game*

Item	Type	Chapter	Description
Level	data	11	Background scenery
Object	data	12	Characters inhabiting the game
Sprites	data	12	Graphical representation of an object
Tiles	data	11	Building blocks of levels
Action functions	code	13	Determine motion of the objects
Controlling functions	code	14	Organize everything
Scrolling functions	code	11	Determine motion of the levels

- **MAP.C** - This file contains code to handle level and tile operations, including loading levels, displaying foreground and background tiles, scrolling, and warping levels. It is presented in Chapter 11.
- **TIMER.ASM** - This assembly-language source code speeds up the system's internal clock for improved timer resolution to normalize frame rates. It is presented in Chapter 12.
- **ACTION.C** - This source code file contains all the action functions that are used to perform sprite animation. It is presented in Chapter 13.
- **MOTION.C** - This source code file contains all the animation-related functions needed to limit the motion of sprites with respect to other sprites and tiles. It is presented in Chapter 13.
- **TOMMY.C** - This is the primary source code file for the *Tommy's Adventures* game. It contains the function **main()** and the functions to initialize the game, load and initialize sprites (including the player sprite), activate levels, and terminate the game. It is presented in Chapter 14.
- **EFFECTS.C** - This source code file contains functions and various drawing and special effects functions. It is presented in Chapter 15.
- **CHAR.C** - This source code file contains code for displaying character strings. The font bitmap data for a 5x5 character font is in the file **FONT5.H**. It was presented in Chapter 9.

Notice that the last file, CHAR.C, was introduced in Chapter 9 when we discussed the game editor. That leaves us six source files and one header file to discuss. We'll present these files as we introduce the key game-programming topics. For instance, when we discuss sprite animation in Chapters 12 and 13, we'll look at the functions in TIMER.ASM, ACTION.C, and MOTION.C.

For the most part, you shouldn't have too much trouble following the code because of the way it is organized. But keep in mind that many of the game components and operations, such as the tiles, sprites, scrolling system, and animation are all tightly integrated. It is difficult to discuss one component of the game without mentioning the other parts of the game, which means this is not a sequential discussion. Please bear with me, and I will try to define the elements of the game as I introduce them, and by the end of Chapter 15 we will have covered everything.

Working with the Source Code

All the C source code has been tested with the Borland C++, Turbo C/C++, Microsoft C/C++ and Microsoft Visual C++ compilers, and should work with other ANSI C/C++ compilers, as well.

Compiling the *Tommy's Adventures* Game

If you have not yet done so, now would be a good time to recompile *Tommy's Adventures.* Be sure to keep a clean copy of the source code and the data files in a backup directory so that you can refer to them later if you need to. Use your favorite C compiler and compile the following source code files:

```
TOMMY.C CHAR.C EFFECTS.C MAP.C MOTION.C
```

This will generate five OBJ files. Link these OBJ files with TIMER.OBJ and the appropriate large model Fastgraph library (FGL.LIB for Fastgraph or FGLL.LIB for Fastgraph/Light). This will give you a new TOMMY.EXE.

A note on troubleshooting: Check for batch files in the \FG\TOMMY subdirectory with compile commands and switches for the most popular compilers. If you are using the Borland C++ or Turbo C/C++ compilers and you want to compile in the IDE, you will need to make a project file. In general, all you need to do is open a project file, add the five source code files plus TIMER.ASM, and the FGL.LIB or FGLL.LIB. If you have any difficulty with this (many people do!), consult your compiler manuals or call Borland.

Do not compile and link the ACTION.C source code file. It is included in the TOMMY.C source code file. I will explain why in Chapter 13.

If you are using Fastgraph/Light, you will need to run the FGDRIVER.EXE program before running TOMMY.EXE. Do not try to use FGDRIVER.EXE in a Windows DOS box. Exit Windows before running programs linked with Fastgraph/Light.

Introducing GAMEDEFS.H

The best place to begin with our game source code is the GAMEDEFS.H header file that is used by all of the source code files. This file contains the definitions for all the constants, data structures, and function prototypes used in the game. In particular, you'll find the sections shown in Table 10.2 in this file.

Let's examine the header file and then we'll discuss some of the more important data structures. Here is the complete GAMEDEFS.H file:

```
/*****************************************************************\
*  GameDefs.h -- Main header file for Tommy's Adventures game     *
*  copyright 1994 Diana Gruber                                    *
*  compile using large model, link with Fastgraph (tm)            *
\*****************************************************************/

/******************** standard include files *******************/
#include <fastgraf.h>             /* Fastgraph function declarations*/
#include <conio.h>
#include <ctype.h>
#include <string.h>
#include <stdio.h>
#include <stdlib.h>
#include <dos.h>
#include <io.h>

/* Borland C and Turbo C have different names for some of the
   standard include files */

#ifdef __TURBOC__
  #include <alloc.h>
  #include <mem.h>
#else
  #include <malloc.h>
```

Table 10.2 *Sections in GAMEDEFS.H*

Section	**Description**
File I/O Variables	Filename strings and file handles for all the files we will open, including level data, sprite data, and so on
Map Declarations	Global variable declarations and data structure definitions for coordinate systems, scrolling, and levels
Sprite Declarations	Global variable declarations and data structure definitions for sprites
Object Declarations	Global variable declarations and data structure definitions for objects
Special Effects	Declarations for arrays and variables used in special effects
Key Declarations	Definitions of the keys and keyboard scan codes
Miscellaneous Definitions and Variables	Declarations and definitions of all the other constants, macros, and global variables
Function Declarations	Function prototypes for all of the main source files including TIMER.ASM, ACTION.C, CHAR.C, EFFECTS.C, MAP.C, MOTION.C, and TOMMY.C

```
  #include <memory.h>
#endif

#ifdef tommy_c
    #define DECLARE                     /* declarations are not extern */
#else
    #define DECLARE extern              /* declarations are extern */
#endif

/********************* file i/o variables ************************/

DECLARE int  nlevels;                   /* total number of levels */
DECLARE int  current_level;             /* current level number */
DECLARE char game_fname[13];            /* filename of game file */
DECLARE char level_fname[13];           /* filename of level data */
DECLARE char background_fname[13];      /* pcx file -- background tiles */
DECLARE char backattr_fname[13];        /* background tile attributes */
DECLARE char foreground_fname[13];      /* pcx file -- foreground tiles */
DECLARE char foreattr_fname[13];        /* foreground tile attributes */

#define MAXLEVELS 6                     /* max 6 levels per episode */
typedef struct levdef                   /* level structure */
{
   char level_fname[13];
   char background_fname[13];
   char backattr_fname[13];
   char foreground_fname[13];
   char foreattr_fname[13];
   char sprite_fname[13];
}  LEVDEF;
DECLARE LEVDEF far level[MAXLEVELS];  /* array of level structures */

DECLARE int  nspritelists;              /* total number of sprite lists */
DECLARE char sprite_fname[13];          /* sprite filename */
DECLARE char list_fname[13];            /* sprite list filename */
#define MAXSPRITELISTS 8                /* max 8 sprite lists per level */
DECLARE char list_fnames[MAXSPRITELISTS][13]; /* array of sprite lists */

DECLARE FILE *stream;                   /* general purpose file handle */
DECLARE FILE *dstream;                  /* used for debugging */
DECLARE FILE *level_stream;             /* file handle: level data */
DECLARE FILE *sprite_stream;            /* file handle: sprite file */

/********************  map declarations ************************/

#define BACKGROUND   0                  /* tile type is background */
#define FOREGROUND   1                  /* tile type is foreground */
DECLARE int tile_type;                  /* foreground or background */

DECLARE int tile_orgx;                  /* tile space x origin */
DECLARE int tile_orgy;                  /* tile space y origin */

DECLARE int screen_orgx;                /* screen space x origin */
DECLARE int screen_orgy;                /* screen space y origin */
```

```
DECLARE int screen_xmax;             /* max screen space x coordinate */
DECLARE int screen_ymax;             /* max screen space y coordinate */

DECLARE int world_x;                 /* world space x origin */
DECLARE int world_y;                 /* world space y origin */
DECLARE int world_maxx;              /* max world space x coordinate */
DECLARE int world_maxy;              /* max world space y coordinate */

DECLARE int vpo;                     /* visual page offset */
DECLARE int vpb;                     /* visual page bottom */
DECLARE int hpo;                     /* hidden page offset */
DECLARE int hpb;                     /* hidden page bottom */
DECLARE int tpo;

#define MAXROWS 200                  /* maximum rows of tiles */
#define MAXCOLS 240                  /* maximum columns of tiles */
DECLARE int nrows;                   /* number of rows */
DECLARE int ncols;                   /* number of columns */

/* tile arrays for levels */
DECLARE unsigned char far background_tile[MAXCOLS][MAXROWS];
DECLARE unsigned char far foreground_tile[MAXCOLS][MAXROWS];

/* tile attribute arrays */
DECLARE unsigned char background_attributes[240];
DECLARE unsigned char foreground_attributes[28];

DECLARE char layout[2][22][15];      /* layout array */

DECLARE int warped;                  /* flag: warped this frame? */
DECLARE int scrolled_left;           /* flag: scrolled left? */
DECLARE int scrolled_right;          /* flag: scrolled right? */
DECLARE int scrolled_up;             /* flag: scrolled up? */
DECLARE int scrolled_down;           /* flag: scrolled down? */

/********************  sprite declarations ************************/

typedef struct _sprite               /* sprite structure */
{
   char far *bitmap;                 /* pointer to bitmap data */
   int width;                        /* width of bitmap */
   int height;                       /* height of bitmap */
   int xoffset;                      /* x offset */
   int yoffset;                      /* y offset */
   int bound_x;                      /* x coord of bounding box */
   int bound_y;                      /* y coord of bounding box */
   int bound_width;                  /* width of bounding box */
   int bound_height;                 /* height of bounding box */
}  far SPRITE;

#define MAXSPRITES 100               /* maximum number of sprites */
DECLARE SPRITE *sprite[MAXSPRITES];  /* sprite array */
DECLARE int nsprites;                /* number of sprites */
```

```
#define STANDFRAMES  3               /* number of frames in sprite list */
#define RUNFRAMES    6
#define JUMPFRAMES   4
#define KICKFRAMES   8
#define SHOOTFRAMES  7
#define SCOREFRAMES  3
#define ENEMYFRAMES  6

DECLARE SPRITE *tom_stand[STANDFRAMES]; /* sprite lists */
DECLARE SPRITE *tom_run  [RUNFRAMES];
DECLARE SPRITE *tom_jump [JUMPFRAMES];
DECLARE SPRITE *tom_kick [KICKFRAMES];
DECLARE SPRITE *tom_shoot[SHOOTFRAMES];
DECLARE SPRITE *tom_score[SCOREFRAMES];
DECLARE SPRITE *enemy_sprite[ENEMYFRAMES];

#define LEFT   0                     /* direction of sprite */
#define RIGHT  1

/************************** object declarations *******************/
DECLARE struct OBJstruct;            /* forward declarations */
typedef struct OBJstruct OBJ, far *OBJp;

typedef void near ACTION (OBJp objp); /* pointer to action function */
typedef ACTION near *ACTIONp;

typedef struct OBJstruct             /* object structure */
{
  OBJp next;                         /* linked list next node */
  OBJp prev;                         /* linked list previous node */
  int x;                             /* x coordinate */
  int y;                             /* y coordinate */
  int xspeed;                        /* horizontal speed */
  int yspeed;                        /* vertical speed */
  int direction;                     /* LEFT or RIGHT */
  int tile_xmin;                     /* tile limits */
  int tile_xmax;
  int tile_ymin;
  int tile_ymax;
  int frame;                         /* frame of animation */
  unsigned long time;                /* time */
  SPRITE *sprite;                    /* pointer to sprite */
  ACTIONp action;                    /* pointer to action function */
};

DECLARE OBJp player;                 /* main player object */
DECLARE OBJp top_node, bottom_node;  /* nodes in linked list */
DECLARE OBJp score;                  /* score object */

#define MAXENEMIES 5
DECLARE OBJp enemy[MAXENEMIES];      /* array of enemy objects */
DECLARE int nenemies;                /* how many enemies */
```

```
/*********************  special effects *************************/
DECLARE char far *slide_array;
DECLARE int slide_arraysize;          /* size of slide array */

DECLARE int player_blink;             /* flag: is Tommy blinking? */
DECLARE int nblinks;                  /* how many times has he blinked? */
DECLARE unsigned long blink_time;     /* how long since the last blink? */
DECLARE char far blink_map[4000];     /* bitmap mask for the blink */

/*********************  key declarations ************************/
#define BS          8              /* bios key values */
#define ENTER      13
#define ESC        27
#define SPACE      32

#define KB_ALT     56              /* low-level keyboard scan codes */
#define KB_CTRL    29
#define KB_ESC      1
#define KB_SPACE   57
#define KB_UP      72
#define KB_LEFT    75
#define KB_RIGHT   77
#define KB_DOWN    80
#define KB_F1      59
#define KB_F2      60
#define KB_W       17
#define KB_D       32

/************ miscellaneous defines and variables ***********/
#define MAX(x,y) ((x) > (y)) ? (x) : (y)
#define MIN(x,y) ((x) < (y)) ? (x) : (y)
#define OFF   0
#define ON    1
#define ERR  -1
#define OK    1
#define FALSE 0
#define TRUE  1

DECLARE int hidden;                   /* hidden page */
DECLARE int visual;                   /* visual page */
DECLARE int seed;                     /* random number generator seed */

DECLARE int white;                    /* colors for status screen */
DECLARE int black;
DECLARE int blue;

DECLARE unsigned long game_time;      /* total clock ticks */
DECLARE unsigned long last_time;      /* time last frame */
DECLARE unsigned long delta_time;     /* time elapsed between frames */
DECLARE unsigned long max_time;       /* how long Tommy stands still */

DECLARE int nbullets;                 /* how many bullets */
DECLARE unsigned long shoot_time;     /* how long between shots */
DECLARE long player_score;            /* how many points */
```

```
DECLARE int show_score;              /* flag: scoreboard on? */

DECLARE int forward_thrust;          /* horizontal acceleration */
DECLARE int vertical_thrust;         /* vertical acceleration */
DECLARE int kicking;                 /* flag: kicking? */
DECLARE int kick_frame;              /* stage of kick animation */
DECLARE int kick_basey;              /* y coord at start of kick */
DECLARE int nkicks;                  /* how many kicks */
DECLARE int nshots;                  /* how many shots */
DECLARE int nhits;                   /* how many hits */
DECLARE int nlives;                  /* how many lives */

DECLARE int warp_to_next_level;      /* flag: warp? */
DECLARE char abort_string[50];       /* display string on exit */

/*****************  function declarations ******************/

void set_rate(int rate);             /* external timer function */

typedef void far interrupt HANDLER (void);
typedef HANDLER far *HANDLERp;
DECLARE HANDLERp oldhandler;

/* action function declarations: action.c */
void  near bullet_go(OBJp objp);
void  near enemy_hopper_go(OBJp objp);
void  near enemy_scorpion_go(OBJp objp);
void  near floating_points_go(OBJp objp);
void  near kill_bullet(OBJp objp);
void  near kill_enemy(OBJp objp);
void  near kill_object(OBJp objp);
void  near launch_bullet(void);
void  near launch_enemy(int x,int y,int type);
void  near launch_floating_points(OBJp objp);
void  near player_begin_fall(OBJp objp);
void  near player_begin_jump(OBJp objp);
void  near player_begin_kick(OBJp objp);
void  near player_begin_shoot(OBJp objp);
void  near player_fall(OBJp objp);
void  near player_jump(OBJp objp);
void  near player_kick(OBJp objp);
void  near player_run(OBJp objp);
void  near player_shoot(OBJp objp);
void  near player_stand(OBJp objp);
void  near put_score(OBJp objp);
void  near update_score(OBJp objp);

/* function declarations: char.c */
void  put_string(char *string,int ix,int iy);
void  center_string(char *string,int x1,int x2,int y);

/* function declarations: effects.c */
void  get_blinkmap(OBJp objp);
void  load_status_screen(void);
```

```
void  redraw_screen(void);
int   status_screen(void);
void  status_shape(int shape,int x,int y);

/* function declarations: map.c */
void  load_level(void);
void  page_copy(int ymin);
void  page_fix(void);
void  put_foreground_tile(int xtile,int ytile);
void  put_tile(int xtile,int ytile);
void  rebuild_background(void);
void  rebuild_foreground(void);
int   scroll_down(int npixels);
int   scroll_left(int npixels);
int   scroll_right(int npixels);
int   scroll_up(int npixels);
void  swap(void);
void  warp(int x,int y);

/* function declarations: motion.c */
int   can_move_down(OBJp objp);
int   can_move_up(OBJp objp);
int   can_move_right(OBJp objp);
int   can_move_left(OBJp objp);
int   collision_detection(OBJp objp1,OBJp objp2);
int   how_far_left(OBJp objp,int n);
int   how_far_right(OBJp objp,int n);
int   how_far_up(OBJp objp,int n);
int   how_far_down(OBJp objp,int n);
int   test_bit(char num,int bit);

/* function declarations: tommy.c */
void  main(void);
void  activate_level(void);
void  apply_sprite(OBJp objp);
void  array_to_level(int  n);
void  fix_palettes(void);
void  flushkey(void);
void  getseed(void);
void  get_blinkmap(OBJp objp);
void  interrupt increment_timer(void);
int   irandom(int  min,int max);
void  init_graphics(void);
void  level_to_array(int n);
void  load_sprite(void);
void  load_status_screen(void);
void  terminate_game(void);
```

Notes on GAMEDEFS.H

Because the GAMEDEFS.H file is included in all the source code files, it could present a problem. Global variables should be declared one time in one source code file, and then seen elsewhere as "extern" variables. This ensures all the functions in all the source code files are looking at the same memory location for a variable. In order to solve this problem, we define a symbol **DECLARE**, as follows:

```
#ifdef tommy_c
    #define DECLARE                 /* declarations are not extern */
#else
    #define DECLARE extern          /* declarations are extern */
#endif
```

This means **DECLARE** will be defined to mean nothing in the TOMMY.C source code file, and elsewhere it will be defined to mean "extern." This solves the problem quite nicely. A global variable can now be declared like this:

```
DECLARE int current_level;
```

The declaration will be extern in all source code files except TOMMY.C. To facilitate the definition of **DECLARE**, we define **tommy_c** at the top of TOMMY.C like this:

```
#define tommy_c
#include "gamedefs.h"
```

Now the **tommy_c** symbol will only be defined in the TOMMY.C source code file, and elsewhere it will be invisible to the compiler.

Exploring the Data Structures

If you look closely at GAMEDEFS.H, you'll see that our game is designed using four data structures to support a layout array, levels, sprites, and objects. You'll need a good understanding of how these structures work in order to follow the game code we'll present in Chapters 11 through 15. When we cover the source code, you'll see how these data structures are used.

Supporting Levels

The game code is designed to support six levels. We define a constant named **MAXLEVELS** in GAMEDEFS.H to specify the number of levels that can be used:

```
#define MAXLEVELS 6
```

If you want to add more levels to the game, you'll need to change this constant.

If you recall from Chapter 9 when we completed the game editor, we explained that the level data is stored in an array named **level**, which is declared like this:

```
DECLARE LEVDEF far level[MAXLEVELS];
```

In the game, we use this same data structure. Recall that it is simply an array of **LEVDEF** structures. This structure simply holds the names of each of the six data files that are used to create the game:

```
typedef struct levdef                /* level structure */
{
   char level_fname[13];
   char background_fname[13];
   char backattr_fname[13];
   char foreground_fname[13];
   char foreattr_fname[13];
   char sprite_fname[13];
}  LEVDEF;
```

Here we have compartments for the filenames of the level data, background tiles, background tile attributes, foreground tiles, foreground tile attributes, and the sprite list. The names of the these files are read by the **main()** function in TOMMY.C and then they are assigned to the level array by calling the **level_to_array()** function, which is also located in TOMMY.C:

```
void level_to_array(int n)
{
   /* update all the levels */
   strcpy(level[n].level_fname,      level_fname);
   strcpy(level[n].background_fname,background_fname);
   strcpy(level[n].backattr_fname,  backattr_fname);
   strcpy(level[n].foreground_fname,foreground_fname);
   strcpy(level[n].foreattr_fname,  foreattr_fname);
   strcpy(level[n].sprite_fname,    sprite_fname);
}
```

Once this data has been read in, it can easily be accessed by the main game functions.

Introducing the layout Array

When we get to Chapter 12, we'll be spending quite a bit of time discussing game animation. In particular, we'll look at how our animated sprites interact with the tiles in our game levels. This type of animation can get a little tricky so we've devoted a few chapters to showing you the subtleties of fast sprite animation. For now, let's explore the data structures that are used.

First, we'll need two arrays to hold pointers to our background and foreground tiles:

```
/* tile arrays for levels */
DECLARE unsigned char far background_tile[MAXCOLS][MAXROWS];
DECLARE unsigned char far foreground_tile[MAXCOLS][MAXROWS];
```

Because **MAXCOLS** is set to 240 and **MAXROWS** is set to 200, these arrays can reference as many as 48,000 tiles for our background and foreground art.

Second, we need an important structure we call the ***layout*** *array*:

```
/* declare the layout array */
DECLARE char layout[2][22][15];
```

The **layout** array holds the information about the status of the tiles displayed on the current screen. We need it to help us keep track of when tiles need to be redrawn on the screen when sprites are being animated. Notice that the **layout** array has three dimensions. The first subscript, **[2]**, refers to the two pages: hidden and visual. Tiles are tracked on both the hidden and visual pages. The second subscript, **[22]**, refers to the number of columns. The third subscript, **[15]**, is the number of rows. It's easy to visualize the **layout** array as an array of Boolean values superimposed on the tiles, as shown in Figure 10.1.

If the array element is assigned a value of 0, the corresponding tile has not changed in the current *animation frame* (see the next Tommy's Tip) and we'll call this a *clean* tile. If the array element is 1, the tile has been overwritten with something, probably a sprite, and it needs to be redrawn. When there are no sprites visible and all the tiles are clean, the **layout** array contains all 0s, as shown in Figure 10.1. As sprites are added, they cover up tiles, and the corresponding elements of the layout array are set to 1, or TRUE.

Tommy's Tip

Animation Success with Animation Frames

Animation in a side scroller consists of displaying many frames very quickly and very smoothly. For the purposes of our discussion, we'll define an *animation frame* to be the sequence of events ending in a page flip. We expect to animate our game at a frame rate of approximately two dozen frames per second. The sequence of events will happen roughly like this:

1. Collect user input and perform any necessary calculations, including scrolling.
2. Rebuild all the background tiles.
3. Put the sprites on top of the background tiles.
4. Put the foreground tiles on top of the sprites.
5. Flip the pages.

We'll elaborate on this sequence as we go along in Chapters 11 through 14. In general, every frame of animation does all five of these steps to a greater or lesser degree. Some frames skip the user interaction part, and not all frames require scrolling, but every frame requires a page flip. So we will use the page flip to define the end of a frame.

The process of rebuilding all the tiles can be the most time-consuming part of the frame. Since we want to maximize our frame rate, we can take a shortcut on this step. Instead of replacing all the tiles every frame, we can update the bare minimum number of tiles that must be redrawn to clear the

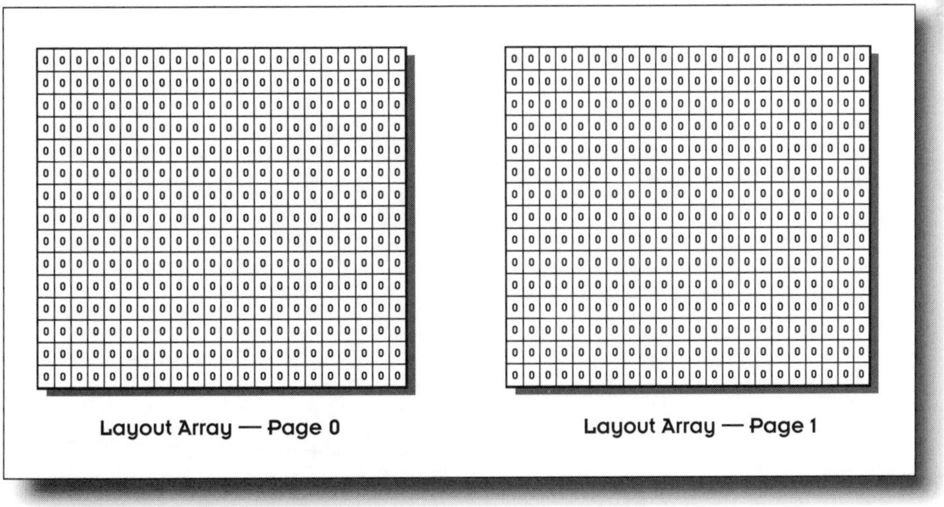

Figure 10.1 *How the layout array is set up.*

screen. If we scrolled during the frame, we will need to update a row or column of tiles along the edges. The only other tiles we'll need to replace are those that were covered by sprites. In order to differentiate these tiles from the "clean" tiles, we need a mechanism to keep track of the tile status. And that's where the **layout** array comes in.

Tile Attributes

Tile attributes are byte values assigned to individual tiles that contain information about how a sprite may interact with the tile. The most important tile attribute is *solid on top* (the sprite "walks" on the tiles that are solid on top). Paths and platforms are made up of tiles with the solid-on-top attribute. Not all tiles are solid on top, of course, or Tommy would walk on walls and in the sky. We want Tommy to keep his feet on the floor, and if he happens to venture out into empty space, we want the rules of physics to apply. Figure 10.2 shows how tile attributes are used to keep Tommy's feet on the ground.

Similarly, we have attributes for solid on the bottom so that Tommy will bump his head on ceilings and ledges if he's not careful, and solid on the left or right, so he won't walk through walls.

Each tile has eight attributes; besides the four attributes for solid on the top, bottom, left, and right, there are four more attributes that you can use for anything you want. You may want to use attributes to flag a tile as the end of a level, as a door, as a remappable tile (as in the case of a flickering torch,

Figure 10.2 *Tile attributes keep Tommy from falling through the floor.*

Table 10.3 Tile Attributes

Bit	Attribute
0	Solid on top
1	Solid on bottom
2	Solid on left
3	Solid on right
4	unassigned
5	unassigned
6	unassigned
7	unassigned

where tiles are replaced periodically), as a starting point for a sprite, or as a hazard, such as spikes. Additionally, passing over a tile may change the action of the sprite. If a tile is a patch of ice, the sprite will slide over it, or a tile may accelerate sprite movement, such as a fan or catapult. There are obviously many ways to use a tile attribute.

Each tile is assigned a tile attribute byte. The eight bits in the byte indicate which attributes are set. Table 10.3 shows how I have assigned the bits.

The tile attributes are assigned to the unique tiles in the tile library. That means that if a tile is a floor, it will be a floor throughout the level. If a tile is solid on the top in one position in the level, every occurrence of that tile in the level will also be solid on the top. Assigning tile attributes to tiles in the tile library is more efficient than assigning attributes to every tile in the level individually. That method would also work, but you would need an array as big as the level to hold the attributes and you would use up much more RAM. I don't do it that way, but I can see how it would be possible for some games to work better with attributes assigned to level positions rather than unique tiles. Feel free to experiment, but for our discussion, we'll assume the attributes are assigned to unique tiles in the tile library.

The attribute bytes are stored in two arrays, which are declared like this in GAMEDEFS.H:

```
char background_attributes[240];
char foreground_attributes[28];
```

Each of the 240 unique background tiles has an attribute byte associated with it, as does each of the 28 unique foreground tiles. The attributes are usually set in the game editor. To check an attribute by testing a bit, either in the game or in the editor, use the following function:

```
test_bit(char num,int bit)
{
   /* test bit flags, used for tile attributes */
   return((num >> bit) & 1);
}
```

This function is found in the file MOTION.C.

Objects and Sprites

Is Tommy a sprite or is Tommy an object? As discussed earlier, Tommy is both, but for the purposes of the code we are going to discuss, Tommy must be defined very precisely. Therefore, we will define a structure of type **object** in GAMEDEFS.H that will completely describe Tommy. The structure looks like this:

```
typedef struct OBJstruct                /* object structure */
{
  OBJp next;                            /* linked list next node */
  OBJp prev;                            /* linked list previous node */
  int x;                                /* x coordinate */
  int y;                                /* y coordinate */
  int xspeed;                           /* horizontal speed */
  int yspeed;                           /* vertical speed */
  int direction;                        /* LEFT or RIGHT */
  int tile_xmin;                        /* tile limits */
  int tile_xmax;
  int tile_ymin;
  int tile_ymax;
  int frame;                            /* frame of animation */
  unsigned long time;                   /* time */
  SPRITE *sprite;                       /* pointer to sprite */
  ACTIONp action;                       /* pointer to action function */
};
```

This structure gives all the information about Tommy: his current position, what he is doing, how long he has been doing it, and what sprite he is currently displayed as. That's right, *Tommy's object keeps track of Tommy's sprite.* There are many sprites that could be the current representation of Tommy. He may be standing still, walking, or running. The chosen sprite is one of the images we created in the sprite editor, and it will be stored in a structure that looks like this:

```
typedef struct _sprite                  /* sprite structure */
{
   char far *bitmap;                    /* pointer to bitmap data */
   int width;                           /* width of bitmap */
   int height;                          /* height of bitmap */
```

```
    int xoffset;                /* x offset */
    int yoffset;                /* y offset */
    int bound_x;                /* x coord of bounding box */
    int bound_y;                /* y coord of bounding box */
    int bound_width;            /* width of bounding box */
    int bound_height;           /* height of bounding box */
}   far SPRITE;
```

So Tommy's object structure points to Tommy's sprite structure. While there is only one object structure for Tommy, there are 37 sprite structures, and Tommy's object can point to any one of them. We will examine this relationship in more detail in Chapter 12.

Object or Tile?

There will be times, as we build our game, that we'll have an item that we don't know what to do with. There are some items that can be represented as either a tile or an object, and it is not always obvious which is the best way to define it.

Take the case of a cheeseburger, for example. Suppose Tommy is running around the level and his energy level goes down. He is hungry. Let's give him a cheeseburger. How are we going to do it?

The cheeseburger can be displayed as either a tile or a sprite. If it is stored as a tile, it should be as a foreground tile, so it can be put anywhere in the level, and the background will show through it. How will we know Tommy has grabbed the cheeseburger? We can use a tile attribute to mark the tile as food. Then every time Tommy passes a foreground tile, we can check it to see if the food attribute is set. If it is, we remove the foreground tile from the **foreground_tile** array and give Tommy the energy boost he has earned.

On the other hand, if the cheeseburger is stored as an object it would have no tile attribute. We would have to use collision detection techniques to determine how the two objects should interact with each other. If a collision is detected, we would remove the cheeseburger object from the linked list and give Tommy his snack.

Both methods would work, and the one you choose is related to space and speed considerations. Since we only have enough room in video memory for 28 foreground tiles, we may want to use them sparingly. On the other hand, sprite and objects take up room in RAM, and if we are facing a RAM crunch, tiles, which are stored in video memory, may be the better option. Video-to-video transparent blits are a little slower than RAM-to-video transparent blits, so a "cheeseburger sprite" would be a little faster than a "cheeseburger tile," with the exception that objects are drawn every frame, and foreground tiles are not. We only redraw tiles when a object passes over them (or behind them). Also, if there are many cheeseburgers on a level, we will have to do a collision check on each one every frame. That would slow us down, but just a little bit.

Are there other factors we have not considered? We only have four unassigned tile attributes, what if we want to use them for something else? What if we want the cheeseburger to use the background palettes rather than the sprite palettes? Do we want the cheeseburger to blink or display a floating score when it is grabbed?

As you can see, the decision on how to store the cheeseburger is complex. The optimal solution is not always obvious during the early design phase of a game. Sometimes a little experimentation is needed. It is a good idea to keep an open mind about things like this. Different games will yield different results.

Function Declarations

At the bottom of GAMEDEFS.H are the function declarations for all the source code files. Function declarations are important to get clean compiles without compiler warnings. The function declarations are organized in the same order as the source code files and are presented in roughly alphabetical order. Notice that ACTION.C is treated as a separate source code file even though it is not compiled alone. Rather, it is included in TOMMY.C using the **#include** preprocessor directive. The reason for **include**ing the file in this manner is all the action functions in ACTION.C are declared to be near, and must reside in the same code segment as the functions that call them. We'll discuss this concept further in Chapter 13.

Getting Organized

Some of the global variables in GAMEDEFS.H are visible in only one source code file, others are visible in several source code files. I have not differentiated between them—all globals variables are universally visible in the *Tommy's Adventures* source code files. I realize this runs contrary to the current programming style of data encapsulation. My only defense of this practice is to say: this is the way I like to do it; it works well for me. Development is speeded up because I always know where my globals are. Having them in one file makes it easy for me to find them. I can modify them or add new globals quickly. I don't waste a lot of time worrying about which variables are visible to which functions, and I don't waste RAM on duplicate copies of variables. It seems like a perfectly efficient way to organize things to me.

You may, of course, feel free to encapsulate your own data with my blessing.

Chapter 11

The world we live in is constantly moving. How can we express this motion on a computer screen?

Supporting Game Levels and Scrolling

Many years ago, in my misspent youth, I took a cross-country trip on a motorcycle. I visited places I had never been to before, and it was quite an adventure. I traveled very light; everything I wore for two weeks fit in one saddlebag of a Honda Gold Wing. I took the bare minimum I needed to survive, and what I didn't have, I didn't miss.

Now that I'm older I've become accustomed to traveling in a different style. With airlines, rental cars, porters, and bell captains, I don't have to travel light. I take everything I can pack; clothes, shoes (lots of them), cosmetics, hair-care supplies, hats, hat boxes, pajamas, books, toys—you name it. I take stuff I don't even need simply because I'm able to.

Software works the same way. When I began designing games years ago, software had to travel light. Our games needed to fit on a single 360K floppy and run in 256K RAM. The games had to work on all platforms and look good. These days, games can take up megabytes of hard disk and RAM space. If you run out of disk space, you can move up to a CD-ROM. Unfortunately, games are starting to get fat and extravagant. We put stuff in them we don't really need. So now, we need to return to the idea of traveling light, particularly where our game code is concerned. Code that is small and tight is easier to debug and port to other platforms. The smaller the code the better, because you can always find a use for any left over room. For example, music and sound effects tend to expand to fill any amount of available RAM, so you should leave some room for them.

In the true spirit of "lean-and-mean" game programming, we need to develop a set of tight functions for loading, displaying, and scrolling our level art. In this chapter, we'll present each of the functions we need to build the foundation of our game code.

Introducing the Game-Scrolling Functions

The scrolling functions, as well as the functions to draw the background for our game, are in the file MAP.C. Here we have functions to load levels, *blit* foreground and background tiles, scroll level art in all directions (up, down, left, right, and even diagonally), and *warp* to a position in a level. Table 11.1 lists the complete set of functions.

Some of these functions may look similar to the ones we used in the game editor. In fact, the theory behind the scrolling is the same as what we saw in Chapter 5. Video memory is resized and rectangular areas for pages and tiles

Table 11.1 *Functions Used in MAP.C*

Function	Description
load_level()	Loads graphics and level data from disk
page_copy()	Copies one page to another
page_fix()	Adjusts tile graphics according to scrolling
put_foreground_tile()	Blits a foreground tile
put_tile()	Blits a background tile
rebuild_background()	Copies all background tiles to hidden page
rebuild_foreground()	Copies all foreground tiles to hidden page
scroll_down()	Performs scrolling calculations to scroll down
scroll_left()	Performs scrolling calculations to scroll left
scroll_right()	Performs scrolling calculations to scroll right
scroll_up()	Performs scrolling calculations to scroll up
swap()	Performs a page flip
warp()	Rebuilds a complete level at any location

are assigned the same way. There are some differences in the way the code behaves, though, as we will see in a minute. But first, let's have a look at the source code in the file MAP.C.

```
/******************************************************************\
*  map.c -- Tommy game map/level source code                       *
*  copyright 1994 Diana Gruber                                     *
*  compile using large model, link with Fastgraph (tm)             *
\******************************************************************/

#include "gamedefs.h"
/******************************************************************/
void load_level()
{
   register int i;

   tile_orgx = 0;          /* initialize global level variables */
   tile_orgy = 0;
   screen_orgx = 0;
   screen_orgy = 0;
   vpo = 0;
   hpo = 240;
   vpb = vpo+239;
   hpb = hpo+239;
   visual = 0;
   hidden = 1;
   tpo = 480;

   /* display the foreground tiles */
   fg_move(0,tpo);
   fg_showpcx(foreground_fname,2);

   /* reorganize the foreground tiles to conserve video memory */
   fg_transfer(0,31,480,591,320,591,0,0);
   fg_transfer(32,63,480,591,320,703,0,0);

   /* display the background tiles */
   fg_move(0,480);
   fg_showpcx(background_fname,2);

   /* fix the foreground palettes */
   fix_palettes();

   /* load the level information */
   if ((level_stream = fopen(level_fname,"rb")) == NULL)
   {
      sprintf(abort_string,"%s not found",level_fname);
      abort_game();
   }

   /* get the rows and columns */
   fread(&ncols,sizeof(int),1,level_stream);
   fread(&nrows,sizeof(int),1,level_stream);

   /* load the background tiles */
   for (i = 0; i < ncols; i++)
      fread(&background_tile[i][0],sizeof(char),nrows,level_stream);
```

```
   /* load the foreground tiles */
   for (i = 0; i < ncols; i++)
      fread(&foreground_tile[i][0],sizeof(char),nrows,level_stream);
   fclose(level_stream);

   /* load the background tile attributes */
   if ((level_stream = fopen(backattr_fname,"rb")) == NULL)
   {
      sprintf(abort_string,"%s not found",backattr_fname);
      abort_game();
   }
   fread(background_attributes,sizeof(char),240,level_stream);
   fclose(level_stream);

   /* calculate the maximum tile origin */
   world_maxx = (ncols - 20) * 16;
   world_maxy = (nrows - 12) * 16 - 8;
}
/*****************************************************************/
void page_copy(int ymin)
{
   /* copy both the video memory and the layout array */

   if (ymin == vpo)          /* visual to hidden */
   {
      fg_transfer(0,351,vpo,vpb,0,hpb,0,0);
      memcpy(layout[hidden],layout[visual],22*15);
   }
   else                      /* hidden to visual */
   {
      fg_transfer(0,351,hpo,hpb,0,vpb,0,0);
      memcpy(layout[visual],layout[hidden],22*15);
   }
}
/*****************************************************************/
void page_fix()
{
   /* if the scrolling flags were set, do the video blits and
      update the layout array */

   register int i;

   if (warped)              /* warped -- just replace all the tiles */
   {
      warp(world_x,world_y);
      return;
   }
   else if (scrolled_left && scrolled_up)    /* diagonal scrolls */
   {
      fg_transfer(0,335,vpo,223+vpo,16,hpb,0,0);
      for(i = 0; i< 15; i++)
         put_tile(0,i);
      for(i = 0; i< 22; i++)
         put_tile(i,0);
      for (i = 0; i < 21; i++)
         memcpy(&layout[hidden][i+1][1],layout[visual][i],14);
   }
   else if (scrolled_left && scrolled_down)
   {
      fg_transfer(0,335,16+vpo,vpb,16,223+hpb,0,0);
```

```
   for(i = 0; i< 15; i++)
      put_tile(0,i);
   for(i = 0; i< 22; i++)
      put_tile(i,14);
   for (i = 0; i < 21; i++)
      memcpy(layout[hidden][i+1],&layout[visual][i][1],14);
}
else if (scrolled_right && scrolled_up)
{
   fg_transfer(16,351,vpo,223+vpo,0,hpb,0,0);
   for(i = 0; i< 15; i++)
      put_tile(21,i);
   for(i = 0; i< 22; i++)
      put_tile(i,0);

   for (i = 0; i < 21; i++)
      memcpy(&layout[hidden][i][1],layout[visual][i+1],14);
}
else if (scrolled_right && scrolled_down)
{
   fg_transfer(16,351,16+vpo,vpb,0,223+hpo,0,0);
   for(i = 0; i< 15; i++)
      put_tile(21,i);
   for(i = 0; i< 22; i++)
      put_tile(i,14);

   for (i = 0; i < 21; i++)
      memcpy(layout[hidden][i],&layout[visual][i+1][1],14);
}
else if (scrolled_left)                /* horizontal scrolls */
{
   fg_transfer(0,335,vpo,vpb,16,hpb,0,0);
   for(i = 0; i< 15; i++)
      put_tile(0,i);
   for (i = 0; i < 21; i++)
      memcpy(layout[hidden][i+1],layout[visual][i],15);
}
else if (scrolled_right)
{
   fg_transfer(16,351,vpo,vpb,0,hpb,0,0);
   for(i = 0; i< 15; i++)
      put_tile(21,i);
   for (i = 0; i < 21; i++)
      memcpy(layout[hidden][i],layout[visual][i+1],15);
}
else if (scrolled_up)                  /* vertical scrolls */
{
   fg_transfer(0,351,vpo,223+vpo,0,hpb,0,0);
   for(i = 0; i< 22; i++)
      put_tile(i,0);
   for (i = 0; i < 22; i++)
      memcpy(&layout[hidden][i][1],layout[visual][i],14);
}
else if (scrolled_down)
{
   fg_transfer(0,351,16+vpo,vpb,0,223+hpo,0,0);
   for(i = 0; i< 22; i++)
      put_tile(i,14);
   for (i = 0; i < 22; i++)
      memcpy(layout[hidden][i],&layout[visual][i][1],14);
```

```
   }
}
/**********************************************************************/
void put_foreground_tile(int xtile,int ytile)
{
   int tile_num;
   int x,y;
   int x1,x2,y1,y2;

   /* get the tile number */
   tile_num = (int)foreground_tile[xtile+tile_orgx][ytile+tile_orgy];

   /* 28 or greater == no foreground tile here */
   if (tile_num <= 27)
   {

      /* calculate the source and destination coordinates */
      y1 = (tile_num/2)*16+480;
      y2 = y1+15;
      x1 = 320+tile_num%2 * 16;
      x2 = x1 + 15;
      x = xtile*16;
      y = ytile*16+15;

      /* transfer the foreground tile (transparent video-video blit) */
      fg_tcxfer(x1,x2,y1,y2,x,y+hpo,0,0);
   }
}
/**********************************************************************/
void put_tile(int xtile,int ytile)
{
   int tile_num;
   int x,y;
   int x1,x2,y1,y2;

   /* get the tile number from the background array */
   tile_num = (int)background_tile[xtile+tile_orgx][ytile+tile_orgy];

   /* calculate source and destination coordinates */
   x1 = (tile_num%20)*16;
   x2 = x1+15;
   y1 = (tile_num/20)*16 + tpo;
   y2 = y1+15;
   x = xtile*16;
   y = ytile*16+15;

   /* transfer the tile */
   fg_transfer(x1,x2,y1,y2,x,y+hpo,0,0);
}
/**********************************************************************/
void rebuild_background()
{
   /* put all the necessary background tiles on the hidden page */
   register int i,j;

   for (i = 0; i < 22; i++)
   {
      for (j = 0; j < 15; j++)
      {
         /* check and make sure you need a tile there */
```

```
            if (layout[hidden][i][j])
            {
               put_tile(i,j);

               /* reset the layout array */
               layout[hidden][i][j] = FALSE;
            }
         }
      }
}
/*****************************************************************/
void rebuild_foreground()
{
   /* put all the necessary foreground tiles on the hidden page */
   register int i,j;

   for (i = 0; i < 22; i++)
   {
      for (j = 0; j < 15; j++)
      {
         /* check and make sure you need a tile there */
         if (layout[hidden][i][j])
            put_foreground_tile(i,j);
      }
   }
}
/*****************************************************************/
int scroll_down(int npixels)
{
   /* scroll more than one column, just redraw the whole screen */
   if (npixels >= 16)
   {
      world_y = tile_orgy*16 + screen_orgy;
      world_y = MIN(world_maxy,world_y+npixels);
      world_x = tile_orgx*16 + screen_orgx;
      warped = TRUE;
   }

   /* less than one column, no need to draw new tiles */
   else if (screen_orgy <= 40-npixels)
   {
      screen_orgy+=npixels;
   }

   /* need to scroll one row down */
   else if (tile_orgy < nrows - 15)
   {
      tile_orgy++;
      screen_orgy-=(16-npixels);
      scrolled_down = TRUE;
   }
   else /* can't scroll down */
   {
      return(ERR);
   }
   return(OK);
}
/*****************************************************************/
int scroll_left(int npixels)
{
```

```
   /* scroll more than one column, just redraw the whole screen */
   if (npixels > 16)
   {
      world_x = tile_orgx*16 + screen_orgx;
      world_x = MAX(0,world_x-npixels);
      world_y = tile_orgy*16 + screen_orgy;
      warped = TRUE;
   }

   /* less than one column, no need to draw new tiles */
   else if (screen_orgx >= npixels)
   {
      screen_orgx-= npixels;
   }

   /* need to scroll one column to the left */
   else if (tile_orgx > 0)
   {
      tile_orgx--;
      screen_orgx+=(16-npixels);
      scrolled_left = TRUE;
   }

   /* can't scroll left */
   else
      return(ERR);

   return(OK);
}
/****************************************************************/
int scroll_right(int npixels)
{
   /* scroll more than one column, just redraw the whole screen */
   if (npixels > 16)
   {
      world_x = tile_orgx*16 + screen_orgx;
      world_x = MIN(world_maxx,world_x+npixels);
      world_y = tile_orgy*16 + screen_orgy;
      warped = TRUE;
   }

   /* less than one column, no need to draw new tiles */
   else if (screen_orgx <= 32-npixels)
   {
      screen_orgx+=npixels;
   }

   /* need to scroll one column to the right */
   else if (tile_orgx < ncols - 22)
   {
      tile_orgx++;
      screen_orgx-=(16-npixels);
      scrolled_right = TRUE;
   }
   else /* can't scroll right */
   {
      return(ERR);
   }
   return(OK);
}
```

```
/**********************************************************************/
int scroll_up(int npixels)
{
   /* scroll more than one column, just redraw the whole screen */
   if (npixels >= 16)
   {
      world_y = tile_orgy*16 + screen_orgy;
      world_y = MAX(0,world_y-npixels);
      world_x = tile_orgx*16 + screen_orgx;
      warped = TRUE;
   }

   /* less than one column, no need to draw new tiles */
   else if (screen_orgy >= npixels)
   {
      screen_orgy-=npixels;
   }

   /* need to scroll one row up */
   else if (tile_orgy > 0)
   {
      tile_orgy--;
      screen_orgy+=(16-npixels);
      scrolled_up = TRUE;
   }
   else /* can't scroll up */
   {
      return(ERR);
   }
   return(OK);
}
/**********************************************************************/
void swap()
{
   /* vpo = visual page offset, vpb = visual page bottom */
   /* hpo = hidden page offset, vpb = hidden page bottom */

   vpo = 240 - vpo;  /* toggle between 0 and 240 */
   hpo = 240 - hpo;

   vpb = vpo+239;
   hpb = hpo+239;

   /* toggle hidden and visual page */
   visual = !visual;
   hidden = !hidden;

   /* pan to the new visual page */
   fg_pan(screen_orgx,screen_orgy+vpo);
}
/**********************************************************************/
void warp(int x,int y)
{
   register int i,j;

   if (x < 16)                    /* calculate the tile x origin */
   {
      tile_orgx = 0;
      screen_orgx = x;
   }
```

```
    else if (x >= world_maxx)
    {
       x = world_maxx;
       tile_orgx = x/16-2;
       screen_orgx = 32;
    }
    else
    {
       tile_orgx = x/16 - 1;
       screen_orgx = x%16 + 16;
    }

    if (y < 16)                      /* calculate the tile y origin */
    {
       tile_orgy = 0;
       screen_orgy = y;
    }
    else if (y >= world_maxy)
    {
       y = world_maxy;
       tile_orgy = y/16-2;
       screen_orgy = 40;
    }
    else
    {
       tile_orgy = y/16 - 1;
       screen_orgy = y%16 + 16;
    }

    for (i = 0; i < 22; i++)     /* draw all the tiles */
    {
       for (j = 0; j < 15; j++)
       {
          put_tile(i,j);
          put_foreground_tile(i,j);
       }
    }
    /* update the layout array */
    memset(layout[hidden],0,15*22);
}
```

Game Scrolling versus Level Editor Scrolling

Let's take a closer look at the game-scrolling functions and compare them to the code used for scrolling in the game editor. The scrolling action performed in the game uses the same video memory layout and data structures as the scrolling code in the level editor. There are, however, some differences in the way the code works. In the level editor, scrolling was a leisurely process. We only scrolled occasionally, and when we did, there was no particular need for speed. We never flipped pages, except when we scrolled beyond the edge of the screen. We also didn't need to perform any animation.

In our game, *Tommy's Adventures*, the action is fast-paced and furious. We expect the screen to be in constant motion, which means we must be ready to scroll immediately at the touch of a key. Not only that, we are constantly animating the screen and flipping pages, whether or not a scroll is involved.

In the level editor, scrolling only occurred in four directions: up, down, left and right. Scrolling was done in 16-pixel increments. In the game, scrolling can happen at any angle. That is, we may want to scroll two pixels up and 10 pixels to the right in one frame. We need to be completely flexible in our ability to scroll.

The scrolling functions in the level editor were also self-contained. The scrolling calculations and blits were all performed in the same function. In the game, the scrolling tasks are handled differently. The scrolling code is spread out over several functions. First, the calculations are done in one or more scrolling functions (**scroll_up()**, **scroll_down()**, **scroll_left()**, **scroll_right()**, or **warp()**), then the screen is updated in a function called **page_fix()**. We'll be exploring the scrolling functions soon, but before we get into that, let's back up a little and start at the beginning, where the level data is loaded and displayed.

Loading the Level

The level data is loaded by the **load_level()** function. Tiles are stored in a manner similar to the way they are stored in the level editor. The foreground tiles are displayed first, and then copied in two chunks to the area where they need to be displayed, as shown in Figure 11.1.

```
/* display the foreground tiles */
fg_move(0,tpo);
fg_showpcx(foreground_fname,2);

/* re-organize the foreground tiles to conserve video memory */
fg_transfer(0,31,480,591,320,591,0,0);
fg_transfer(32,63,480,591,320,703,0,0);
```

The background tiles are then loaded into the area where the foreground tiles used to be, covering them up. At this point, the screen looks like Figure 11.2.

```
/* display the background tiles */
fg_move(0,480);
fg_showpcx(background_fname,2);
```

PCX files can potentially change the palette colors. Since tile colors are unpredictable, it is possible the PCX files may have clobbered the sprite colors. To fix this, the next thing **load_level()** does is call **fix_palettes()** to fix the first 32 palette colors. (The **fix_palettes()** function is in the TOMMY.C source file.)

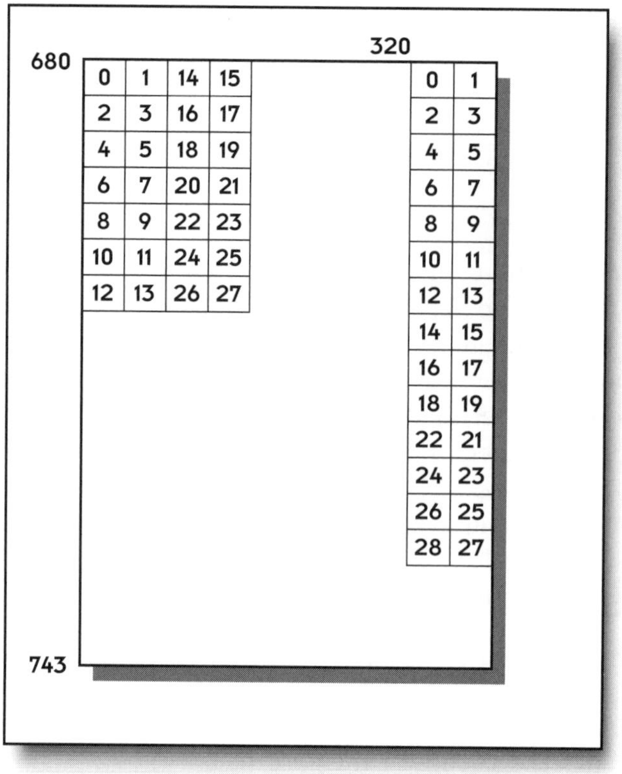

Figure 11.1 *Loading the foreground tiles.*

```
/* fix the foreground palettes */
fix_palettes();
```

We're now ready to load in the actual level data from a single binary file that is created by the game editor. Once the background tiles are read in, they are stored in the array **background_tile**; the foreground tiles are stored in **foreground_tile**. Later, these arrays will be used by the display functions, such as **put_tile()** and **put_foreground_tile()**, to display the tiles. To read in the data, only a few simple **for** loops are required:

```
/* load the level information */
if ((level_stream = fopen(level_fname,"rb")) == NULL)
{
   sprintf(abort_string,"%s not found",level_fname);
   abort_game();
}

/* get the rows and columns */
fread(&ncols,sizeof(int),1,level_stream);
fread(&nrows,sizeof(int),1,level_stream);
```

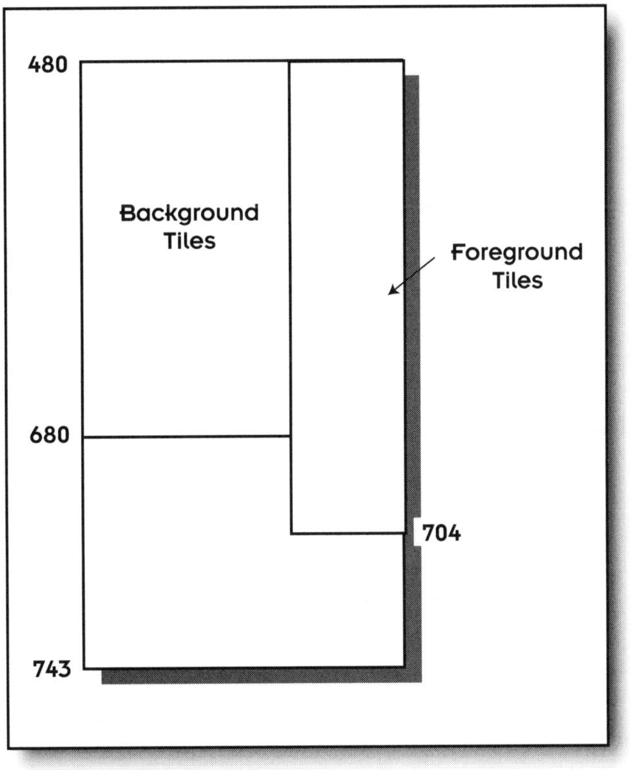

Figure 11.2 *Loading the background tiles.*

```
/* load the background tiles */
for (i = 0; i < ncols; i++)
   fread(&background_tile[i][0],sizeof(char),nrows,level_stream);

/* load the foreground tiles */
for (i = 0; i < ncols; i++)
   fread(&foreground_tile[i][0],sizeof(char),nrows,level_stream);
fclose(level_stream);
```

Once we've read in the foreground and background tile data for the level, we need to read in the attributes for the background tiles. Recall that the attribute data is stored in its own binary file. The attribute data is stored in the array **background_attributes**:

```
/* load the background tile attributes */
if ((level_stream = fopen(backattr_fname,"rb")) == NULL)
{
   sprintf(abort_string,"%s not found",backattr_fname);
   abort_game();
}
fread(background_attributes,sizeof(char),240,level_stream);
fclose(level_stream);
```

Once the tile data and attributes are safe and snug in their arrays, we need to set two key variables that are used by the scrolling functions:

```
/* calculate the maximum tile origin */
world_maxx = (ncols - 20) * 16;
world_maxy = (nrows - 12) * 16 - 8;
}
```

We're now ready to draw our first screen.

Building Screens

Recall that all of our game screens are built of tiles. The **rebuild_background()** function builds the background from tiles. It does this quickly, because it does not blit every tile in the background. It only blits the tiles that have changed since the last frame. The function knows which tiles to blit because it examines the **layout** array. The **layout** array (discussed Chapter 10) holds a Boolean value for each tile on the screen. If the value in the **layout** array is 0, the tile has not been changed and does not need to be redrawn. If the layout array value is 1, the tile has been changed, and must be redrawn. When **rebuild_background()** recognizes that a tile must be redrawn, it calls the **put_tile()** to blit the tile. After the tile is drawn, the associated value in the layout array is set to 0. This process is simple, but it is quite important because it is responsible for the speed of screen updates. The process of examining and updating the **layout** array ensures only the parts of the screen that have changed since the last frame will be redrawn.

```
void rebuild_background()
{
   /* put all the necessary background tiles on the hidden page */
   register int i,j;

   for (i = 0; i < 22; i++)
   {
      for (j = 0; j < 15; j++)
      {
         /* check and make sure you need a tile there */
         if (layout[hidden][i][j])
         {
            put_tile(i,j);

            /* reset the layout array */
            layout[hidden][i][j] = FALSE;
         }
      }
   }
}
```

Notice that we are using register variables for loop indexes to give the funtion a further speed boost.

When the **put_tile()** function is called, it obtains the actual tile number from the **background_tile** array, calculates the coordinates for displaying the tile, and then displays the tile by calling Fastgraph's video-to-video blit function, **fg_transfer().**

```
void put_tile(int xtile,int ytile)
{
   int tile_num;
   int x,y;
   int x1,x2,y1,y2;

   /* get the tile number from the background array */
   tile_num = (int)background_tile[xtile+tile_orgx][ytile+tile_orgy];

   /* calculate source and destination coordinates */
   x1 = (tile_num%20)*16;
   x2 = x1+15;
   y1 = (tile_num/20)*16 + tpo;
   y2 = y1+15;
   x = xtile*16;
   y = ytile*16+15;

   /* transfer the tile */
   fg_transfer(x1,x2,y1,y2,x,y+hpo,0,0);
}
```

Rebuilding the foreground is very similar to rebuilding the background. In this case, the function **rebuild_foreground()** function is called, which in turn calls **put_foreground_tile()** to display the foreground tiles, if there are any.

Using Foreground Tiles

We've already encountered foreground tiles in the game editor. Let's take a closer look at them now. Foreground tiles are stored and displayed in a manner similar to background tiles, but with some important differences. Since foreground tiles are displayed *after* the sprite, they show up in front of it. This gives the appearance of a sprite moving behind things, such as walking behind a pillar or a wall. Foreground tiles also have a transparent color so you can see through them. This is useful for odd-shaped tiles like bushes and trees, and also for semi-transparent tiles like screens or tunnels with small windows.

I have allowed for 28 foreground tiles in the our game. That isn't very many, but we are starting to run out of video memory, and that's how many I could conveniently fit in on the right side of video memory, as shown in Figure 11.3.

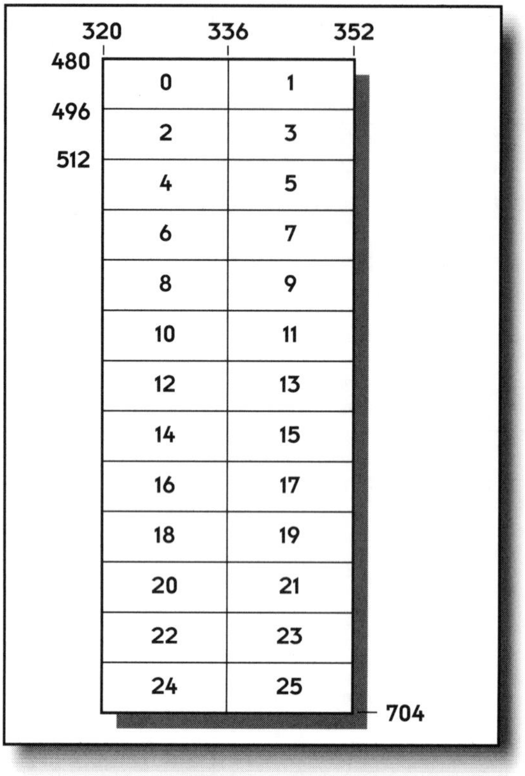

Figure 11.3 *Foreground tiles in video memory.*

I arranged the foreground in two columns of 14 tiles in the area just to the right of the background tiles. They occupy an area 32x224 pixels. Both the game and the level editor store the foreground tiles in this area. As we saw in Chapter 10, foreground tile information for the level is stored in an array similar to the background tile array:

```
unsigned char far foreground_tile[MAXCOLS][MAXROWS];
```

Foreground tiles are displayed using the **put_foreground()** function:

```
void put_foreground_tile(int xtile,int ytile)
{
   int tile_num;
   int x,y;
   int x1,x2,y1,y2;

   /* get the tile number */
   tile_num = (int)foreground_tile[xtile+tile_orgx][ytile+tile_orgy];
```

```
   /* 28 or greater == no foreground tile here */
   if (tile_num <= 27)
   {

      /* calculate the source and destination coordinates */
      y1 = (tile_num/2)*16+480;
      y2 = y1+15;
      x1 = 320+tile_num%2 * 16;
      x2 = x1 + 15;
      x = xtile*16;
      y = ytile*16+15;

      /* transfer the foreground tile (transparent video-video blit) */
      fg_tcxfer(x1,x2,y1,y2,x,y+hpo,0,0);
   }
}
```

The **put_foreground_tile()** function is very similar to the **put_tile()** function listed earlier, except that the source coordinates are calculated differently, and a different Fastgraph video-to-video blit function is called. The **fg_tcxfer()** function is the transparent color version of Fastgraph's **fg_transfer()** function. It's a bit slower than **fg_transfer()**, so when speed is a consideration (as it always is), the use of foreground tiles should be kept to a minimum. Areas in the level with no foreground tiles are given a value of 255 to indicate no foreground tile is there. The **put_foreground_tile()** function checks the **foreground_tile** array to see if a foreground tile number is greater than 28. If it is, the **put_foreground_tile()** function returns without trying to place a foreground tile.

Fastgraph Tip

fg_tcxfer()

The **fg_tcxfer()** function copies a rectangular region from any position on any video page to any position on any video page, excluding any pixels whose color is transparent. The transparent colors are defined by the **fg_tcmask()** function.

```
void fg_tcxfer(int minx, int maxx, int miny, int maxy,
   int newx, int newy, int source_page, int dest_page);
```

- *minx* is the x coordinate of the source region's left edge. Its value is reduced to a byte boundary if necessary.
- *maxx* is the x coordinate of the source region's right edge. It must be greater than or equal to the value of *minx*. Its value is extended to a byte boundary if necessary.
- *miny* is the y coordinate of the source region's top edge.

- *maxy* is the y coordinate of the source region's bottom edge. It must be greater than or equal to the value of *miny*.
- *newx* is the x coordinate of the destination region's left edge. Its value is reduced to a byte boundary if necessary.
- *newy* is the y coordinate of the destination region's bottom edge.
- *source_page* is the video page number containing the source region.
- *dest_page* is the video page number for the destination region.

The **fg_tcxfer()** function does a video-to-video blit with any number of transparent colors. Fastgraph's **fg_tcmask()** function is used to define the transparent colors. I usually use palette 0 as the transparent color, to be consistent with the sprite transparent color.

Fastgraph Tip

fg_tcmask()

The **fg_tcmask()** function defines which of the first 16 color values the **fg_tcxfer()** function will consider transparent.

```
void fg_tcmask(int mask);
```

- *mask* is a 16-bit mask, where each bit indicates whether the corresponding color value is transparent. For instance, if bit 0 (the rightmost bit) is 1, then color 0 will be transparent. If bit 0 is 0, color 0 will not be transparent.

Warping

There will be times when we want to update an entire screen of tiles, for example, when we display the first frame of a new level. This process is called *warping*.

Tommy's Tip

Warps

A *warp* is a jump from one area of a level to a completely different area of the same level, or even an entirely different level. It forces every tile on the screen to be redrawn.

A warp describes a method by which a character can be in one area and almost instantaneously appear somewhere else, as if he had entered a *Star Trek* transporter. An elevator is a common device to achieve a visually appealing warp. A character steps into an elevator, the background changes, and he or she steps out of the elevator somewhere else.

In our game, pressing the letter W will warp our main character Tommy to the next level.

To support warping, we've included a function called **warp()**.

```
void warp(int x,int y)
{
   register int i,j;

   if (x < 16)                  /* calculate the tile x origin */
   {
      tile_orgx = 0;
      screen_orgx = x;
   }
   else if (x >= world_maxx)
   {
      x = world_maxx;
      tile_orgx = x/16-2;
      screen_orgx = 32;
   }
   else
   {
      tile_orgx = x/16 - 1;
      screen_orgx = x%16 + 16;
   }

   if (y < 16)                  /* calculate the tile y origin */
   {
      tile_orgy = 0;
      screen_orgy = y;
   }
   else if (y >= world_maxy)
   {
      y = world_maxy;
      tile_orgy = y/16-2;
      screen_orgy = 40;
   }
   else
   {
      tile_orgy = y/16 - 1;
      screen_orgy = y%16 + 16;
   }

   for (i = 0; i < 22; i++)     /* draw all the tiles */
   {
      for (j = 0; j < 15; j++)
      {
         put_tile(i,j);
         put_foreground_tile(i,j);
      }
   }
```

```
   /* update the layout array */
   memset(layout[hidden],0,15*22);
}
```

The **warp()** function calculates the new screen origin and then draws all the tiles. Since this effectively clears all the tiles, the **layout** array is set to all 0s. We call C's **memset()** function to accomplish this task quickly.

Flipping Pages

The **warp()** function only updates the hidden page. This is desireable, because we want the tiles to be drawn in offscreen video memory so we don't create any kind of flickering or screen fragmentation. After the warp, we want to make the hidden page visible. This involves a page flip. We will do many page flips in our game, and all of them are done by calling the function **swap()**.

```
void swap()
{
   /* vpo = visual page offset, vpb = visual page bottom */
   /* hpo = hidden page offset, vpb = hidden page bottom */

   vpo = 240 - vpo;  /* toggle between 0 and 240 */
   hpo = 240 - hpo;

   vpb = vpo+239;
   hpb = hpo+239;

   /* toggle hidden and visual page */
   visual = !visual;
   hidden = !hidden;

   /* pan to the new visual page */
   fg_pan(screen_orgx,screen_orgy+vpo);
}
```

The **swap()** function changes the variables that define the hidden and visual pages. Recall the **vpo** is the *visual page offset* and the **hpo** is the *hidden page offset*. These values that will be added to the y coordinate of any item that is displayed on one of the pages, such as tiles, sprites, or text. For example, to display text at y=100 on the visual page, you would display the text at y=100+vpo.

Two global variables, **hidden** and **visual**, are toggled. These variables will be equal to either 0 or 1. If **hidden** is 0, then the page at the top is the hidden page and the page at the bottom is the visual page. Similarly, if **hidden** is 1, the page at the bottom is the hidden page and the page at the top is the visual page. Which ever page is not the hidden page is the visual page. We keep track of these values in the **swap()** function so we don't need to worry about them elsewhere.

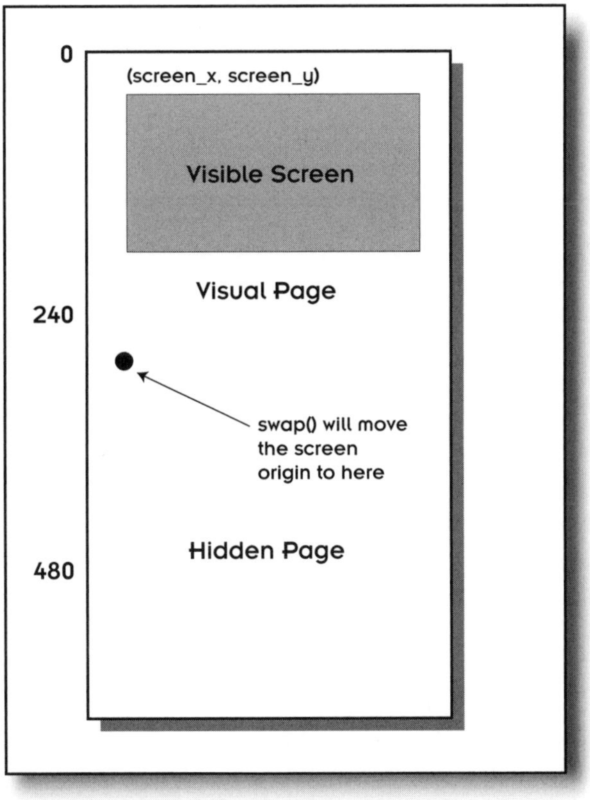

Figure 11.4 *The swap() function changes the origin of the visual page.*

Finally, the **swap()** function changes the screen origin with a call to **fg_pan()**. This is where the page flip occurs. We are now looking at a completely different part of video memory as shown in Figure 11.4.

Copying Pages

Let's assume we are performing our first frame of animation. First, we perform a *warp* to draw the screen on the hidden page. Then we do a *page flip* to make the hidden page visible. There is one more step we need to perform. At this point, the hidden page and the visual page won't match. In fact, the new hidden page will be blank, because we haven't drawn anything on it yet. We could rebuild all the tiles on the hidden page with another call to **warp()**, but that is not very efficient. A call to **warp()** causes 330 tile blits (22 columns x 15 rows) to be performed, each one involving a bit of unnecessary overhead. It will be much faster to just copy the visual page to the hidden page. Then we will have matching pages, which is what we want. The **page_copy()**

function handles the work of copying the visual page to the hidden page (or, less commonly, it can be used to copy the hidden page to the visual page):

```
void page_copy(int ymin)
{
   /* copy both the video memory and the layout array */

   if (ymin == vpo)          /* visual to hidden */
   {
      fg_transfer(0,351,vpo,vpb,0,hpb,0,0);
      memcpy(layout[hidden],layout[visual],22*15);
   }
   else                      /* hidden to visual */
   {
      fg_transfer(0,351,hpo,hpb,0,vpb,0,0);
      memcpy(layout[visual],layout[hidden],22*15);
   }
}
```

We pass the value **ymin**, which is the y coordinate of the top of either the hidden page or the visual page, to **page_copy()**. Usually we will pass **vpo** to **page_copy()**, to signify we want to copy the visual page to the hidden page.

The **page_copy()** function calls Fastgraph's **fg_transfer()** function to do a video-to-video blit. The entire page is copied in one quick function call. Since the two pages now match, their **layout** arrays should also match. The simplest way to make the **layout** arrays match is to use C's **memcpy()** function to copy the appropriate array elements.

Once the pages and the **layout** arrays match, we can go about the business of updating the hidden page for the next frame. Since the next frame will probably closely resemble the last frame, this will probably involve changing only a few tiles. In general, it is more efficient to call the **page_copy()** function after every warp and scroll, and then update only the tiles that need to change, than to rebuild the hidden page from scratch.

Scrolling Functions

As you've seen, warping involves rebuilding the entire hidden page from the set of tiles. But the warping function is not the fastest way to scroll a background because it requires 330 blits to redraw the page. Whenever possible, we want to minimize the number of blits. One large blit will always execute faster than several hundred small blits. That is the basis of our fast scrolling technique. As we saw in Chapter 5, we can copy large areas from the visual page to the hidden page, and then fill in a row or column of tiles around the edges to achieve a fast scroll.

There are four scrolling functions in the MAP.C file. These are **scroll_down()**, **scroll_left()**, **scroll_right()**, and **scroll_up()**. They all work approximately the same way. Let's look at one of them in closer detail to see what is going on behind the scenes:

```
int scroll_right(int npixels)
{
   /* scroll more than one column, just redraw the whole screen */
   if (npixels > 16)
   {
      world_x = tile_orgx*16 + screen_orgx;
      world_x = MIN(world_maxx,world_x+npixels);
      world_y = tile_orgy*16 + screen_orgy;
      warped = TRUE;
   }

   /* less than one column, no need to draw new tiles */
   else if (screen_orgx <= 32-npixels)
   {
      screen_orgx+=npixels;
   }

   /* need to scroll one column to the right */
   else if (tile_orgx < ncols - 22)
   {
      tile_orgx++;
      screen_orgx-=(16-npixels);
      scrolled_right = TRUE;
   }
   else /* can't scroll right */
   {
      return(ERR);
   }
   return(OK);
}
```

The **scroll_right()** function shown here is a little different than the **scroll_right()** function we saw in the level editor. In this version of **scroll_right()**, nothing is changed on the screen. No tiles are redrawn, no areas are copied to the hidden page, and no page flipping occurs. All that happens is some global variables are adjusted. The **world_x** and **world_y** variables are updated to reflect the new coordinates of the upper-left corner of the screen. The **screen_x** and **screen_y** coordinates are similarly updated. Two Boolean variables, **scrolled_right** and **warped**, are updated if necessary to indicate a scroll or a warp has occurred. The work of updating the screen is done after the scroll, in the **page_fix()** function.

The page_fix() Function

The **page_fix()** function is called in any frame where a scroll or warp has occurred. Its job is to do the necessary blits to fix the hidden page. It also updates the **layout** array as needed to reflect the new state of the tiles. Here is the complete function:

```
void page_fix()
{
   /* if the scrolling flags were set, do the video blits and
      update the layout array */

   register int i;

   if (warped)            /* warped--just replace all the tiles */
   {
      warp(world_x,world_y);
      return;
   }
   else if (scrolled_left && scrolled_up)    /* diagonal scrolls */
   {
      fg_transfer(0,335,vpo,223+vpo,16,hpb,0,0);
      for(i = 0; i< 15; i++)
         put_tile(0,i);
      for(i = 0; i< 22; i++)
         put_tile(i,0);
      for (i = 0; i < 21; i++)
         memcpy(&layout[hidden][i+1][1],layout[visual][i],14);
   }
   else if (scrolled_left && scrolled_down)
   {
      fg_transfer(0,335,16+vpo,vpb,16,223+hpb,0,0);
      for(i = 0; i< 15; i++)
         put_tile(0,i);
      for(i = 0; i< 22; i++)
         put_tile(i,14);
      for (i = 0; i < 21; i++)
         memcpy(layout[hidden][i+1],&layout[visual][i][1],14);
   }
   else if (scrolled_right && scrolled_up)
   {
      fg_transfer(16,351,vpo,223+vpo,0,hpb,0,0);
      for(i = 0; i< 15; i++)
         put_tile(21,i);
      for(i = 0; i< 22; i++)
         put_tile(i,0);

      for (i = 0; i < 21; i++)
         memcpy(&layout[hidden][i][1],layout[visual][i+1],14);
   }
   else if (scrolled_right && scrolled_down)
   {
      fg_transfer(16,351,16+vpo,vpb,0,223+hpo,0,0);
      for(i = 0; i< 15; i++)
         put_tile(21,i);
      for(i = 0; i< 22; i++)
         put_tile(i,14);

      for (i = 0; i < 21; i++)
         memcpy(layout[hidden][i],&layout[visual][i+1][1],14);
   }
   else if (scrolled_left)              /* horizontal scrolls */
   {
      fg_transfer(0,335,vpo,vpb,16,hpb,0,0);
      for(i = 0; i< 15; i++)
         put_tile(0,i);
      for (i = 0; i < 21; i++)
```

```
         memcpy(layout[hidden][i+1],layout[visual][i],15);
   }
   else if (scrolled_right)
   {
      fg_transfer(16,351,vpo,vpb,0,hpb,0,0);
      for(i = 0; i< 15; i++)
         put_tile(21,i);
      for (i = 0; i < 21; i++)
         memcpy(layout[hidden][i],layout[visual][i+1],15);
   }
   else if (scrolled_up)              /* vertical scrolls */
   {
      fg_transfer(0,351,vpo,223+vpo,0,hpb,0,0);
      for(i = 0; i< 22; i++)
         put_tile(i,0);
      for (i = 0; i < 22; i++)
         memcpy(&layout[hidden][i][1],layout[visual][i],14);
   }
   else if (scrolled_down)
   {
      fg_transfer(0,351,16+vpo,vpb,0,223+hpo,0,0);
      for(i = 0; i< 22; i++)
         put_tile(i,14);
      for (i = 0; i < 22; i++)
         memcpy(layout[hidden][i],&layout[visual][i][1],14);
   }
}
```

The **page_fix()** function is called once for each frame. It is called before the sprites are displayed, and after the scrolling functions, which may or may not be called during a frame. The globals that were set in the scrolling functions tell **page_fix()** whether to do a simple horizontal or vertical scroll, a diagonal scroll, or a complete screen redraw.

The following are the ten cases that **page_fix()** must consider:

1. warp
2. scroll left and up
3. scroll left and down
4. scroll right and up
5. scroll right and down
6. scroll left
7. scroll right
8. scroll up
9. scroll down
10. no scroll

If no scrolling functions were called during a frame, the **page_fix()** function returns without doing anything.

Adjusting the layout Array

The screen updates in the **page_fix()** function do not have any affect on the sprites. If there were sprites on the visual page, they will be copied to the hidden page. That means the hidden page will contain both clean tiles and tiles covered with sprites. We will need to have access to that information for the next frame. We will need to know which tiles will need to be updated. The **layout** array for the hidden page will need to be updated to show the location of the sprites that were copied from the visual page. Unfortunately, we can't simply copy the visual page **layout** array to the hidden page **layout** array as we did in the **page_copy()** function. This time, the graphics on the hidden page have shifted slightly, in one or two directions. We will have to copy the **layout** array in such a way as to reflect the shift.

A horizontal scroll is simpler than a diagonal scroll, so let's look at that cases first. When the screen scrolls to the right, the code looks like this:

```
else if (scrolled_right)
{
   fg_transfer(16,351,vpo,vpb,0,hpb,0,0);
   for(i = 0; i< 15; i++)
      put_tile(21,i);
   for (i = 0; i < 21; i++)
      memcpy(layout[hidden][i],layout[visual][i+1],15);
}
```

The graphics are copied from the visual page to the hidden page, shifted 16 pixels to the left. A new row of graphics will appear on the right. Then the visual page **layout** array is copied into the hidden page **layout** array, and all the columns are shifted, as shown in Figure 11.5.

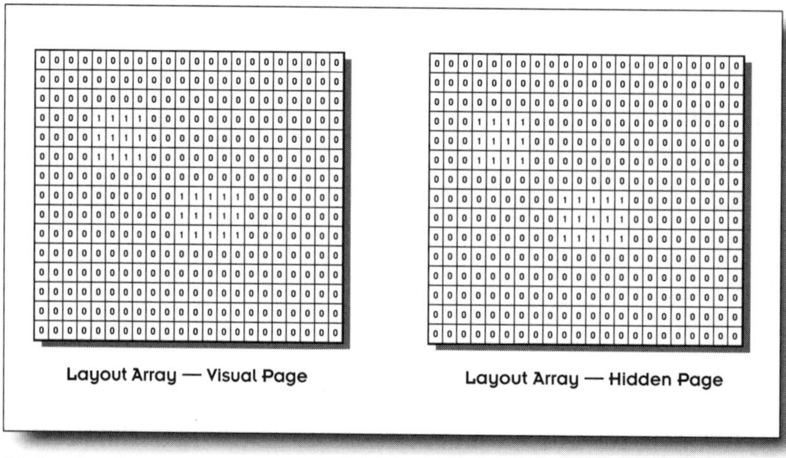

***Figure 11.5** Copying the layout array during a scroll.*

The C runtime library function **memcpy()** is used to copy 21 columns of tiles, shifted one column to the left. Column 1 becomes column 0, column 2 becomes column 1, and so on. Fifteen tiles are copied in each column, representing the 15 rows of tiles.

Diagonal Scrolling

To scroll the screen diagonally, we must handle both the horizontal and the vertical cases at the same time. This is tricky. The code for copying the graphics and the **layout** array left and up looks like this:

```
else if (scrolled_left && scrolled_up)    /* diagonal scrolls */
{
   fg_transfer(0,335,vpo,223+vpo,16,hpb,0,0);
   for(i = 0; i< 15; i++)
      put_tile(0,i);
   for(i = 0; i< 22; i++)
      put_tile(i,0);
   for (i = 0; i < 21; i++)
      memcpy(&layout[hidden][i+1][1],layout[visual][i],14);
}
```

This code is condensed and not too obvious, but it works well and is quite fast. In this example, the screen is being scrolled up and to the left. As Figure 11.6 shows, area 'A' is copied from the visual page to the hidden page. Row 14 and column 21 on the visual page are discarded. A new row 0 and column 0 are generated on the hidden page. The visual page **layout** array is then copied into the hidden page **layout** array, properly shifted up and to the left.

The **page_fix()** function is necessary to handle the case of diagonal scrolling. If it were not for the case of diagonal scrolling, we could do the screen

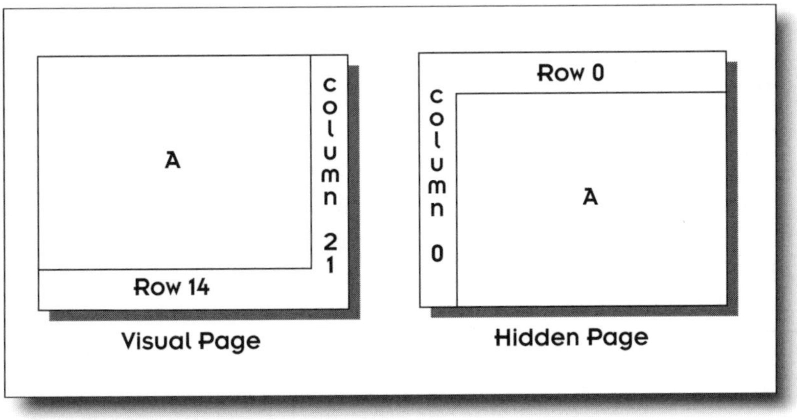

Figure 11.6 *The process of scrolling diagonally.*

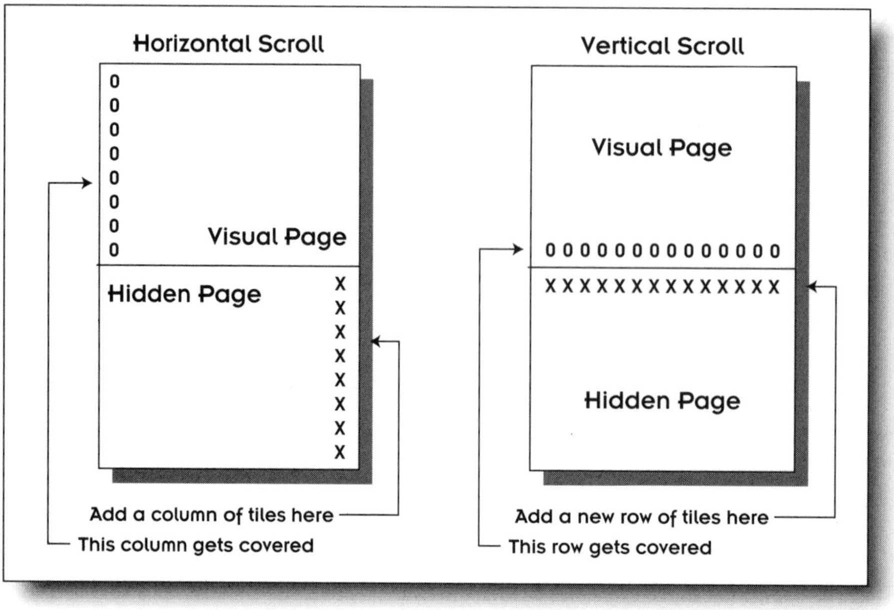

Figure 11.7 *Diagonal scrolling.*

blits and level array updates in the scrolling functions. It would be simpler if we could perform the diagonal scrolling in two steps—first scrolling left, then scrolling down—but unfortunately, this won't work. Not only would it be slower, it would also cause the vertical scroll to wipe out the horizontal scroll. Figure 11.7 shows what the hidden page and visual page look like during a diagonal scroll.

If you need to scroll both left and up in one frame, you can not do it in two functions. You must handle the diagonal scrolling as a separate case in the **page_fix()** function.

Speed Considerations

Throughout this chapter I have stressed certain optimizations. The most important is to try to only update the part of the screen that needs to be changed. Screen blits, either from RAM to video, or from video to video, are one of the most time consuming parts of game programming. It is usually worthwhile to take whatever steps you can to reduce screen blits. Clever background processing of the layout array can help to optimize operations, such as diagonal scrolling. It is much faster to perform tricky string copies in RAM than to do unnecessary screen blits.

Chapter 12

Explore the intricacies of sprite animation through the use of data structures memory allocation, and timing issues.

On the Road to Sprite Animation

We're now about to embark on a two part adventure into the mysteries of sprite animation. And as you can imagine, sprite animation is tricky business. In this chapter, we will focus on how sprites are stored. We first looked at the sprite and object structures in Chapter 10, and now we are going to examine them in detail, along with the various arrays and lists that keep them organized. We'll also explore the mechanisms for allocating space to hold the sprite information and detail about how sprite actions are timed. The data structures are complex and a bit convoluted, but they are powerful. They hold all the information needed to perform the high-speed animation in the game. In the next chapter, we will add code to the data structures and finally see how to make a sprite move.

First, though, we need to develop a general strategy for storing and displaying our sprites.

Storing Sprites: RAM versus Video Memory

Where shall we store our sprites? Your first impulse may be to put the game sprites in video memory. If so, your second impulse should be to disregard your first one. There's no way we are going find enough video memory to store all of the sprites used in a game. We have already used most of the available video memory for our pages and tiles. There will be some empty corners of video memory left around, but not enough for the sprites. We plan to have a lot of sprites, after all, and we don't want to limit the number of sprites we can use to the tiny amount of video memory we have available.

Our only alternative is to store our sprites in RAM. Unfortunately, we don't have a lot of RAM either. Remember, we are writing this game in DOS real mode. We *could* choose to use protected mode DOS, in which case we would have plenty of room for sprites, but as of this writing, that is only a semi-practical idea. There are still plenty of computers in the home entertainment market that have 1Mb or less of installed RAM. I expect this to change in the next few years, so if, by the time you read this book, you have access to 8Mb of RAM, then by all means use it. In the mean time, we will design our game to work in 640K DOS memory. We can make it work, we just have to plan carefully, and be conservative in our use of sprites.

Conserving Sprite Memory

In the 256-color modes, a sprite bitmap takes one byte of RAM per pixel. So a bitmap that is 40x40 pixels will require 1,600 bytes of RAM. If a game has a variety of characters in different positions, you can see how bitmaps can eat up RAM in a hurry.

When designing games, remember our golden rule: *conserve everything.* This especially applies to RAM. Games will expand to fill any amount of RAM you have available. Any room that is left over after the code and sprites have eaten their share will be needed for music and sound effects.

A good way to conserve RAM is to plan your sprites out in advance—before you get too carried away with the details of your game. Try to find ways to optimize the size of your sprites or the number of animation frames you'll need for each of them. For instance, does your menacing scorpion really need a three-inch tail? (Shortening the tail could save you several kilobytes.) Or, does each enemy need a four-stage walk or will a two-stage walk do? (A four-stage walk will look better because the enemy will have more frames of animation and thus appear to be moving more smoothly. In contrast, the two-stage walk won't look as smooth because the enemy will have only two frames of animation. See the next Tommy's Tip for more information.) These are the kinds of sprite design tradeoffs that we need to consider. We can create a few elaborate enemies with smooth motion, or we can have more enemies with choppier motion. These decisions are usually made by trial and error, and that is why it is so important to have a game editor. We can insert and delete sprites into our game conveniently, keeping track of how much space we have, and fine-tune our sprites as we go along.

Tommy's Tip

Stages of Animation

A four-stage walk indicates that a sprite uses four different graphics to achieve a walking effect. Similarly, a two-stage walk indicates only two images are needed to make a sprite walk. In general, a main character sprite uses more stages for each motion, and an enemy sprite can get by with fewer stages. For example, our main character Tommy has a six-stage walk, a four-stage left kick, and a two-stage right kick. The enemy scorpion has a two-stage walk and a one-stage death.

The other way to conserve RAM is to allocate it only as it's needed and free it when we are done with the task. We'll allocate room for our sprites as they appear and we'll only load them when they are used for a level. When we switch levels, we'll free all of the sprite memory and load new sprites for the next level. We'll also allocate objects as we need them. Bullets, for example, can be allocated and freed continuously, since they appear and disappear quite rapidly.

Working with the Sprite Data Structures

As we saw in Chapter 10, our sprites are stored in structures. But the hierarchy of these structures and the pointers that are used to access them can get a little tricky. Let's work out the details now so that you can see how our coding strategy will allow us to allocate the exact amount of memory at any point during program execution.

Tommy's Tip

The Mystery Word "Sprite"

The word *sprite* actually has two meanings. Generally, a sprite is a character in our story. In our game, Tommy is a sprite, and the pink scorpion he battles with is a sprite. When we're discussing our game code, however, the word *sprite* has a more precise meaning. It refers to a structure that contains a bitmap. As Figure 12.1 shows, our Tommy character is actually composed of many sprites, one for each stage or *frame* of animation. For example, to support his six-stage walk, we use six different sprites—one for each frame.

Declaring and Displaying Bitmaps

Since a sprite is essentially a bitmap image, we need to look at how bitmaps are stored and displayed before we move on and implement our structures for storing sprites. Bitmaps are rectangular picture images stored in RAM. But when they show up in a game, they are typically displayed as irregular-shaped objects, such as bullets, walking boys, jumping frogs—you get the idea. So how can we convert our bitmaps from the rectangular world of RAM to the irregular-shaped world of a game? We'll need to use a simple transparency trick.

For example, let's take the case of a bullet bitmap. As Figure 12.2 shows, the bullet bitmap is stored in memory as a rectangular block, however when it is displayed it looks like a bullet and not a square-shaped object. Instead of just storing the bullet as a rectangular set of color pixel values, we include the

Figure 12.1 *Using six different sprites to make Tommy walk.*

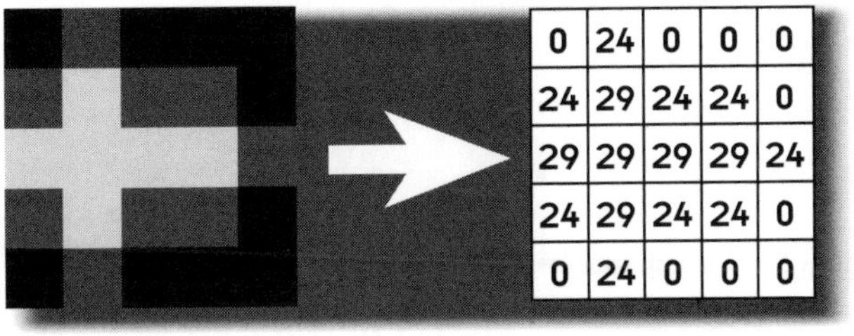

Figure 12.2 *Storing a sprite using a transparent color.*

value 0 to represent a transparent color. When the bitmap is displayed, the non-zero pixels appear and the pixels with a value of 0 are ignored. That means the background art will show through wherever a bitmap has a 0 pixel.

In our game, bitmaps are declared as pointers to arrays of type **char**. They are also declared as **far** pointers to save room in the default data segment. Here's the declaration from GAMEDEFS.H

```
char far *bitmap;
```

This declaration only allocates space for the pointer to a bitmap. The actual space for the data must be allocated at runtime. This is handled in the **load_sprite()** function, which we'll look at in a minute.

Declaring Sprites

The bitmap data is just part of the information needed to display a sprite. We also need to know the width and height of the bitmap. I find it convenient to store both the bitmap and size specifications together in a data structure. Since this is a data structure we will refer to often, we'll use C's **typedef** facility to define our **SPRITE** structure as a data type. Every sprite image in our game will then be stored in a data structure of type **SPRITE**. The structure actually includes the bitmap pointer (***bitmap**) that we just defined as a *member.* The other members include the width, height, x and y offsets, and extents of the bounding box used for the sprite. Here is the complete structure as defined in GAMEDEFS.H:

```
typedef struct _sprite          /* sprite structure */
{
   char far *bitmap;            /* pointer to bitmap */
   int width;                   /* width of bitmap */
   int height;                  /* height of bitmap */
   int xoffset;                 /* x offset */
   int yoffset;                 /* y offset */
```

```
   int bound_x;               /* x coord of bounding box */
   int bound_y;               /* y coord of bounding box */
   int bound_width;           /* width of bounding box */
   int bound_height;          /* height of bounding box */
}  far SPRITE;
```

Let's look at these members in a little more detail:

- The **bitmap** member is a pointer to the bitmap data, which is the actual image that will be displayed to represent the sprite.
- The **width** and **height** members represent the horizontal and vertical size of the bitmap in pixels.
- The **xoffset** and **yoffset** members represent how far away from an object's x and y position the bitmap is displayed. This helps align sprites with related sprites. For example, when Tommy is shooting to the left, the **xoffset** field is adjusted to the left, so that Tommy himself appears to be standing still, only his arm is extended.
- The **bound_x** and **bound_y** members represent the origin of the sprite's bounding box. The bounding box is sometimes used for collision detection. For example, a bullet will not actually kill an object unless it penetrates the bounding box. Shooting between an insect's antennae is not enough to kill it. The bounding box will specify a part of the sprite as the "kill range."
- The **bound_width** and **bound_height** members specify the width and the height of the bounding box.

The Sprite Array

To help us access all of the different sprites used in a game, we'll generate an array of pointers to the sprites at compile-time. We're storing the sprite pointers in an array rather than a linked list because we'll be using a fixed number of them, and it is more efficient to address elements of an array than nodes of a linked list. We'll use one large array to hold all of the sprites, which is declared like this:

```
#define MAXSPRITES 100
SPRITE *sprite[MAXSPRITES];
```

You can find this declaration in the file GAMEDEFS.H. This declaration gives us an array called **sprite** that holds 100 pointers to structures of type **SPRITE**. Although the declaration limits us to using 100 sprites or less, this is a reasonably generous number. If you need more sprites, change the value of

MAXSPRITES. Don't make the value too big, though. Memory for the sprite array is allocated at compile-time, and it is fixed. There is no reason to use up more RAM than you need to.

The sprite array declaration only allocates room for the pointers to the sprites. It does not allocate room for the spites themselves. Room for the sprite must be dynamically allocated at runtime, in the function **load_sprite()**.

Loading Sprites

I find it convenient to allocate sprite space when the sprite is read from a file. The function **load_sprite()** in the file TOMMY.C handles the work of allocating room for bitmaps and sprites, and assigning values to the sprite structure members:

```
void load_sprite()              /* load sprite data from files */
{
   SPRITE *new_sprite;
   register int i,j;
   int n,nbytes;
   int width,height;
   int xorg,yorg;
   int bound_x,bound_y;
   int bound_width,bound_height;
   char far *bitmap;

   if ((stream = fopen(sprite_fname,"rt")) == NULL)
   {
      sprintf(abort_string,"%s not found",sprite_fname);
      terminate_game();
   }

   i = 0;
   fscanf(stream,"%d",&nspritelists);
   for (j = 0; j < nspritelists; j++)
   {
      fscanf(stream,"%s",list_fname);

      if ((sprite_stream = fopen(list_fname,"rb")) == NULL)
      {
         sprintf(abort_string,"%s not found",list_fname);
         terminate_game();
      }

      fread(&nsprites,sizeof(int),1,sprite_stream);
      for (n = 0; n < nsprites; n++)
      {
         fread(&width,sizeof(int),1,sprite_stream);
         fread(&height,sizeof(int),1,sprite_stream);
         nbytes = width * height;
```

```
         if ((bitmap = (char far *)malloc(nbytes)) == (char *)NULL)
         {
            sprintf(abort_string,"out of bitmap memory");
            terminate_game();
         }

         if ((new_sprite = (SPRITE *)malloc(sizeof(SPRITE)))
            == (SPRITE *)NULL)
         {
            sprintf(abort_string,"out of sprite memory");
            terminate_game();
         }

         sprite[i] = new_sprite;
         fread(&xorg,sizeof(int),1,sprite_stream);
         fread(&yorg,sizeof(int),1,sprite_stream);
         fread(&bound_x,sizeof(int),1,sprite_stream);
         fread(&bound_y,sizeof(int),1,sprite_stream);
         fread(&bound_width,sizeof(int),1,sprite_stream);
         fread(&bound_height,sizeof(int),1,sprite_stream);

         fread(bitmap,sizeof(char),nbytes,sprite_stream);

         sprite[i]->bitmap = bitmap;
         sprite[i]->width = width;
         sprite[i]->height = height;
         sprite[i]->bound_x = bound_x;
         sprite[i]->bound_y = bound_y;
         sprite[i]->bound_width = bound_width;
         sprite[i]->bound_height = bound_height;
         sprite[i]->xoffset = 0;
         sprite[i]->yoffset = 0;
         i++;
      }
      fclose(sprite_stream);
   }
   fclose(stream);

   /* assign the sprites to some more meaningful names */
   j = 0;
   for (i = 0; i < STANDFRAMES; i++)
      tom_stand[i] = sprite[j++];
   for (i = 0; i < RUNFRAMES; i++)
      tom_run[i] = sprite[j++];
   for (i = 0; i < JUMPFRAMES; i++)
      tom_jump[i] = sprite[j++];
   for (i = 0; i < KICKFRAMES; i++)
      tom_kick[i] = sprite[j++];
   for (i = 0; i < SHOOTFRAMES; i++)
      tom_shoot[i] = sprite[j++];
   for (i = 0; i < SCOREFRAMES; i++)
      tom_score[i] = sprite[j++];
   for (i = 0; i < ENEMYFRAMES; i++)
      enemy_sprite[i] = sprite[j++];
}
```

The **load_sprite()** function opens the sprite list files that were created in the sprite editor. For each sprite in the sprite list, we must allocate room for both the sprite structure and the bitmap. The space needed for the sprite structure is allocated like this:

```
new_sprite = (SPRITE *)malloc(sizeof(SPRITE));
```

This call to **malloc()** only allocates room for the structure, not for the data the structure contains. That is, 20 bytes are allocated to hold the pointer to the bitmap, the sprite's width and height, and so on. To allow enough room for the sprite's bitmap data, we need to call **malloc()** again. The size of the bitmap is its width multiplied by its height. We must read the width and height from the sprite file, and then use **malloc()** to allocate memory for the bitmap:

```
fread(&width,sizeof(int),1,sprite_stream);
fread(&height,sizeof(int),1,sprite_stream);
nbytes = width * height;

if ((bitmap = (char far *)malloc(nbytes)) == (char *)NULL)
{
   sprintf(abort_string,"out of bitmap memory");
   terminate_game();
}
```

If for some reason we are unable to allocate enough room for the bitmap, we exit the program gracefully with a call to **terminate_game()**.

After space for the sprite and the bitmap are allocated, we can read the values from the file and assign the appropriate values to the sprite as shown here:

```
sprite[i]->bitmap = bitmap;
sprite[i]->width = width;
sprite[i]->height = height;
sprite[i]->bound_x = bound_x;
sprite[i]->bound_y = bound_y;
sprite[i]->bound_width = bound_width;
sprite[i]->bound_height = bound_height;
sprite[i]->xoffset = 0;
sprite[i]->yoffset = 0;
i++;
```

This process is repeated for each sprite until all the sprite data is stored in structures, which are pointed to by elements in the sprite array.

Renaming Sprites

Since we have several dozen (up to 100) sprites, we will find it helpful to give some of them more meaningful names. For convenience, we'll declare some pointers in GAMEDEFS.H that represent locations into the array so that we can easily reference selected sprites:

```
#define STANDFRAMES  3
#define RUNFRAMES    6
#define JUMPFRAMES   4
#define KICKFRAMES   8
#define SHOOTFRAMES  7
#define SCOREFRAMES  3
#define ENEMYFRAMES  6

DECLARE SPRITE *tom_stand[STANDFRAMES];
DECLARE SPRITE *tom_run  [RUNFRAMES];
DECLARE SPRITE *tom_jump [JUMPFRAMES];
DECLARE SPRITE *tom_kick [KICKFRAMES];
DECLARE SPRITE *tom_shoot[SHOOTFRAMES];
DECLARE SPRITE *tom_score[SCOREFRAMES];
DECLARE SPRITE *enemy_sprite[ENEMYFRAMES];
```

These declarations correspond to six sprite lists that define Tommy's motions and the sprite list holding Tommy's enemies. Tommy has three standing frames (with different facial expressions), six running frames, four jumping frames (including shooting while jumping), eight kicking frames (including a two-stage forward kick and a six-stage backward spin-kick), and seven shooting frames (including shooting while standing, shooting while walking, recoil, and a bullet sprite). The score sprite list includes sprites for the scoreboard, the energy bar, and the one-ups. The enemy sprite list includes two motion frames and a death frame for both the grasshopper and the scorpion. We give these sprite lists logical names and assign them to the appropriate **sprite** array elements. We place the code to accomplish this task toward the end of the **load_sprite()** function:

```
/* assign the sprites to some more meaningful names */
j = 0;
for (i = 0; i < STANDFRAMES; i++)
   tom_stand[i] = sprite[j++];
for (i = 0; i < RUNFRAMES; i++)
   tom_run[i] = sprite[j++];
for (i = 0; i < JUMPFRAMES; i++)
   tom_jump[i] = sprite[j++];
for (i = 0; i < KICKFRAMES; i++)
   tom_kick[i] = sprite[j++];
```

```
for (i = 0; i < SHOOTFRAMES; i++)
   tom_shoot[i] = sprite[j++];
for (i = 0; i < SCOREFRAMES; i++)
   tom_score[i] = sprite[j++];
for (i = 0; i < ENEMYFRAMES; i++)
   enemy_sprite[i] = sprite[j++];
```

Having multiple names for sprites is not wasteful. We are not declaring duplicate space for the sprites, merely duplicate pointers. The pointers only take a couple of bytes each. This tiny extravagance in wasted space is well worth the savings in terms of more readable (and therefore more easily debugged) code.

Declaring Objects

The sprite structures for Tommy are allocated once at the beginning of the game (load-time) and are not freed until the end of the game. Certain other sprites are also present throughout the game, including the scoreboard and the bullets. This might sound like a contradiction to what we said earlier—that bullets are constantly being allocated and freed—but it's not. They are two different kinds of structures. The bullet as a *sprite* is allocated once. The bullet as an *object* is allocated and freed many times.

Recall that the object structure is declared like this in GAMEDEFS.H:

```
DECLARE struct OBJstruct;              /* forward declarations */
typedef struct OBJstruct OBJ, far *OBJp;

typedef void near ACTION (OBJp objp); /* pointer to action function */
typedef ACTION near *ACTIONp;

typedef struct OBJstruct               /* object structure */
{
  OBJp next;                           /* linked list next node */
  OBJp prev;                           /* linked list previous node */
  int x;                               /* x coordinate */
  int y;                               /* y coordinate */
  int xspeed;                          /* horizontal speed */
  int yspeed;                          /* vertical speed */
  int direction;                       /* LEFT or RIGHT */
  int tile_xmin;                       /* tile limits */
  int tile_xmax;
  int tile_ymin;
  int tile_ymax;
  int frame;                           /* frame of animation */
  unsigned long time;                  /* time */
  SPRITE *sprite;                      /* pointer to sprite */
  ACTIONp action;                      /* pointer to action function */
};
```

This is a pretty scary-looking declaration! It involves a forward declaration, a pointer to a **near** function, a linked list, a pointer to a sprite structure, and a bunch of integer values. Seeing a declaration like this is enough to make you wonder if you should quit programming and join a rock band. But don't let the object declaration throw you off. Well-designed data structures are going to save us a lot of code later on. This is the worst one, and once you've conquered it, the rest are going to be easy.

Let's explore the members of the **OBJstruct** in more detail:

- The **next** and **prev** structure fields are pointers to adjacent nodes in a linked list. While sprites are allocated once per game or once per level, objects are allocated and freed much more often. Storing them in a linked list makes it easier to keep track of them.
- The **x** and **y** fields show the current position of the object, and are stored in *world space* coordinates. That is, when x is 0, the object is at the far left side of the level. An object's x coordinate increments as the object moves right, and continues to increment as the screen scrolls. So **x** can be much larger than the horizontal screen resolution and, similarly, **y** can be much greater than the vertical screen resolution.
- The **xspeed** and **yspeed** fields are the horizontal and vertical speed components of the object's motion. The speed of an object is measured in pixels per frame. Speed will vary, depending on what the object is doing. An object may walk at a rate of four pixels per frame, or run at a rate of eight pixels per frame. If Tommy is falling, his speed will gradually increase to simulate acceleration due to gravity. Similarly, if he is jumping, his vertical speed will gradually slow. Pressing an arrow key will also affect Tommy's speed.

  In general, Tommy's position in each frame is calculated by simply adding **xspeed** to **x** and **yspeed** to **y**, although we allow ourselves flexibility here to account for Tommy's special motions, such as jump kicks. Speed can be positive or negative, depending on whether the object is moving to the left or to the right.
- The **direction** field indicates which way the object is facing. This value is either **LEFT** or **RIGHT**, defined as follows:

```
#define LEFT   0
#define RIGHT  1
```

The direction of the object determines whether the sprite is displayed in a regular or flipped format. Some sprite motion depends on the direction, such as whether Tommy does a forward kick or a backward spin-kick. Also, when Tommy shoots, his direction determines the initial direction of the bullet.

- The **tile_xmin**, **tile_xmax**, **tile_ymin**, and **tile_ymax** fields are values for the minimum and maximum tile extents of a sprite on the screen. In Tommy's case, the tile extents determine when it is time to scroll the screen. If Tommy's x coordinate moves beyond **tile_xmax**, then the screen must scroll to the right. We try not to let the main character walk off the edge of the screen. Instead, we move the screen to keep him within a central tolerance area. If other objects move beyond their tile extents, they will either die (as in the case of a bullet), or simply not be drawn. Tile extents are calculated in layout space, ranging from 0 to 22 in the horizontal direction and 0 to 15 in the vertical direction.
- The **frame** field is used for different purposes for different objects. In Tommy's case, this variable keeps track of the current stage in Tommy's six-stage walk. The **frame** field is also useful for keeping track of which sprite to point to. In other objects, you can use this field for anything you want. In general, its purpose is to keep track of the current state of the animation.
- Similarly, the **time** field keeps track of the state of animation of an object, and can be used for different purposes for different objects. In Tommy's case, his **frame** field increments as a function of his **time** field. Tommy's **time** field increments as the real-time clock increments (as we discussed in Chapter 10), and when enough time passes, Tommy will take another step or do whatever his next action is. Keeping the animation synchronized with the real-time clock makes objects move at approximately the same speed on many different computers. Accelerating the clock allows us to measure these motions with precision. We will see how to accelerate the clock later in this chapter.
- The **sprite** field is a pointer to a structure of type **SPRITE**. This is the bitmap currently being displayed. An object can have many different sprites associated with it, but only one of them can be displayed each frame. The **sprite** field determines which one to display this frame.

  The relationship between objects and sprites is illustrated in Figure 12.3. An object may point to any of several sprites, and several objects may point to the same sprite. For example, Tommy's object may point to any of 37 sprites, and up to 9 bullet objects may point to the same bullet sprite.

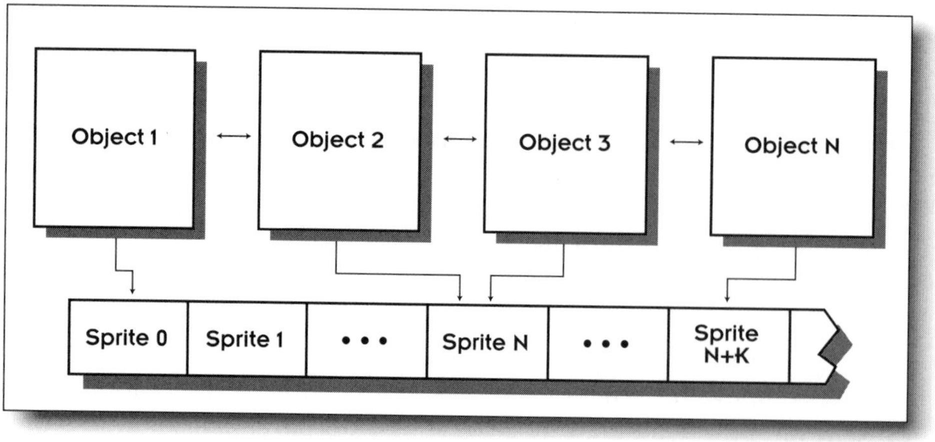

Figure 12.3 *Objects structures and sprite structures.*

- The **action** field is a pointer to a **near** function. We'll discuss these in detail in Chapter 13. In general, one action function will be executed for each object in each animation frame. The object function for Tommy will determine if he is walking, falling, shooting, kicking, or standing still. The current state of the game will determine which action function is executed. So if Tommy is walking and he comes to the edge of a platform, he will be falling in the next frame. The current frame's action function checks the floor, the keyboard, the other sprites, and so on, and then sets the action function for the next frame.

Declaring Tommy

The **OBJstruct** structure is declared to be a data type of type **OBJstruct** using C's **typedef** facility. This is done in the forward declaration:

```
DECLARE struct OBJstruct;
typedef struct OBJstruct OBJ, far *OBJp;
```

The **OBJp** data type is a pointer to a **far** structure of type **OBJ**. We will find the **OBJp** data type to be very useful to us. All our objects are described this way. We will use this label when accessing structure members, when passing objects to action functions, and when traversing the linked list of objects. Though the declaration is cumbersome, using the object pointer is easy. All our objects will be declared as object pointers. Let's look at how Tommy is declared:

```
DECLARE OBJp player;
```

That's all there is to it! Tommy is declared. He still needs to be allocated and initialized, but his declaration is handled in one line of code in GAMEDEFS.H. This file is where Tommy is born.

Note that I call Tommy "player." This is how we refer to Tommy throughout the source code, as the player or the main player sprite. This was done in the spirit of re-usable code—you may want to use the game engine for a different game, and you won't want to rename all the data structures and functions. In the Quickfire demo, for example, the player is an airplane, but the declarations and some of the action functions are the same.

Declaring Other Objects

It is convenient to declare a few other object pointers in GAMEDEFS.H. Since we know we are going to be traversing a linked list, let's declare pointers to the top and bottom nodes:

```
DECLARE OBJp top_node, bottom_node;
```

Also, we know the scoreboard is going to be an object, so we can declare that too:

```
DECLARE OBJp score;
```

We are going to need some enemies. We know we will have at least two, and we may want to add some later. Let's declare pointers to five.

```
#define MAXENEMIES 5
DECLARE OBJp enemy[MAXENEMIES];
```

That takes care of the global object declarations. We will be declaring some other objects later, but those will either be local variables, or they will be dynamically allocated at runtime. We have enough global objects declared to keep us organized.

Allocating Objects

Like the sprite structures, the object structures must be allocated before they can be used. Enemies and bullets are allocated as needed. We will look at code to launch bullet and enemy objects in Chapter 13. Tommy also needs to be allocated. He gets allocated just once, at the beginning of the game. You will find Tommy's allocation code in function **main()** in the file TOMMY.C. Here is what it looks like:

```
player = (OBJp)malloc(sizeof(OBJ));  /* allocate the player */
```

After Tommy is allocated, we can assign values to his structure members. For example, we assign these values to his tile extremities:

```
player->tile_xmin = 4;
player->tile_xmax = 14;
player->tile_ymin = 5;
player->tile_ymax = 11;
```

These lines indicate Tommy's tolerance area. When Tommy is standing on a tile that is closer than 4 tiles away from the left border, or farther than 14 tiles away, it is time to scroll the level either to the left or the right to keep Tommy within his tolerance area. Similarly, when Tommy is fewer than 5 tiles from the top of the screen or more than 11 tiles away, it is time to scroll the level up or down.

Other initializations are done at the beginning of each level:

```
player->x = 32;                 /* initialize player */
player->y = 200;
player->frame = 0;
player->time = 0;
player->xspeed = 0;
player->yspeed = 0;
player->sprite = tom_stand[0];
player->direction = RIGHT;
player->action = player_run;
```

This code tells us Tommy is starting out at a position (x=32, y=200) in world space. His initial speed is 0. His initial image is frame 0 of the **tom_stand[]** sprite list. His initial action function is **player_run()**.

Timing Tricks

Sprite animation requires careful timing. We are going to need a precise timing resolution for our game, which means we will need to speed up the system clock. The only practical way to do this is to re-vector one of the PC's interrupts. This involves a little more programming muscle in the form of "lean-and-mean" assembly code. If you are not an assembly-language programmer, don't worry about it. You should be able to use the assembly code we'll present without modifications. For the purposes of this book, we are more interested in how the timer function can be used in our game than how the assembly-language code actually works.

Accelerating the Clock

Usually, when you write a high-speed arcade game, you want it to run at approximately the same speed on many different computers. While it's convenient to base animation speed on the real-time clock, a problem occurs when the clock increments at a rate slower than the frame rate. Suppose, for example, that we are animating at 25 frames per second. Since, by default, the clock only increments 18.2 times per second, we'll have frames in which no clock tick occurs. If we base our animation on incrementing clock ticks, we will have whole frames of animation in which nothing happens.

Here's an example to consider. Think of a sprite falling off a ledge. The longer it falls, the more its speed increases as shown in Figure 12.4. First, it falls one pixel per clock tick. Then, it falls two pixels per clock tick and then three pixels per clock tick, and so on. This continues until it reaches a maximum speed of 10 pixels per clock tick. The fall looks realistic because the sprite has acceleration at the top of the fall and terminal velocity at the bottom. But if the clock-tick resolution isn't granular enough, the sprite is going to miss frames and the motion will look jerky. Speeding up the clock allows us to smooth out the curve.

Figure 12.4 *Animating a falling sprite.*

The BIOS clock-tick interrupt normally occurs 18.2 times per second and is implemented through interrupt 08 hex. The interrupt handler assigned to interrupt 08 hex performs two important tasks. First, it increments the BIOS time-of-day clock value (the time-of-day value represents the number of clock ticks since midnight). Second, it calls interrupt 1C hex just before exiting. Interrupt 1C hex is a user-definable interrupt whose default handler is simply an IRET (*interrupt return*) instruction. If you supply your own handler for interrupt 1C hex, it will automatically be executed every time interrupt 08 hex is issued (that is, 18.2 times per second). This process is often called *hooking* the clock-tick handler. Figure 12.5 illustrates the default relationship between these interrupt vectors.

It's possible to make the clock-tick interrupt occur at rates faster than 18.2 times per second to achieve a higher timing resolution. Accelerating the clock is itself rather straightforward, but we must re-vector an interrupt if we want the time of day clock to remain accurate.

After we accelerate the clock, interrupt 08 hex will be called more often. For example, if we double the clock-tick rate, interrupt 08 hex will be called 36.4 times per second instead of its usual 18.2 times per second.

As I mentioned earlier, the interrupt 08 hex handler updates the BIOS time-of-day value. If we simply multiply the clock-tick interrupt rate by eight, the value will be incremented eight times as often as before and the time of day clock will be running at eight times its normal speed. This time warp is undesirable because midnight will occur much sooner than we expected, and at midnight our computer turns into a pumpkin, the real-time clock becomes a pair of white mice, and disk accesses become as elusive as a lost glass slipper. Let's avoid this particular trip into the Twilight Zone by managing our clock interrupts carefully.

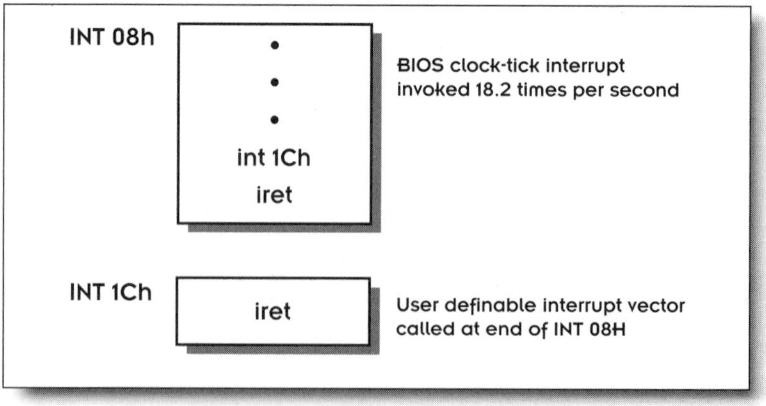

Figure 12.5 *Relationship between 1C hex and 08 hex.*

Writing a Replacement Interrupt Handler

What we need to do is write a replacement handler for interrupt 08 hex that calls the original BIOS time-of-day interrupt only when needed to update the real-time clock. If we wanted to double the clock-tick rate, for example, our new interrupt handler would call the original time-of-day handler every other invocation and thus keep the clock accurate. The general scheme is to save the address of the original interrupt 08 hex vector and then have our new interrupt 08 hex handler pass control to the original interrupt vector when it must update the time-of-day clock. After doing this, our interrupt vectors will look like the ones shown in Figure 12.6.

Note that if we've defined a handler for interrupt 1C hex, it will now be called 36.4 times per second. Half of these calls will be issued through the original BIOS time-of-day handler, but we must explicitly issue the other interrupt 1C hex calls through our replacement handler.

One other point worth mentioning is how the original interrupt 08 hex code is executed. As it is an interrupt routine, the original interrupt 08 hex code ends with an IRET instruction, but the code is no longer callable as an interrupt (because its vector isn't in the DOS interrupt table). Hence, we simulate the execution of an INT instruction by pushing the flags register and then

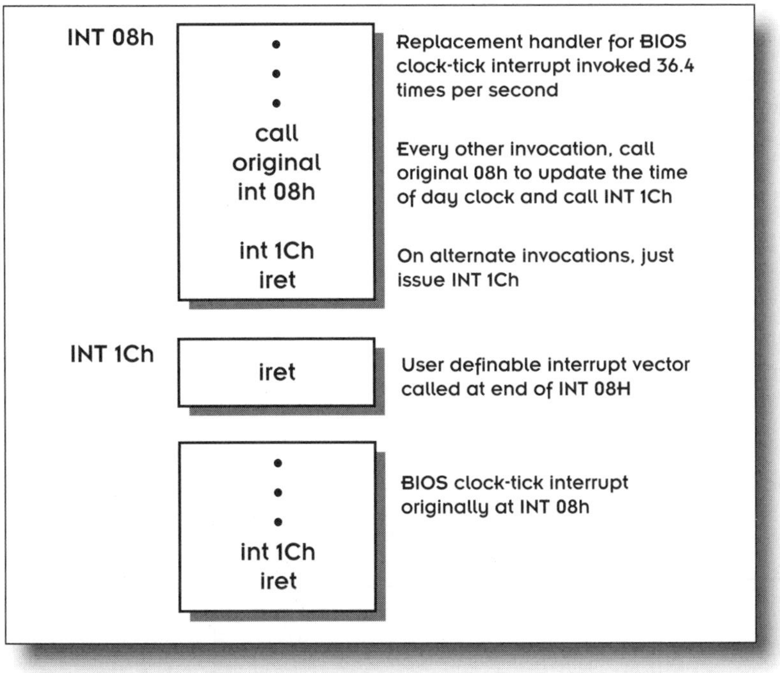

***Figure 12.6** Re-vectored interrupt.*

branching to the original interrupt 08 hex code using a far call. In essence, that mimics the behavior of an INT instruction.

The file TIMER.ASM includes an assembly-language function callable from C or C++ to manage the clock-tick interrupt rate and its associated interrupts:

```
; TIMER.ASM
;
; Copyright (c) 1993-1994 Ted Gruber Software.  All rights reserved.
;
; This is a C or C++-callable function illustrating a simple way to
; change the BIOS clock-tick interrupt rate under DOS while maintaining
; an accurate time of day clock value.
;
; To accelerate the clock-tick interrupt rate, use
;
;         set_rate(factor);
;
; where "factor" represents the acceleration factor for the clock-tick
; rate. For example, to quadruple the clock-tick rate, specify a factor
; of 4. If the clock-tick rate is already accelerated, nothing further
; happens.
;
; To revert to the normal clock-tick rate, use
;
;         set_rate(0);
;
; If the clock is already running at its normal rate, nothing happens.
; You must restore the normal clock-tick rate before your program exits
; to DOS.
;
; This function is written for the medium or large memory models.
; It can be modified to support the small memory model if you do the
; following:
;
;    - Change the segment name from "time_TEXT" to "_TEXT".
;    - Change the "far" reference in the PROC declaration to "near".
;    - Change the arg1 definition from "[bp+6]" to "[bp+4]".
;
;***********************************************************************

rate_TEXT SEGMENT byte public 'CODE'
          ASSUME  cs:rate_TEXT

_set_rate PROC    far
          PUBLIC  _set_rate

arg1      equu    [bp+6]         ; address of the function's argument
chan_0    equ     40h            ; port address for channel 0
cmd_reg   equ     43h            ; port address for command register
fp        equ     <far ptr>      ; shorthand for far pointer override
```

```
          push    bp              ; save caller's BP register
          mov     bp,sp           ; make BP point to argument list

          mov     dx,arg1         ; DX = clock acceleration factor
          cmp     dx,1            ; restore clock to normal rate?
          jle     regular         ; yes, go do it

accel:    cmp     cs:speed,1      ; clock already accelerated?
          jg      return          ; yes, nothing more to do
          mov     cs:speed,dx     ; set speed indicator to accelerated
          mov     cs:countdown,dx ; initialize the timer countdown value
          call    fast            ; accelerate clock tick interrupt rate
          jmp     short return    ; and return to the caller

regular:  cmp     cs:speed,1      ; clock already at normal speed?
          jle     return          ; yes, nothing to do
          mov     cs:speed,dx     ; set speed indicator to normal
          call    normal          ; restore clock to 18.2 ticks/second

return:   xor     ax,ax           ; set function return value to zero
          pop     bp              ; restore caller's BP register
          ret                     ; return to the caller

countdown dw      ?               ; clock-tick interrupt countdown value
old_int08 dd      ?               ; address of original INT 08h handler
speed     dw      0               ; clock acceleration factor

_set_rate ENDP

;----------------------------------------------------------------------

fastclock PROC    far             ; interrupt handler to replace INT 08h

          push    ax              ; save altered registers

          dec     cs:countdown    ; decrement the countdown value
          jz      blastoff        ; update time when countdown expires
          int     1Ch             ; otherwise just call interrupt 1Ch
          mov     al,20h
          out     20h,al          ; re-enable lower-level interrupts
          pop     ax              ; restore altered registers
          iret                    ; go back where we came from

blastoff: pushf                   ; simulate next call as an interrupt
          call    cs:[old_int08]; call original clock tick interrupt
          mov     ax,cs:speed     ; AX = clock acceleration factor
          mov     cs:countdown,ax; reset countdown value
          mov     al,20h
          out     20h,al          ; re-enable lower-level interrupts
          pop     ax              ; restore altered registers
          iret                    ; go back where we came from

fastclock ENDP
```

```
;--------------------------------------------------------------------------

fast      PROC    near           ; accelerate the clock by a factor of DX

          cli                    ; disable interrupts
          xor     ax,ax          ; zero AX
          mov     es,ax          ; point ES to start of memory

          mov     bx,08h*4       ; interrupt vector 08h
          mov     ax,es:[bx]     ; put the interrupt vector offset in AX
          mov     cx,es:[bx+2]   ; put the interrupt vector segment in CX
          lea     bx,old_int08   ; where to save original INT 08h handler
          mov     cs:[bx],ax     ; save original INT 08h offset
          mov     cs:[bx+2],cx   ; save original INT 08h segment

          mov     bx,08h*4       ; interrupt vector 08h
          lea     ax,fastclock   ; CS:AX = addr of accelerated clock handler
          mov     es:[bx],ax
          mov     es:[bx+2],cs   ; point INT 08h to the new handler

          mov     al,36h         ; initialize channel 0 for mode 3
          out     cmd_reg,al     ; send above byte to command register

          mov     bx,dx          ; BX = the clock acceleration factor
          mov     dx,1
          xor     ax,ax          ; DX:AX = 65,536
          div     bx             ; AX = counter for desired acceleration
          out     chan_0,al      ; send low byte of counter to channel 0
          mov     al,ah          ; put high byte of counter in AL
          out     chan_0,al      ; send high byte

          sti                    ; re-enable interrupts
          ret

fast      ENDP

;--------------------------------------------------------------------------

normal    PROC    near           ; reset clock to 18.2 ticks/second

          cli                    ; disable interrupts
          mov     al,36h         ; initialize channel 0 for mode 3
          out     cmd_reg,al     ; send above byte to command register

          xor     ax,ax          ; counter for 18.2 ticks per second
          mov     es,ax          ; point ES to start of memory

          out     chan_0,al      ; send low byte of counter to channel 0
          out     chan_0,al      ; send high byte (same as low byte)

          lea     bx,old_int08   ; address of original INT 08h handler
          mov     ax,cs:[bx]     ; AX = original INT 08h offset
          mov     cx,cs:[bx+2]   ; CX = original INT 08h segment
          mov     bx,08h*4       ; interrupt vector 08h
```

```
        mov     es:[bx],ax
        mov     es:[bx+2],cx   ; restore original INT 08h vector

        sti                    ; re-enable interrupts
        ret

normal  ENDP

;-----------------------------------------------------------------------

rate_TEXT ENDS
        END
```

Now the time of day clock is still updated 18.2 times per second, but interrupt 1C occurs eight times per clock tick. The following code re-vectors interrupt 1C hex to increment our own internal timer, which is available to our program as a global variable.

```
#include <dos.h>
void  interrupt increment_timer(void);
void  interrupt (*oldhandler) (void);
long game_time;
void main()
{
   unsigned long time1, time2;

   /* get the current interrupt vector for 0X1C */
   oldhandler = _dos_getvect(0x1C);

   /* re-vector the interrupt to myu function */
   _dos_setvect(0x1C,increment_timer);

   /* initialize the global */
   game_time = 0;

   /* speed up the clock rate */
   set_rate(8);

   /*** do the game ***/

   /* slow down the clock rate to normal */
   set_rate(0);

   /* put the interrupt back the way it was */
   _dos_setvect(0x1C,oldhandler);

   exit(0);
}

/******************************************************************/
void interrupt increment_timer()
```

```
{
   game_time++;
}
```

Now we have a global value, **game_time**, which is incrementing nice and fast. We can determine the elapsed time down to a fine resolution and gauge our animation accordingly. This accuracy is convenient for our game, but there are still some other considerations to watch for. Disk drive accesses are often dependent on the clock interrupts, so you don't want to read or write a file while the clock rate is accelerated. Be sure to return the clock rate to normal before each disk access. Also, some music and sound drivers speed up the clock interrupt. You'll want to coordinate your clock speed with whatever the music or sound library expects. Eight times the normal clock speed is pretty standard for games, but if you're not sure, check the documentation for your music and sound drivers.

Taking Control

We now have our sprites and objects right where we want them. Sprites are stored in sprite structures, along with the information that applies to them: bitmap data, width, height, and so on. sprite structures are stored in a sprite array and also may be referred to by arrays with convenient logical names like *tomstand.* Objects are stored in object structures, along with information needed to describe fully describe them: position, image, action function, and so on. These we will keep in a linked list so we can conveniently keep track of a variable number of them and process each object each frame. All the sprites and objects are properly declared and allocated. We have also taken control of the clock interrupt and we are prepared to time our sprite motion with proper precision. Things seem to be well under control. It's time to make our sprites move.

Chapter 13

Combining action functions with your creativity is a sure-fire way to create a game with smooth animation, interesting characters, and challenging enemies.

Unlocking the Mysteries of Sprite Animation

Now that you know how to store sprites and display them on the screen, let's see if we can make their movements more interesting. In this chapter, we'll see how action functions are executed for each animation frame. The action function looks at the forces applied to the sprite and adjusts the sprite's position accordingly. The action function is also where sprite-related decisions are made, such as spawning new objects or changing the score or energy level.

The most common forces applied to sprites are background tile attributes, user interaction (keyboard input), interaction with other objects (collision detection), gravity, momentum, friction, and artificial intelligence. To understand how these forces interact, you will first need a thorough understanding of the physics of motion. Get out your high-school physics text and look up the formulas for velocity, acceleration, friction, and momentum. (Just kidding—you don't need to do that!) For the purpose of sprite animation, we will act not as scientists, but as artists. We'll subscribe to the philosophy "feels right is good enough." Most of our sprite motion is accomplished through trial and error. The ideas in this chapter will get you off to a good start on sprite motion, but are by no means the final word on the subject. Your own imagination is what will make your sprites come to life.

The Secret of Sprite Motion: The Action Functions

The sprite action functions are the foundation of sprite motion. All the action functions are found in the source code file, ACTION.C. We put them all in one source code file because they are all declared **near**. The **near** declaration allows us to address these functions as integer fields in the sprite structures. (Recall from Chapter 12 that the sprite action function has an integer address that is a member of the object structure.) To support the action functions, we'll also be using a second source file named MOTION.C. This file contains functions that perform collision detection operations and determine how sprites can move. The action functions frequently call some of the functions in MOTION.C when they need to make decisions about sprite motion.

The functions in ACTION.C are listed in Table 13.1 and the functions in MOTION.C are listed in Table 13.2.

Table 13.1 *Functions Used in ACTION.C*

Function	**Description**
bullet_go()	Bullet action
enemy_hopper_go()	Grasshopper action
enemy_scorpion_go()	Scorpion action
floating_points_go()	Floating score action
kill_bullet()	Removes a bullet when it is no longer needed
kill_enemy()	Removes an enemy after it has died
kill_object()	Removes any object from a linked list
launch_bullet()	Spawns a bullet object
launch_enemy()	Spawns an enemy object
launch_floating_points()	Spawns a floating-score object
player_begin_fall()	Begins falling
player_begin_jump()	Begins jumping

continued

Table 13.1 Functions Used in ACTION.C (Continued)

Function	Description
player_begin_kick()	Begins kicking
player_begin_shoot()	Begins shooting
player_fall()	Falling action
player_jump()	Jumping action
player_kick()	Kicking action
player_run()	Running action
player_shoot()	Shooting action
player_stand()	Standing action
put_score()	Calculates the position of the scoreboard
update_score()	Changes the score

Table 13.2 Functions Used in MOTION.C

Function	Description
can_move_down()	Checks if the adjacent tile is solid on top
can_move_left()	Checks if the adjacent tile is solid on the right
can_move_right()	Checks if the adjacent tile is solid on the left
can_move_up()	Checks if the adjacent tile is solid on the bottom
collision_detection()	Checks if two objects intersect
how_far_left()	Checks to see how far we can move left
how_far_right()	Checks to see how far we can move right
how_far_up()	Checks to see how far we can move up
how_far_down()	Checks to see how far we can move down
test_bit()	Tests a tile attribute

Tommy's Tip

Adding Your Own Action Funtions

To extend the *Tommy's Adventures* game, the first thing you'll probably want to do is add your own sprite animation or change the animation of one of the exising sprites. This is easy to do by adding new action functions or modifying existing ones. Be sure to add the action function to the ACTION.C source code file so it can be addressed as a **near** function.

A Closer Look at Action Functions

Although an object, such as a bullet, may have several action functions, only one action function will be called for each frame of animation. In general, the action function performs the following tasks:

- *Calculates the object's position.* The position will change according to the forces applied to the object, such as user interaction, artificial intelligence, interaction with the background, and interaction with other sprites.
- *Determines the object's sprite.* If a character has a six-stage walk, the action function decides which stage we are on currently on, and points the object structure to the right sprite structure.
- *Collision detection.* This function determines if the object runs into anything during the frame. If so, the action function determines what should be done.
- *Spawns new objects and kills off old ones.* If a sprite performs an action, such as firing a bullet, the action function must spawn a new object during the frame—in this case, a bullet. This is accomplished by calling a function to create the new object. If an object is killed, a function must also be called to remove the object from the linked list and free the allocated memory.
- *Chooses the action function for the next frame.* If an object gets to a transition stage, such as reaching the end of a ledge, a new action function will be assigned to the object, which will be executed during the next animation frame.

Examining ACTION.C

Let's look at the complete listing for ACTION.C.

```
/******************************************************************\
*  action.c -- Tommy game action functions source code             *
*  copyright 1994 Diana Gruber                                     *
*  compile using large model, link with Fastgraph (tm)             *
\******************************************************************/

void near bullet_go(OBJp objp)
{
   int min_x,max_x;
   register int i;

   /* increment the bullet's horizontal position */
   objp->x += objp->xspeed;
```

```
   /* collision detection */
   for (i = 0; i < nenemies; i++)
   {
      if (enemy[i]->frame < 6 && objp->x>enemy[i]->x
          && objp->x<enemy[i]->x+enemy[i]->sprite->width
          && objp->y<enemy[i]->y
          && objp->y>enemy[i]->y-enemy[i]->sprite->height)
      {
         launch_floating_points(enemy[i]);
         enemy[i]->frame = 6;
         objp->action = kill_bullet;
      }
   }

   /* check if the bullet has moved off the screen */
   max_x = (tile_orgx + objp->tile_xmax) * 16;
   min_x = (tile_orgx + objp->tile_xmin) * 16;

   /* if it has moved off the screen, kill it by setting the action
      function to kill for the next frame */

   if (objp->x > max_x || objp->x < min_x)
      objp->action = kill_bullet;

   if (objp->direction == RIGHT && !can_move_right(objp))
      objp->action = kill_bullet;
   else if (objp->direction == LEFT && !can_move_left(objp))
      objp->action = kill_bullet;
}
/*****************************************************************/
void near enemy_hopper_go(OBJp objp)
{
   if (objp->frame > 4)   /* is this enemy dying? */
   {
      /* after 100 frames, kill this enemy off */
      objp->frame++;
      if (objp->frame > 100)
         objp->action = kill_enemy;
      objp->sprite = enemy_sprite[5];

      /* enemy can fall while dying */
      objp->yspeed = how_far_down(objp,12);
      if (objp->yspeed > 0)
         objp->y += objp->yspeed;

      /* no point in doing anything else while dying */
      return;
   }

   /* this enemy moves every 12 clock ticks */
   objp->time += delta_time;
   if (objp->time < 12)
      return;
```

```
   else
      objp->time = 0;

   objp->yspeed = how_far_down(objp,12);    /* falling? */
   if (objp->yspeed > 0)
      objp->y += objp->yspeed;
   else
   {
      /* increment the object's horizontal position */
      if (objp->direction == LEFT)
      {
         if (!can_move_left(objp))
         {
            objp->direction = RIGHT;
            objp->xspeed = 12;
         }
      }
      else if (objp->direction == RIGHT)
      {
         if (!can_move_right(objp))
         {
            objp->direction = LEFT;
            objp->xspeed = -12;
         }
      }
      objp->x += objp->xspeed;
   }
   objp->frame = 7-objp->frame;           /* increment the frame */
   objp->sprite = enemy_sprite[objp->frame];

   /* if the player hasn't been hit recently, can we hit him now? */
   if (!player_blink)
   {
      if (collision_detection(objp, player) && !kicking)
      {
         player_blink = TRUE;             /* make the player blink */

         nhits++;                         /* seven hits per life */
         if (nhits > 7)
         {
            nlives--;
            if (nlives == 0)              /* three lives per game */
               nlives = 3;
            nhits = 0;
         }

         /* update the action function for the score */
         score->action = update_score;
      }
   }
}
/**********************************************************************/
void near enemy_scorpion_go(OBJp objp)
```

```
{
   if (objp->frame > 1)                    /* is this enemy is dying? */
   {
      objp->frame++;

      /* after 100 frames, kill this enemy off */
      if (objp->frame > 100)
         objp->action = kill_enemy;

      objp->sprite = enemy_sprite[2];

      /* enemy can fall while dying */
      objp->yspeed = how_far_down(objp,12);
      if (objp->yspeed > 0)
         objp->y += objp->yspeed;

      /* no point in doing anything else while dying */
      return;
   }

   /* this enemy moves every 16 clock ticks */
   objp->time += delta_time;
   if (objp->time < 16)
      return;
   else
      objp->time = 0;

   objp->yspeed = how_far_down(objp,12);  /* falling? */
   if (objp->yspeed > 0)
      objp->y += objp->yspeed;
   else
   {
      /* increment the object's horizontal position */
      if (objp->direction == LEFT)
      {
         if (!can_move_left(objp))
         {
            objp->direction = RIGHT;
            objp->xspeed = 12;
         }
      }
      else if (objp->direction == RIGHT)
      {
         if (!can_move_right(objp))
         {
            objp->direction = LEFT;
            objp->xspeed = -12;
         }
      }
      objp->x += objp->xspeed;
   }
   objp->frame = 1-objp->frame;           /* increment frame */
   objp->sprite = enemy_sprite[objp->frame];
```

```
   /* if the player hasn't been hit recently, can we hit him now? */
   if (!player_blink)
   {
      if (collision_detection(objp, player) && !kicking)
      {
         player_blink = TRUE;            /* make the player blink */
         /* seven hits per life */
         nhits++;                        /* seven hits per life */
         if (nhits > 7)
         {
            nlives--;
            if (nlives == 0)             /* three lives per game */
               nlives = 3;
            nhits = 0;
         }

         /* update the scoreboard */
         score->action = update_score;
      }
   }
}
/********************************************************************/
void near floating_points_go(OBJp objp)
{
   /* update the vertical position */
   objp->y += objp->yspeed;

   /* score goes up 75 frames, then disappears */
   objp->frame++;
   if (objp->frame > 75)
      objp->action = kill_object;
}
/********************************************************************/
void near kill_bullet(OBJp objp)
{
   /* decrement the bullet count and kill the bullet */
   nbullets--;
   kill_object(objp);
}
/********************************************************************/
void near kill_enemy(OBJp objp)
{
   register int i;
   int enemy_no;

   for (i = 0; i < nenemies; i++)         /* which enemy is it? */
   {
      if (enemy[i] == objp)
      {
         enemy_no = i;
         break;
      }
   }
   nenemies--;                            /* decrement the enemy count */
```

```
   for (i = enemy_no; i < nenemies; i++) /* update the array */
      enemy[i] = enemy[i+1];
   enemy[nenemies] = (OBJp)NULL;         /* last enemy points to NULL */
   kill_object(objp);                    /* remove node from list */
   player_score += 100;                  /* increment the score */
   score->action = update_score;
}
/******************************************************************/
void near kill_object(OBJp objp)         /* remove node from list */
{
   OBJp node;

   node = objp;
   if (node == bottom_node)              /* remove bottom node */
   {
      bottom_node = node->next;
      if (bottom_node != (OBJp) NULL)
         bottom_node->prev = (OBJp)NULL;
   }
   else if (node == top_node)            /* remove top node */
   {
      top_node = node->prev;
      top_node->next = (OBJp)NULL;
   }
   else                                  /* remove middle node */
   {
      node->prev->next = node->next;
      node->next->prev = node->prev;
   }
   free(node);
}
/******************************************************************/
void near launch_bullet()                /* start a new bullet */
{
   OBJp node;

   if (nbullets > 9) return;             /* max 9 bullets */

   node = (OBJp)malloc(sizeof(OBJ)+3);   /* allocate space */
   if (node == (OBJp)NULL) return;

   if (player->direction == RIGHT)       /* assign values */
   {
      node->direction = RIGHT;
      node->xspeed = 13;
      if (player->sprite == tom_jump[2])  /* jumping */
      {
         node->x = player->x+player->sprite->xoffset+46-node->xspeed;
         node->y = player->y-25;
      }
      else if (player->sprite == tom_jump[3]) /* falling */
      {
         node->x = player->x+player->sprite->xoffset+46-node->xspeed;
```

```
         node->y = player->y-25;
      }
      else if (fg_kbtest(KB_RIGHT))      /* running */
      {
         node->x = player->x+player->sprite->xoffset+40-node->xspeed;
         node->y = player->y-26;
      }
      else                               /* standing */
      {
         node->x = player->x+player->sprite->xoffset+40-node->xspeed;
         node->y = player->y-28;
      }
   }
   else
   {
      node->direction = LEFT;
      node->xspeed = -13;
      node->x = player->x+player->sprite->xoffset-node->xspeed-5;
      if (player->sprite == tom_jump[2])      /* jumping */
         node->y = player->y-25;
      else if (player->sprite == tom_jump[3]) /* falling */
         node->y = player->y-25;
      else if (fg_kbtest(KB_LEFT))           /* running */
         node->y = player->y-26;
      else                                   /* standing */
         node->y = player->y-28;
   }
   node->yspeed    = 0;
   node->tile_xmin = 1;
   node->tile_xmax = 21;
   node->tile_ymin = 0;
   node->tile_ymax = 14;
   node->sprite = tom_shoot[6];             /* assign the sprite */

   node->action = bullet_go;                /* assign action function */

   /* insert the new object at the top of the linked list */
   if (bottom_node == (OBJp)NULL )
   {
      bottom_node = node;
      node->prev = (OBJp)NULL;
   }
   else
   {
      node->prev = top_node;
      node->prev->next = node;
   }
   top_node = node;
   node->next = (OBJp)NULL;

   nbullets++;                              /* increment bullet count */
}
/**********************************************************************/
void near launch_enemy(int x, int y, int type)  /* start a new enemy */
```

```
{
   OBJp node;

   node = (OBJp)malloc(sizeof(OBJ));          /* allocate space */
   if (node == (OBJp)NULL) return;

   node->direction = RIGHT;                   /* assign values */
   node->x = x;
   node->y = y;
   node->xspeed = 8;
   node->yspeed = 0;
   node->tile_xmin = 1;
   node->tile_xmax = 21;
   node->tile_ymin = 0;
   node->tile_ymax = 14;
   node->time = 0;

   /* assign the sprite and action function */
   if (type == 0)
   {
      node->frame = 0;
      node->action = enemy_scorpion_go;
   }
   else
   {
      node->frame = 3;
      node->action = enemy_hopper_go;
   }
   node->sprite = enemy_sprite[node->frame];

   /* insert the new object at the top of the linked list */
   if (bottom_node == (OBJp)NULL )
   {
      bottom_node = node;
      node->prev = (OBJp)NULL;
   }
   else
   {
      node->prev = top_node;
      node->prev->next = node;
   }
   top_node = node;
   node->next = (OBJp)NULL;

   enemy[nenemies] = node;                    /* update enemy array */
   nenemies++;                                /* increment enemy counter */
}
/****************************************************************/
void near launch_floating_points(OBJp objp)
{
   OBJp node;

   node = (OBJp)malloc(sizeof(OBJ)+3);        /* allocate space */
   if (node == (OBJp)NULL) return;
```

```
   node->direction = RIGHT;                   /* assign values */
   node->xspeed = 0;
   node->yspeed = -1;
   node->x = objp->x+16;
   node->y = objp->y-8;
   node->frame = 0;
   node->tile_xmin = 1;
   node->tile_xmax = 21;
   node->tile_ymin = 0;
   node->tile_ymax = 14;
   node->sprite = tom_score[2];               /* assign the sprite */
   node->action = floating_points_go;         /* assign action function */

   /* insert the new object at the top of the linked list */
   if (bottom_node == (OBJp)NULL )
   {
      bottom_node = node;
      node->prev = (OBJp)NULL;
   }
   else
   {
      node->prev = top_node;
      node->prev->next = node;
   }
   top_node = node;
   node->next = (OBJp)NULL;
}
/******************************************************************/
void near player_begin_fall(OBJp objp)
{
   /* called once at the start of a fall */

   objp->yspeed = 1;                          /* initialize variables */
   vertical_thrust = 0;
   shoot_time = 0;

   /* any thrust from the arrow keys? */
   if (fg_kbtest(KB_LEFT) || fg_kbtest(KB_RIGHT))
      forward_thrust = 100;
   else
      forward_thrust = 0;

   if (objp->direction == LEFT)
      tom_jump[3]->xoffset = -10;
   else
      tom_jump[3]->xoffset = -0;

   if (fg_kbtest(KB_ALT))                     /* shooting while falling */
      objp->frame = 3;
   else
      objp->frame = 1;

   objp->sprite = tom_jump[objp->frame];      /* assign the sprite */
```

```
   objp->action = player_fall;             /* assign action function */
}
/**********************************************************************/
void near player_begin_jump(OBJp objp)
{
   /* called once at the start of a jump */

   objp->yspeed = -15;                     /* initialize variables */
   objp->frame = 0;
   shoot_time = 0;

   if (fg_kbtest(KB_LEFT) || fg_kbtest(KB_RIGHT)) /* walking? */
      forward_thrust = 50;
   else
      forward_thrust = 0;

   if (objp->direction == LEFT)
      tom_jump[3]->xoffset = 25;
   else
      tom_jump[3]->xoffset = 0;

   objp->sprite = tom_jump[objp->frame];   /* assign sprite */
   objp->action = player_jump;             /* assign action function */
}
/**********************************************************************/
void near player_begin_kick(OBJp objp)
{
   /*  called once at the start of a kick */

   int i;

   kicking = TRUE;                         /* initialize variables */
   objp->time = 0;
   nkicks = 0;

   /* is this a left (backward) or a right (forward) kick? */
   if (objp->direction == LEFT)
   {
      objp->frame = 0;
      kick_frame = 3;
      kick_basey = objp->y;
      objp->sprite = tom_kick[objp->frame]; /* assign sprite */

      /* back him up a little if needed */
      player->x += 36;
      for (i = 0; i < 36; i++)
      if (can_move_left(player))
         player->x--;
   }
   else
   {
      objp->frame = 6;
      kick_frame = 7;
```

```
      kick_basey = objp->y;
      objp->sprite = tom_kick[objp->frame]; /* assign sprite */

      /* back him up a little if needed */
      player->x -= 24;
      for (i = 0; i < 24; i++)
      if (can_move_right(player))
         player->x++;
   }
   objp->action = player_kick;             /* assign action function */
}
/****************************************************************/
void near player_begin_shoot(OBJp objp)
{
   /* called once at the start of shooting */

   register int i;

   objp->frame = 0;                        /* initialize variables */
   objp->time = 0;
   nshots = 0;

   if (objp->direction == RIGHT)
   {
      tom_shoot[0]->xoffset = 2;
      tom_shoot[1]->xoffset = 2;
      tom_shoot[2]->xoffset = 2;

      /* back him up a little if needed */
      if (fg_kbtest(KB_RIGHT))             /* running while shooting? */
      {
         objp->sprite = tom_shoot[3];
         player->x -= 24;
         for (i = 0; i < 24; i++)
         if (can_move_right(player))
            player->x++;
      }
      else
         objp->sprite = tom_shoot[0];      /* assign sprite */
   }
   else
   {
      tom_shoot[0]->xoffset = -1;
      tom_shoot[1]->xoffset = -20;
      tom_shoot[2]->xoffset = -15;
      if (fg_kbtest(KB_LEFT))              /* running while shooting? */
         objp->sprite = tom_shoot[3];      /* assign sprite */
      else
         objp->sprite = tom_shoot[0];
   }
   objp->action = player_shoot;            /* assign action function */
}
/****************************************************************/
void near player_fall(OBJp objp)
```

```
{
   int tile_x,tile_y;

   /* less than 5 clock ticks? Then skip this function */
   objp->time += delta_time;
   shoot_time += delta_time;
   if (objp->time > 5)
      objp->time = 0;
   else
      return;

   if (fg_kbtest(KB_ALT))                    /* shooting while falling? */
   {
      objp->frame = 3;

      /* start a new bullet every 15 clock ticks */
      if (shoot_time > 15)
      {
         launch_bullet();
         shoot_time = 0;
      }
   }
   else
      objp->frame = 1;

   objp->sprite = tom_jump[objp->frame];    /* assign sprite */

   /* increase the rate of speed of the fall */
   if (objp->yspeed < 15)
      objp->yspeed += (vertical_thrust++);

   /* vertical position is based on yspeed */
   objp->y += objp->yspeed;

   /* check the arrow keys, starting with left arrow */
   if (objp->direction == LEFT)
   {
      /* horizontal speed */
      if (fg_kbtest(KB_LEFT))
      {
         objp->xspeed = -1;
         if (forward_thrust > 50)
            objp->xspeed *= 3;
         else if (forward_thrust > 0)
            objp->xspeed *= 2;
      }
      else
         objp->xspeed = 0;

      /* check for walls, etc. */
      objp->xspeed = -how_far_left(objp,-objp->xspeed);

      /* increment the x position according to the speed */
      objp->x += objp->xspeed;
```

```
      /* Are we still on visible screen? If not, scroll */
      tile_x = objp->x/16 - tile_orgx;
      if (tile_x < objp->tile_xmin)
         scroll_left(-objp->xspeed);
   }

   /* same thing for right arrow key */
   else
   {
      if (fg_kbtest(KB_RIGHT))
      {
         objp->xspeed = 1;
         if (forward_thrust > 50)
            objp->xspeed *= 3;
         else if (forward_thrust > 0)
            objp->xspeed *= 2;
      }
      else
         objp->xspeed = 0;

      tom_jump[3]->xoffset = 0;
      objp->direction = RIGHT;
      objp->xspeed = how_far_right(objp,objp->xspeed);
      objp->x += objp->xspeed;

      /* are we still on visible screen? If not, scroll */
      tile_x = objp->x/16 - tile_orgx;
      if (tile_x > objp->tile_xmax)
         scroll_right(objp->xspeed);
   }

   /* decrement the forward thrust */
   forward_thrust--;

   /* are we close to the bottom of the screen? If so, scroll */
   tile_y = objp->y/16 - tile_orgy;
   if (tile_y > objp->tile_ymax)
      scroll_down(objp->yspeed);

   /* have we hit a solid tile yet? If so, stop falling */
   if (!can_move_down(objp))
   {
      objp->y = ((objp->y+1)/16) * 16; /* land on top of tile */
      objp->yspeed = 0;
      objp->action = player_stand;
   }
}
/**********************************************************************/
void near player_jump(OBJp objp)
{
   int tile_x,tile_y;
   register int i;
```

```
/* increment the timer, if it is less than 5, skip it */
objp->time += delta_time;
shoot_time += delta_time;
if (objp->time > 5L)
   objp->time = 0;
else
   return;

/* check for arrow keys, left arrow first */
if (fg_kbtest(KB_LEFT))
{
   objp->direction = LEFT;
   objp->xspeed = -3;

   /* forward thrust gives a little boost at start of jump */
   if (forward_thrust > 30)
      objp->xspeed *= 4;
   else if (forward_thrust > 0)
      objp->xspeed *= 2;

   /* move left, checking for walls, etc. */
   objp->xspeed = -how_far_left(objp,-objp->xspeed);
   objp->x += objp->xspeed;

   /* need to scroll the screen left? */
   tile_x = objp->x/16 - tile_orgx;
   if (tile_x < objp->tile_xmin)
      scroll_left(-objp->xspeed);
}

/* same for right arrow key */
else if (fg_kbtest(KB_RIGHT))
{
   objp->xspeed = 3;
   if (forward_thrust > 50)
      objp->xspeed *= 4;
   else if (forward_thrust > 0)
      objp->xspeed *= 2;
   objp->direction = RIGHT;
   objp->xspeed = how_far_right(objp,objp->xspeed);

   tile_x = objp->x/16 - tile_orgx;
   if (tile_x > objp->tile_xmax)
      scroll_right(objp->xspeed);
   objp->x += objp->xspeed;
}

/* decrement forward thrust */
forward_thrust--;

/* additional upward thrust if you hold down the Ctrl key */
if (fg_kbtest(KB_CTRL))
   objp->yspeed++;
```

```
    else
       objp->yspeed/=4;

    /* check bumping head on ceiling */
    objp->yspeed = how_far_up(objp,objp->yspeed);
    objp->y += objp->yspeed;

    /* check if we are shooting */
    if (fg_kbtest(KB_ALT))
    {
       /* Tommy's jumping and shooting frame */
       objp->frame = 2;

       /* space the bullets 15 clock ticks apart */
       if (shoot_time > 15)
       {
          launch_bullet();
          shoot_time = 0;
       }
    }

    /* not shooting, just use Tommy jumping frame */
    else
       objp->frame = 0;

    /* set sprite to the correct frame */
    objp->sprite = tom_jump[objp->frame];

    /* Too close to top of screen? Scroll the screen up. */
    tile_y = objp->y/16 - tile_orgy;
    if (tile_y < objp->tile_ymin)
       scroll_up(-objp->yspeed);

    /* Reached top of arc? Tommy start descent. */
    if (objp->yspeed >= 0)
       objp->action = player_begin_fall;
}
/******************************************************************/
void near player_kick(OBJp objp)
{
   register int i;
   int tile_x,tile_y;

   /* collision detection -- did we kick an enemy? */
   for (i = 0; i < nenemies; i++)
   {
      /* frame 6 is the enemy hit frame. enemies are only hit once */
      if (enemy[i]->frame < 6 && collision_detection (objp,enemy[i]))
      {
         /* if you are kicking left, you can only hit enemy
            left of you */

         if (objp->direction == LEFT && enemy[i]->x < objp->x)
         {
```

```
         launch_floating_points(enemy[i]);
         enemy[i]->frame = 6;
      }

      /* likewise, right kicks kill enemies on the right */
      else if (objp->direction == RIGHT && enemy[i]->x > objp->x)
      {
         launch_floating_points(enemy[i]);
         enemy[i]->frame = 6;
      }
   }
}

/* increment the frame every 10 clock ticks */
objp->time += delta_time;
if (objp->time > 10)
{
   /* case of the left (backwards) kick */
   if (objp->direction == LEFT)
   {
      /* where are we in this kick? */
      if (objp->frame == kick_frame && nkicks < 4
          && fg_kbtest(KB_SPACE))
      {
          /* keep kicking */
      }

      else
      {
         /* increment the frame */
         objp->frame++;

         /* end of kick */
         if (objp->frame > 5)
         {
            objp->y = kick_basey; /* end kick where you started */
            objp->sprite = tom_stand[0];
            kicking = FALSE;

            /* new action function */
            objp->action = player_stand;
         }

         /* still kicking, set the sprite */
         else
         {
            objp->sprite = tom_kick[objp->frame];

            /* horizontal motion */
            if (can_move_left(objp))
            {
               if (fg_kbtest(KB_LEFT))
                  objp->xspeed = -3;
```

```
            else
               objp->xspeed = -1;

            objp->x += objp->xspeed;

            /* moved past edge of screen? scroll left */
            tile_x = objp->x/16 - tile_orgx;
            if (tile_x < objp->tile_xmin)
               scroll_left(-objp->xspeed);
         }
      }
   }
}

/* case of the right (forward) kick */
else
{
   /* choose frame */
   if (objp->frame == kick_frame && nkicks < 4
       && fg_kbtest(KB_SPACE))
   {
       /* keep kicking */
   }
   else
   {
      objp->frame++;
      if (objp->frame > 9)
      {
         objp->y = kick_basey; /* end kick where you started */
         objp->sprite = tom_stand[0];
         kicking = FALSE;
         objp->action = player_stand;
      }
      else
      {
         if (objp->frame > 8)
         {
            objp->sprite = tom_stand[0];
         }
         else if (objp->frame > 7)
         {
            objp->sprite = tom_kick[6];
         }
         else
            objp->sprite = tom_kick[objp->frame];

         /* horizontal motion */
         if (can_move_right(objp))
         {
            if (fg_kbtest(KB_RIGHT))
               objp->xspeed = 3;
            else
               objp->xspeed = 1;
```

```
               objp->xspeed = how_far_right(objp,objp->xspeed);
               objp->x += objp->xspeed;

               tile_x = objp->x/16 - tile_orgx;
               if (tile_x > objp->tile_xmax)
                  scroll_right(objp->xspeed);

            }
         }
      }
   }

   /* vertical motion */
   if (objp->frame == kick_frame)
   {
      /* put a little vertical bounce in the kick */
      if (objp->y == kick_basey)
      {
         objp->yspeed = -3;

         /* barrier above? */
         objp->yspeed = how_far_up(objp,objp->yspeed);
         objp->y += objp->yspeed;

         /* need to scroll up? */
         tile_y = objp->y/16 - tile_orgy;
         if (tile_y < objp->tile_ymin)
            scroll_up(-objp->yspeed);
      }
      else
      {
         objp->y = kick_basey;
         nkicks++;
      }
   }

   /* falling? */
   if (objp->y == kick_basey && can_move_down(objp))
   {
      kicking = FALSE;
      objp->action = player_begin_fall;
   }

   /* set the timer back to 0 */
   objp->time = 0;
  }
}
/*****************************************************************/
void near player_run(OBJp objp)
{
   int tile_x;

   /* case where the player is facing left */
   if (objp->direction == LEFT)
```

```
   {
      /* gradually increase the speed */
      if (objp->xspeed > -8)
         objp->xspeed--;

      /* change the horizontal position according to the speed */
      if (can_move_left(objp))
      {
         objp->x += objp->xspeed;
         tile_x = objp->x/16 - tile_orgx;

         /* if you have moved out of the visible area, scroll left */
         if (tile_x < objp->tile_xmin)
            scroll_left(-objp->xspeed);
      }
   }

   /* case where the player is facing right */
   else
   {
      if (objp->xspeed < 8)
         objp->xspeed++;

      if (can_move_right(objp))
      {
         objp->x += objp->xspeed;
         tile_x = objp->x/16 - tile_orgx;
         if (tile_x > objp->tile_xmax)
            scroll_right(objp->xspeed);
      }
   }

   /* is it time to increment the the walking stage yet? */
   objp->time += delta_time;
   if (objp->time > 3)
   {
      objp->time = 0;
      objp->frame++;

      /* it's a six-stage walk */
      if (objp->frame > 5) objp->frame = 0;
      objp->sprite = tom_run[objp->frame];
   }

   /* are we pressing any arrow keys? */
   if (fg_kbtest(KB_LEFT))
   {
      /* change the direction if necessary */
      if (objp->direction == RIGHT)
      {
         /* slow down speed in the middle of a direction change */
         objp->xspeed = 0;
         objp->direction = LEFT;
      }
```

```
    }
    else if (fg_kbtest(KB_RIGHT))
    {
       if (objp->direction == LEFT)
       {
          objp->xspeed = 0;
          objp->direction = RIGHT;
       }
    }

    /* if we aren't pressing any keys, then we aren't walking. Change
       the action function to standing. */

    else
       objp->action = player_stand;

    /* are we falling? */
    if (can_move_down(objp))
       objp->action = player_begin_fall;

    /* or kicking or jumping or shooting? */
    else if (fg_kbtest(KB_SPACE))
       objp->action = player_begin_kick;
    else if (fg_kbtest(KB_CTRL))
       objp->action = player_begin_jump;
    else if (fg_kbtest(KB_ALT))
       objp->action = player_begin_shoot;
}
/******************************************************************/
void near player_shoot(OBJp objp)
{
   register int i;
   unsigned long max_shoottime;
   int tile_x,tile_y;

   objp->time += delta_time;

   /* check for horizontal motion -- arrow keys pressed? */
   if (fg_kbtest(KB_RIGHT))
   {
      /* Changing direction? Start shooting all over. */
      if (objp->direction == LEFT)
      {
         objp->direction = RIGHT;
         objp->action = player_begin_shoot;
      }
      else
      {
         /* spawn bullets more often when walking */
         max_shoottime = 3;
         if (objp->time > max_shoottime)
         {
            if (objp->sprite == tom_shoot[3])
            {
```

```
                objp->sprite = tom_shoot[4];
                launch_bullet();
             }
             else if (objp->sprite == tom_shoot[4])
                objp->sprite = tom_shoot[5];
             else
                objp->sprite = tom_shoot[3];

             /* move forward during walking frames */
             if (can_move_right(objp))
             {
                /* move right, checking for barriers */
                objp->xspeed = how_far_right(objp,8);
                objp->x += objp->xspeed;

                /* need to scroll the screen right? */
                tile_x = objp->x/16 - tile_orgx;
                if (tile_x > objp->tile_xmax)
                   scroll_right(objp->xspeed);
             }
             objp->time = 0;
          }
       }

       if (!fg_kbtest(KB_ALT))                /* done shooting? */
          objp->action = player_run;

       else if (can_move_down(objp))          /* falling? */
       {
          objp->yspeed = how_far_down(objp,5);
          objp->y += objp->yspeed;

          /* Are we close to the bottom of the screen? If so, scroll. */
          tile_y = objp->y/16 - tile_orgy;
          if (tile_y > objp->tile_ymax)
             scroll_down(objp->yspeed);
       }
       else if (fg_kbtest(KB_CTRL))            /* jumping? */
          objp->action = player_begin_jump;
    }

    /* same thing for left arrow key */
    else if (fg_kbtest(KB_LEFT))
    {
       if (objp->direction == RIGHT)
       {
          objp->direction = LEFT;
          objp->action = player_begin_shoot;
       }
       else
       {
          max_shoottime = 3;
          if (objp->time > max_shoottime)
          {
```

```
            if (objp->sprite == tom_shoot[3])
            {
               objp->sprite = tom_shoot[4];
               launch_bullet();
            }
            else if (objp->sprite == tom_shoot[4])
               objp->sprite = tom_shoot[5];
            else
               objp->sprite = tom_shoot[3];

            if (can_move_left(objp))
            {
               objp->xspeed = -8;
               objp->x += objp->xspeed;
               tile_x = objp->x/16 - tile_orgx;
               if (tile_x < objp->tile_xmin)
               scroll_left(-objp->xspeed);
            }
            objp->time = 0;
         }
      }

      if (!fg_kbtest(KB_ALT))               /* done shooting? */
         objp->action = player_run;

      else if (can_move_down(objp))         /* falling? */
      {
         objp->yspeed = how_far_down(objp,5);
         objp->y += objp->yspeed;

         /* are we close to the bottom of the screen? If so, scroll */
         tile_y = objp->y/16 - tile_orgy;
         if (tile_y > objp->tile_ymax)
            scroll_down(objp->yspeed);
      }
      else if (fg_kbtest(KB_CTRL))          /* jumping? */
         objp->action = player_begin_jump;

   }

   /* no arrow keys pressed, standing still */
   else
   {
      max_shoottime = 16;
      if (objp->time > max_shoottime)
      {
         /* pull out gun */
         if (objp->frame == 0)
         {
            objp->frame++;
               objp->sprite = tom_shoot[objp->frame];
         }
         else if (objp->frame == 1)         /* shooting */
         {
```

```
            /* done shooting */
            if (!fg_kbtest(KB_ALT))
               objp->frame++;
            nshots++;

            objp->sprite = tom_shoot[objp->frame];
            launch_bullet();
         }
         else if (objp->frame == 2)         /* recoil */
         {
            if (fg_kbtest(KB_ALT))
               objp->frame = 1; /* shoot again */
            else
            {
               objp->frame++;
               objp->sprite = tom_shoot[2];
            }
         }
         else if (objp->frame == 3)         /* done shooting */
         {
            objp->frame = 0;
            objp->sprite = tom_stand[0];
            objp->action = player_stand;
         }
         objp->time = 0;
      }
      if (!fg_kbtest(KB_ALT))               /* done shooting? */
         objp->action = player_stand;
      else if (can_move_down(objp))         /* falling? */
         objp->action = player_begin_fall;
      else if (fg_kbtest(KB_CTRL))          /* jumping? */
         objp->action = player_begin_jump;
   }

}
/******************************************************************/
void near player_stand(OBJp objp)
{
   /* Standing still. Start walking? */
   if (fg_kbtest(KB_RIGHT))
   {
      objp->frame = 0;
      objp->xspeed = 1;
      objp->direction = RIGHT;
      objp->action = player_run;
   }
   else if (fg_kbtest(KB_LEFT))
   {
      objp->frame = 0;
      objp->xspeed = -1;
      objp->direction = LEFT;
      objp->action = player_run;
   }
```

```
/* start kicking, jumping or shooting? */
else if (fg_kbtest(KB_SPACE))
{
   objp->action = player_begin_kick;
}
else if (fg_kbtest(KB_CTRL))
{
   objp->action = player_begin_jump;
}
else if (fg_kbtest(KB_ALT))
{
   objp->action = player_begin_shoot;
}

/* look down, look up */
else if (fg_kbtest(KB_DOWN))
{
   if (objp->y - tile_orgy*16 > 48)
      scroll_down(1);
}
else if (fg_kbtest(KB_UP))
{
   if (objp->y - tile_orgy*16 < 200)
      scroll_up(1);
}

/* just standing there */
else if (objp->sprite != tom_stand[0] && objp->frame < 7)
{
   objp->frame = 0;
   objp->sprite = tom_stand[objp->frame];
}
else
{
   /* change Tommy's facial expression */
   objp->time += delta_time;
   if (objp->time > max_time)
   {
      if (objp->frame == 0)
      {
         objp->frame = irandom(7,8);
         objp->time = 0;
         objp->sprite = tom_stand[objp->frame-6];

         /* how long we smile or frown is random */
         max_time = (long)irandom(200,400);
      }
      else
      {
         objp->frame = 0;
         objp->time = 0;
         objp->sprite = tom_stand[0];
```

```
            /* how long we stand straight without smiling */
            max_time = (long)irandom(500,1000);

         }
      }
   }
}
/*******************************************************************/
void near put_score(OBJp objp)
{
   /* determine x and y coords based on the screen origin */
   objp->x = tile_orgx*16 + screen_orgx + 2;
   objp->y = tile_orgy*16 + screen_orgy + 43;
}
/*******************************************************************/
void near update_score(OBJp objp)  /* called when score has changed */
{
   char string[128];
   SPRITE *scoremap;
   int y;
   register int i;

   /* Convert the (long) score to a character string.  Assume 10 digits
      is enough */

   ltoa(player_score,string,10);

   /* clear an area in video memory below the tile space where nothing
      else is going on */

   fg_setcolor(0);
   fg_rect(0,319,680,724);

   /* draw the scoreboard in offscreen memory */
   scoremap = tom_score[0];
   fg_move(0,724);
   fg_drwimage(scoremap->bitmap,scoremap->width,scoremap->height);

   /* set the color to black and display the score */
   fg_setcolor(1);
   center_string(string,5,56,720);

   /* the status bar indicates how many times you have been hit */
   y = nhits*3;

   fg_setcolor(14);
   if (nhits == 0)            /* all blue */
   {
      fg_setcolor(18);
      fg_rect(62,67,701,723);
   }
   else if (nhits >= 8)       /* all white */
   {
```

```
      fg_setcolor(14);
      fg_rect(62,67,701,723);
   }
   else
   {                          /* white and blue */
      fg_setcolor(14);
      fg_rect(62,67,701,700+y);
      fg_setcolor(18);
      fg_rect(62,67,700+y,723);
   }

   scoremap = tom_score[1];    /* tommy one-ups */
   for (i = 0; i < nlives; i++)
   {
      fg_move(80+i*10,716);
      fg_drwimage(scoremap->bitmap,scoremap->width,scoremap->height);
   }

   /* do a getimage to put the score in a bitmap in RAM */
   objp->sprite->width = 80+10*nlives;
   fg_move(0,724);
   fg_getimage(objp->sprite->bitmap,
            objp->sprite->width,objp->sprite->height);

   /* update the x and y coords */
   objp->x = tile_orgx*16 + screen_orgx + 2;
   objp->y = tile_orgy*16 + screen_orgy + 43;

   /* assign action function */
   objp->action = put_score;
}
```

Examining MOTION.C

The functions in MOTION.C are often called by the action functions to modify the position of an object, or make decisions about an object's actions. Here is the complete code:

```
/******************************************************************\
*  motion.c -- Tommy game source code file                         *
*  copyright 1994 Diana Gruber                                     *
*  compile using large model, link with Fastgraph (tm)             *
\******************************************************************/

#include "gamedefs.h"
/******************************************************************/
int can_move_down(OBJp objp)
{
   /* can the object fall? */

   int tile_x,tile_y,tile_num;
```

```
   /* test left side */
   tile_x = (objp->x)/16;
   if (tile_x < 0)
      return(FALSE);

   tile_y = (objp->y+1)/16;
   tile_num = (int)background_tile[tile_x+1][tile_y];

   /* are we at the bottom of the map? */
   if (tile_y >= nrows)
      return(FALSE);

   /* is the tile solid on the top? */
   if (test_bit(background_attributes[tile_num],0))
      return(FALSE);

   /* test the right side too */
   tile_x = (objp->x + objp->sprite->bound_width)/16;
   tile_num = (int)background_tile[tile_x-1][tile_y];
   return (!test_bit(background_attributes[tile_num],0));
}
/****************************************************************/
int can_move_left(OBJp objp)
{
   int tile_x,tile_y,tile_num;

   /* test the bottom of the sprite */
   tile_x = (objp->x-1)/16;
   if (tile_x <= 0)
      return(FALSE);
   tile_y = objp->y/16;
   tile_num = (int)background_tile[tile_x][tile_y];

   /* is the tile solid on the right? */
   if (test_bit(background_attributes[tile_num],3))
      return(FALSE);

   /* check the top of the sprite too */
   tile_y = (objp->y - objp->sprite->height)/16;
   tile_num = (int)background_tile[tile_x][tile_y];
   return (!test_bit(background_attributes[tile_num],2));
}
/****************************************************************/
int can_move_right(OBJp objp)
{
   int tile_x,tile_y,tile_num;
   int width;

   tile_x = (objp->x + objp->sprite->bound_width)/16;
   if (tile_x >= ncols-1)
      return(FALSE);

   /* test the bottom of the sprite */
   tile_y = objp->y/16;
```

```
   tile_num = (int)background_tile[tile_x][tile_y];

   /* is the tile solid on the left? */
   if (test_bit(background_attributes[tile_num],2))
      return(FALSE);

   /* check top of sprite too */
   tile_y = (objp->y - objp->sprite->height)/16;
   tile_num = (int)background_tile[tile_x][tile_y];
   return (!test_bit(background_attributes[tile_num],3));
}
/****************************************************************/
int can_move_up(OBJp objp)
{
   int tile_x,tile_y,tile_num;

   tile_x = objp->x/16;      /* test left side */
   tile_y = (objp->y-objp->sprite->height-1)/16;
   if (tile_y < 0)           /* test top of map */
      return(FALSE);

   tile_num = (int)background_tile[tile_x][tile_y];

   /* is the tile solid on the bottom? */
   if (test_bit(background_attributes[tile_num],1))
      return(FALSE);

   /* test the right side too */
   tile_x = (objp->x + objp->sprite->width)/16;
   tile_num = (int)background_tile[tile_x][tile_y];

   return (!test_bit(background_attributes[tile_num],1));
}
/****************************************************************/
int collision_detection (OBJp objp1,OBJp objp2)
{
   int xmin1,xmax1,xmin2,xmax2;
   int ymin1,ymax1,ymin2,ymax2;

   /* x coordinates of object 1 */
   xmin1 = objp1->x+objp1->sprite->xoffset;
   xmax1 = xmin1+objp1->sprite->width;

   /* x coordinates of object 2 */
   xmin2 = objp2->x+objp2->sprite->xoffset;
   xmax2 = xmin2+objp2->sprite->width;

   /* y coordinates of object 1 */
   ymax1 = objp1->y+objp1->sprite->yoffset;
   ymin1 = ymax1-objp1->sprite->height;

   /* y coordinates of object 2 */
   ymax2 = objp2->y+objp2->sprite->yoffset;
   ymin2 = ymax2-objp2->sprite->height;
```

```
   /* object 2 entirely to the left of object 1 */
   if (xmax2 < xmin1) return(FALSE);

   /* object 2 entirely to the right of object 1 */
   if (xmin2 > xmax1) return(FALSE);

   /* object 2 entirely to the below object 1 */
   if (ymax2 < ymin1) return(FALSE);

   /* object 2 entirely to the above object 1 */
   if (ymin2 > ymax1) return(FALSE);

   /* the objects overlap */
   return(TRUE);
}
/******************************************************************/
int how_far_down(OBJp objp,int n)
{
   register int i;
   register int temp;

   temp = objp->y;         /* save the current position */

   /* increment the position until you can't move right any further */
   for (i = 0; i < n; i++)
   {
      objp->y++;
      if (!can_move_down(objp))
      {
          objp->y = temp;
          return(i);
      }
   }
   objp->y = temp;         /* restore the current position */
   return(n);              /* return how far right */
}
/******************************************************************/
int how_far_left(OBJp objp,int n)
{
   register int i;
   register int temp;

   temp = objp->x;        /* save the current position */

   /* increment the position until you can't move left any further */
   for (i = 0; i < n; i++)
   {
      objp->x--;
      if (!can_move_left(objp))
      {
         objp->x = temp;
         return(i);
      }
   }
```

```
   objp->x = temp;       /* restore the current position */
   return(n);            /* return how far left */
}
/****************************************************************/
int how_far_right(OBJp objp,int n)
{
   register int i;
   register int temp;

   temp = objp->x;      /* save the current position */

   /* increment the position until you can't move right any further */
   for (i = 0; i < n; i++)
   {
      objp->x++;
      if (!can_move_right(objp))
      {
         objp->x = temp;
         return(i);
      }
   }

   objp->x = temp;      /* restore the current position */
   return(n);           /* return how far right */
}
/****************************************************************/
int how_far_up(OBJp objp,int n)
{
   register int i;
   register int temp;

   temp = objp->y;      /* save the current position */

   /* increment the position until you can't move right any further */
   for (i = 0; i > n; i--)
   {
      objp->y--;
      if (!can_move_up(objp))
      {
          objp->y = temp;
          return(i);
      }
   }
   objp->y = temp;     /* restore the current position */
   return(n);          /* return how far right */
}

/****************************************************************/

test_bit(char num,int bit)
{
   /* test bit flags, used for tile attributes */
   return((num >> bit) & 1);
}
```

A Simple Action Function

Let's start by looking at a simplified action function to see how it is constructed:

```
void near player_stand(OBJp objp)
{
   if (fg_kbtest(KB_CTRL))
      objp->action = player_start_jump;
}
```

This isn't the actual **player_stand()** function used in ACTION.C. Here we've reduced this function down to its basic components so we can discuss how it works.

Notice that the action function is declared as **void near**. None of the action functions return values and they are all declared **near** to force all of the code to be stored in the same code segment. We do this for two reasons. First, **near** functions will execute a bit faster—in this kind of game every millisecond counts. Since the action functions are executed many times per second, keeping them in near memory makes sense. Second, the near address allows us to store the pointer to this function as an integer field in the object structure. This is important because a sprite's action function will change constantly as it confronts different obstacles. For instance, to execute the proper action function each frame, we let Tommy's object point to it. If the action changes, the object points to a new function.

We don't have a lot of room in a code segment, only 64K, so we must allocate that space carefully. By default, functions may reside in separate code segments and are activated through far calls in the medium and large memory models. We are using the large memory model, so we expect all functions to reside in other code segments unless we explicitly declare them **near**. We will only declare the action functions to be near, so we will have room for as many of them as possible.

Returning to **player_stand()**, notice that only one argument is passed—a pointer to a structure of type **OBJp**. In this case, the object will always be the player. We won't pass a grasshopper or a scorpion to this action function, or any of the other player action functions. That makes things a little easier. Our main player, Tommy, has his own set of action functions which he doesn't share with any of the other objects. Only one of Tommy's action functions will be executed in a given frame.

A Chain of Action Functions

An object's action functions can be thought of in terms of a chain of events. Each time an action function is executed, it is a link in a chain. The next link may be the same action function, or it may be a different one. The current action function determines the next link in the chain.

For example, the **player_stand()** action function will continue to be executed once every frame until a Ctrl keypress is detected. At that point, the **player_stand()** function determines it is time for a change. It decides it is time for Tommy to stop standing and start jumping. Rather than handle the jumping action itself, the **player_stand()** function passes control to another function. It does this by assigning the object's action function pointer to another function. In this case, it tells the object to point to **player_start_jump()**. Subsequently, in the next frame, the **player_stand()** function will not be executed, but the **player_start_jump()** function will. The **player_start_jump()** function will execute for one frame, and then will pass control on to another function, the **player_jump()** function. That function, in turn, will execute for a while and then pass control on to something else, most likely the **player_start_fall()** function. Eventually, Tommy will be finished with his jumping and falling, and control will return to the **player_stand()** function. This sequence of events is repeated many times during the game. The various action functions will pass control to each other depending on the variables and forces they are aware of. Nearly all the animation in the game is controlled by this chain of action functions.

The Low-Level Keyboard Handler

One of the most common forces acting on the player object is the keyboard. As you press keys, you expect Tommy to run, jump, kick, and shoot in a responsive manner. The player action functions intercept these keystrokes and perform actions accordingly. In the the **player_stand()** function we discussed earlier, the Ctrl key is detected and causes Tommy to begin jumping. We detect this key by using Fastgraph's low-level keyboard handler. The low-level keyboard handler replaces the BIOS keyboard handler for interrupt 09 hex. Keystrokes are intercepted before they get to the BIOS keyboard handler. The result is fast, continuous detection of keypresses without the problem of filling up the BIOS keyboard buffer. It also has the advantage of being able to detect two keypresses at the same time, for example the Ctrl and left arrow key detected simultaneously will cause Tommy to jump to the left. A low-level keyboard handler is an essential element of responsive action arcade games.

Fastgraph's **fg_kbtest()** function is used to detect keypresses in the player action functions.

Fastgraph Tip

fg_kbtest()

The **fg_kbtest()** function determines if the key having the specified scan code is now pressed or released.

```
int fg_kbtest (int scan_code);
```

- *scan_code* is the scan code of the key to check.

The Player Action Functions

When we discussed the **player_stand()** function we didn't look at everything this function does. Let's take a closer look at the entire function now:

```
void near player_stand(OBJp objp)
{
   /* Standing still. Start walking? */
   if (fg_kbtest(KB_RIGHT))
   {
      objp->frame = 0;
      objp->xspeed = 1;
      objp->direction = RIGHT;
      objp->action = player_run;
   }
   else if (fg_kbtest(KB_LEFT))
   {
      objp->frame = 0;
      objp->xspeed = -1;
      objp->direction = LEFT;
      objp->action = player_run;
   }

   /* start kicking, jumping or shooting? */
   else if (fg_kbtest(KB_SPACE))
   {
      objp->action = player_begin_kick;
   }
   else if (fg_kbtest(KB_CTRL))
   {
      objp->action = player_begin_jump;
   }
   else if (fg_kbtest(KB_ALT))
   {
      objp->action = player_begin_shoot;
   }
```

```
   /* look down, look up */
   else if (fg_kbtest(KB_DOWN))
   {
      if (objp->y - tile_orgy*16 > 48)
         scroll_down(1);
   }
   else if (fg_kbtest(KB_UP))
   {
      if (objp->y - tile_orgy*16 < 200)
         scroll_up(1);
   }

   /* just standing there */
   else if (objp->sprite != tom_stand[0] && objp->frame < 7)
   {
      objp->frame = 0;
      objp->sprite = tom_stand[objp->frame];
   }
   else
   {
      /* change Tommy's facial expression */
      objp->time += delta_time;
      if (objp->time > max_time)
      {
         if (objp->frame == 0)
         {
            objp->frame = irandom(7,8);
            objp->time = 0;
            objp->sprite = tom_stand[objp->frame-6];

            /* how long we smile or frown is random */
            max_time = (long)irandom(200,400);
         }
         else
         {
            objp->frame = 0;
            objp->time = 0;
            objp->sprite = tom_stand[0];

            /* how long we stand straight without smiling */
            max_time = (long)irandom(500,1000);

         }
      }
   }
}
```

Here, keystrokes are processed as before, but we look at more cases. If a right or left arrow key is pressed, Tommy begins to run to the right or left. The appropriate structure fields are then modified: the direction is set to **RIGHT** or **LEFT**, the speed is set to 1 or -1, the frame is set to 0, and the action function is set to **player_run()**. Similarly, if keys are intercepted for jumping, kicking, or shooting, the appropriate action function pointer is assigned to the **objp->action** field. If no keystroke is intercepted, the frame is set to 0 and the sprite image is set to **tom_stand[0]**, which is Tommy's standing still frame. As long as Tommy is not moving, the **tom_stand()** action function will continue to execute once each frame.

Making Tommy Fidget

Characters are most endearing when they seem to have a mind of their own. Tommy is no exception. When he is supposed to be standing still, his personality shows through. He fidgets. Sometimes he grins and shrugs his shoulders. Other times he frowns. This is done at random intervals in the **player_stand()** function.

Looking at the Time

To keep track of the random time intervals, we need to look at two variables. One of them is the **time** member of Tommy's object structure. The other is a global variable called **delta_time**. Whenever Tommy is doing nothing, the time interval is added to Tommy's **time** field, as follows:

```
objp->time += delta_time;
```

The **delta_time** variable is the amount of time elapsed since the last frame. As you recall from Chapter 12, the system clock has been accelerated to eight times the normal speed. That means the clock interrupt is called 145 times per second. The **delta_time** variable represents the number of clock ticks between the beginning of the last frame and the beginning of the current frame. Tommy's **time** field is increased by **delta_time** and then it is compared to a target value called **max_time**:

```
if (objp->time > max_time)
```

When the target is reached, it is time to change Tommy's expression.

Changing Tommy's expression is as easy as reassigning Tommy's sprite image. The structure field we are interested in is **objp->image**. This field points to the sprite representing the current incarnation of Tommy. If he is standing still and neither smiling nor shrugging, **objp->image** will point to **tom_stand[0]**. When he smiles or shrugs, **objp->image** will point at either **tom_stand[1]** or **tom_stand[2]**.

If Tommy is currently smiling or frowning, we set **max_time** to a random interval between 200 and 400 clock ticks. If Tommy is standing still, **max_time** is a random interval between 500 and 1,000 clock ticks. We give him a longer time interval for standing still than fidgeting. There is no exact formula to determine when Tommy should fidget. The above numbers were derived through trial and error. If you run the game and watch Tommy, you will see him smile and frown at random intervals. If you think Tommy should smile more often, you can decrease the range of values for **max_time**.

Tommy's **frame** member keeps track of his current frame of animation. Since Tommy has a six-stage walk, frames 1 through 6 are are associated with his walking frames. When his frame is 0, Tommy is standing still. We assign frames 7 and 8 to his fidget frames: When Tommy's frame is 7, his image is **tom_stand[1]**; when his frame is 8, his image is **tom_stand[2]**.

Looking Up and Down

There are times when we want Tommy to stand still and have a look around. For example, we may want to look above us to see what is up there—a platform? an enemy? money? Similarly, we may want to make Tommy look down and check out the scenery below him. There could be anything down there—hazards, enemies, or maybe a secret passage—so it is wise to look before we leap. Also, we may want to time our jump to coincide with a an event happening below. For example, we would want to wait for the scorpion to get out of the way before jumping into his territory.

Looking up and down is a simple process. When the *up* arrow is pressed, the screen scrolls *down*, and when the *down* arrow is pressed, the screen scrolls *up*. That may sound backwards, but it isn't. Looking up requires the screen to scroll down, as shown in Figure 13.1.

Similarly, looking down requires the screen to scroll up as in Figure 13.2. The code to do this is in the **tom_stand()** function.

```
/* look down, look up */
else if (fg_kbtest(KB_DOWN))
{
   if (objp->y - tile_orgy*16 > 48)
      scroll_down(1);
}
else if (fg_kbtest(KB_UP))
{
   if (objp->y - tile_orgy*16 < 200)
      scroll_up(1);
}
```

The screen scrolls by one-pixel increments until a maximum value is reached. The screen will scroll beyond Tommy's usual tolerance area, but Tommy will not completely disappear from the screen.

Figure 13.1 Pressing the up arrow scrolls the screen down.

Figure 13.2 Pressing the down arrow scrolls the screen up

Making Tommy Jump

When the **player_stand()** action function detects a Ctrl keypress, it passes control of the Tommy sprite to the **player_begin_jump()** function. This function retains control for only one frame, as it prepares Tommy for his jump:

```
void near player_begin_jump(OBJp objp)
{
   /* called once at the start of a jump */

   objp->yspeed = -15;                     /* initialize variables */
   objp->frame = 0;
   shoot_time = 0;

   if (fg_kbtest(KB_LEFT) || fg_kbtest(KB_RIGHT)) /* walking? */
      forward_thrust = 50;
   else
      forward_thrust = 0;

   if (objp->direction == LEFT)
      tom_jump[3]->xoffset = 25;
   else
      tom_jump[3]->xoffset = 0;

   objp->sprite = tom_jump[objp->frame];    /* assign sprite */
   objp->action = player_jump;              /* assign action function */
}
```

Tommy's vertical speed is initialized to -15 at the start of the jump. As the jump progresses, the vertical speed will be incremented until it reaches 0. When upward speed is 0, Tommy is no longer going up and he will start to fall.

The **player_start_jump()** function introduces two new global variables: **shoot_time** and **forward_thrust**. The **shoot_time** variable determines the amount of time between bullets. When the fire key (Alt) is pressed, bullets will be spawned at the rate of approximately one every 15 clock ticks. The value of **shoot_time** is incremented until it reaches 15, then the bullet is spawned, and **shoot_time** is set back to 0. Again, this value was chosen by trial and error.

The **forward_thrust** variable affects the horizontal motion when an arrow key is pressed. If a left or right arrow is pressed, Tommy will move forward during the jump, but his amount of forward motion decreases, so he will move in a natural-looking arc. When the arrow key is released, **forward_thrust** is reset to 0.

Next, Tommy's frame is set to 0. This coincides with the frame in the **tom_jump[]** sprite list. The 0 frame is the image of Tommy jumping upward without shooting. This image will continue to be displayed until Tommy begins descending or starts shooting.

Finally, Tommy's action function is set to **player_jump(),** which will be active as long as Tommy is accelerating. Let's take a closer look at **player_jump()**.

```
void near player_jump(OBJp objp)
{
```

```
   int tile_x,tile_y;
   register int i;

   /* increment the timer, if it is less than 5, skip it */
   objp->time += delta_time;
   shoot_time += delta_time;
   if (objp->time > 5L)
      objp->time = 0;
   else
      return;

   /* check for arrow keys, left arrow first */
   if (fg_kbtest(KB_LEFT))
   {
      objp->direction = LEFT;
      objp->xspeed = -3;

      /* forward thrust gives a little boost at start of jump */
      if (forward_thrust > 30)
         objp->xspeed *= 4;
      else if (forward_thrust > 0)
         objp->xspeed *= 2;

      /* move left, checking for walls, etc. */
      objp->xspeed = -how_far_left(objp,-objp->xspeed);
      objp->x += objp->xspeed;

      /* need to scroll the screen left? */
      tile_x = objp->x/16 - tile_orgx;
      if (tile_x < objp->tile_xmin)
         scroll_left(-objp->xspeed);
   }

   /* same for right arrow key */
   else if (fg_kbtest(KB_RIGHT))
   {
      objp->xspeed = 3;
      if (forward_thrust > 50)
         objp->xspeed *= 4;
      else if (forward_thrust > 0)
         objp->xspeed *= 2;
      objp->direction = RIGHT;
      objp->xspeed = how_far_right(objp,objp->xspeed);

      tile_x = objp->x/16 - tile_orgx;
      if (tile_x > objp->tile_xmax)
         scroll_right(objp->xspeed);
      objp->x += objp->xspeed;
   }

   /* decrement forward thrust */
   forward_thrust--;

   /* additional upward thrust if you hold down the Ctrl key */
```

```
   if (fg_kbtest(KB_CTRL))
      objp->yspeed++;
   else
      objp->yspeed/=4;

   /* check bumping head on ceiling */
   objp->yspeed = how_far_up(objp,objp->yspeed);
   objp->y += objp->yspeed;

   /* check if we are shooting */
   if (fg_kbtest(KB_ALT))
   {
      /* Tommy's jumping and shooting frame */
      objp->frame = 2;

      /* space the bullets 15 clock ticks apart */
      if (shoot_time > 15)
      {
         launch_bullet();
         shoot_time = 0;
      }
   }

   /* not shooting, just use Tommy jumping frame */
   else
      objp->frame = 0;

   /* set sprite to the correct frame */
   objp->sprite = tom_jump[objp->frame];

   /* Too close to top of screen? Scroll the screen up. */
   tile_y = objp->y/16 - tile_orgy;
   if (tile_y < objp->tile_ymin)
      scroll_up(-objp->yspeed);

   /* Reached top of arc? Tommy start descent. */
   if (objp->yspeed >= 0)
      objp->action = player_begin_fall;
}
```

The **player_jump()** function begins by regulating sprite motion according to the real-time clock. If fewer than five clock ticks have passed since the last frame, we skip the rest of the action function this frame. That means Tommy will be displayed at the same position this frame as he was in the last frame. So while the frame rate will vary on different computers, Tommy will move at approximately the same speed. Tommy's speed is dependent on the system clock, not the frame rate.

The **shoot_time** variable is also incremented every frame. Bullets are released at the rate of approximately one every 15 clock ticks, regardless of whether Tommy has moved or not. We have to increment the **shoot_time** variable every frame in order for the bullets to be evenly spaced, whether or not Tommy is moving or shooting during this particular frame.

If sufficient time has passed, the action function goes to work. The first thing it does is check for specific key presses, starting with the left arrow key. If the left arrow key is pressed, Tommy's horizontal speed is set appropriately. The speed is modified by the amount of horizontal thrust, which was set in the **player_start_jump()** function, and is decremented later in this function. This is how Tommy jumps to the left.

How Far Can He Go?

The horizontal speed is modified by the function **how_far_left()**, which determines how far away Tommy is from a wall or other barrier. So while Tommy's speed determines how far left he will move, this value can be cut short by **how_far_left()**. The **how_far_left()** function is in the file MOTION.C and looks like this:

```
int how_far_left(OBJp objp,int n)
{
   register int i;
   register int temp;

   temp = objp->x;        /* save the current position */

   /* increment the position until you can't move left any further */
   for (i = 0; i < n; i++)
   {
      objp->x--;
      if (!can_move_left(objp))
      {
         objp->x = temp;
         return(i);
      }
   }
   objp->x = temp;        /* restore the current position */
   return(n);             /* return how far left */
}
```

The **how_far_left()** function saves Tommy's x position in a temporary variable called **temp**. It then decrement's Tommy's x coordinate and calls **can_move_left()** sequentially, until either **can_move_left()** fails, or we have gone as far as we wanted to go in the first place. Then the temporary variable is copied back into Tommy's x coordinate. The purpose of this function is not to actually modify the x coordinate, just to report how much it can be modified in the left direction.

The **can_move_left()** function calls the **test_bit()** function to check the tile attributes of the adjacent tile. If the tile is solid on the right, the object can not move left.

```
int can_move_left(OBJp objp)
{
   int tile_x,tile_y,tile_num;

   /* test the bottom of the sprite */
   tile_x = (objp->x-1)/16;
   if (tile_x <= 0)
      return(FALSE);
   tile_y = objp->y/16;
   tile_num = (int)background_tile[tile_x][tile_y];

   /* is the tile solid on the right? */
   if (test_bit(background_attributes[tile_num],3))
      return(FALSE);

   /* check the top of the sprite too */
   tile_y = (objp->y - objp->sprite->height)/16;
   tile_num = (int)background_tile[tile_x][tile_y];
   return (!test_bit(background_attributes[tile_num],2));
}
```

For good measure, tiles at the top and the bottom of the sprite are checked. Tommy cannot move forward if either his head or his feet will bump into a wall.

Both **how_far_left()** and **can_move_left()** work on other objects besides Tommy. Bullets and enemies are also restricted in their motion. Bullets should not shoot through walls, for example. The other motion functions work in a similar manner: **how_far_right()** calls **can_move_right()**, **how_far_up()** calls **can_move_up()**, and **how_far_down()** calls **can_move_down()**.

The **test_bit()** function is quite simple. It just returns the value of a bit in a byte.

```
test_bit(char num,int bit)
{
   /* test bit flags, used for tile attributes */
   return((num >> bit) & 1);
}
```

Time to Scroll

We can't let Tommy move too far left or he will move off the edge of the screen. We need to calculate Tommy's position with respect to the tile origin. If he has moved beyond the minimum tile tolerance, the screen needs to scroll. We choose to scroll the screen left the same number of pixels as Tommy moved left. The scroll will look smoother if it scrolls at the same speed as

Tommy's horizontal movement. Here is the code to check Tommy's position relative to the tile origin and then scroll left:

```
tile_x = objp->x/16 - tile_orgx;
if (tile_x < objp->tile_xmin)
   scroll_left(-objp->xspeed);
```

The **scroll_left()** function expects a positive number as the number of pixels to scroll. Since Tommy's **xspeed** field is negative when he walks left, we pass the negative **xspeed** to **scroll_left()** and it works out to a positive number.

The same code is executed for the right arrow key. Obviously, Tommy can't move left and right at the same time, so if both the left and right arrow keys are pressed, the left motion will take precedence over the right motion.

Shooting while Jumping

Tommy can also shoot while he is jumping. The **player_jump()** function next checks for the Alt key, which signals that Tommy is shooting at something while he jumps. The shooting while jumping image is frame 3 in the **tom_jump[]** sprite list. The frame is set to 3 whether or not a bullet is going to be released this frame. As we said earlier, bullets are only started when **shoot_time** exceeds 15, which means at least 15 clock ticks have elapsed since the last time a bullet was spawned. The function **start_bullet()** spawns a bullet and adds it to the linked list. More about **start_bullet()** in a minute.

If Tommy is not shooting, his image is set to frame 0 of the **tom_jump[]** sprite list. Once Tommy's image is set to the proper sprite, it's time to consider vertical motion.

As with horizontal motion, the amount Tommy moves depends on whether a key is being pressed. If the Ctrl key is pressed, Tommy will move up faster than when the Ctrl key is released. A slight tap on the Ctrl key makes Tommy jump a tiny amount, and a prolonged press of the Ctrl key causes Tommy to reach his maximum height. As with horizontal movement, Tommy can only move vertically until he reaches a barrier. The **how_far_up()** function modifies the vertical speed so that he will not continue going up if he bumps his head on the ceiling.

Again, Tommy's position is compared to the edge of the screen. If he has moved beyond the minimum vertical tile tolerance, the screen will scroll vertically to accommodate him.

What's Next?

When Tommy ascends, his vertical speed is negative. The vertical speed is decreased a little each frame, either by incrementing it when the Ctrl key is pressed, or by dividing it by four when the Ctrl key is not pressed. Either way, eventually Tommy's vertical speed will reach 0. When that happens, Tommy is no longer moving up. He has reached the top of his jump and is ready to start descending. When Tommy's vertical speed reaches 0, the **player_jump** action function is replaced by **player_start_fall()**. The **player_start_fall()** action function initializes the falling variables in a manner similar to **player_start_jump()**. It then sets the action function to **player_fall()**. The **player_fall()** function is very similar to the **player_go_up()** function, so I'm not going to list it here. The biggest difference between the jumping and falling functions is that Tommy's vertical speed increases in the falling function, and he will continue to go down until he hits a solid tile. The **player_fall()** function, along with all of Tommy's action functions, are included on the companion disk.

Bullet Action Functions

So far, we have only looked at Tommy's action functions, but Tommy is not the only object that has them. All the objects have action functions. In fact, one action function is executed for each object every frame. The non-Tommy action functions are interesting when they modify the linked list. For an example of some action functions that are not Tommy's, let's take a look at the bullets.

Launching Bullets

Bullets are spawned and killed quite often. Every time the Alt key is pressed, Tommy fires a bullet, at the rate of one every 15 clock ticks. Tommy can fire a bullet while standing, running, or jumping. If Tommy's action function determines it is time to fire a bullet, it will call the **launch_bullet()** function. While **launch_bullet()** is not an action function itself (it is not called as a pointer to a function in an object structure), it launches a new object and assigns control of that object to its associated action function. Let's take a look at how this works:

```
void near launch_bullet()                /* start a new bullet */
{
   OBJp node;

   if (nbullets > 9) return;             /* max 9 bullets */

   node = (OBJp)malloc(sizeof(OBJ)+3);   /* allocate space */
   if (node == (OBJp)NULL) return;

   if (player->direction == RIGHT)       /* assign values */
   {
```

```
      node->direction = RIGHT;
      node->xspeed = 13;
      if (player->sprite == tom_jump[2])  /* jumping */
      {
         node->x = player->x+player->sprite->xoffset+46-node->xspeed;
         node->y = player->y-25;
      }
      else if (player->sprite == tom_jump[3]) /* falling */
      {
         node->x = player->x+player->sprite->xoffset+46-node->xspeed;
         node->y = player->y-25;
      }
      else if (fg_kbtest(KB_RIGHT))       /* running */
      {
         node->x = player->x+player->sprite->xoffset+40-node->xspeed;
         node->y = player->y-26;
      }
      else                                /* standing */
      {
         node->x = player->x+player->sprite->xoffset+40-node->xspeed;
         node->y = player->y-28;
      }
   }
   else
   {
      node->direction = LEFT;
      node->xspeed = -13;
      node->x = player->x+player->sprite->xoffset-node->xspeed-5;
      if (player->sprite == tom_jump[2])      /* jumping */
         node->y = player->y-25;
      else if (player->sprite == tom_jump[3]) /* falling */
         node->y = player->y-25;
      else if (fg_kbtest(KB_LEFT))           /* running */
         node->y = player->y-26;
      else                                   /* standing */
         node->y = player->y-28;
   }
   node->yspeed    = 0;
   node->tile_xmin = 1;
   node->tile_xmax = 21;
   node->tile_ymin = 0;
   node->tile_ymax = 14;
   node->sprite = tom_shoot[6];              /* assign the sprite */

   node->action = bullet_go;                 /* assign action function */

   /* insert the new object at the top of the linked list */
   if (bottom_node == (OBJp)NULL )
   {
      bottom_node = node;
      node->prev = (OBJp)NULL;
   }
   else
```

```
    {
       node->prev = top_node;
       node->prev->next = node;
    }
    top_node = node;
    node->next = (OBJp)NULL;

    nbullets++;                          /* increment bullet count */
}
```

The first thing **launch_bullet()** does is see how many bullets are currently active. Through trial and error, I determined nine bullets on the screen at one time are about enough. If Tommy stands in the middle of the screen and fires towards one edge, the first bullet must go off the edge of the screen before the ninth bullet is spawned. Even when Tommy is standing at the edge of the screen, there is no noticeable gap between bullets when the maximum is set to nine. Feel free to change this number if you want to. As with most of the arbitrary values in this game, the programmer should choose unique values so his game will not look like everybody else's.

We keep track of the number of bullets in the variable **nbullets**. This value is incremented as bullets are added, and decremented when bullets are killed. If there are fewer than nine bullets are currently flying, **launch_bullet()** proceeds to launch a new one. It starts by using the C runtime library function **malloc()** to allocate space for the object. If **malloc()** is unable to allocate space for the bullet (which may happen if there are already many objects on the screen), we return without creating this bullet. In most cases, there will be no problem allocating the room for the bullet, so we proceed to initialize the object by plugging values into the members of the object structure.

The direction of the bullet depends on the direction of the player. If the player is facing right, the bullet will move to the right, and if the player is facing left, the bullet will move to the left. The x and y position of the bullet also depends on the position of the player. We want the bullet to come out of the end of Tommy's gun, not out of his knee or his foot. The exact location of the end of Tommy's gun depends on what Tommy is currently doing. We look at Tommy's image and the keyboard to determine if Tommy is currently jumping, falling, running, or standing still, and calculate the x and y position accordingly.

The bullet has no vertical speed; it always moves horizontally at the rate of 13 pixels per frame. The tile extents are set so the bullet will be killed if it goes beyond the edge of the screen in any direction. The image field for the bullet is set to **tom_shoot[6]**. The bullet's action function is set to **bullet_go()**.

Sharing Action Functions

The pointer to the object structure, **objp**, is always passed to the action function. In the case of Tommy, the object will always be the player—we only have one main character. That is not the case for most of our objects, however. Most objects have multiple copies. You may have up to nine bullets on the screen at one time, for example. When that happens, all the bullet objects will point to the same action function, as shown in Figure 13.3.

A Linked List of Objects

To keep our objects properly organized, we store them in a linked list. The bullet is added to the top of the linked list, and the pointers to the next and previous nodes are properly initialized. The bullet becomes the top node of the linked list. Objects are always added to the top of the list, and the last object spawned is always the top node. It is a safe bet this bullet won't stay on top for long. It is very likely another bullet will be spawned in about 15 clock ticks, and this bullet will move down the list and the next bullet will become the top node. Bullets come and go frequently.

As we said earlier, **launch_bullet()** is not an action function. It does, however, assign an action function to the bullet, called **bullet_go()**. The **bullet_go()** function is the main action function for the bullet.

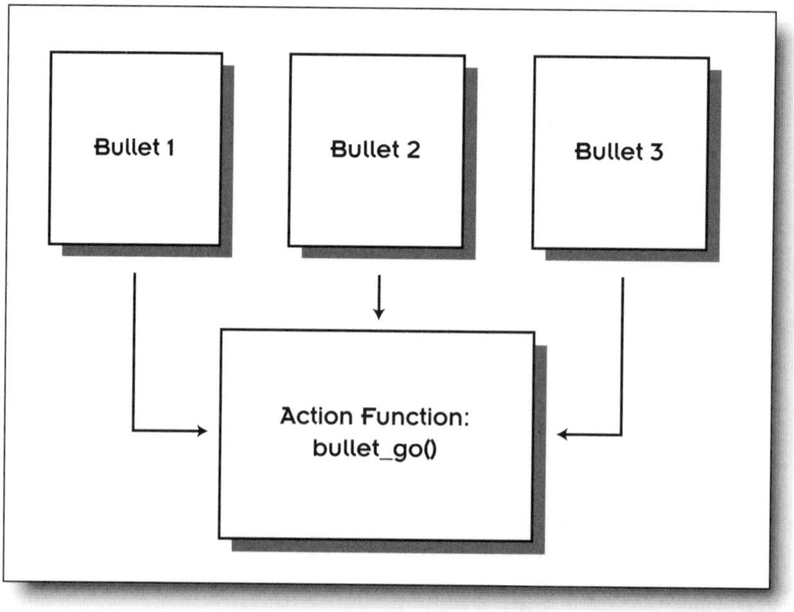

Figure 13.3 Several objects pointing to the same action function.

```
void near bullet_go(OBJp objp)
{
   int min_x,max_x;
   register int i;

   /* increment the bullet's horizontal position */
   objp->x += objp->xspeed;

   /* collision detection */
   for (i = 0; i < nenemies; i++)
   {
      if (enemy[i]->frame < 6 && objp->x>enemy[i]->x
          && objp->x<enemy[i]->x+enemy[i]->sprite->width
          && objp->y<enemy[i]->y
          && objp->y>enemy[i]->y-enemy[i]->sprite->height)
      {
         launch_floating_points(enemy[i]);
         enemy[i]->frame = 6;
         objp->action = kill_bullet;
      }
   }

   /* check if the bullet has moved off the screen */
   max_x = (tile_orgx + objp->tile_xmax) * 16;
   min_x = (tile_orgx + objp->tile_xmin) * 16;

   /* if it has moved off the screen, kill it by setting the action
      function to kill for the next frame */

   if (objp->x > max_x || objp->x < min_x)
      objp->action = kill_bullet;

   if (objp->direction == RIGHT && !can_move_right(objp))
      objp->action = kill_bullet;
   else if (objp->direction == LEFT && !can_move_left(objp))
      objp->action = kill_bullet;
}
```

The first thing **bullet_go()** does is increment (or decrement) the horizontal position of the bullet as determined by the bullet's speed. In other words, the bullet moves 13 pixels to the left or the right. Then the action function checks for a collision between the bullet and any of Tommy's enemies. It does this by scanning an array of pointers to enemy objects. If a collision is detected, the enemy object is flagged by setting its frame number to 6. The enemy's action function will handle the death throes of the enemy. The bullet's action function is only concerned with the activity of the bullet.

Collision Detection

We are often quite interested in happens when two objects collide. When a bullet collides with an enemy, we will want to initiate the sequence of events that leads to the death of both the bullet and the enemy, and more points for Tommy. To detect a collision, we call the **collision_detection()** function.

```
int collision_detection (OBJp objp1, OBJp objp2)
{
   int xmin1,xmax1,xmin2,xmax2;
   int ymin1,ymax1,ymin2,ymax2;

   /* x coordinates of object 1 */
   xmin1 = objp1->x+objp1->image->xoffset;
   xmax1 = xmin1+objp1->image->width;

   /* x coordinates of object 2 */
   xmin2 = objp2->x+objp2->image->xoffset;
   xmax2 = xmin2+objp2->image->width;

   /* y coordinates of object 1 */
   ymax1 = objp1->y+objp1->image->yoffset;
   ymin1 = ymax1-objp1->image->height;

   /* y coordinates of object 2 */
   ymax2 = objp2->y+objp2->image->yoffset;
   ymin2 = ymax2-objp2->image->height;

   /* object 2 entirely to the left of object 1 */
   if (xmax2 < xmin1) return(FALSE);

   /* object 2 entirely to the right of object 1 */
   if (xmin2 > xmax1) return(FALSE);

   /* object 2 entirely to the below object 1 */
   if (ymax2 < ymin1) return(FALSE);

   /* object 2 entirely to the above object 1 */
   if (ymin2 > ymax1) return(FALSE);

   /* the objects overlap */
   return(TRUE);
}
```

This function uses a simple rectangular collision detection. It checks for two objects and one of four cases: If object 2 is entirely to the left or the right of object 1, or if it is entirely above or below object 1, then there is no collision. Otherwise, there is a collision. See Figure 13.4 for a diagram of the collision detection scheme.

Note that the **collision_detection()** function only detects collisions between two objects. Collisions between objects and tiles are detected in the motion functions, such as **can_move_left()**.

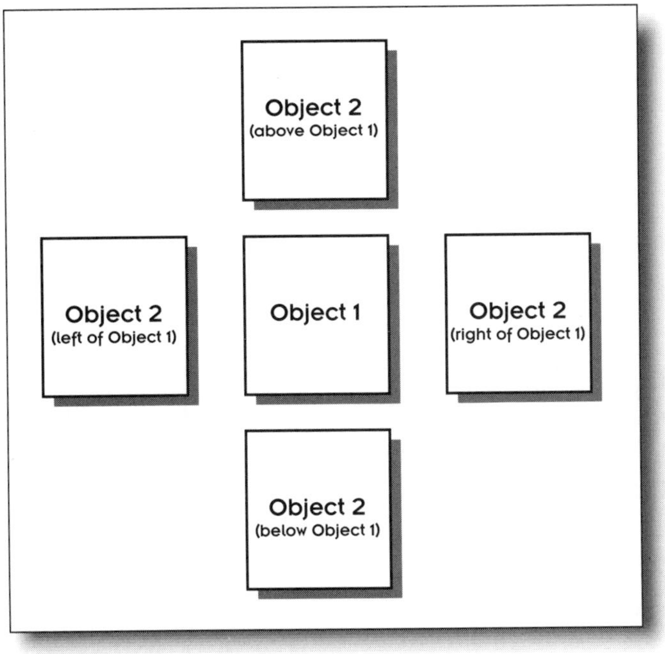

Figure 13.4 *The collision_detection() function checks for four cases.*

There are more accurate and complicated collision detection alogrithms. Our function is inexact, but exact collision detection is not required for this kind of game. The action in *Tommy's Adventures* is fast and furious, it is difficult to see whether a bullet has actually hit an enemy, or just brushed past its tail. In an action game like *Street Fighter* or *Mortal Kombat*, accuate collision detection is more critical. You would not want your player to get points for throwing air punches!

The feel of our collision detection scheme was gauged through trial and error. After trying the simple detection, and discovering it felt reasonable, I discarded the more complicated collision detection algorithms. Most side-scroller games use a simple rectangular collision detection.

The accuracy of the collision detection function could be improved somewhat by using the bounding box information as the basis of the collisions, instead of the position and width and height of the sprite. For some odd-shaped sprites, that enhancement could be useful, but implementing bounding box collision detection is left as an excercise for you.

Killing Bullets

Bullets don't do much. They move forward until they die. They die when they collide with an enemy, hit a wall, or if they go off the edge of the screen. If any of these events happens, the bullet is not killed immediately. Instead, its action function is set to **kill_bullet()**, and the object is killed on the next frame. Here is the **kill_bullet()** action function.

```
void near kill_bullet(OBJp objp)
{
   /* decrement the bullet count and kill the bullet */

   nbullets--;
   kill_object(objp);
}
```

This function decrements the number of bullets, and also calls **kill_object()**. The **kill_object()** function removes an object from the linked list. Any killable objects, such as bullets and enemies, are killed using this function. Here is the **kill_object()** function.

```
void near kill_object(OBJp objp)
{
   /* remove the object from the linked list */

   OBJp node;

   node = objp;
   if (node == bottom_node)
   {
      bottom_node = node->next;
      if (bottom_node != (OBJp) NULL)
         bottom_node->prev = (OBJp)NULL;
   }
   else if (node == top_node)
   {
      top_node = node->prev;
      top_node->next = (OBJp)NULL;
   }
   else
   {
      node->prev->next = node->next;
      node->next->prev = node->prev;
   }
   free(node);
}
```

The **kill_object()** function uses a traditional method for removing a node from a linked list—It checks the position of the object within the list and reassigns the pointers accordingly. The object is then freed using C's **free()** function. The memory allocated for this node is now free to be re-allocated for a new object.

Enemy Action Functions

The other major kind of objects in our game are enemies. Enemies are important because they add an element of challenge to the game. Producing unusual and creative enemy sprites is one of the most important elements of a game's success.

Something usually triggers the spawning of an enemy. For example, an enemy may be launched when Tommy moves into a new area in a level. Tommy may step on a tile that triggers the spawning of an enemy. Sometimes enemies are time based, and a new enemy will appear every minute or two. Sometimes enemies appear at random. Most often, all the enemies are created at the beginning of the level in fixed locations, and once they are killed they are gone for good. This last method seems to be the most appealing to players. It's okay to have an occasional random enemy, but if most of your enemies are in fixed locations, the player will have a chance to learn the level and anticipate the appearance of enemies.

Tommy's Tip

Boss Enemies

It is customary in side-scrolling games to have a boss enemy. This is a large, fierce enemy usually encountered at the end of a level or at the end of an episode. It is usually very difficult to defeat. Unlike the regular enemies, it must be hit many times at just the right angle in order to be killed. Boss enemies serve as a dramatic climax to a game, and prolong the play time of a game at the end because they are so hard to kill.

Different classes of enemies have different action functions. In our game, Tommy faces some huge, scary insects. One is a grasshopper, and the other is a scorpion. We use the same code to launch both types of enemies because they are so similar.

```
void near launch_enemy(int x, int y, int type)  /* start a new enemy */
{
   OBJp node;

   node = (OBJp)malloc(sizeof(OBJ));          /* allocate space */
   if (node == (OBJp)NULL) return;

   node->direction = RIGHT;                   /* assign values */
   node->x = x;
```

```
   node->y = y;
   node->xspeed = 8;
   node->yspeed = 0;
   node->tile_xmin = 1;
   node->tile_xmax = 21;
   node->tile_ymin = 0;
   node->tile_ymax = 14;
   node->time = 0;

   /* assign the sprite and action function */
   if (type == 0)
   {
      node->frame = 0;
      node->action = enemy_scorpion_go;
   }
   else
   {
      node->frame = 3;
      node->action = enemy_hopper_go;
   }
   node->sprite = enemy_sprite[node->frame];

   /* insert the new object at the top of the linked list */
   if (bottom_node == (OBJp)NULL )
   {
      bottom_node = node;
      node->prev = (OBJp)NULL;
   }
   else
   {
      node->prev = top_node;
      node->prev->next = node;
   }
   top_node = node;
   node->next = (OBJp)NULL;

   enemy[nenemies] = node;                  /* update enemy array */
   nenemies++;                              /* increment enemy counter */
}
```

The grasshopper enemy is not terribly complicated. All it does is walk left or right at a fixed speed. If it comes to the end of a platform, it falls off. If it is hit by a bullet or kicked, it dies. Here is the grasshopper's main action function:

```
void near enemy_hopper_go(OBJp objp)
{
   if (objp->frame > 4)   /* is this enemy dying? */
   {
      /* after 100 frames, kill this enemy off */
      objp->frame++;
      if (objp->frame > 100)
         objp->action = kill_enemy;
      objp->sprite = enemy_sprite[5];
```

```
      /* enemy can fall while dying */
      objp->yspeed = how_far_down(objp,12);
      if (objp->yspeed > 0)
         objp->y += objp->yspeed;

      /* no point in doing anything else while dying */
      return;
   }

   /* this enemy moves every 12 clock ticks */
   objp->time += delta_time;
   if (objp->time < 12)
      return;
   else
      objp->time = 0;

   objp->yspeed = how_far_down(objp,12);     /* falling? */
   if (objp->yspeed > 0)
      objp->y += objp->yspeed;
   else
   {
      /* increment the object's horizontal position */
      if (objp->direction == LEFT)
      {
         if (!can_move_left(objp))
         {
            objp->direction = RIGHT;
            objp->xspeed = 12;
         }
      }
      else if (objp->direction == RIGHT)
      {
         if (!can_move_right(objp))
         {
            objp->direction = LEFT;
            objp->xspeed = -12;
         }
      }
      objp->x += objp->xspeed;
   }
   objp->frame = 7-objp->frame;            /* increment the frame */
   objp->sprite = enemy_sprite[objp->frame];

   /* if the player hasn't been hit recently, can we hit him now? */
   if (!player_blink)
   {
      if (collision_detection(objp, player) && !kicking)
      {
         player_blink = TRUE;              /* make the player blink */

         nhits++;                          /* seven hits per life */
         if (nhits > 7)
         {
```

```
            nlives--;
            if (nlives == 0)              /* three lives per game */
               nlives = 3;
            nhits = 0;
         }

         /* update the action function for the score */
         score->action = update_score;
      }
   }
}
```

When hit, the grasshopper dies slowly. It appears as a dead grasshopper sprite, which stays on the screen for 75 frames. The object's **frame** field is used to count the dying frames. Meanwhile, a floating score is launched and moves upward as the grasshopper dies. After the prolonged death throes of the grasshopper, it is killed the same way a bullet is killed: its action function is set to **kill_enemy()**, which removes it from the enemy array and the linked list. At this point, you could say the enemy is out of the loop.

Tommy's Tip

Floating Scores

A floating score has become traditional in Apogee-style, side-scrolling games. It is a number, usually a three-digit number, that floats upward over the corpse of an enemy. It indicates how many points you earned for the kill.

It is always good to give the player some satisfaction for defeating enemy sprites. Similar reward devices include making the enemy flicker, change into something else, or explode.

In non-violent games, it is common for enemies to be stunned rather than killed, or to be changed into something friendly. In Goodbye Galaxy, for example, enemies look dazed when shot, as indicated by a halo of stars circling above their heads. And in Sonic the Hedgehog, evil robots are turned into happy woodland creatures.

The enemy action function has an interesting anomaly—it modifies the action function of another object. That is, when the grasshopper dies, it sets the action function of the score object to **update_score()**. In general, action functions only change the actions of their own objects but this is a special case. We'll discuss the score object some more in the next section.

The scorpion behaves in a manner very similar to the grasshopper (for the purposes of this book, we've kept our enemies *very* simple-minded). I'm sure you can come up with better enemies than these. Enemies that fly or jump are interesting. Enemies that have enough artificial intelligence to hunt you down and kill you are also fun. This is one of the areas of game design where your creative ideas will separate an excellent game from an ordinary game. I encourage you to spend a lot of time designing interesting enemies.

Score Action Functions

The score object is a special object. It is displayed in the same place in the upper-left corner of the screen every frame unless it is turned off, in which case it is not displayed in any frame. To optimize the score for speed, we don't redraw the numbers every frame. If there are four digits in the score, it would require four bitmaps to be drawn every frame, as well as the outline of the scoreboard. This would cause only a tiny speed degradation, but even tiny ones are significant when added up over hundreds of frames. To avoid drawing unnecessary characters every frame, we'll update the score only when it changes.

In the frames when the score has not changed, the **put_score()** action function looks like this:

```
void near put_score(OBJp objp)
{
   /* determine x and y coords based on the screen origin */
   objp->x = tile_orgx*16 + screen_orgx + 2;
   objp->y = tile_orgy*16 + screen_orgy + 43;
}
```

This function simply adjusts the x and y coordinates according to the screen origin so the score will appear in the same place every frame, but does nothing to change the sprite bitmap.

If the score has changed, for example, when Tommy shoots a grasshopper, then the sprite must be updated to reflect the new score. This is done in the **update_score()** action function:

```
void near update_score(OBJp objp)  /* called when score has changed */
{
   char string[128];
   SPRITE *scoremap;
   int y;
   register int i;

   /* Convert the (long) score to a character string.  Assume 10 digits
      is enough */

   ltoa(player_score,string,10);
```

```
/* clear an area in video memory below the tile space where nothing
   else is going on */

fg_setcolor(0);
fg_rect(0,319,680,724);

/* draw the score box in offscreen memory */
scoremap = tom_score[0];
fg_move(0,724);
fg_drwimage(scoremap->bitmap,scoremap->width,scoremap->height);

/* set the color to black and display the score */
fg_setcolor(1);
center_string(string,5,56,720);

/* the status bar indicates how many times you have been hit */
y = nhits*3;

fg_setcolor(14);
if (nhits == 0)             /* all blue */
{
   fg_setcolor(18);
   fg_rect(62,67,701,723);
}
else if (nhits >= 8)        /* all white */
{
   fg_setcolor(14);
   fg_rect(62,67,701,723);
}
else
{                           /* white and blue */
   fg_setcolor(14);
   fg_rect(62,67,701,700+y);
   fg_setcolor(18);
   fg_rect(62,67,700+y,723);
}

scoremap = tom_score[1];     /* Tommy one-ups */
for (i = 0; i < nlives; i++)
{
   fg_move(80+i*10,716);
   fg_drwimage(scoremap->bitmap,scoremap->width,scoremap->height);
}

/* do a getimage to put the score in a bitmap in RAM */
objp->sprite->width = 80+10*nlives;
fg_move(0,724);
fg_getimage(objp->sprite->bitmap,
            objp->sprite->width,objp->sprite->height);

/* update the x and y coords */
objp->x = tile_orgx*16 + screen_orgx + 2;
objp->y = tile_orgy*16 + screen_orgy + 43;
```

```
   /* assign action function */
   objp->action = put_score;
}
```

The **update_score()** action function creates a new bitmap. It does this by drawing the scoreboard in offscreen video memory. First the **fg_rect()** function is used to draw a rectangle. Then **fg_drwimage()** is used to put the scoreboard outline on top of the rectangle. Finally, the score is drawn on top of the scoreboard. Fastgraph's **fg_getimage()** function is used to grab the image and store it in a sprite bitmap in RAM. See Figure 13.5 for a picture of video memory with the score sprite being redrawn below the tile area.

The shaded area in Figure 13.5 is where the score is redrawn in video memory. Tommy one-ups are also drawn in this area. The one-ups are represented as miniature pictures of Tommy.

Tommy's Tip

One-Ups

A *one-up* is an extra life for the main player. Traditionally, a character begins a game with three one-ups. Every time a character dies, the number of one-ups decreases. If the character dies three times, it uses the last one-up, and the game is over.

Some games allow the player to find one-ups in the level, or earn additional one-ups by finding other objects. One-ups should not be confused with *energy*, which is reduced incrementally as the player encounters hazards, or *continues*, which are chances to restart the game at the current level when all the one-ups are exhausted.

The Creativity of Sprite Animation

This chapter has covered the basic elements of controlling sprite movements through action functions. Once again, I would like to stress that creativity is an absolute necessity in this part of game programming. The action functions we have looked at are the bare-bones minimum amount of code needed to create sprite motion. You can use these functions as templates for your own sprites, but plan on modifying and adding to them. A game needs to have interesting sprites to be a success, and you'll spend a lot of time designing them. Sprite design is an inexact science. The best way to approach it is through trial and error. Implement your ideas, try them out, and see if they feel right. Keep experimenting with the action functions until you are satisfied that your sprites express the personality, emotion, and challenge that will set your game apart from all the others.

Figure 13.5 *Score sprite being redrawn in offscreen video memory.*

Chapter 14

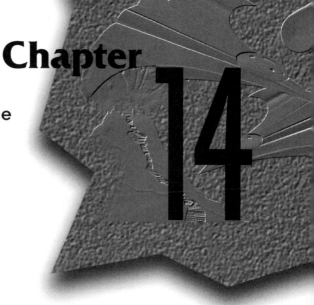

Ready to put it all together? Find out how we combine all the pieces we've discussed so far into a real live game.

It's Show Time

Now that we've assembled all of the ingredients we need for fast, side-scrolling-style animation, it's time to put them all together. We have built our game editor, and then we have used it to build our sprites and our levels. We have designed our data structures and action functions. Now it's time to look at the main controlling functions for our game. These functions are found in the file TOMMY.C. In this chapter, I'll present this source code file so you can see how the game is loaded and how the other functions are called. We'll also look at the details of completing a frame of animation.

Lights . . . Camera . . . Action!

Every C program starts with a **main()** function and ours is no exception. The **main()** function, along with the other useful functions for game initialization and termination, are found in the file TOMMY.C. Let's examine the functions, listed in Table 14.1, found in this file.

Table 14.1 Functions Used in TOMMY.C

Function	Description
main()	Initializes the game by loading in the files and starting the main event loop
activate_level()	Provides the main event loop to control the game and it calls the action functions for sprite animation
apply_sprite()	Draws a bitmapped sprite and updates the layout array
array_to_level()	Loads level data from far array into variables
fix_palettes()	Adjusts the first 32 colors to match sprite colors
flushkey()	Clears out the keystroke buffer
getseed()	Obtains a seed for the random number generator
increment_timer()	Increments the game timer
init_graphics()	Initializes the graphics for the game
irandom()	Generates a random number
level_to_array()	Copies level data from a specified location in in layout array to the level variables
load_sprite()	Loads sprite data from the sprite list file
terminate_game()	Shuts down the game by resetting the video mode and clock speed, and returning to DOS

TOMMY.C

The source code for TOMMY.C is bigger than it looks! That's because ACTION.C is included. Since we already listed ACTION.C in the last chapter, let's look at the rest of the file now.

```
/******************************************************************\
*  Tommy.c -- Tommy game source code file                          *
*  copyright 1994 Diana Gruber                                     *
*  compile using large model, link with Fastgraph (tm)             *
\******************************************************************/

#define tommy_c
#include "gamedefs.h"
#include "action.c"

/* #define debug */
/******************************************************************/
void main()
{
   register int i;
   char *bitmap;
```

```
   SPRITE *score_sprite;
   OBJp node;
   OBJp next_node;

   if (fg_testmode(20,4) == 0)        /* VGA or better required */
   {
      printf("\nVGA required\n");
      exit(0);
   }

#ifdef debug
   /* text file used for debugging purposes */
   dstream = fopen("debug.dat","wt");
#endif

#ifdef __TURBOC__
   oldhandler = getvect(0x1C);          /* get the vector for 0X1C */
   setvect(0x1C,increment_timer);       /* set timer interrupt function */
#else
   oldhandler = _dos_getvect(0x1C);     /* get the vector for 0X1C */
   _dos_setvect(0x1C,increment_timer); /* set timer interrupt function */
#endif

   /* open the game data file */
   if ((stream = fopen("game.dat","rt")) == NULL)
   {
      sprintf(abort_string,"Bad or missing file: Game.dat.");
      terminate_game();
   }

   /* read all the file names, store in structures */
   fscanf(stream,"%d",&nlevels);
   for (i = 0; i < nlevels; i++)
   {
      fscanf(stream,"%s",level_fname);
      fscanf(stream,"%s",background_fname);
      fscanf(stream,"%s",backattr_fname);
      fscanf(stream,"%s",foreground_fname);
      fscanf(stream,"%s",foreattr_fname);
      fscanf(stream,"%s",sprite_fname);
      level_to_array(i);
   }
   fclose(stream);

   current_level = 0;                 /* start with the first level */
   array_to_level(current_level);     /* get level data from array */

   init_graphics();                   /* initialize the VGA graphics */
   fg_showpcx("tommy.pcx",0);         /* display intro screen */
   fg_waitkey();                      /* wait for a keystroke */
   fg_setcolor(0);                    /* clear the screen */
   fg_rect(0,351,0,479);
   load_level();                      /* load the level data */
```

```
load_sprite();                    /* load the sprite data */
load_status_screen();             /* load the status screen data */

player = (OBJp)malloc(sizeof(OBJ));  /* allocate the player */
player->tile_xmin = 4;
player->tile_xmax = 14;
player->tile_ymin = 5;
player->tile_ymax = 11;

/* initialize the score sprite */
if ((bitmap = (char *)malloc(160*42)) == (char *) NULL)
{
    sprintf(abort_string,"Out of sprite memory.");
    terminate_game();
}

if ((score_sprite = (SPRITE *)malloc(sizeof(SPRITE)))
   == (SPRITE *)NULL)
{
    sprintf(abort_string,"Out of sprite memory.");
    terminate_game();
}
score_sprite->bitmap  = bitmap;
score_sprite->width   = 160;
score_sprite->height  = 42;
score_sprite->xoffset = 0;
score_sprite->yoffset = 0;

/* initialize the score object */
score = (OBJp)malloc(sizeof(OBJ));
score->sprite = score_sprite;
score->action = update_score;
score->direction = RIGHT;

/* start the linked list */
bottom_node = (OBJp)NULL;
top_node = (OBJp)NULL;
next_node = (OBJp)NULL;

/* initialize some global variables */
max_time = 500L;
player_score = 0L;
show_score = TRUE;

fg_tcmask(1);                        /* mask for fg_tcxfer */

fg_kbinit(1);                        /* start the keyboard handler */
game_time = 0;                       /* start the timer */
set_rate(8);                         /* speed up the clock rate */
score->action(score);                /* start the score */

for (;;)                             /* main program loop */
{
```

```
/* initialize some global variables */
nbullets = 0;
nenemies = 0;
player_blink = FALSE;
nblinks = 0;
nhits = 0;
nlives = 3;
blink_time = 0;
kicking = FALSE;

warp(16,80);                     /* warp to starting position */
swap();                          /* swap pages */
page_copy(vpo);                  /* copy visual page to hidden */

player->x = 32;                  /* initialize player */
player->y = 200;
player->frame = 0;
player->time = 0;
player->xspeed = 0;
player->yspeed = 0;
player->sprite = tom_stand[0];
player->direction = RIGHT;
player->action = player_run;

launch_enemy(120,120,0);         /* launch some enemies */
launch_enemy(900,120,1);

warp_to_next_level = FALSE;
do                               /* continuous loop */
{                                /* activate the level */
   activate_level();
   if (warp_to_next_level)
      break;
}
while(!status_screen());         /* check for program exit */

if (!warp_to_next_level)         /* done -- exit */
{
   abort_string[0] = '\n';
   terminate_game();
}

for (node=bottom_node; node!=(OBJp)NULL; node=next_node)
{
    next_node = node->next;
    kill_object(node);
}
current_level++;                 /* do the next level */
if (current_level == nlevels)
   current_level = 0;
array_to_level(current_level);

fg_setcolor(0);                  /* clear the screen */
fg_rect(0,351,0,479);
```

```
      set_rate(0);                      /* set the clock rate to normal */
      load_level();                     /* load the level */
      set_rate(8);                      /* reset the clock rate */
   }
}
/**************************************************************************/
void activate_level()
{
   register int i,j;
   unsigned long time;
   OBJp node; /* index for linked list */
   OBJp next_node; /* pointer to next node */

   next_node = (OBJp)NULL;
   for(;;)  /* loop continuously */
   {
      /* determine how much time has passed since the last frame */
      time = game_time;
      delta_time = time - last_time;
      delta_time = MAX(1L,delta_time);
      last_time = time;

      if (fg_kbtest(KB_ESC))  /* check for Esc key */
         return;

      if (fg_kbtest(KB_F1))   /* check for the scoreboard toggle */
         show_score = TRUE;
      else if (fg_kbtest(KB_F2))
         show_score = FALSE;
      else if (fg_kbtest(KB_W))
      {
         warp_to_next_level = TRUE;
         fg_waitfor(10);
         return;
      }

      /* do the action function for the player */
      player->action(player);

      /* if any scrolling occurred, adjust the screen & arrays */
      page_fix();

      /* do the action functions for all the sprites */
      for (node=bottom_node; node!=(OBJp)NULL; node=next_node)
      {
         next_node = node->next;
         node->action(node);        /* do the action function */
      }

      /* do the action function for the score */
      score->action(score);

      /* rebuild all the background tiles on the hidden page */
```

```
      rebuild_background();
      rebuild_foreground();
      for (i = 0; i < 22; i++)
         for (j = 0; j < 15; j++)
            layout[hidden][i][j] = FALSE;

      /* apply all the sprites on the hidden page */
      for (node=bottom_node; node!=(OBJp)NULL; node=node->next)
         apply_sprite(node);

      /* apply the player sprite */
      apply_sprite(player);

      /* apply any foreground tiles */
      rebuild_foreground();

      /* if the scoreboard is visible, put it on last */
      if (show_score)
         apply_sprite(score);

      /* swap the pages */
      swap();

      /* if the page has scrolled, copy the visual page to the
         hidden page */

      if (scrolled_left || scrolled_right || scrolled_up ||
          scrolled_down || warped)
         page_copy(vpo);

      /* reset all the scrolling globals to false */
      scrolled_left = FALSE;
      scrolled_right = FALSE;
      scrolled_up = FALSE;
      scrolled_down = FALSE;
      warped = FALSE;
   }
}
/*****************************************************************/
void apply_sprite(OBJp objp)
{
   register int i,j;
   int x,y;
   int tile_x1,tile_y2;
   int tile_x2,tile_y1;
   int width, height;
   char *p;

   /* calculate the location, width and height */
   x = objp->x + objp->sprite->xoffset;
   y = objp->y + objp->sprite->yoffset;
   width = objp->sprite->width;
   height = objp->sprite->height;
```

```
/* which tiles are going to be covered up? */
tile_x1 = x/16 - tile_orgx;
tile_y2 = y/16 - tile_orgy;
tile_x2 = (x+width)/16 - tile_orgx;
tile_y1 = (y-height)/16 - tile_orgy;

/* if we are off the screen, forget it */
if (tile_x2 < 0 || tile_x1 > 21 || tile_y1 > 14 || tile_y2 < 0)
   return;

tile_x1 = MAX(tile_x1,0);
tile_x2 = MIN(21,tile_x2);
tile_y1 = MAX(tile_y1,0);
tile_y2 = MIN(14,tile_y2);

/* update the layout array */
for (i = tile_x1; i <= tile_x2; i++)
{
   p = layout[hidden][i] + tile_y1;
   for (j = tile_y1; j <= tile_y2; j++)
   {
      *p++ = TRUE;
   }
}

/* convert world space coordinates to screen space */
x = x - (tile_orgx*16);
y = y - (tile_orgy*16) + hpo;

/* set the clipping limits */
fg_setclip(0,351,hpo,hpb);
fg_move(x,y);

/* if the player is blinking, alternate black and regular */
if (objp == player && player_blink)
{
   blink_time += delta_time;
   if (blink_time > 5)
   {
      blink_time = 0;
      nblinks++;
      if (nblinks == 30)
      {
        player_blink = FALSE;
        nblinks = 0;
        blink_time = 0;
      }
   }
   if (nblinks%2 == 0)
   {
      get_blinkmap(objp);
      if (objp->direction == RIGHT)
          fg_clpimage(blink_map,width,height);
```

```
         else
            fg_flpimage(blink_map,width,height);
         fg_setclip(0,351,0,726);
         return;
      }
   }

   /* not blinking, just display the bitmap */
   if (objp->direction == RIGHT)
      fg_clpimage(objp->sprite->bitmap,width,height);
   else
      fg_flpimage(objp->sprite->bitmap,width,height);

   fg_setclip(0,351,0,726);
}
/******************************************************************/
void array_to_level(int n)
{
   /* update the current level */
   strcpy(level_fname,      level[n].level_fname);
   strcpy(background_fname,level[n].background_fname);
   strcpy(backattr_fname,  level[n].backattr_fname);
   strcpy(foreground_fname,level[n].foreground_fname);
   strcpy(foreattr_fname,  level[n].foreattr_fname);
   strcpy(sprite_fname,    level[n].sprite_fname);
}
/******************************************************************/
void fix_palettes()
{
   /* the first 32 palettes are fixed sprite colors */
   static char game_palette[] = {
    0, 0, 0, 18, 7, 0, 27,13, 3, 36,21,10, 45,31,19, 54,42,32, 63,55,47,
    0, 0, 0, 14,14,14, 21,21,21, 28,28,28, 35,35,35, 42,42,42, 49,49,49,
   56,56,56, 63,63,63,  0, 0,42,  8, 8,52, 21,21,63, 21,37,61, 21,53,60,
   36, 0, 0, 45, 0, 0, 54, 0, 0, 63, 0, 0, 56,44,47,  0,35, 0,  0,57, 0,
   21,63, 0, 63,63, 0, 51, 0,51, 63, 0,63};

   register int i;
   int color;
   int white_value,black_value;
   int blue_value;
   int distance;

   /* set the palettes for the first 32 colors (sprite colors) */
   fg_setdacs(0,32,game_palette);

   /* find the closest colors to white, black and blue. */
   white_value = 0;
   black_value = 63*63;
   white = 15;
   black = 0;
   blue_value = 63*63*3;
```

```
   for (i = 0; i < 32*3; i+=3)
   {
      color = game_palette[i]+game_palette[i+1]+game_palette[i+2];
      if (color > white_value) /* biggest total color is white */
      {
         white = i/3;
         white_value = color;
      }
      if (color < black_value) /* smallest total color is black */
      {
         black = i/3;
         black_value = color;
      }
      /* find closest blue color using least squares method */
      distance =
         (63 - game_palette[i+2]) * (63 - game_palette[i+2]) +
         (21 - game_palette[i+1]) * (21 - game_palette[i+1]) +
         (21 - game_palette[i]) * (21 - game_palette[i]);

      if (distance < blue_value)
      {
         blue = i/3;
         blue_value = distance;
      }
   }
}
/******************************************************************/
void flushkey()
{
   unsigned char key,aux;

   /* clear out the keystroke buffer */
   do {
         fg_intkey(&key,&aux);
      }
      while (key+aux > 0);
}
/******************************************************************/
void getseed()
{
   /* get a seed for the random number generator */
   seed = (int)(fg_getclock() & 0x7FFF);
}
/******************************************************************/
void interrupt increment_timer()
{
   game_time++;
}
/******************************************************************/
void init_graphics()
{
   fg_setmode(20);              /* set the video mode to Mode X */
   fg_resize(352,744);          /* resize video memory */
```

```
   fg_setclip(0,351,0,726);   /* set the clipping limits */
   getseed();                 /* start the random number generator */
   fix_palettes();            /* get the palette information */
}
/****************************************************************/
int irandom(int min, int max) /* random number generator */
{
   register int temp;

   temp = seed ^ (seed >> 7);
   seed = ((temp << 8) ^ temp) & 0x7FFF;
   return((seed % (max-min+1)) + min);
}
/****************************************************************/
void level_to_array(int n)    /* update all the levels */
{
   strcpy(level[n].level_fname,     level_fname);
   strcpy(level[n].background_fname,background_fname);
   strcpy(level[n].backattr_fname,  backattr_fname);
   strcpy(level[n].foreground_fname,foreground_fname);
   strcpy(level[n].foreattr_fname,  foreattr_fname);
   strcpy(level[n].sprite_fname,    sprite_fname);
}
/****************************************************************/
void load_sprite()            /* load sprite data from files */
{
   SPRITE *new_sprite;
   register int i,j;
   int n,nbytes;
   int width,height;
   int xorg,yorg;
   int bound_x,bound_y;
   int bound_width,bound_height;
   char far *bitmap;

   if ((stream = fopen(sprite_fname,"rt")) == NULL)
   {
      sprintf(abort_string,"%s not found",sprite_fname);
      terminate_game();
   }

   i = 0;
   fscanf(stream,"%d",&nspritelists);
   for (j = 0; j < nspritelists; j++)
   {
      fscanf(stream,"%s",list_fname);

      if ((sprite_stream = fopen(list_fname,"rb")) == NULL)
      {
         sprintf(abort_string,"%s not found",list_fname);
         terminate_game();
      }
```

```
      fread(&nsprites,sizeof(int),1,sprite_stream);
      for (n = 0; n < nsprites; n++)
      {
         fread(&width,sizeof(int),1,sprite_stream);
         fread(&height,sizeof(int),1,sprite_stream);
         nbytes = width * height;

         if ((bitmap = (char far *)malloc(nbytes)) == (char *)NULL)
         {
            sprintf(abort_string,"out of bitmap memory");
            terminate_game();
         }

         if ((new_sprite = (SPRITE *)malloc(sizeof(SPRITE)))
            == (SPRITE *)NULL)
         {
            sprintf(abort_string,"out of sprite memory");
            terminate_game();
         }

         sprite[i] = new_sprite;
         fread(&xorg,sizeof(int),1,sprite_stream);
         fread(&yorg,sizeof(int),1,sprite_stream);
         fread(&bound_x,sizeof(int),1,sprite_stream);
         fread(&bound_y,sizeof(int),1,sprite_stream);
         fread(&bound_width,sizeof(int),1,sprite_stream);
         fread(&bound_height,sizeof(int),1,sprite_stream);

         fread(bitmap,sizeof(char),nbytes,sprite_stream);

         sprite[i]->bitmap = bitmap;
         sprite[i]->width = width;
         sprite[i]->height = height;
         sprite[i]->bound_x = bound_x;
         sprite[i]->bound_y = bound_y;
         sprite[i]->bound_width = bound_width;
         sprite[i]->bound_height = bound_height;
         sprite[i]->xoffset = 0;
         sprite[i]->yoffset = 0;
         i++;
      }
      fclose(sprite_stream);
   }
   fclose(stream);

   /* assign the sprites to some more meaningful names */
   j = 0;
   for (i = 0; i < STANDFRAMES; i++)
      tom_stand[i] = sprite[j++];
   for (i = 0; i < RUNFRAMES; i++)
      tom_run[i] = sprite[j++];
   for (i = 0; i < JUMPFRAMES; i++)
      tom_jump[i] = sprite[j++];
```

```
   for (i = 0; i < KICKFRAMES; i++)
      tom_kick[i] = sprite[j++];
   for (i = 0; i < SHOOTFRAMES; i++)
      tom_shoot[i] = sprite[j++];
   for (i = 0; i < SCOREFRAMES; i++)
      tom_score[i] = sprite[j++];
   for (i = 0; i < ENEMYFRAMES; i++)
      enemy_sprite[i] = sprite[j++];
}
/******************************************************************/
void terminate_game()
{
   /* clean up and exit to DOS */
   fg_kbinit(0);         /* turn off the low-level keyboard handler */

   fg_setmode(3);        /* reset the video mode */
   fg_reset();           /* reset screen attributes */

   fg_setcolor(15);      /* print the exit string */
   printf(abort_string);
   printf("\n");

   set_rate(0);          /* put the clock speed back to a normal rate */
#ifdef __TURBOC__
   setvect(0x1C,oldhandler);      /* restore the interrupt */
#else
   _dos_setvect(0x1C,oldhandler); /* restore the interrupt */
#endif

   exit(0);
}
```

Inside main()

Tommy's Adventures begins execution, as expected, with a function called **main()**. The **main()** function in TOMMY.C initializes the video environment and data structures, assigns values to global variables, and launches levels. We don't need to discuss the entire function in detail since much of the code is just simple assignment statements, however, we'll need to look at some of the control code.

One piece of interesting code that you'll encounter right away is this conditional macro used for debugging purposes:

```
#ifdef debug
   /* text file used for debugging purposes */
   dstream = fopen("debug.dat","wt");
#endif
```

We are checking for a debugging flag that can be set in TOMMY.C. If the flag is set, information to help us debug the game will be written to the

DEBUG.DAT file. In Chapter 16, we'll see some helpful ways to use this file.

The code in the next section of **main()** consists of a number of assignment statements and simple function calls to set up the game. It is here that we initialize the interrupt vectors for the game timer, open the game data file (GAME.DAT) and read in the six game files, initialize the first level, initialize the VGA graphics, load the level data and status screen, and initialize the player, score sprite, score object, and a few other global variables. This sounds like a lot but the code is quite simple.

The actual game control begins with a continous **for** loop used as the main program loop:

```
for (;;)                            /* main program loop */
{
   /* initialize some global variables */
   nbullets = 0;
   nenemies = 0;
   player_blink = FALSE;
   nblinks = 0;
   nhits = 0;
   nlives = 3;
   blink_time = 0;
   kicking = FALSE;

   warp(16,80);                     /* warp to starting position */
   swap();                          /* swap pages */
   page_copy(vpo);                  /* copy visual page to hidden */

   player->x = 32;                  /* initialize player */
   player->y = 200;
   player->frame = 0;
   player->time = 0;
   player->xspeed = 0;
   player->yspeed = 0;
   player->sprite = tom_stand[0];
   player->direction = RIGHT;
   player->action = player_run;

   launch_enemy(120,120,0);         /* launch some enemies */
   launch_enemy(900,120,1);

   warp_to_next_level = FALSE;
   do                               /* continuous loop */
   {                                /* activate the level */
      activate_level();
      if (warp_to_next_level)
         break;
   }
   while(!status_screen());         /* check for program exit */
```

```
   if (!warp_to_next_level)          /* done -- exit */
   {
      abort_string[0] = '\n';
      terminate_game();
   }

   next_node = node->next;           /* clean up last level */
   for (node=bottom_node; node!=(OBJp)NULL; node=next_node)
   {
       next_node = node->next;
       kill_object(node);
   }
   current_level++;                  /* do the next level */
   if (current_level == nlevels)
      current_level = 0;
   array_to_level(current_level);

   fg_setcolor(0);                   /* clear the screen */
   fg_rect(0,351,0,479);
   set_rate(0);                      /* set the clock rate to normal */
   load_level();                     /* load the level */
   set_rate(8);                      /* reset the clock rate */
}
```

The loop controls the game and specifies when the game should terminate or when a new level should be displayed. The first part of the loop initializes the variables used in the current level. Then, we come to the main control code:

```
warp_to_next_level = FALSE;
do                                /* continuous loop */
{                                 /* activate the level */
   activate_level();
   if (warp_to_next_level)
      break;
}
while(!status_screen());          /* check for program exit */
```

Take a close look at the inner control loop. As it begins, we initialize a flag called **warp_to_next_level**. It is set to **FALSE**, indicating we are not ready to warp. Then, we call **activate_level()** in a continuous loop. The **activate_level()** function controls all the level animation, as we'll see in the next section. It executes for many frames and it returns to **main()** if something interrupts it—if the user presses the Esc key, for example. We could interrupt the **activate_level()** function for many reasons. The user may want online help or to pause the game. We display a status screen by calling **status_screen()** with the purpose of asking the user, "what do you want to do now?" (The status screen is also a special effect, so we'll discuss it in detail in Chapter 15.) If **status_screen()** returns **TRUE**, we are ready to quit this level. If it returns **FALSE**, we continue.

When the level is terminated, two options are available. We can either warp to another level, or we can quit the game. The setting of the **warp_to_next_level** determines which path is taken. Pressing the W key, in either the status screen or during level play, will set this flag. If it is set, we clear the current level and load the next level:

```
if (!warp_to_next_level)          /* done -- exit */
{
   abort_string[0] = '\n';
   terminate_game();
}

next_node = node->next;           /* clean up last level */
for (node=bottom_node; node!=(OBJp)NULL; node=next_node)
{
    next_node = node->next;
    kill_object(node);
}
current_level++;                  /* do the next level */
if (current_level == nlevels)
   current_level = 0;
array_to_level(current_level);

fg_setcolor(0);                   /* clear the screen */
fg_rect(0,351,0,479);
set_rate(0);                      /* set the clock rate to normal */
load_level();                     /* load the level */
set_rate(8);                      /* reset the clock rate */
```

Taking Control of the World with activate_level()

The **activate_level()** function called by **main()** is one big continuous loop as shown here:

```
void activate_level()
{
   register int i,j;
   unsigned long time;
   OBJp node; /* index for linked list */
   OBJp next_node; /* pointer to next node */

   next_node = (OBJp)NULL;
   for(;;)  /* loop continuously */
   {
      /* determine how much time has passed since the last frame */
      time = game_time;
```

```
delta_time = time - last_time;
delta_time = MAX(1L,delta_time);
last_time = time;

if (fg_kbtest(KB_ESC))  /* check for Esc key */
   return;

if (fg_kbtest(KB_F1))   /* check for the scoreboard toggle */
   show_score = TRUE;
else if (fg_kbtest(KB_F2))
   show_score = FALSE;
else if (fg_kbtest(KB_W))
{
   warp_to_next_level = TRUE;
   fg_waitfor(10);
   return;
}

/* do the action function for the player */
player->action(player);

/* if any scrolling occurred, adjust the screen & arrays */
page_fix();

/* do the action functions for all the sprites */
for (node=bottom_node; node!=(OBJp)NULL; node=next_node)
{
   next_node = node->next;
   node->action(node);         /* do the action function */
}

/* do the action function for the score */
score->action(score);

/* rebuild all the background tiles on the hidden page */
rebuild_background();
rebuild_foreground();
for (i = 0; i < 22; i++)
   for (j = 0; j < 15; j++)
      layout[hidden][i][j] = FALSE;

/* apply all the sprites on the hidden page */
for (node=bottom_node; node!=(OBJp)NULL; node=node->next)
   apply_sprite(node);

/* apply the player sprite */
apply_sprite(player);

/* apply any foreground tiles */
rebuild_foreground();

/* if the scoreboard is visible, put it on last */
if (show_score)
   apply_sprite(score);
```

```
      /* swap the pages */
      swap();

      /* if the page has scrolled, copy the visual page to the
         hidden page */

      if (scrolled_left || scrolled_right || scrolled_up ||
          scrolled_down || warped)
         page_copy(vpo);

      /* reset all the scrolling globals to false */
      scrolled_left = FALSE;
      scrolled_right = FALSE;
      scrolled_up = FALSE;
      scrolled_down = FALSE;
      warped = FALSE;
   }
}
```

Each iteration through the loop represents one frame. Here are the events that occur in each frame:

- Time variables are updated.
- Keys are checked and processed.
- The player's action function is executed.
- If the player's action function triggered any scrolling, the screen is updated in the function **page_fix()**.
- The action functions for all the other objects (enemies, bullets) are executed. This is accomplished by traversing the linked list of objects.
- The action function for the scoreboard is executed.
- The background is rebuilt by replacing all the necessary tiles on the hidden page.
- The foreground is fixed up too, as needed.
- All the sprites, except the player sprite and the scoreboard sprite, are placed on top of the background.
- The player sprite is drawn.
- Foreground tiles are drawn.
- The scoreboard is drawn.
- Pages are swapped. This technically completes the frame
- If needed, the hidden page is updated by copying the visual page to it.
- Flag variables are updated.

The order of these actions is important. For example, the background must be updated before the sprites can be applied. The foreground tiles must be placed after the sprites, so the sprites appear to walk behind them. Also, although we execute the player's action function before the other action functions, we draw the player after we draw the other sprites. So if our player intersects an enemy, the player will appear to walk in front of the enemy.

You may change the order in which objects are drawn to suit your preference. For example, you may want to draw the scoreboard before the sprites are drawn so it doesn't cover up the action—an easy change to make.

Notice that the foreground tiles are replaced twice, once before the sprites are drawn and once after. The first time, the foreground tiles that were affected by the last frame's sprites are redrawn. Then after the sprites are drawn this frame, the foreground tiles must be replaced again.

Processing User Input

The **activate_level()** function processes these keystrokes:

- The Esc key returns control to **main()**, which in turn calls the status screen to prompt the user for quitting or warping.
- The F1 and F2 keys turn the scoreboard on and off. It would be convenient but impractical to use one key, for example the F1 key, to toggle the scoreboard both on and off. By the time you take your finger off the F1 key, several frames will have passed. The scoreboard would flicker on and off several times, and its final state would be random. This is not the desired result. Using a single keystroke as a toggle does not work well when the low-level keyboard handler is enabled.
- The W key sets the **warp_to_next_level** flag and returns control to **main()**, which imediately initiates the next level.

Traversing a Linked List to Execute Action Functions

As we've seen, objects are stored in a linked list. The list is traversed twice each frame. The first time through, all the action functions are executed. The second time through, all the sprites are drawn. The list is traversed in the traditional way: we declare a pointer of type **OBJp** and call it **node**. The **node** pointer starts at one end of the list, and points to consecutive nodes until it comes to the end of the list. We know it has reached the end when it points to **(OBJp)NULL**, which is what the last (top) node points to. The list traversal code in the function **activate_level()** used to apply the sprite looks like this:

```
for (node=bottom_node; node!=(OBJp)NULL; node=node->next)
      apply_sprite(node);
```

An interesting thing happens when the action functions are executed. It is possible for an action function to delete an object from the list. For example, the **kill_bullet()** function will remove a bullet from the linked list. When this happens, pointers may become confused. We solve this problem by declaring another object pointer called **next_node**. This pointer is assigned before the action function is executed. That way, if the object is deleted during the action function, the pointer will not be lost. Here is the code in **activate_level()** that calls the action function for each sprite:

```
/* do the action functions for all the sprites */
for (node=bottom_node; node!=(OBJp)NULL; node=next_node)
{
   next_node = node->next;
   /* do the action function */
   node->action(node);
}
```

Completing the Frame

We have defined the end of a frame to be official when a page flip occurs. However, before starting the next frame, there are a couple more details to handle.

As we saw in Chapter 11, scrolling is done in two steps. In the process, some flags are set, including **scrolled_left**, **scrolled_right**, **scrolled_down**, **scrolled_up**, and **warped**. At the end of the frame, we look at these flags. If any of them have been set to **TRUE**, we know the hidden page and the visual page no longer match. We fix this situation right up with a call to **page_copy()**:

```
if (scrolled_left || scrolled_right || scrolled_up ||
   scrolled_down || warped)
   page_copy(vpo);
```

Passing **vpo** (visual page offset) to **page_copy()** means we are copying the visual page to the hidden page. The visual page is just the way we want it, because we just completed the frame, and copying it to the hidden page prepares the hidden page for the next frame.

We are done with the flags, so if any of them were **TRUE**, we set them all to **FALSE**. This is the last thing done at the bottom of the loop:

```
/* reset all the scrolling globals to false */
scrolled_left = FALSE;
```

```
scrolled_right = FALSE;
scrolled_up = FALSE;
scrolled_down = FALSE;
warped = FALSE;
```

That's it! We've done it! A frame of animation has been successfully completed. We will continue in this manner infinitely, as long as the game is played.

Next Level, Please

The **activate_level()** function we've been discussing is the primary function for controlling level animation. It is "blind" to the level contents. That is, it doesn't care if we are running Tommy's Egyptian level or his space platform level. The tiles can change, the sprites can change, the level size and shape can change, and even the action functions can change, and **activate_level()** won't care. It runs the same way no matter what the level looks like.

The *Tommy's Adventures* game has two levels to play with. Warping from one to the other is as easy as pressing the letter W. When this happens, **activate_level()** returns control of program execution to function **main()**, which examines the **warp_to_next_level flag**, and initiates the warp. This involves the same initializations as the previous level: Tommy's coordinates are initialized, level data and sprite data is loaded from disk as needed, and then **activate_level()** is called. Game execution continues in this manner until the user has had enough and decides to quit.

It is nice to do a fancy little special effect when prompting the user to quit. We will discuss a nifty one in the next chapter.

Keeping Oriented in Time and Space

I'm a great believer in using global variables. In this game, I depend strongly on certain global variables, such as the time variables, to keep everthing organized. The time variables are changed once each frame, and may be accessed from any action function. This is especially useful for timing Tommy's motion, the release of bullets, and so on.

The screen origins, level origins, and tile origins are useful for making sure everything is displayed in the right location. When we rebuild a screen from tiles and sprites, we have to know where to apply everything relative to everything else.

Putting the Accelerated Clock to Good Use

One of the first things we do in the **activate_level()** function is update certain time variables. As you recall from Chapter 12, we have re-vectored an interrupt to give us a finer time resolution. The **increment_timer()** function updates a global variable called **game_time** approximately 145 times per second. This variable is available to us to regulate activities in our game. We actually only look at this variable once per frame. The real quantity that interests us is not the total number of clock ticks that have elapsed, but the number of ticks that have elapsed since the beginning of the last frame. We get this by subtracting the old time value, called **last_time**, from the current time value in **activate_level()**, as follows:

```
/* determine how much time has passed since the last frame */
time = game_time;
delta_time = time - last_time;
delta_time = MAX(1L,delta_time);
last_time = time;
```

The value **delta_time** is the number of clock ticks that have elapsed since the last frame, and it is the value we will be examining in the action functions.

Working in Multiple Coordinate Systems

Applying sprites involves several coordinate conversions. Before we get to actual sprite application (discussed in the next section), let's review the four overlapping coordinate systems we're using:

- World space is the x and y pixel coordinates of the entire level, from **x = 0** to **x = maxcols * 16**, and **y = 0** to **y = maxrows * 16**.
- Screen space is the x and y pixel coordinates of the physical page, ranging from **x = 0** to **x = 351** and **y = 0** to **y = 239**. The hidden page offset (hpo) or visual page offset (vpo) is usually added to the y coordinate in screen space.
- Tile space is the column and row coordinates of tiles in the levels. These range from **col = 0** to **col = maxcols** and **row = 0** to **row = maxrows**. Only a subset of tile space will be displayed in video memory at any time. The tile in the upper-left corner of the screen has coordinates called **tile_orgx** and **tile_orgy**.
- Layout space is the column and row coordinates of tiles in the physical page. These range from **col = 0** to **col = 21** and **row = 0** to **row = 14**.

These descriptions are a bit confusing, but with time, you'll get used to the coordinates systems. The diagram in Figure 14.1 may help you visualize the various coordinate system conversions.

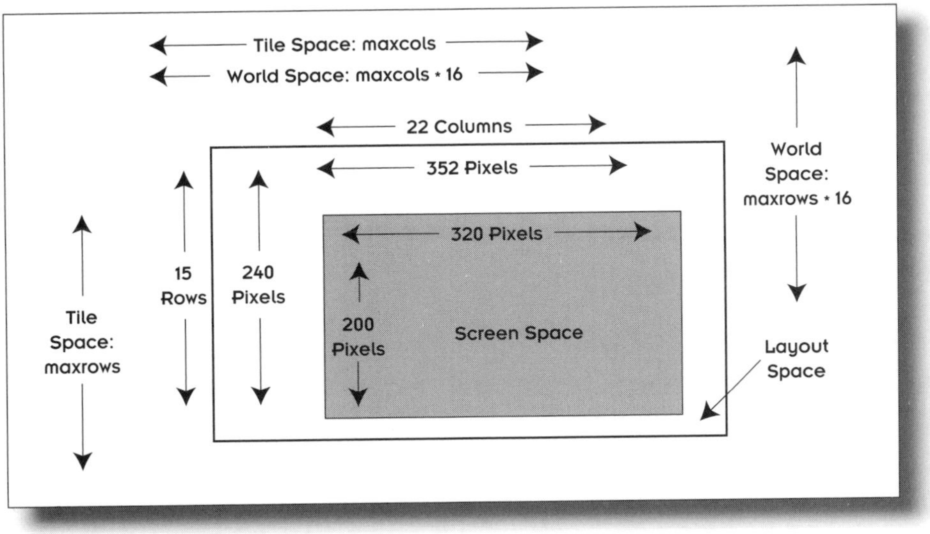

Figure 14.1 *The overlapping coordinate systems used in the game.*

Applying Sprites

There is more to applying sprites than just drawing a bitmap. You also must update the **layout** array in preparation of rebuilding the screen the next frame. (Recall the **rebuild_hidden()** function, discussed in Chapter 11, which examines the **layout** array and places tiles accordingly.) The **apply_sprite()** function handles the job of updating the **layout** array and drawing the sprite bitmap. All sprites are drawn using this function because it is assumed the **layout** array must be updated every time any sprite is drawn. In the next few sections we'll take a closer look at **apply_sprite()**.

```
void apply_sprite(OBJp objp)
{
   register int i,j;
   int x,y;
   int tile_x1,tile_y2;
   int tile_x2,tile_y1;
   int width, height;
   char *p;

   /* calculate the location, width and height */
   x = objp->x + objp->sprite->xoffset;
   y = objp->y + objp->sprite->yoffset;
   width = objp->sprite->width;
   height = objp->sprite->height;
```

```
/* which tiles are going to be covered up? */
tile_x1 = x/16 - tile_orgx;
tile_y2 = y/16 - tile_orgy;
tile_x2 = (x+width)/16 - tile_orgx;
tile_y1 = (y-height)/16 - tile_orgy;

/* if we are off the screen, forget it */
if (tile_x2 < 0 || tile_x1 > 21 || tile_y1 > 14 || tile_y2 < 0)
   return;

tile_x1 = MAX(tile_x1,0);
tile_x2 = MIN(21,tile_x2);
tile_y1 = MAX(tile_y1,0);
tile_y2 = MIN(14,tile_y2);

/* update the layout array */
for (i = tile_x1; i <= tile_x2; i++)
{
   p = layout[hidden][i] + tile_y1;
   for (j = tile_y1; j <= tile_y2; j++)
   {
      *p++ = TRUE;
   }
}

/* convert world space coordinates to screen space */
x = x - (tile_orgx*16);
y = y - (tile_orgy*16) + hpo;

/* set the clipping limits */
fg_setclip(0,351,hpo,hpb);
fg_move(x,y);

/* if the player is blinking, alternate black and regular */
if (objp == player && player_blink)
{
   blink_time += delta_time;
   if (blink_time > 5)
   {
      blink_time = 0;
      nblinks++;
      if (nblinks == 30)
      {
        player_blink = FALSE;
        nblinks = 0;
        blink_time = 0;
      }
   }
   if (nblinks%2 == 0)
   {
      get_blinkmap(objp);
      if (objp->direction == RIGHT)
```

```
            fg_clpimage(blink_map,objp->sprite->width,
                        objp->sprite->height);
         else
            fg_flpimage(blink_map,objp->sprite->width,
                        objp->sprite->height);
         fg_setclip(0,351,0,726);
         return;
      }
   }

   /* not blinking, just display the bitmap */
   if (objp->direction == RIGHT)
      fg_clpimage(objp->sprite->bitmap,width,height);
   else
      fg_flpimage(objp->sprite->bitmap,width,height);
   fg_setclip(0,351,0,726);
}
```

Calculating Coordinates

The first task **apply_sprite()** performs is calculate the x and y positions in world space. This is done by adding the x and y offsets to the **x** and **y** fields in the object structure.

```
/* calculate the location, width and height */
x = objp->x + objp->sprite->xoffset;
y = objp->y + objp->sprite->yoffset;
```

We also grab the width and the height of the sprite as follows:

```
width = objp->sprite->width;
height = objp->sprite->height;
```

Next, we calculate which tiles will be covered by this sprite. The x and y coordinates are then converted to layout space by dividing them by 16 and subtracting the tile origin:

```
tile_x1 = x/16 - tile_orgx;
tile_y2 = y/16 - tile_orgy;
```

Since a sprite will typically cover more than one tile, we also calculate the maximum x tile and the minimum y tile, based on the width and height of the sprite:

```
tile_x2 = (x+width)/16 - tile_orgx;
tile_y1 = (y-height)/16 - tile_orgy;
```

Now that we know which tiles the sprite will occupy, we can check if the sprite is completely off the screen. It is acceptable for the sprite to be partially off the screen because we are going to clip it when we display it. If it is totally off the screen, there is no point in drawing it at all. Here is the line of code that checks for this condition:

```
if (tile_x1 > 21 || tile_x2 < 0 || tile_y1 > 14 || tile_y2 < 0)
   return;
```

A sprite can go over the edge of the screen, but a tile cannot. When updating the **layout** array, we need to be careful not to write to an array element outside the array extents. That is, the sprite may cover a tile position at **tile_x1 = -1**, as in Figure 14.2, but we would not assign **layout_array[-1]** to **TRUE**. Doing so would result in an "array out of bounds" error. To be safe, we'll set the tile minimums and maximums to the edges of the screen:

```
tile_x1 = MAX(tile_x1,0);
tile_x2 = MIN(21,tile_x2);
tile_y1 = MAX(tile_y1,0);
tile_y2 = MIN(14,tile_y2);
```

Updating the layout Array

Now we're ready to update the **layout** array. Each tile that is covered by a sprite will have its corresponding **layout_array[]** element marked **TRUE**. We

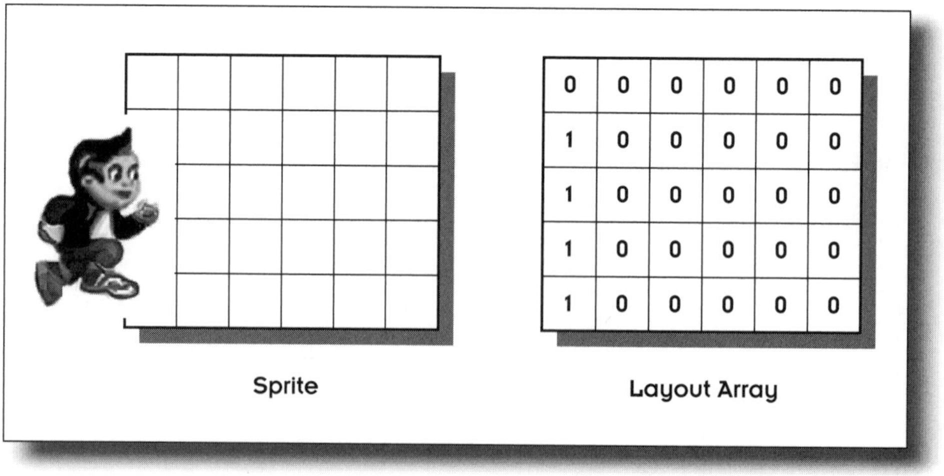

Figure 14.2 *A sprite going off the edge of the screen.*

work down the columns, starting with the first column covered by the sprite. We use a pointer, ***p**, to speed up the process:

```
/* update the layout array */
for (i = tile_x1; i <= tile_x2; i++)
{
   p = layout[hidden][i] + tile_y1;
   for (j = tile_y1; j <= tile_y2; j++)
   {
      *p++ = TRUE;
   }
}
```

Notice we are updating the **layout** array for the hidden page, because that is where we are planning to put the sprite.

Displaying the Sprite

It's time to display the sprite. First, though, we need to do a few more coordinate calculations. We convert the world space x and y coordinates to screen space x and y coordinates by subtracting the origins in level space. This will give us a value for x between 0 and 351 and a value for y between 0+hpo and 239+hpo. (The hpo value will be either 0 or 240 depending on which page is currently the hidden page.)

```
x = x - (tile_orgx*16);
y = y - (tile_orgy*16) + hpo;
```

Notice how the screen origins are calculated on the fly by multiplying the tile origins by 16 (see Figure 14.3).

Setting the Clipping Region

Since the sprite can go over the edge of the screen, it's important that we set the clipping limits. We're drawing the sprite on the hidden page, so we'll clip it at the top and bottom of the hidden page. If we neglected to do this, we would find remnants of our sprite on the hidden page or, worse, in the tile area. The clipping area is set by using the Fastgraph **fg_setclip()** function shown here:

```
fg_setclip(0,351,hpo,hpb);
```

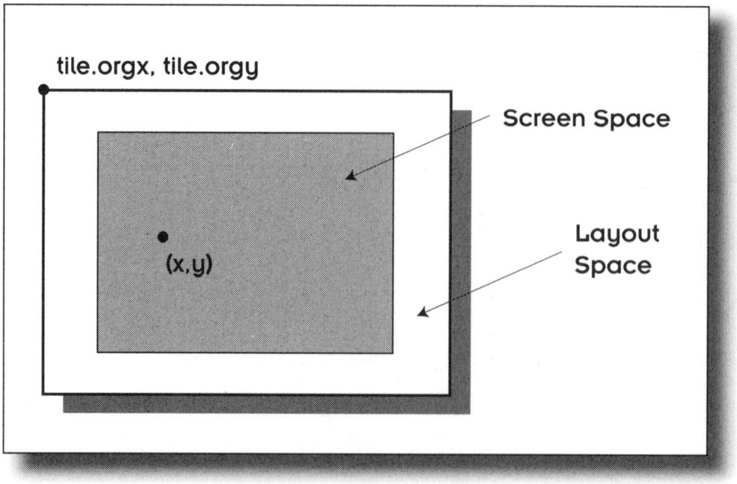

Figure 14.3 Screen origins are calculated on the fly.

fg_setclip()

The **fg_setclip()** function defines the clipping region in screen space. The clipping region is a rectangular area outside of which graphic display is suppressed.

```
void fg_setclip (int minx, int maxx, int miny, int maxy);
```

- *minx* is the screen space x coordinate of the clipping region's left edge.
- *maxx* is the screen space x coordinate of the clipping region's right edge. It must be greater than or equal to the value of *minx*.
- *miny* is the screen space y coordinate of the clipping region's top edge.
- *maxy* is the screen space y coordinate of the clipping region's bottom edge. It must be greater than or equal to the value of *miny*.

We then move to the calculated location to display the sprite.

```
fg_move(x,y);
```

If the sprite is facing right, we use **fg_clpimage()** to display it in a clipped, forward-facing direction. If the sprite is facing left, we use **fg_flpimage()** to display it in a reversed, or "flipped," direction. Here's the code that controls this operation:

```
if (objp->direction == RIGHT)
   fg_clpimage(objp->sprite->bitmap,width,hight);
else
   fg_flpimage(objp->sprite->bitmap,width,height);
```

Fastgraph Tip

fg_clpimage()

The **fg_clpimage()** function displays a clipped image strored as a mode-specific bitmap. The image will be positioned so that its lower-left corner is at the graphics cursor position. Only the part of the image that falls within the current clipping limits will be displayed.

```
void fg_clpimage (char *map_array, int width, int height);
```

- *map_array* is the arbitrary-length array containing the bitmap.
- *width* is the width in bytes of the bitmap.
- *height* is the height in bytes (pixel rows) of the bitmap.

Fastgraph Tip

fg_flpimage()

The **fg_flpimage()** function displays a reversed clipped image stored as a mode-specific bitmap. The image will be positioned so that its lower-left corner is at the graphics cursor position. Only the part of the image that falls within the current clipping limits will be displayed.

```
void fg_flpimage (char *map_array, int width, int height);
```

- *map_array* is the arbitrary-length array containing the bitmap.
- *width* is the width in bytes of the bitmap.
- *height* is the height in bytes (pixel rows) of the bitmap.

Notice what we are passing to **fg_clpimage()** and **fg_flpimage()**.

```
fg_clpimage(objp->image->bitmap,width,height);
```

The object points to the sprite, which points to the bitmap data.

Changing Tommy's Orientation

Using the same bitmap for left- and right-facing sprites saves RAM. In the case of Tommy, it also causes an interesting anomaly. You may notice that when he is facing right, he holds the gun in his right hand, and when he faces left, he is a left-handed gunslinger. His gun arm is always the arm in front. That's because the same bitmap is being used for shooting in both directions. We allow this blooper because it saves RAM. Most players won't notice that Tommy changes gun hands, and if they do, it does not detract from the playability of the game. Once again, conservation of sprite memory is a priority. An ambidextrous Tommy is a small price to pay for the several kilobytes of RAM saved using this strategy.

The last thing **apply_sprite()** does is return the clipping limits to encompass all of video memory. The sprite is now drawn on the hidden page, and will be visible the next time we do a page flip.

You may have noticed there is a special case in **apply_sprite** where Tommy is blinking. In this case, instead of Tommy's sprite bitmap being displayed, a special bitmap called **blinkmap** is displayed. I'll describe where this bitmap comes from in the next chapter when we talk about special effects.

Exiting the Game

Graceful exit from any game involves restoring the system to the way it was. The **terminate_game()** function does this.

```
void terminate_game()
{
   /* clean up and exit to DOS */
   fg_kbinit(0);           /* turn off the low-level keyboard handler */

   fg_setmode(3);          /* reset the video mode */
   fg_reset();             /* reset screen attributes */

   fg_setcolor(15);        /* print the exit string */
   printf(abort_string);
   printf("\n");

   set_rate(0);            /* put the clock speed back to a normal rate */
   _dos_setvect(0x1C,oldhandler); /* restore the interrupt */

   exit(0);
}
```

Actually, this function should look familiar, we since terminated several programs in earlier chapters (the tile ripper for example). The only differences we see here is there are some additional tasks involved in the clean-up process: we must set the clock speed back to normal, restore the clock interrupt to what it was before, and we must also terminate the low-level keyboard handler. Failing to do any of these things can be disasterous. If the low-level keyboard handler is not disabled, the user will not be able to type in any DOS commands or even reboot! And failing to restore the clock interrupt can cause problems with disk accesses.

The polite thing to do is leave the system in the same state in which you found it.

Chapter 15

Nothing adds more life and drama to your game than special effects. Take a look at this chapter to see how you can create interesting effects to make your game more appealing.

Creating Special Effects

Special effects are the best part of game programming. They are the icing on the cupcake, so to speak. They are also fun to write, because when it comes to special effects, you can break all the rules. You don't have to use your game editor to create special effects. You can use other tools that you already have or you can experiment with new ones. Here's your chance to play with that frame grabber card that has been gathering dust in your system. You can also create some great effects with your scanner or use some interesting ray tracing and image processing techniques. When creating special effects, let your imagination run wild. Try to show your users something they've never seen before.

I like to work on special effects when I get bored with programming the other parts of my games. Many of the game parts are just plain tedious and sometimes it feels good to take a break and work on something else. Once you visualize a special effect, try to think of ways to bring your idea to life. When it comes to special effects, you're no longer constrained by tiles, sprites, and predefined data structures. Nearly any trick you can think of to accomplish your special effect is perfectly acceptable.

In this chapter, we'll explore the special effects file EFFECTS.C, which is used in *Tommy's Adventures.* This is the final source final we need to complete our game. We'll start by discussing a few general guidelines for programming special effects and then we'll look at how the two special effects in our game are programmed.

The Golden Rule for Special Effects—Save RAM

There are a few limitations on what you can do with special effects. In most cases, you won't want to wipe out everything that is currently in video memory. You have to find a way to squeeze your special effects into whatever room is available. When we designed our use of video memory in Chapter 5, we left a little room for our special effects. (Recall the room we left available at the bottom of the video page.) I always try to leave a little room in video memory for special effects; think of this as allowing room for future creativity.

Unfortunately, special effects can take up a lot of RAM. Thus, you should try to optimize your use of RAM. If you have two special effects that never occur at the same time, see if you can share memory space. Also, plan ahead in terms of disk accesses. There are times when disk access is appropriate, such as when you save a game or warp to another level. Other times, a disk access simply won't work. For example, if you put in an explosion effect, you'll need it to be instantaneous. You can't read explosion data from disk. If the player of your game has to wait for an explosion to occur, your game won't be very exciting!

One way to conserve RAM is to use the same array space for more than one item. For example, you can store data for a popup help window and an explosion in the same array. The way to do this is to load the explosion data in the array and leave it there. That way, it will always be accessible when you need it. When you need the popup help data, read it from disk and overwrite the explosion array. Then, display the help data. When you're done, read the explosion data from the disk and overwrite the help window again. With this technique, the explosion will be reloaded into RAM and ready for instant display when you need it. This strategy assumes that the player will never want popup help in the middle of an explosion. That is a pretty safe assumption. If the user pauses the game by asking for help in the middle of the explosion, he or she will have to wait the few seconds it takes for the two disk accesses.

Creating Special Effects with EFFECTS.C

Table 15.1 lists the five functions provided in EFFECTS.C. The two special effects we are going to look at are:

- A slide projector screen that appears when you press the Esc key
- A technique for making the main character sprite blink when he is hit by an enemy

Here is the complete source file for EFFECTS.C:

```
/******************************************************************\
*  effects.c -- Tommy game source code file                        *
*  copyright 1994 Diana Gruber                                     *
*  compile using large model, link with Fastgraph (tm)             *
\******************************************************************/

#include "gamedefs.h"
/******************************************************************/
void get_blinkmap(OBJp objp)
{
   /* create a bitmap based on the sprite bitmap. If the pixel is
      any color except 0, make it black. 0 colors are transparent */

   register int i;
   register int nchar;
   char *p;

   /* p points to the bitmap of the object we want to copy */
   p = objp->sprite->bitmap;

   /* figure out the width and height */
   nchar = objp->sprite->width * objp->sprite->height;
```

Table 15.1 *Functions Used in EFFECTS.C*

Function	Description
get_blinkmap()	Gets a mask bitmap for the blinking sprite
load_status screen()	Reads the slide projector screen from a file
redraw_screen()	Updates all of the tiles
status_screen()	Displays the slide projector screen
status_shape()	Helps build the slide projector screen

```
   /* make the silhouette copy */
   for (i = 0; i < nchar; i++)
   {
      if (p[i] == 0)
         blink_map[i] = 0;
      else
         blink_map[i] = 7;
   }
}
/******************************************************************/
void load_status_screen()
{
   /* read in the slide projector screen */
   long filesize;

   if ((stream = fopen("slide.spr","rb")) == NULL)
   {
      strcpy(abort_string,"slide.spr not found");
      terminate_game();
   }
   /* allocate room for the slide projector screen */
   filesize = filelength(fileno(stream));
   slide_array = malloc((int)filesize);
   if (slide_array == (int)NULL)
   {
      strcpy(abort_string,"Out of memory: slide_array");
      terminate_game();
   }
   fread(slide_array,sizeof(char),(unsigned int)filesize,stream);
   slide_arraysize = (int)filesize;
   fclose(stream);
}
/******************************************************************/
void redraw_screen()
{
   OBJp node;
   register int i,j;

   for (i = 0; i < 22; i++)       /* draw background tiles */
      for (j = 0; j < 15; j++)
            put_tile(i,j);

   apply_sprite(player);         /* draw the sprites */
   for (node=bottom_node; node!=(OBJp)NULL; node=node->next)
      apply_sprite(node);
                                 /* draw foreground tiles */
   for (i = 0; i < 22; i++)
         if (layout[hidden][i][j])
            put_foreground_tile(i,j);

   if (show_score)               /* draw the score sprite */
      apply_sprite(score);
}
/******************************************************************/
```

```
int status_screen()
{
   /* assemble a slide projector screen (special effect) */

   int nruns;
   unsigned char key,aux;
   register int y;
   static char *string[] = {
   "Tommy's",
   "Adventures",
   "Q - Quit",
   "W - Warp",
   "copyright 1994",
   "Diana Gruber"};

   /* display the RLE in offscreen memory */
   nruns = slide_arraysize/2;
   fg_move(0,726);
   fg_display(slide_array,nruns,320);
   fg_tcmask(1);

   redraw_screen();            /* frame 1: screen & legs folded */
   status_shape(3,156,150);
   status_shape(7,160,110);
   status_shape(4,160,91);
   status_shape(5,160,142);
   status_shape(6,160,99);
   swap();
   fg_waitfor(1);

   redraw_screen();            /* frame 2: legs open */
   status_shape(2,128,168);
   status_shape(7,160,136);
   status_shape(7,160,110);
   status_shape(4,160,91);
   status_shape(5,160,142);
   status_shape(6,160,99);
   swap();
   fg_waitfor(1);

   redraw_screen();            /* frame 3: screen turns 90 degrees */
   status_shape(2,128,168);
   status_shape(7,160,136);
   status_shape(7,160,110);
   status_shape(4,160,91);
   status_shape(1,100,128);
   swap();

   fg_waitfor(1);              /* frame 4: top goes up */
   redraw_screen();
   status_shape(2,128,168);
   status_shape(7,160,136);
   status_shape(7,160,110);
   status_shape(4,160,74);
```

```
   status_shape(1,100,128);
   swap();

   for (y = 123; y > 50; y-= 8) /* move the screen up */
   {
      fg_tcxfer(0,127,683,695,100+screen_orgx,y+vpo+screen_orgy,0,0);
      fg_waitfor(1);
   }
   fg_tcxfer(0,127,683,695,100+screen_orgx,48+vpo+screen_orgy,0,0);

   fg_setcolor(black);
   center_string(string[0],105+screen_orgx,219+screen_orgx,
                 50+vpo+screen_orgy);
   center_string(string[1],105+screen_orgx,219+screen_orgx,
                 60+vpo+screen_orgy);

   fg_setcolor(blue);
   center_string(string[2],105+screen_orgx,219+screen_orgx,
                 77+vpo+screen_orgy);
   center_string(string[3],105+screen_orgx,219+screen_orgx,
                 87+vpo+screen_orgy);

   fg_setcolor(black);
   center_string(string[4],105+screen_orgx,219+screen_orgx,
                 105+vpo+screen_orgy);
   center_string(string[5],105+screen_orgx,219+screen_orgx,
                 115+vpo+screen_orgy);

   fg_kbinit(0);              /* turn off the keyboard handler */
   flushkey();
   fg_getkey(&key,&aux);      /* wait for a keypress */


   if ((key|32) == 'q')       /* quit */
   {
      fg_kbinit(1);
      return (TRUE);
   }
   else if ((key|32) == 'w')  /* warp */
   {
      fg_kbinit(1);
      warp_to_next_level = TRUE;
      return (TRUE);
   }
   else                       /* don't quit */
   {
      redraw_screen();
      swap();
      redraw_screen();
      fg_kbinit(1);
      return (FALSE);
   }
}
/******************************************************************/
```

```
void status_shape(int shape,int x,int y)
{
   /* pieces of the slide projector screen */
   static int x1[] = {  0,  0,128,196,208,216,232,208};
   static int x2[] = {127,127,195,207,215,223,247,215};
   static int y1[] = {683,697,683,683,683,683,683,689};
   static int y2[] = {695,704,714,723,725,726,726,725};

   fg_tcxfer(x1[shape],x2[shape],y1[shape],y2[shape],
            x+screen_orgx,y+screen_orgy+hpo,0,0);
}
```

Slides Ahead

When I was a younger, my father used to torture my siblings and me by showing us slides of his travels to other countries. Usually his pictures would have some historical or geographical significance, but to us they always looked like a picture of a cow in a field. How little we appreciated such things back then. Even now I look forward to slide shows with something less than enthusiasm.

When I designed the *Tommy's Adventures* game, I pictured Tommy as a small child tormented by large crawling insects and adults with slide projectors. I decided to incorporate a slide projector screen in the game as a special effect. It has some advantages as special effects go. It's roughly rectangular in shape, it can be easily drawn and built by graphic components, it's easy to recognize, it moves but it doesn't move too much, and it has a large white area that can be used to frame whatever gems of information I want to pass along to my users, such as "Quit Y/N?"

I began creating my special effect by drawing the slide projector screen. I just pulled out the screen from the back of the closet and set it up in the living room. The result of my effort is shown in Figure 15.1.

When I was satisfied with my drawing, I organized the drawing in such a way as to optimize space. Figure 15.2 shows the final state of the slide projector screen graphics. As you can see, the projector screen has been broken down into components. Since I planned to store the graphic in an *RLE* (discussed shortly), I organized the graphic into a shape that is long in the horizontal direction and narrow in the vertical direction.

Tommy's Tip

What Is an RLE?

An RLE is a *run-length-encoded image*. It's sometimes called a *packed bitmap*. RLEs are stored as a series of pixel runs, organized in a repeating color, count sequence. The first byte is the color of the pixel, the second byte is the number of pixels in a line of that color.

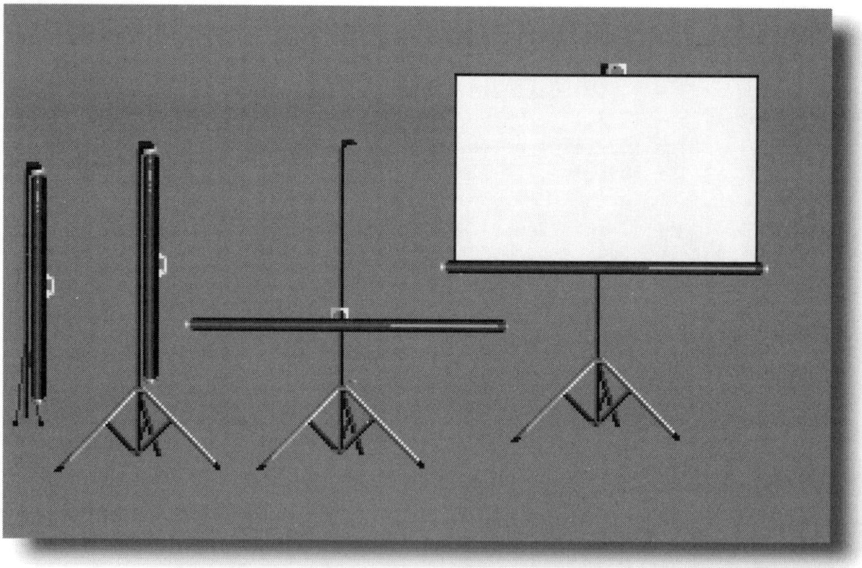

Figure 15.1 The slide projector screen.

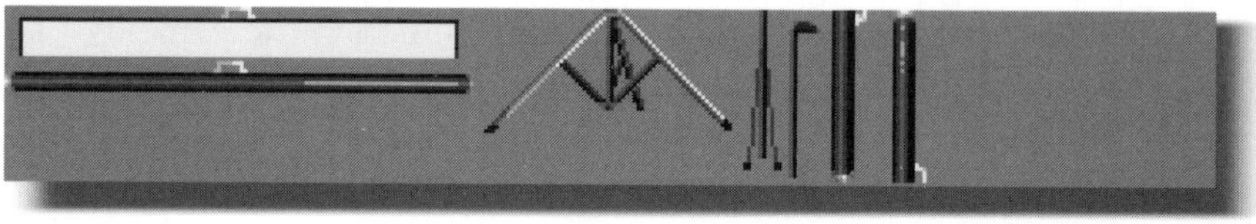

Figure 15.2 Slide projector screen, reduced to components.

RLE Images

RLE images have properties that are different from other image formats. This gives them certain advantages and disadvantages:

Advantages:

- RLEs don't provide header information. Header information in a PCX file can be very wasteful. The palette information, in particular, takes up 768 bytes in a 256-color image. If your image is small, the PCX header can be larger than the data! If you have a number of small images all using the same palette set, you will want to avoid the PCX format.
- RLEs may be blitted to video memory directly from disk, or they may be read into RAM and blitted to video memory as needed. The RAM to video memory blit is relatively fast.
- RLEs work independently of the video mode. If you are writing a game to work in both 16-color and 256-color modes, you will find RLEs very useful.

- RLE size will be very small if the data is blocky (long horizontal rows of identical pixels).

Disadvantages:

- RLEs don't provide header information. If you need to preserve the palette information, you should use a PCX or GIF file format.
- Standard paint programs do not support the RLE or SPR file format. You can create an RLE using Fastgraph's SNAPSHOT utility, described in the following Tommy's Tip.
- RLE formats can be very large if the data is dithered, if it has vertical stripes, or if for some other reason horizontally adjacent pixels do not match.

Tommy's Tip

Using the SNAPSHOT and CLIP Utilities

Fastgraph's SNAPSHOT utility is a terminate-and-stay-resident program (TSR) used to capture graphic images into an RLE format. To capture an image from any paint program, or any other source, load the SNAPSHOT utility, then display the image. Press Alt+Left Shift to activate SNAPSHOT. SNAPSHOT will capture whatever is on the screen and store it in a file with a numerical extension, for example SNAPSHOT.000, SNAPSHOT.001, and so on. These files are RLE images with a width equal to the width of the screen in the current graphics mode (in Mode X the width of the RLE will be 320 pixels).

Fastgraph's CLIP utility is an interactive utility you can use to reduce the size of an RLE image generated with Fastgraph's SNAPSHOT utility. Use CLIP to trim excess pixels of the edges of the RLE.

Loading the Status Screen

Traditionally, RLE files have an SPR (standard pixel run) extension. The RLE file containing the slide projector screen is stored in the file SLIDE.SPR. Since I wanted the slide projector screen to display instantaneously, I decided to load the RLE into RAM and leave it there. The function **load_status_screen()** in the EFFECTS.C file loads the RLE like this:

```
void load_status_screen()
{
   /* read in the slide projector screen */
   long filesize;
```

```
    if ((stream = fopen("slide.spr","rb")) == NULL)
    {
       strcpy(abort_string,"slide.spr not found");
       terminate_game();
    }
    /* allocate room for the slide projector screen */
    filesize = filelength(fileno(stream));
    slide_array = malloc((int)filesize);
    if (slide_array == (int)NULL)
    {
       strcpy(abort_string,"Out of memory: slide_array");
       terminate_game();
    }
    fread(slide_array,sizeof(char),(unsigned int)filesize,stream);
    slide_arraysize = (int)filesize;
    fclose(stream);
}
```

The slide RLE is stored in an array called **slide_array[]** which is declared in GAMEDEFS.H like this:

```
DECLARE unsigned char far *slide_array;
```

The room for the slide array must be allocated at runtime. Calculating the size of the slide array is as easy as looking at the file size. C's **filelength()** function returns the size of the SLIDE.SPR file, which is the size of the RLE. The SLIDE.SPR file is only 3K, which seemed like a reasonable investment in RAM usage for a special effect we'll be using often.

Building a Picture from Parts

There is a problem with storing the slide screen RLE in RAM. The screen is built in parts. First the legs are unfolded, then the bar is raised, the screen swings down, and the screen moves up incrementally. To accomplish this effect, I need to be able to blit parts of the image to the screen in sequence. It's very difficult to blit from RAM to video memory when you are extracting part of an RLE. The alternative is to store the image in RAM as a regular unpacked bitmap, but that would take more space—approximately 14K! My solution was to unpack the bitmap to video memory, and then perform video-to-video blits to copy the components of the slide projector from a hidden area in video memory to the visual page.

Recall the shape of video memory we designed earlier. It's a large rectangle with two pages at the top for page swapping, a foreground and background tile area, and an area below that is sometimes used to display the scoreboard. Our video memory scheme is shown in Figure 15.3.

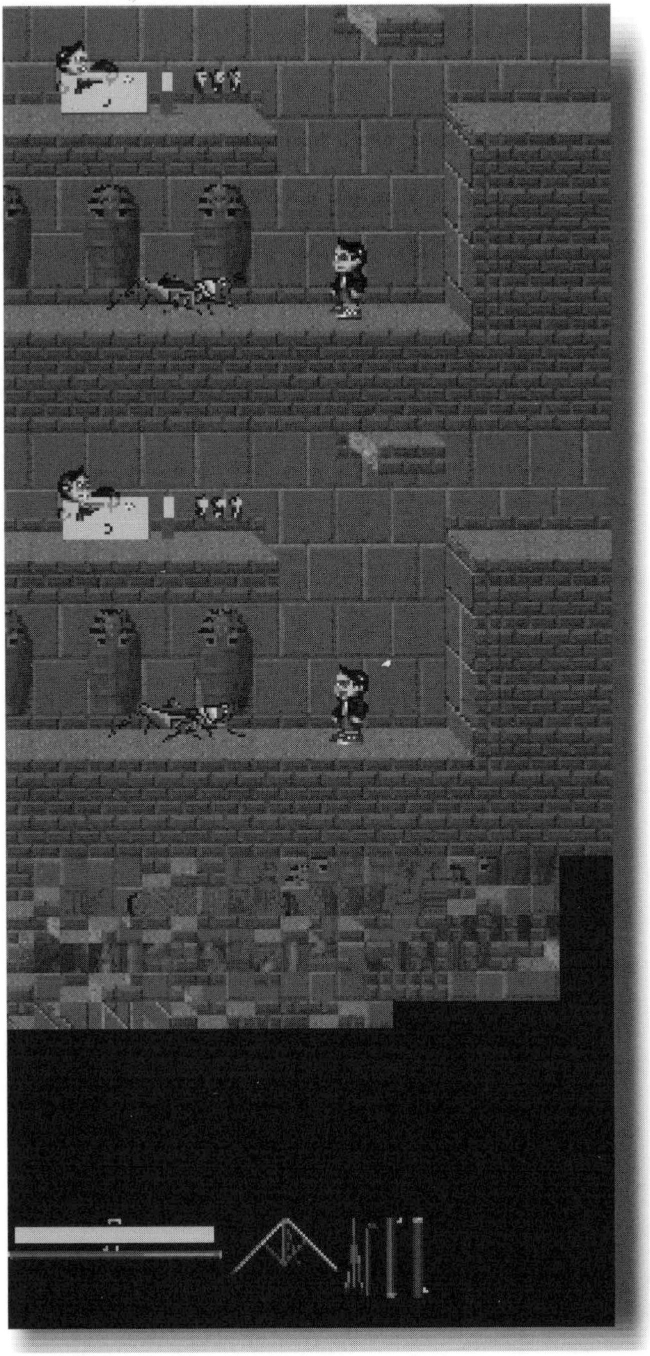

Figure 15.3 *Available video memory.*

Sharing Space

Recall that the scoreboard is only displayed in video memory periodically—when the score has changed and a new bitmap must be built. The rest of the time, the area below row 673 is not used. Since it's impossible for the score to change while the status screen (slide projector screen) is being displayed, we can safely re-use this area of video memory for our special effect.

The **status_screen()** function in the EFFECTS.C file handles the job of displaying the RLE in video RAM and reconstructing the slide projector screen from its parts:

```
int status_screen()
{
   /* assemble a slide projector screen (special effect) */

   int nruns;
   unsigned char key,aux;
   register int y;
   static char *string[] = {
   "Tommy's",
   "Adventures",
   "Q - Quit",
   "W - Warp",
   "copyright 1994",
   "Diana Gruber"};

   /* display the RLE in offscreen memory */
   nruns = slide_arraysize/2;
   fg_move(0,726);
   fg_display(slide_array,nruns,320);
   fg_tcmask(1);

   redraw_screen();          /* frame 1: screen & legs folded */
   status_shape(3,156,150);
   status_shape(7,160,110);
   status_shape(4,160,91);
   status_shape(5,160,142);
   status_shape(6,160,99);
   swap();
   fg_waitfor(1);

   redraw_screen();          /* frame 2: legs open */
   status_shape(2,128,168);
   status_shape(7,160,136);
   status_shape(7,160,110);
   status_shape(4,160,91);
   status_shape(5,160,142);
   status_shape(6,160,99);
   swap();
   fg_waitfor(1);
```

```
redraw_screen();              /* frame 3: screen turns 90 degrees */
status_shape(2,128,168);
status_shape(7,160,136);
status_shape(7,160,110);
status_shape(4,160,91);
status_shape(1,100,128);
swap();

fg_waitfor(1);                /* frame 4: top goes up */
redraw_screen();
status_shape(2,128,168);
status_shape(7,160,136);
status_shape(7,160,110);
status_shape(4,160,74);
status_shape(1,100,128);
swap();

for (y = 123; y > 50; y-= 8) /* move the screen up */
{
   fg_tcxfer(0,127,683,695,100+screen_orgx,y+vpo+screen_orgy,0,0);
   fg_waitfor(1);
}
fg_tcxfer(0,127,683,695,100+screen_orgx,48+vpo+screen_orgy,0,0);

fg_setcolor(black);
center_string(string[0],105+screen_orgx,219+screen_orgx,
              50+vpo+screen_orgy);
center_string(string[1],105+screen_orgx,219+screen_orgx,
              60+vpo+screen_orgy);

fg_setcolor(blue);
center_string(string[2],105+screen_orgx,219+screen_orgx,
              77+vpo+screen_orgy);
center_string(string[3],105+screen_orgx,219+screen_orgx,
              87+vpo+screen_orgy);

fg_setcolor(black);
center_string(string[4],105+screen_orgx,219+screen_orgx,
              105+vpo+screen_orgy);
center_string(string[5],105+screen_orgx,219+screen_orgx,
              115+vpo+screen_orgy);

fg_kbinit(0);                 /* turn off the keyboard handler */
flushkey();
fg_getkey(&key,&aux);         /* wait for a keypress */


if ((key|32) == 'q')          /* quit */
{
   fg_kbinit(1);
   return (TRUE);
}
else if ((key|32) == 'w')     /* warp */
{
```

```
      fg_kbinit(1);
      warp_to_next_level = TRUE;
      return (TRUE);
   }
   else                          /* don't quit */
   {
      redraw_screen();
      swap();
      redraw_screen();
      fg_kbinit(1);
      return (FALSE);
   }
}
```

We display the RLE array from RAM to the desired part of video memory using Fastgraph's **fg_display()** function:

```
fg_move(0,726);
fg_display(far_slidearray,nruns,320);
```

Fastgraph Tip

fg_display()

The **fg_display()** function displays an image stored in Fastgraph's standard pixel run format, where the image resides in an array. The image will be positioned so that its lower-left corner is at the graphics position.

```
void fg_display (char *map_array, int runs, int width);
```

- *map_array* is the arbitrary-length array containing the pixel run map. The pixel runs are represented by a (color,count) pair, as shown here:

  [0] color for run 1
  [1] count for run 1
  [2] color for run 2
  [3] count for run 2
  .
  .
  .
  [2n-2] color for run n
  [2n-1] color for run n

  Each "color" element is a value between 0 and 255 specifying the color index for that pixel run. Each "count" element is a value between 0 and 255 specifying the length in pixels of that pixel run.

- *runs* is the number of pixel runs to display from the pixel run map. It's normally half the size of the *map_array* array.
- *width* is the width of the image in pixels. It must be greater than zero.

Notice how we calculate the number of runs in the RLE bitmap. Since each pixel run takes exactly two bytes, the number of runs is the array size divided by two:

```
nruns = slide_arraysize/2;
```

Also, notice that the width of the RLE is 320, which is equal to the width of the screen. Actually, the image itself is slightly less than 320. I chose the 320 value because I found it easier to work with. Extra blank space at the right side of an RLE adds no additional overhead in terms of disk space or RAM space. The amount of extra time it takes to blit the RLE is negligible, but the savings in development time is significant. Recalculating the width every time the art changes, trimming the image, and then editing and recompiling the code is time consuming. Using the full screen width for this image is a reasonable shortcut.

Animating the Status Screen

We're calling the effect a *status screen* because its purpose is to report the status of the game, such as when the game has been paused or saved. It takes five frames to animate the setting up of the screen, and then another nine frames in a loop to slide the screen up. There are eight components of the slide projector screen. Not all these components are displayed in every frame.

I found it simplified the code to have a separate function called **status_shape()** to display the individual pieces of the screen. The x and y coordinates are stored in static arrays that are initialized in the function. The **fg_tcxfer()** function is used to do a transparent blit from video memory to video memory to build the screen:

```
void status_shape(int shape,int x,int y)
{
   /* pieces of the slide projector screen */
   static int x1[] = {  0,   0,128,196,208,216,232,208};
   static int x2[] = {127,127,195,207,215,223,247,215};
   static int y1[] = {683,697,683,683,683,683,683,689};
   static int y2[] = {695,704,714,723,725,726,726,725};
```

```
    fg_tcxfer(x1[shape],x2[shape],y1[shape],y2[shape],
              x+screen_orgx,y+screen_orgy+hpo,0,0);
}
```

When I originally wrote the function, I put multiple calls to **fg_tcxfer()** in the **status_screen()** function, but I didn't like the way the code looked (it looked messy). Isolating the calls to **fg_tcxfer()** in a separate function made the code easier to read and debug.

Each frame of animation is accomplished by redrawing the hidden page, applying the components to the hidden page, and swapping pages. Only a small part of the white and blue slide projector screen is stored in the RLE. This is expanded into a full-size screen by copying parts of it in sequence to give the effect of motion as the screen "unrolls" upward, as shown in Figure 15.4.

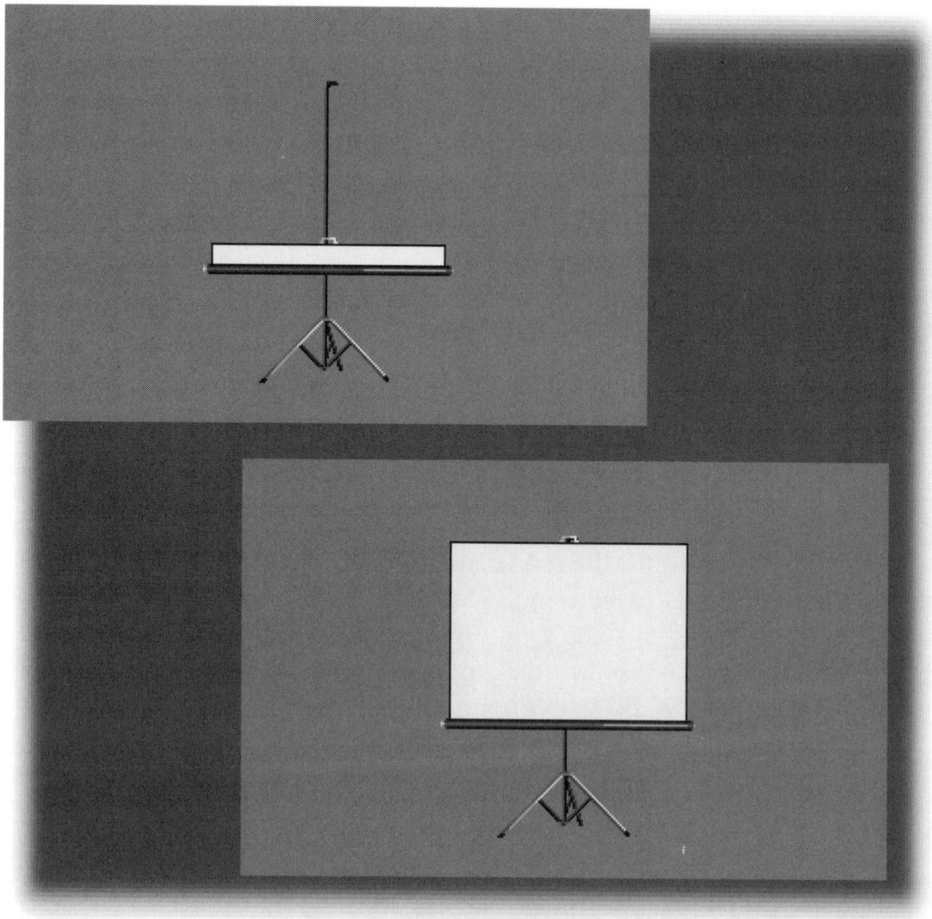

Figure 15.4 *Sequential video blits give the effect of motion.*

```
for (y = 123; y > 50; y -= 8)
{
   fg_tcxfer(0,127,683,695,100+screen_orgx,y+vpo+screen_orgy,0,0);
   fg_waitfor(1);
}
```

After the screen has been completely drawn, text is added to it. In a bigger game, I would probably use variable text. That is, I would re-use the effect but put different text on it depending on what the game was doing. For example, at the end of the game, I might display "You lose!" on the status screen.

Different Kinds of Keyboard Handlers

After the screen is displayed, animated, and has the text drawn on it, it's time to wait for user input. At this point, I disable the low-level keyboard handler by calling **fg_kbinit(0)**. I find it easier to use the regular BIOS keyboard handler with the keyboard buffer for accepting text input. The low-level handler is more appropriate for the kind of high speed input we need during game play. Status screens work better when you can collect keystrokes and process them one at a time.

Fastgraph Tip

fg_kbinit()

The **fg_kbinit()** function enables or disables the Fastgraph low-level keyboard handler. If the keyboard handler is already in the requested state, nothing happens.

```
void fg_kbinit (int state);
```

- *state* is a flag specifying if the keyboard handler is to be enabled (*state* = 1) or disabled (*state* = 0).

I only process three kinds of user input in this function. I'm looking for instructions to quit, warp to the next level, or continue. This is a somewhat simplified function. In a more sophisticated game, you would offer the user more choices, or perhaps a menu with a floating highlight bar. For our purposes, the three choices are enough to demonstrate this example of a special effect.

Making Tommy Blink

Most games give some kind of a blink effect when the character encounters an enemy or hazard. (I don't mean the character's eyes blink—I mean his whole body flashes on and off, as if in an emotional response to the trauma of having encountered a giant pink scorpion). I've seen this in so many games, I decided I needed to duplicate it. I consider blinking sprites a special effect, but it isn't really that special.

The way I make a sprite blink is by creating another bitmap that is an exact mask of the original bitmap. That is, all the transparent pixels in the original bitmap remain transparent, and all the non-transparent pixels are set to black, as shown in Figure 15.5. Then I alternate displaying the regular bitmap and the bitmap mask. The effect is a sprite that blinks to black at a specified interval.

The mask bitmap is made on the fly. We don't want to create a mask bitmap for every sprite ahead of time because that would waste a lot of space. We don't know exactly what Tommy is going to be doing when he needs to blink. He could touch an enemy while running, jumping, kicking, or shooting. To complicate matters further, Tommy doesn't stand still after he has been hit. He continues running, jumping, kicking, and shooting even while blinking. Whatever Tommy is doing, he has to continue doing it, and he has to simultaneously blink. Therefore, we will need to make many mask bitmaps as Tommy moves along.

The Blink Map

I allocate space at load-time for the blink mask bitmap. Four thousand bytes seems to be about enough space. The declaration for the blink mask bitmap is found in GAMEDEFS.H and shown here:

```
char far blink_map[4000];
```

***Figure 15.5** A sprite along with an exact mask of the original bitmap.*

This array will be used to hold the mask data. It will be filled on the fly by comparing it to the sprite bitmap (in this case, always Tommy), and setting the bytes to 0 or 1. This task is accomplished in the function **get_blinkmap()**:

```
void get_blinkmap(OBJp objp)
{
   /* create a bitmap based on the sprite bitmap. If the pixel is
      any color except 0, make it black. 0 colors are transparent */

   register int i;
   register int nchar;
   char *p;

   /* p points to the bitmap of the object we want to copy */
   p = objp->image->bitmap;

   /* figure out the width and height */
   nchar = objp->image->width * objp->image->height;

   /* make the silhouette copy */
   for (i = 0; i < nchar; i++)
   {
      if (p[i] == 0)
         blink_map[i] = 0;
      else
         blink_map[i] = 7;
   }
}
```

In GAMEDEFS.H we also declare a global variable to tell us when Tommy is blinking, and another one to tell us how many times he has blinked so far:

```
int player_blink;
int nblinks;
```

Also, since the blink is time dependent, we'll need another variable to keep track of the time since the last blink:

```
unsigned long blink_time;
```

Since this is a time variable, we declare it unsigned long so it will match the other time variables.

Counting Blinks

Every time Tommy hits an enemy, **player_blink** is set to **TRUE** and **nblinks** is set to 0. Tommy will continue to blink until **nblinks** hits a target value. In our game, the target value is 30. That is, Tommy blinks 30 times each time he is hit.

The code to handle the blinking is part of the **apply_sprite()** function from TOMMY.C, which we reviewed in the last chapter. Let's take another look at this function, especially the last part, where the bitmap is displayed:

```
void apply_sprite(OBJp objp)
{
   register int i,j;
   int x,y;
   int tile_x1,tile_y2;
   int tile_x2,tile_y1;
   int width, height;
   char *p;

   /* calculate the location, width and height */
   x = objp->x + objp->sprite->xoffset;
   y = objp->y + objp->sprite->yoffset;
   width = objp->sprite->width;
   height = objp->sprite->height;

   /* which tiles are going to be covered up? */
   tile_x1 = x/16 - tile_orgx;
   tile_y2 = y/16 - tile_orgy;
   tile_x2 = (x+width)/16 - tile_orgx;
   tile_y1 = (y-height)/16 - tile_orgy;

   /* if we are off the screen, forget it */
   if (tile_x2 < 0 || tile_x1 > 21 || tile_y1 > 14 || tile_y2 < 0)
      return;

   tile_x1 = MAX(tile_x1,0);
   tile_x2 = MIN(21,tile_x2);
   tile_y1 = MAX(tile_y1,0);
   tile_y2 = MIN(14,tile_y2);

   /* update the layout array */
   for (i = tile_x1; i <= tile_x2; i++)
   {
      p = layout[hidden][i] + tile_y1;
      for (j = tile_y1; j <= tile_y2; j++)
      {
         *p++ = TRUE;
      }
   }

   /* convert world space coordinates to screen space */
   x = x - (tile_orgx*16);
   y = y - (tile_orgy*16) + hpo;

   /* set the clipping limits */
   fg_setclip(0,351,hpo,hpb);
   fg_move(x,y);
```

```
   /* if the player is blinking, alternate black and regular */
   if (objp == player && player_blink)
   {
      blink_time += delta_time;
      if (blink_time > 5)
      {
         blink_time = 0;
         nblinks++;
         if (nblinks == 30)
         {
           player_blink = FALSE;
           nblinks = 0;
           blink_time = 0;
         }
      }
      if (nblinks%2 == 0)
      {
         get_blinkmap(objp);
         if (objp->direction == RIGHT)
             fg_clpimage(blink_map,width,height);
         else
             fg_flpimage(blink_map,width,height);
         fg_setclip(0,351,0,726);
         return;
      }
   }

   /* not blinking, just display the bitmap */
   if (objp->direction == RIGHT)
      fg_clpimage(objp->sprite->bitmap,width,height);
   else
      fg_flpimage(objp->sprite->bitmap,width,height);

   fg_setclip(0,351,0,726);
}
```

Recall that **apply_sprite()** is a general purpose function. It's called when any sprite is applied. The only case we are concerned with is when the sprite is Tommy, and Tommy is blinking. If that's the case, the first thing we do is add **delta_time** to **blink_time**. We are only going to change the blink status if five or more clock ticks have elapsed. Tommy is not going to change every frame. He could have two or three black frames in a row, followed by two or three regular frames. It depends on the speed of the computer, and what else is happening during the frame, such as scrolling. Tying the blink to the clock is the cleanest way to get a consistent looking blink.

If five clock ticks have passed, the **nblinks** variable is incremented. This variable serves two purposes. Besides counting the total number of blinks, we use it to keep track of the current blink state. If **nblinks** is an even number, then we display the mask bitmap. If it is odd, we display the regular bitmap.

Each time we display the mask bitmap, we build a new mask. We assume the sprite has changed since the last time we displayed the mask bitmap. It's a pretty safe assumption. If Tommy was recently hit, his first instinct will be to move really fast, either to get away or to shoot back. It's not worth the effort to check and see if the sprite image has changed. Skipping the **get_blinkmap()** function in the rare case where the sprite image has not changed is not worth the overhead in doing the check every time. Besides, **get_bitmap()** is a reasonably fast function, since all it does is manipulate an array in RAM.

The status screen effect and the sprite blinking effect are just two simple examples of the kinds of special effects people like to see in games. Special effects add drama and life to your game and should be used liberally and ingeniously. The suggestions given here are just guidelines. Let your imagination be your guide when it comes to special effects. The more of them you have, the better your game will be.

Chapter 16

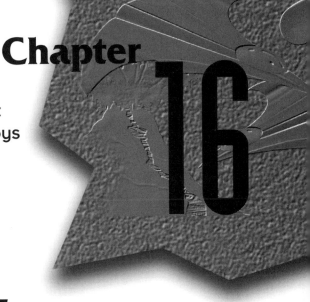

Don't let bugs get the best of you! Debugging skills are what separates the men from the boys (or in my case, the girls).

Debugging Games

If programming special effects is the best part of game programming, debugging is surely the worst. It's the most time-consuming, aggravating, niggling, nit-picking, unforgiving, tedious aspect of game programming. It will slow your progress and cause you to miss deadlines, age prematurely, and lose your sense of equanimity, if not your breakfast. In short, it is a ghastly process that we all would avoid if we could.

Unfortunately, we can't avoid debugging games. Debugging is part of the development process. Bugs are a given—I have never known a program to be developed without introducing at least one bug. I am sure, at some point, even *Hello World* was once spelled *Hello Wolrd.*

We can't avoid bugs, all we can do is find ways to deal with them. Our goal, when debugging games, should be to minimize the debugging process. That is, we should strive to get it done (and get it done *right*) in the shortest amount of time possible. This could still be a considerable amount of time, so be warned! The gremlins that plague us are sneaky and persistent, and as we gird our loins and march into battle, we must prepare ourselves for a long seige.

Tracking Down Gremlins

Bugs can occur practically anyplace in the development process. Let's begin by looking at the process itself and examine the places where bugs are often introduced:

1. *The first compile.* You would be suprised at how many people get stuck the first time they compile. One of the most common technical support questions I hear is "How do I make a project file?" The answer to this question, and many others, is in your manuals, including your compiler manual, your Fastgraph manual, and the installation instructions at the beginning of this book. Also check the release notes on any disks you may handle, including the Fastgraph installation disks and the disk in the back of this book. Don't feel bad if it takes you a while to get past your first compile. You are not alone. Many people have problems setting up their compilers and libraries. Here are a few common problems to watch for:

   - *Project File.* If you are using Borland C++ or the Turbo C/C++ Integrated Development Environment (IDE), you need a project file! Honest, you do. Please don't call me and ask me if this is true; call Borland's technical support.
   - *Paths.* Be sure your libraries and include files are in the directories where the linker expects to find them! With Borland C++ and Turbo C/C++, there is more than one way to goof up the path. Check your manuals.
   - *Mixed Models.* Don't try to compile in the large model and link with medium model libraries! That doesn't work. You may get a helpful, user-friendly message such as *segment fixup overflow.*
   - *Compiler not installed properly.* This happens! Be sure to run the install program, and whenever possible, accept the default values (such as the path name defaults). If your compiler won't work, try re-installing it, recompiling all your source-code modules, and relinking.
   - *Libraries not installed properly.* In my experience, this is less of a problem, but it happens! Re-install Fastgraph for the compiler and memory model you are using.
   - *Floating-Point Problems.* Why are you using floating point anyway? Don't you know gamers go to extreme measures to avoid floating-point arithmetic? It bulks up your code and slows it down! If you must use it, be sure you link with *two* Fastgraph libraries (one is specific to your compiler) and don't rely on the math coprocessor—not everybody has one.

2. *Syntax Errors.* These are common, and usually easy to fix. For example, your compiler will tell you if you are missing a semi-colon or a curly bracket. There are, however, a few tricky syntax errors that are hard to spot. These can slow you down. Here are some examples:

   - *Nested comments.* With most compilers, nested comments don't work. The beginning of the inner comment is not seen and the end of the inner comment is assumed to be the end of the outer comment. The rest of your comment is interpreted as code that doesn't compile. This is usually an easy bug to spot.
   - *Missing end of comment.* This bug is difficult to spot. You can spend hours wondering "Why are these four lines of code not being executed?" when in fact they have been inadvertently commented out. The "*/" was left off the comment line above the code, and everything between this line and the end of the next comment line is interpreted to be a comment. This is a most aggravating bug.

3. *Garbled code problems.* These occur when your code doesn't run the way you think it should. These are the hard bugs to locate! Here are some examples:

   - *Mismatched else.* This bug illustrates the importance of careful code formatting. You intended an *else* or an *else if* to go with an *if* but it went with another *if.* This can mess you up for days.
   - *Incrementing problems.* I have discovered that most bugs, at some level, can be reduced to an incrementing problem. For example, your **i++** went one **+** to far. Or you incremented when you should have decremented. Or you set a target value less than your starting value so that you'll never reach the target. Or, you set a target value larger than it should be and you end up writing to out-of-bounds array elements. Incrementing problems are the worst.
   - *Operator precedence problems.* These are really aggravating! You thought you plussed a variable and then timesed it but you actually timesed it and then plussed it. An especially tricky variation of this problem happens with pointers. Notice that ***p++** equals ***(p++)**, not **(*p)++**. This is also considered (guess what!) an incrementing problem.

Now let's look at some other specific problems, and what you can do about them.

What Mode Is This Anyway?

Ideally, you want your game program to be executed from mode 3 (text mode), set the video mode to mode 20 (Mode X graphics), execute for a while, then return to mode 3 and exit. In an ideal world, the mode you end up with is the mode you started with. But in an ideal world, we wouldn't have any bugs, would we?

If a program terminates abnormally, you could end up in mode 20, or you could end up in some other video mode. If your screen looks strange upon exit, you probably had an abnormal termination. You may even have a DOS error message on the screen (such as "Integer divide by 0") that you can't read. To read this message, turn on your printer, redirect DOS output to your printer (Ctrl+Print Scrn ought to do it), and hopefully your error message will print on your printer and shed some light on why you had an abnormal termination.

To set your video environment back to mode 3, use the DOS MODE command, as in "MODE CO80." This will probably fix the problem, but if your abnormal termination was serious, something else in your system memory may have been clobbered, and you'll have to reboot.

How Code Gets Clobbered

An abnormal termination, as we just explored, is a good indication your code has been clobbered. This happens when the copy of the program that is in RAM is somehow overwritten or corrupted. It no longer works the way you expect it to, because it is no longer capable of working. Something has caused it to break.

When your code gets clobbered, your program may not be the only code affected. Other parts of memory may be damaged as well. Your TSRs may no longer work, you may lose some of your environment variables, you can even (horrors!) overwrite your CMOS. When this happens, you may reboot and get the message "fixed disk C: not found". Don't panic! Your hard disk has most likely not been damaged, only the chip that keeps track of it has been overwritten. You can run your system's SETUP program to get your hard disk back.

This is one of the worst things that can happen when your data is out of control. Try to avoid this kind of bug if you can. Let's look at some ways code can be clobbered.

Data Out of Control

This most often happens when you write beyond the end of an array. An incrementing problem will do it. When the array has been filled, and data continues to be written, it has to go somewhere. Very often, data will be written to the code segment. Whole functions can be wiped out this way. A data overflow in one part of your program can destroy a function in a completely unrelated part of your program. This is what makes this kind of bug so hard to find: You have to look in places other than in the function in which the bug appears to happen.

Even one byte out of bounds can destroy a whole function, and it is nearly impossible to predict which function will be affected. This is a bug that is difficult to avoid and difficult to find!

Null Pointers

Null pointers happen when an item, such as an array or a structure, is declared but space is not allocated for it. For example, the following code will result in a null pointer error:

```
char *p;
p[0] = 0;
```

When a pointer is declared, it begins life pointing to an integer 0, which is called NULL. This thing, NULL, is supposed to be nothing. That is, by definition, a pointer pointing to NULL points to nothing. Except that it doesn't. It points to something. I don't know exactly what it points to, but whatever it is, you can write to it and mess up your program.

My Microsoft C compiler manual says a null pointer points to the NULL segment, which is a special area in low memory that is normally not used. Writing to this segment will trigger a *null pointer assignment* error message. I suspect this is compiler specific, though. I would not expect other compilers' null pointers to point to the same thing Microsoft's null pointers point to.

Whatever your null pointer points to, don't write to that area. Instead, allocate space somewhere else and point your pointer to it. Here are two better ways to write the previous code:

```
char p[ARRAYSIZE];
p[0] = 0;
```

Note that the space for the array is allocated at compile-time. In this example, space for the array is allocated at runtime:

```
char *p;
p = malloc(ARRAYSIZE);
p[0] = 0;
```

Either method is fine, as long as space is allocated for the data and the pointer is directed to point to that space. Until this happens, the pointer points to NULL.

When working with structures, null pointers are especially easy to incorporate into your code. In Chapter 12, we discussed declaring structures and allocating space for them. You may recall, that this was a rather complicated process. If your code has been clobbered, examine your structures carefully. They are a very likely candidate for a null pointer assignment.

Dangling Nodes

Dangling nodes occur when you are working with a linked list of structures. We saw an example of this in Chapter 14. The code shown here may result in a dangling node:

```
/* do the action functions for all the objects */
for (node=bottom_node; node!=(OBJp)NULL; node=node->next)
{
   node->action(node);
}
```

This code looks simple enough, but a problem occurs when the action function for the object deletes a node from the list. When the node is deleted, so is the pointer to the next node. The result is that **node=node->next** doesn't know what to point to.

This bug is specific to the compiler, and results are unpredictable. I found the code executed perfectly with the Microsoft C compiler, and hung tighter than a drum with the Borland compiler. Worse, I had no idea where to look for the source of the bug. It took me days to track this bug down and fix it. This is a bad bug! Avoid it if you can.

Dangling nodes also occur when you remove or reassign the pointer to a node before you free it. Improperly freed nodes will fill up RAM over a period of time. Your program will run fine for a while, then it will just crash. Don't you just hate when that happens?

Mouse Droppings

Mice introduce their own special problems into a program. Fortunately, we don't use a mouse in our game. Unfortunately, we do use a mouse in our game editor. Therefore, we will have to deal with mouse bugs.

Mouse droppings occur when fragments of the mouse cursor are left on the screen when the mouse moves. The most common cause of this is failing to turn the mouse cursor off when writing to the screen. The best solution is to *always turn the mouse cursor off* when writing anything to any part of the screen, or doing anything else to video memory, like a page flip. This is a rule. Everybody has to do this. I am not making this up. It is a big pain, and it causes your mouse to flicker, but you still have to do it, every single time.

There are exceptions. It is possible to constrain mouse motion to one part of the screen while writing to another part of the screen. It is also possible to fix the mouse in one position, and constrain screen writes to areas that do not touch the mouse cursor. These solutions are often more trouble than they are worth, but occasionally they may be useful.

You may also turn the mouse cursor off altogether, and use your own cursor, as we did in the level editor in Chapter 6.

Mind Your Xs and Ys

In the interest of fast, optimized code, Fastgraph does very little error checking. That means, functions are not automatically clipped at the edge of the screen. You may draw off the edge of the screen with unpredictable results (usually an image will wrap around and end up on a different part of the screen). Fastgraph also does not check arguments that are passed to functions. You can pass nonsensical values to Fastgraph functions, and the functions will execute to the best of their ability, sometimes with disasterous results. For example, I once called **fg_paint()** and passed (x,y) coordinates to it that were outside the closed polygon area I wanted to paint. The resulting flood fill filled to the edge of the screen, over the edge of the screen, and kept right on filling. It filled video memory, it filled RAM, and then it filled my CMOS! That was bad! By the way, since then Ted has written a version of **fg_paint()** called **fg_flood()** that checks for clipping limits (which, by default, are the screen extents). The fill function with clipping is a bit slower than the function without it. When speed is critical, error checking must be left out of the low-level code, and it is up to the programmer to check for errors at the high level. Here are some examples of common coordinate errors to check for.

A Pixel Too Far

Remember, screen coordinates start at 0 and go to a value one less than the length or width of the screen. So don't try to draw a rectangle by calling:

```
fg_rect(0,320,0,200);
```

That is a mistake! You have gone too far! What you really wanted was:

```
fg_rect(0,319,0,199);
```

Similarly, remember the width of a rectangle is x2-x1+1. Don't forget the +1! If you want to transfer 20 rows and 20 columns starting at x = 100, y = 100, the proper code is

```
fg_transfer(100,119,100,119,0,19,0,0);
```

not:

```
fg_transfer(100,120,100,120,0,20,0,0);
```

Parallel Dimensions

Parallel dimensions are something you find in the Twilight Zone—a coordinate system that appears logical, but is actuallly unrelated to the reality you are working in. You enter a parallel dimension when you try to address screen coordinates in a manner that does not describe them as they actually are.

My point is: Fastgraph addresses rectangles on the screen in an (X1,X2,Y1,Y2) sequence. Other graphics libraries may address the screen in an (X1,Y1,X2,Y2) sequence. The first method addresses the edges of the rectangle, the second method addresses the corners. Neither strategy is "right" or "wrong," they are just different. Problems arise when you try to mix them, the biggest problem being you forget which is which. It is quite easy to mangle your x and y coordinates, especially when you have developed the habit of working in one system and you must change to the other. Sometimes a simple conversion function or a macro will help.

Can't Even Reboot!

Have you ever exited a program that left your computer in such a mangled state, you had to reboot, but found you could not? That is, a *soft* reboot (pressing Ctrl+Alt+Delete) failed to work. You may be able to press a reset key on your computer to reboot, or you may have to turn your computer off and on again to get a reboot. (Warning! When powering down your computer, give the hard disk a little break. Let it spin down and come to a stop before restarting the system. The extra few seconds this takes may save wear and tear on your hard drive.) What causes this inability to reboot?

One likely cause is abnormal termination of your game. Remember, we have done some tricky things to the system. For example, we have installed a low-level keyboard handler to trap and process all keystrokes before the BIOS keyboard handler gets them. That includes Ctrl+Alt+Delete. The BIOS won't initiate the reboot, because it never sees the keystroke combination.

We have also re-vectored the timer interrupt to increase the clock tick rate. If the program terminates abnormally, this may not be restored to the default 18.2 clock ticks per second. Since disk controllers depend on the 18.2 tick per second rate, you may find you have trouble reading and writing files. The best thing to do after an abnormal program termination is power down.

The Debugging Process

We've discussed a number of bugs and their causes, but the question is, how do you find them and fix them? Understanding the nature of bugs does not solve this problem. You still have to develop a debugging process, and develop methods for tracking down and killing bugs.

This is not as easy as it sounds. There are few hard-and-fast rules when it comes to debugging. Experienced programmers develop a feel for the debugging process. They go through certain steps, but they may not even be sure what those steps are. As their debugging skills improve, they find themselves looking first for obvious potential problems, then for non-obvious potential problems, then for unique and unusual bugs they have never seen before. Less experienced programmers tend to focus on the obvious sources for bugs, and it takes them weeks to work their way through to the non-obvious ones. It is important to remember, the source of your bug may be completely unrelated to what you think is causing your bug! Don't waste too much time focusing on the same lines of code over and over. You may be missing the point altogether.

Here are some suggested steps in the debugging process.

Isolating the Problem

If you can isolate a bug, you can fix it. Isolating a bug consists of identifying the function or functions the bug occurs in, then finding which lines of code in those functions are responsible for the bug. This may involve reducing the code to the smallest amount of code needed to reproduce the problem. If you have a program with 10,000 lines of code, you may have trouble isolating a bug. One solution is to write another program. That is, if you think your problem is in one function, try writing a small program with just that function and function **main()** that calls it. Does the same bug appear? If it does, then you were right, the bug is in that function. If not, your bug may very well be in some other part of the code you have not examined yet. I find the code reduction method is most helpful with very tricky bugs. It is time consuming, but it will give you consistent results.

The first step in isolating a bug is being able to reproduce it. That means, you run the program to the same point, do the same thing, and the same bug occurs every time. This isn't always easy. Some bugs appear to be perfectly random, and efforts to reproduce them are futile. Keep trying, though. Usually there is a sequence of events that triggers the bug, you just haven't discovered it yet.

Dumping Values to a File

When I was debugging *Tommy's Adventures*, I had many bugs relating to redrawing tiles after scrolling. I knew I wanted to adjust the **layout** array and redraw the proper tiles that had been covered by sprites, but for some reason I had many problems. For example, I mistakenly adjusted the **layout** array for the visual page when I should have adjusted the **layout** array for the hidden page. In retrospect, that mistake seems obvious, but during development I found it quite a hard bug to find. The symptoms of the bug were kind of cute—when Tommy ran around, he would leave remnants of little red tennis shoes all over the screen. The long, long hours of tracking down the source of the bug were not so cute, though.

One way I isolated the problem was by dumping values to a file. I dumped all the values I could think of—Tommy's x and y position, the coordinates of the tiles he covered, their tile attributes, the tile origins, the **layout** array, and so on. I finally discovered the values in the **layout** array were not the values I expected them to be, and I was able to isolate and fix the problem.

To dump values to a file, I open a file called DEBUG.DAT for writing in text mode. Since I use this file so often, I code it into my program. I use a preprocessor directive to define a term called **debug**, and I only open the file if the term has been defined, as follows:

```
#define debug

#ifdef debug
   /* text file used for debugging purposes */
   dstream = fopen("debug.dat","wt");
#endif
```

I leave this code in the program even when I am not debugging. It makes it convenient for me to open a file and dump values to it when I need to. If don't want to open the debug file, I comment out the definition, like this:

```
/* #define debug */
```

Alternatively, you can use a conditional compilation to turn debugging on and off. For example, with some compilers you can use a flag such as "/Ddebug" when compiling.

Sometimes I want to be able to dump values to a file at the press of a keystroke. I press the D key to debug. This code, if placed somewhere in the **activate_level()** function, will trap the keystroke, pause program execution, and dump values to the debug file:

```
#ifdef debug
      /* if needed, dump a bunch of debug information to a file */

      if (fg_kbtest(KB_D)) /* press 'd' for debug */
      {
         /* unload keyboard handler, slow down clock rate */
         fg_kbinit(0);
         set_rate(0);

         fprintf(dstream,"Tommy is at x = %d y = %d\n",player->x,player->y);

         tile_x = (player->x)/16;
         tile_y = (player->y+1)/16;
         fprintf(dstream,"tile_x = %d tile_y = %d \n",tile_x,tile_y);

         /* tile number */
         tile_num = (int)backtile[tile_x][tile_y];
         fprintf(dstream,"tile_num = %d \n",tile_num);

         /* tile attributes */
         fprintf(dstream,"tile attributes: ");
         for (i = 0; i < 8; i++)
           fprintf (dstream,"%d ",
                    test_bit(background_attributes[tile_num],i));
         fprintf(dstream,"\n");

         /* bounding box info */
         fprintf(dstream,"bound_x = %d bound_width = %d\n",
                 player->image->bound_x,player->image->bound_width);

         /* flush the output file */
         fflush(dstream);

         /* wait for a keystroke */
         fg_waitkey();

         /* restore keyboard handler and clock rate */
         fg_kbinit(1);
         set_rate(8);
      }
#endif
```

Notice that I set the clock rate to the normal 18.2 ticks per second before writing to the file. Also notice that I disabled the low-level keyboard handler. This change makes it easy to wait for a keystroke using Fastgraph's

fg_waitkey() function. I print out information about the sprite, about the tiles, and about the sprite bounding box. After waiting for a keypress, the clock rate and low-level keyboard handler are restored to the state they need to be in for game play, and the game continues. I can then exit the game, and look at the contents of DEBUG.DAT, which will contain conveniently labeled and formatted debugging information.

Don't Forget to Flush!

Dumping values to a file is great if your bug is not the sort of bug that causes your system to hang. If your system hangs, you may discover your debug file is empty. That is because disk I/O is buffered. The output information is only written to a file when a certain amount of it has accumulated, perhaps 256 or 512 bytes. Unfortunately, your system may hang before that much data has accumulated.

The solution is to flush the output buffer before continuing. This is simple to do. A call to C's **fflush()** function will handle the job for you.

Debugging Tools

In an effort to make a programmer's life easier, many companies have developed tools to help you debug. Some of these are useful. Whether you choose to use them is a matter of personal preference. Some people swear by one tool or another, others forge ahead without them. Personally, I rarely use debugging tools, but I think they have value.

An interactive debugger such as Borland's *Turbo Debugger* or Microsoft's *CodeView* will let you step through your code one line or one function at a time, set break points, examine the contents of memory locations or registers, and in general watch everything your code does as it executes. This sounds wonderful, and in fact it is. There are only a few problems. For one thing, they are time-consuming to master. By the time you install them and learn how to use them, you could have (arguably) already found your bug. The biggest problem, though, seems to be in swapping from a graphics video mode to a text video mode. In general, debuggers are not aware of Mode X, and even if they were, they tend to wipe out whatever was in video memory when they take over the screen to display your debugging information. That means your pages and tiles are gone! It is theoretically possible to swap video graphics to RAM (or extended or expanded memory) and then swap it back to video memory as needed, but I have never tried that, and to be perfectly honest, I don't want to. It sounds like a very difficult and time-consuming solution.

A Dual-Monitor System

Debuggers are sometimes run in a dual-monitor mode, and I know programmers who swear by this method. It involves installing two video cards in your system, one a monochrome text card and the other a regular VGA card. The debugger information is displayed on the monochrome screen, and the program runs on the VGA screen. The reason I have never tried this is because I don't have enough room on my desk for another monitor. I think it sounds like a good idea, though, and it seems to work for many people. I have heard it tends to slow down your program. That is, the monochrome display will slow down what is happening on the VGA display. This is not necessarily a bad thing. Sometimes slowing down the action of a game while debugging allows you to see what is happening more clearly.

Other Tools

A text reformatter such as Gimpel's *PC-lint* will check your code for a variety of problems and formatting inconsistencies. You may be surprised at what you will find when you run your source code through PC-lint.

A memory checking program such as *Bounds-Checker* by Nu-Mega Technologies or *MemCheck* by StratosWare Corporation will help you locate problems such as array overflows. I have not tried either of these programs, but again, some programmers swear by them. If you think you need help in this area, I encourage you to check them out.

Preventing Problems

The best debugging happens before bugs occur. If you design and write your code carefully, develop good coding habits, and test your code thoroughly, you can minimize your debugging problems.

Writing Clean Code

I feel like your mother, nagging you to do what you already know you should do. Be consistent in your indentations! Use meaningful variable names! Include lots of comments! Keep your elbows off the table!

You know how to write clean code. Just do it.

Beta Testing

I have heard people say there is no such thing as a bug-free program. I don't believe that. My background is in mathematics, where there is aways a correct solution to any problem. I believe, with any program, there will be one correct way to write it. There may also be 100,000 incorrect ways. Some of the incorrect ways involve major bugs, and some of them involve bugs that are so obscure they may not surface for years.

Beta testers are your first line of defense against both the obvious and the obscure bugs. Use them liberally. You may notice, not all beta testers are created equal. There are certain beta testers that find more than their share of bugs. I don't know why this is. Perhaps they spend more time with the program, or they are more experimental with keystroke combinations, or perhaps they are more aggressive in their quest to find your mistakes. (Their attitude may be "Aha! Gotcha! You may be a brilliant game programmer, but I found your big mistake!") When it comes to finding bugs, perhaps some people are just lucky that way. Use and appreciate the people that can find your bugs. Give them free copies of your game, and if possible, mention their name somewhere in your documentation. It doesn't cost much to keep a beta tester happy, and it is worth every penny. Every bug found before your release will save you a lot of pain after your release.

Those Wild and Crazy Bugs

Have you ever accidently put an **fopen()** call inside a loop? This would cause the same file to be opened over and over, allocating a 512 byte buffer each time, so eventually your program would ran out of room and crash. That's bad! Don't do that!

Have you ever used C's **memcpy()** function to copy one array into another array, without noticing one array was declared **int** and the other was declared **char**. That's dangerous! Don't do that either!

Some bugs just defy description. Even if you are an experienced C programmer and you think you have already encountered every bug known to man, a new one will crop up that will leave you baffled. The worst part about it is, when you finally figure it out, you will not feel relieved or triumphant, you will probably just feel dumb.

Debugging is a painful, but necessary, part of the development cycle. I hope this chapter gives you some ideas to make the process a little easier for you. The only other thing I can offer you is a few words of encouragement—hang in there! It's hard, but you can do it!

Chapter 17

Time to put some finishing touches on our game. Here are some helpful hints to get you from game amateur to game professional.

Putting It All Together

No two games are alike. Every game is the product of its author's imagination, training, innovation, and perseverance. But despite all their differences, most games generally follow a standard format. And if you want your game to have mass appeal, you should follow this standard as well. By including the essential elements of a side scroller, you'll ensure that your users know what to expect and will feel comfortable with your game. Standardizing will increase your profits and also reduce your technical support costs. If your users see all the standard elements in your game, they will be less likely to call you and ask you questions.

The Install Program

The first thing a user needs to do with your game is install it. Because most side scrollers are shareware, let's assume that you can't depend on a printed manual to describe the install procedure. Even if you have a printed manual, chances are your player won't read it until after he's tried (and probably failed) to play the game. Game players, in general, are not big on manuals. They like to dive in and play.

The install program should be on the disk (the first disk if your game is distributed on more than one) and should be in the form of an INSTALL.EXE or an INSTALL.BAT program. Usually an executable install program, such as the one in Figure 17.1, is more reliable than a batch file, but if your install procedure is simple, a batch file will work fine.

Install programs perform several tasks. Usually they begin by creating a subdirectory for the game. This subdirectory should have a unique, descriptive name. If your game is called *Willie and the Window Washers*, don't try to create a subdirectory called "Windows." Find a better—and more unique—name.

The install program should allow the game to be installed on any disk. Don't restrict installation to the C: drive. Also, don't assume the user is installing from the A: drive or the B: drive. With shareware games, it's common to unzip the program into a temporary directory, run the install program, then delete everything in the temporary directory. It's also possible to install a program into the directory that it currently resides in. Try to design your install program to handle all such cases.

Once the directory is created or found, the install program typically copies all the program files into the directory. If the original files are distributed in a .ZIP, .ARJ, or in another archived format, the install program should handle the unarchiving for the user. Don't assume a user knows how to unarchive a program. Always assume he just bought his computer yesterday, and make the installation procedure as painless as possible.

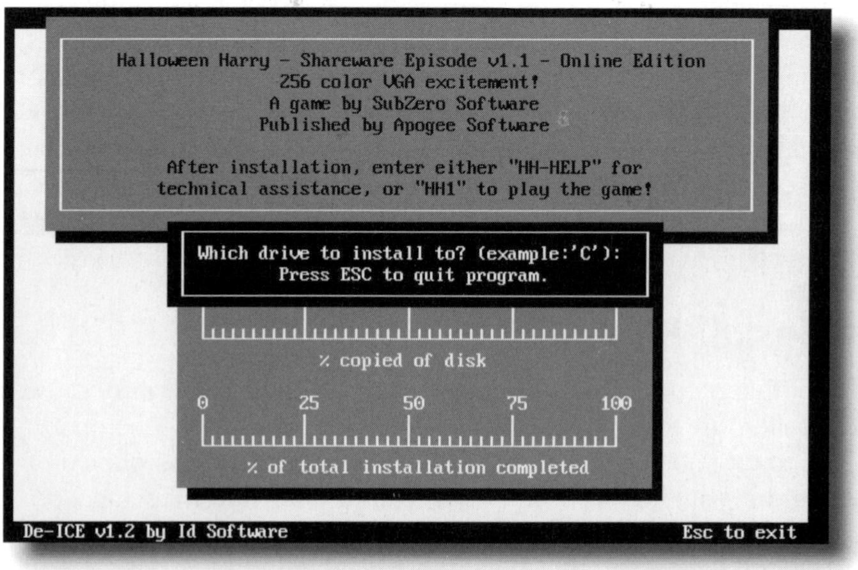

Figure 17.1 *Create an executable install program like this one for your game.*

Don't modify the user's CONFIG.SYS or AUTOEXEC.BAT files without the user's permission. You'll lose friends in a hurry if you do that. If you absolutely *must* modify those files, inform the user, and give him the option of aborting the install procedure. Also, make backup copies of the files before you modify them so that the user can put his system back the way it was.

The Setup Program

Setup programs are not necessary for all games, but they seem to be pretty common. The install program may call the setup program, or the game may call it the first time it runs. Also, the setup program may be called by itself or from within the game when the hardware or user's preferences change.

Typically, the setup program will ask questions about the user's system and preferences, such as "Do you prefer to use the joystick or keyboard?" Then it will write the information to a small file, usually with the extension CFG. In my *Willie and the Window Washers* example, I would probably call the setup file WILLIE.CFG. When the game starts, it looks for the CFG file and uses those settings. If it can't find the CFG file, it runs the setup program and creates it.

The best setup programs auto-detect the user's hardware, such as the mouse, joystick, and sound card, and suggest default settings. The user may then opt for keyboard over joystick, or no music and sound. A graphical representation of the options, as in Figure 17.2, looks nice and will give your game a professional touch.

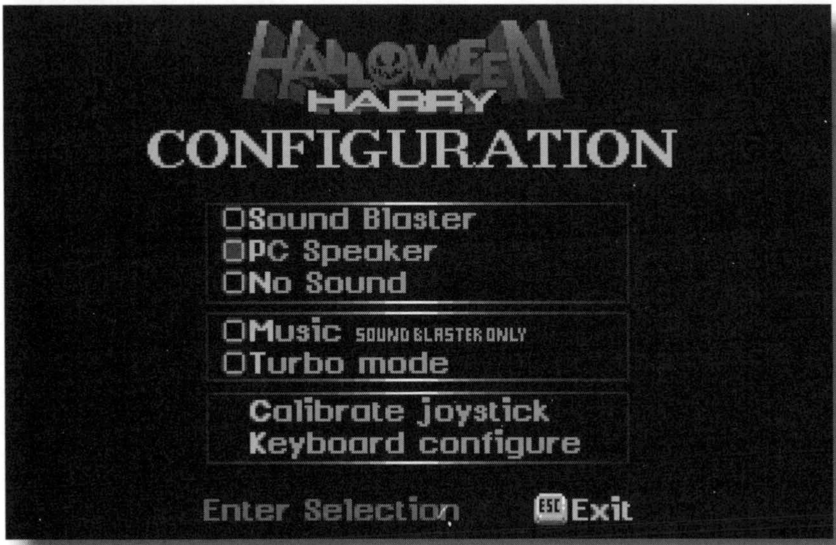

Figure 17.2 *This type of setup screen helps users to customize their hardware settings.*

The Intro

Every time the game is started, there should be some kind of intro sequence. Some games have very elaborate cinematics at the beginning to get the player ready to play. The opening cinematics set up the story line and show off the game's ability to provide visually dazzling graphics, great music, and sound effects. Figure 17.3 shows some very elaborate opening cinematics in Karen Crowther's game, *Pickle Wars.*

Unfortunately, not all opening cinematics are well received, especially after they've been seen a few times. Players don't want to sit through several minutes of introductory material before playing, so always provide an easy way to bypass the opening cinematics. Pressing any key should be enough to interrupt the sequence and let players go directly to the game.

Title Screen

The title screen is very important and needs to have excellent artwork. It will be used to sell your game, and may be used in such things as catalog art, screen shots, and packaging. It offers many people their first glimpse of your game, and reflects its overall quality. An attractive title screen, such as the one in Figure 17.4, will give your game a professional look.

Figure 17.3 *Opening cinematics like these from Pickle Wars grab user interest.*

Figure 17.4 *An attractive title screen gives your game a professional look.*

Opening Credits

Opening credits can go on the title screen or on one or several screens by themselves. Give everybody who worked on the game credit—developers, artists, musicians. It doesn't cost anything to mention somebody's name, and it will build goodwill. Make sure to give yourself credit too. It's not necessary to mention beta testers, but if there are not too many and they made a significant contribution, it doesn't hurt to mention them. See Figure 17.5 for an example of opening credits.

Some licensing agreements require that you mention the developer tools in the credits or documentation. Check the licensing agreements for all your programming tools. (Fastgraph has no such requirement, so it's not *necessary* to mention it.)

Demo Mode

Demos are important for selling your game. If you have an excellent demo, you may find your game running continuously in computer stores or at trade shows. This is obviously desirable, so put a little extra work into creating an attractive demo. The demo should show the sprite moving through several levels of the game and should last several minutes. At the end of the demo, display the opening cinematics again, then run the demo again. The demo should be continuous, so that if no key is pressed, it will run indefinitely.

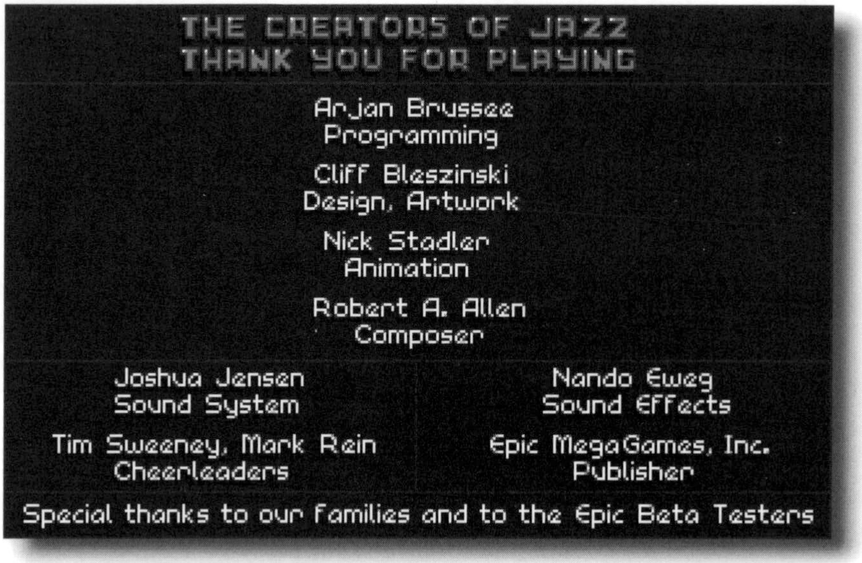

Figure 17.5 *Opening credits offer much appreciated acknowledgment for a job well done.*

The Game

Side-scroller games are typically broken up into episodes, and the episodes contain levels. How many levels you include in an episode depends on how complex the levels are and how the game is marketed. The traditional shareware trilogy model calls for three episodes containing approximately ten levels each. The first episode is distributed as shareware, and the other two episodes are sold through mail order.

How you present each episode is a personal choice; levels may flow smoothly from one to the next, or they may have transitional screens. Sometimes you'll see story line development, including dialog from the main character or primary enemy, or you'll see cinematics or some other artistic expression. If scoring is an important part of the game, you may see the score screen displayed between levels, but this is less common.

Sometimes levels are grouped together in collections called *zones*. You may have three levels from a garden zone, for example, followed by three levels in a space ship zone. This works well because it balances the need for unique and interesting graphics with the need to recycle artwork to save disk space and development costs.

The Control Panel

The player should have an option—usually the Esc or F1 key—to pause the game. When the key is pressed, the game is interrupted and a control panel, like the one in Figure 17.6 is displayed.

The player selects an option from the control panel. Typical control panel options include:

- *Return to Game:* If the game is interrupted in the middle, the player can use this option to return to the same location.
- *New Game:* If the player has lost too many lives or too much energy, he may want to start over from the beginning. Some games also offer the option to restart the current level at the beginning.
- *Save Game:* Saving a side scroller in the middle of a level is difficult. You need to save everything to a file, including the current position of the background, the current locations and action functions of all the sprites, and whatever timing and environmental information is relevant to the game. Some games simplify the save function by returning the player to the beginning of a level, which is less satisfying than a full save. A compromise is the *milepost* method, which involves setting flags (mileposts) as the player passes them. When the player returns to the game, he starts

Figure 17.6 *A control panel provides options for the user.*

at the most recently passed milepost. However you choose to save a game, the save and restore functions are essential to game play, and most players expect them.

- *Restore Game:* Usually more than one game can be saved, and the player is given a menu of games to be restored. Five save/restore game files are usually enough for this option.
- *View High Scores:* Scores should be saved in a file and viewed at the end of the game, with the option of viewing them during the game. Usually the top 10 high scores are saved, and a player can add his name to the scores file only if he beats one of these. Competing with yourself or your family members adds one more level of enjoyment to playing the game.
- *The Story:* Since many people like to skip the opening cinematics, it's nice to give them the option of taking a break from the intense game play to catch up on the story. Either a couple of text screens or cinematics are appropriate at this point.
- *Demo:* The player should be able to choose Demo mode from the menu. Once the game goes into Demo mode, it's not necessary to restore the game to the same state it was in before pausing. Use the same demo code here that was executed at the beginning of the game.
- *Setup:* The player should be able to change the setup options at any time, including turning off the sound and music, or changing from keyboard control to joystick control.
- *Ordering Information:* If this is a shareware game, or if other games are available through direct mail, tell the player this as often as you can. Ordering information should be available at the end of the game, in the documentation, and as an option from the menu.
- *Help:* It's a good idea to list the keystrokes used to play the game here. You don't want a player to have to exit the game to get help with game commands. Help on all functions should be available from within the game.
- *Quit:* If the player selects Quit, ask "Are you sure?" Some games insult the player at this point: "Are you going to wimp out?" I don't really like to be insulted by a computer game, so be careful with your creativity. Also, it's a good idea to ask the user if he wants to save his game before exiting.

The Level

The object of an action/adventure game is to beat the level. If you beat all the levels, you win the game. Beating the level usually involves achieving one or more of the following goals:

- Reaching a location, such as the far-right side of the level. The end of the level may be marked with a signpost.
- Finding something. You may be looking for a hidden object, like a crystal shard or an elevator.
- Rescuing somebody.
- Solving a key/door problem. The door to exit the level is locked. You must find a key in some other part of the level and bring it back to the door.
- Defeating the boss enemy. Some levels, especially the last level, have a large, difficult-to-defeat enemy called the *boss enemy.* If you can defeat the boss enemy, you not only beat the level, you may beat the game.

There really aren't very many new ideas when it comes to exiting levels. Most levels in side-scroller games are exited by some variation of these concepts. Of course, there *is* one other way to exit the level: Dying. Death is a natural part of side-scroller games. People expect to die, and some even like it. While you could write a game where nobody dies, these don't seem to sell as well as the more traditional kill-or-be-killed games.

There are many ways for a character to die. He can die incrementally by degrees, losing a little energy each time he touches a forbidden object, such as an enemy or a torch. Or he can die all at once, such as by falling into a pit of spikes or a pool of hot lava.

Usually after death, a player may be resurrected at the beginning of the current level. This uses up one of his lives, or *one-ups.* Typically, a player will start the game with three one-ups, and when his supply is exhausted, he must start from the beginning, or from the last place he saved a game. If a player continues the game, he may be able to start over at the beginning of the level or zone he died in with a new supply of one-ups. Remember, these are just guidelines; you may vary these parameters to suit your own creative impulses.

In the Level

The player expects to see certain things in the level. A scoreboard or status area is customary. This area displays the current score, the amount of ammunition or energy, if relevant, and the number of one-ups remaining. In *Tommy's Adventures,* the scoreboard is small, and may be turned off, which speeds up the game.

The player expects to encounter certain obstacles in getting through the level. The most common obstacles are enemies, as in Figure 17.7. Enemies can walk, fly, slither, jump, spit, or shoot. The more creative your enemies are, the better.

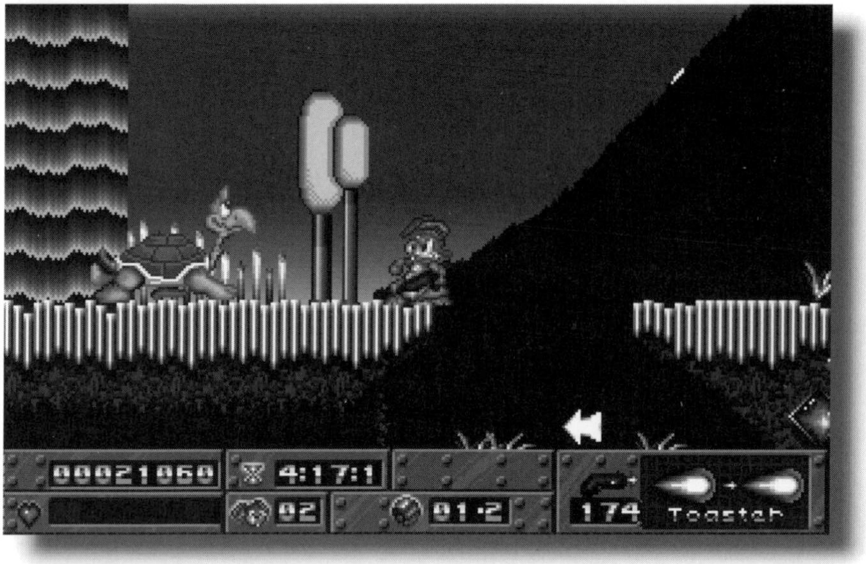

***Figure 17.7** Confronting the enemy.*

Other hazards, such as moving platforms, bottomless lakes, electrical currents, hot lava, and spikes, add interest. The player should interact with both the environment and the other characters in the story. The path through the level may be obvious or subtle, and there may be more than one way to get through a level, such as through hidden passages or shortcuts. There may also be rewards, such as additional ammunition or one-ups, for exploring non-obvious areas of the level. The player commonly depletes supplies of ammunition or energy as he works his way through the level, and picks up more in the form of bullets, food and drink, or first aid supplies. Figure 17.8 shows one way of finding more ammunition.

Sometimes hints and problem-solving skills may be required. For example, a sequence of numbers seen early in the level may open a combination lock later in a level, or a password must be remembered in order to get past a gate guard. Use creativity in designing levels, but remember that obstacles should be fun, not annoying. Listen to your beta testers. If they tell you they hate a certain problem-solving sequence, leave it out.

End of Game

It will usually take several weeks to beat a good side-scroller game. During that time, the player will start and exit the game many times. The exit sequence should be planned carefully. After asking the player if he wants to save his game, you'll probably want to record his high score. After that, consider what information you want left on the screen after the program exits.

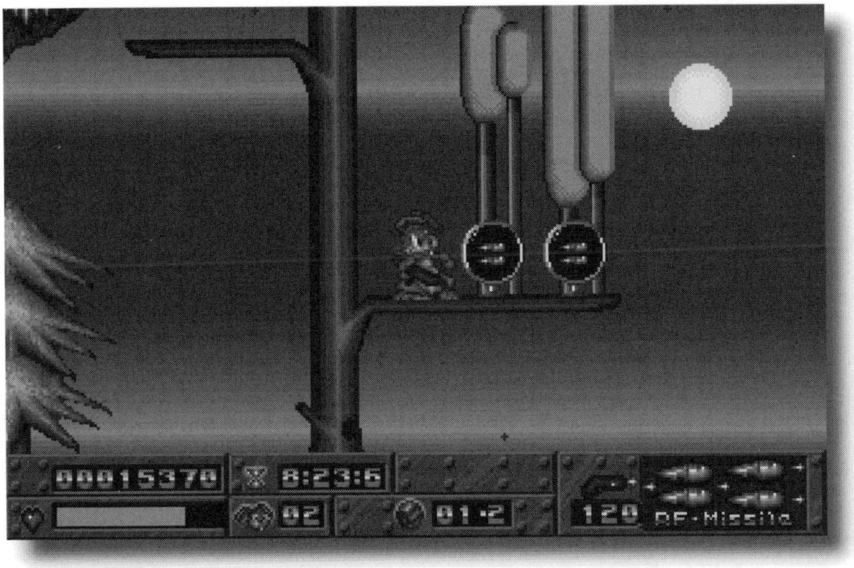

Figure 17.8 *Finding more ammunition.*

If you're serious about running a shareware or mail order game business, you'll want to put some advertising on the exit screen. Display some previews of the other episodes available, including an advance glimpse at artwork or story lines, as in Figure 17.9. You should also display ordering information,

Figure 17.9 *Exit screens offer the perfect opportunity for advertising.*

including the price and description of the game, your address, and phone number. Study how other games are sold and use their style, and don't be shy about using superlatives. This is not the time for shyness.

There should be a balance between advertising on the exit sequence and the ability to exit the game swiftly. Have some sympathy for the guy playing your game at work whose boss might walk in any second. Let him clear the screen and exit to DOS quickly and discretely. You may also want to consider incorporating a *boss key.*

Tommy's Tip

A Boss Key

A boss key is a keystroke sequence that simulates a shell to DOS. The idea is if you're playing a game at work and your boss walks in, you can pretend you're working, or at least not goofing off. Most boss keys don't really exit to DOS, they just draw a C:\ prompt in the upper-left corner. If you want to be really fancy with your boss key, you can display a PCX file that looks like a Windows session with several programs running simultaneously, though that's probably overkill.

Documentation

All games require some kind of documentation. Even games that can be played with virtually no training or help should still be documented. Printed manuals are appropriate for registered versions and retail games, while on-disk manuals are more practical for shareware versions. Documentation that is complete and attractive will give your game a professional look. Comprehensive documentation should include the following features:

- *Getting Started:* Usually the first thing a user wants to do is know how to install and play the game. Put this information near the beginning of the documentation, so the player can get going right away.
- *Introduction:* Give the story line, or some carefully crafted explanation of the player's predicament and goals. You want to generate sympathy, humor, and anticipation of game play. Some parts of the story line can be left to the player's imagination, or can be developed during the game.
- *Background:* Is this a shareware game or retail? Who wrote it and what else have they written? Users are interested in the authors of their games. Be brief, but try to generate some interest in your company and yourself.

- *Files on the Disk:* Include an inventory of files and what they do. If any files can be deleted, such as drivers for sound cards that were not installed, document them here for players who have limited disk space.
- *Instructions:* List all the keys used in your game and what they do. Give specific details about the menu choices, how to save and restore games, and so on.
- *Hints:* If there are certain areas of the game that gave your beta testers a lot of trouble, offer suggestions on how to get past them.
- *Distribution Information:* This is very important for shareware games. Encourage your users to pass your game along. Satisfied users are an important distribution channel. If you have limitations on catalog or rack vending (for example, if you require written permission to distribute), say so here and refer vendors to your license agreement.
- *Ordering Information:* If your writing a shareware game, tell users how to order and register the game, and refer them to the ORDER.FRM file. Remember, to sell the game, you need to convince potential buyers how exciting the other episodes will be. Be sure to thank them for supporting the shareware concept.

If you're writing a retail game, include information about how to order your other games direct through mail order.

Other Disk Files

If you're writing a shareware game, you'll want to include some standard files in your distribution. Check currently popular shareware for current styles in shareware documentation.

FILE_ID.DIZ

This is a small text file, usually 45 characters wide and 10 lines long. It contains the file description for bulletin board distribution. Usually, but not always, it will be automatically extracted by the bulletin board software. When uploading a program, you should always type in a good description in case the FILE_ID.DIZ program is not extracted.

Some bulletin boards give the option of displaying one- or two-line descriptions. Design your FILE_ID.DIZ carefully. The most important information should go in the first line, followed by other vital information in decreasing importance. Here is an example of a FILE_ID.DIZ file:

```
Tommy's Adventures! Side-scrolling Action
Arcade game with outstanding 256-color
VGA graphics, HOT animation. Guide Tommy
through 10 exciting levels, rescue his
mom from giant carnivorous insects, and
save the planet from a fiery destruction!
Requires VGA graphics, sound card optional.
```

LICENSE.DOC

This file is also sometimes called VENDOR.DOC. LICENSE.DOC describes the means by which a program may be legally distributed. It's important to have a legally binding license agreement in order to protect your copyright on shareware distributions. If you have any questions about copyrights, shareware distribution, and how to protect your software, contact a knowledgeable attorney.

Here's a sample LICENSE.DOC file. This one is copied from the game RAPTOR, with permission from Apogee Software. The file was written by attorney Charles Kramer.

```
"RAPTOR: CALL OF THE SHADOWS"
Copyright 1994 CYGNUS STUDIOS, INC.
Licensed for exclusive distribution to APOGEE SOFTWARE
P.O. Box 496389, Garland, TX 75049, TEL: 214-271-2137 ("Apogee")

BY COPYING, USING OR DISTRIBUTING THIS SHAREWARE PROGRAM, YOU
INDICATE YOUR AGREEMENT TO THE TERMS OF THIS vendor.doc.

====================
KEY POINTS
====================

[*] Everyone can - and is encouraged! - to copy, upload and
    generally pass around this Program without charging for it.

[*] If you want to distribute it in a retail location (such as
    on a rack), or as part of a hardware or software bundle, or
    on CD-ROM you must get PRIOR signed written permission from
    Apogee.  Apogee reserves its right to withhold permission.

[*] If you want to distribute it as provided in this Vendor.doc
    by catalog, advertisement, BBS, on-line service, or direct
    mail, no written permission is needed.  Apogee highly
    recommends, however, that distribution be made from a copy
    from Apogee or from one of its authorized sources, such as
    our home BBS (Software Creations BBS: 508-365-2359) to
    prevent the sale of older versions.

[*] All advertising of the Program must include "Apogee" in the
    description.
```

```
[*] The Program is marked "Shareware" and contains "episode #1".
    No right is given by this Vendor.Doc to copy, use or
    distribute any other version, including any version that is
    registered, or not marked shareware, or that contains any
    episode other than #1.

======================
LICENSE
======================

[1] DEFINITIONS:  "Program" means RAPTOR and its related files,
including this one.  The "Trademarks" consists of "Apogee", the
Apogee "comet logo", and "Raptor".

[2] OWNERSHIP: Except to the extent expressly licensed,
Apogee owns and reserves the exclusive right to distribute
the Program, and to use the Trademarks in connection
with it.  Its content, layout and format are the property of
Apogee to the extent permitted by law.

[3] GRANT AND CONDITIONS:  Apogee grants a non-exclusive license
to distribute the Program on IBM compatible media under the
Trademarks subject to the following conditions:

 [A] CONDITIONS FOR ALL DISTRIBUTION

  [1] All of the Program's files, including this one, as
      released by us must be included without modification.
      The following files must always be included to
      constitute a legal version for shareware distribution:

        setup    .exe     64,287 04-01-94   1:00p
        rap      .exe    411,441 04-01-94   1:00p
        file0000.glb     529,919 04-01-94   1:00p
        file0001.glb   3,945,602 04-01-94   1:00p
        rap-help.exe      13,995 04-01-94   1:00p
        catalog .exe      58,749 04-01-94  12:00a
        order   .frm       6,237 04-01-94  12:00a
        dealers .exe       8,651 04-01-94  12:00a

      The catalog.exe, order.frm, and dealers.exe files are periodically
      updated.  These may be replaced with newer versions as they are made
      available from Apogee.

      These files are also included in the BBS version of the shareware episode
      but are not required for distribution:

        vendor  .doc       7,994 04-01-94   1:00p
        contest .zip      11,866 04-01-94   1:00p

  [2] No copyright or trademark information may be removed.

  [3] You must not [a] distribute any version of the Program
      with unauthorized changes, such as additional or different
```

levels, or changed characters or mazes; or
[b] characterize such versions as an "add-on" or "extension" of any Apogee product; or [c] distribute any unauthorized third party utility designed to alter any Apogee game, game level, game episode or saved game.

[B] ADDITIONAL CONDITIONS IF YOU CHARGE: If your distribution involves a disk or other physical medium, you must also:

[1] Clearly market the Program as shareware, which requires (among other things) using "try before you buy" or similar words on packaging for the Programs.

[2] Include "Apogee" and the "comet" logo (we encourage use of the 4 color version) on the front cover of the package.

[3] Include the your name, address and phone number on the packaging and in any added documentation. This can be imprinted on the package or may be in the form of a label affixed to the box, carton or folder.

[4] Any description of the Program included in a re-sellers catalog, sales brochure, on special packaging or handouts, must include "An Apogee Game", "Released by Apogee" or "Published by Apogee" if the word count of the description is more than 14 words in length.

[5] Distribute copies only after the programs on newly created master diskettes have been thoroughly tested. Always use high quality media and duplication technology.

[6] Try to sell only the most current version of the Program.

[7] Although Apogee discourages the practice, you may add an installation routine if it does not interfere with the proper operation or installation of the Program.

[8] Program updates, recommended descriptions and "screen shots" will be provided upon request, and are available in the re-seller / dealer conference of Apogee's main BBS.

[C] ADDITIONAL CONDITIONS FOR BUNDLES, CD-ROMS, AND RACKS: If you wish to distribute in a retail location (such as on a rack), or as part of a hardware or software bundle, or on CD-ROM, you must get PRIOR signed written permission from Apogee, which is in Apogee's discretion and may be subject to royalty or other conditions.

[4] TERM: Unless terminated for cause, your grants under this VENDOR.DOC terminate 30 days after you receive written notice, or such longer period as the notice may provide. Following such termination, you may distribute the Program only until the earlier of 60 days after the termination date in the notice, or distribution of the copies you have in stock. Sections [2], [5], and [6] survive termination.

```
[5] LIMITED WARRANTY AND LIMITATION OF REMEDIES: If Apogee
provides a physically defective copy of the Program, Apogee will
replace it upon submission of the defective one.  Aside from
this, the Program IS PROVIDED "AS-IS", AND NO WARRANTIES OF ANY
KIND (INCLUDING IMPLIED WARRANTIES OF MERCHANTABILITY OR FITNESS
FOR A PARTICULAR PURPOSE), EXPRESS OR IMPLIED, ARE MADE AS TO IT
OR ANY MEDIUM IT MAY BE ON.  OUR ENTIRE LIABILITY AND YOUR
EXCLUSIVE REMEDY IS SUCH REPLACEMENT, AND UNDER NO CIRCUMSTANCES
WILL WE PROVIDE ANY OTHER REMEDY FOR DIRECT, INDIRECT, SPECIAL,
CONSEQUENTIAL, PUNITIVE, INCIDENTAL OR OTHER DAMAGES ARISING
FROM IT, INCLUDING SUCH FROM NEGLIGENCE, STRICT LIABILITY, OR
BREACH OF WARRANTY OR CONTRACT, EVEN AFTER NOTICE OF THE
POSSIBILITY OF SUCH DAMAGES.

[6] MISCELLANY

 [A] Since we would be irreparably damaged if Section [3], [4]
or [6][D] were not specifically enforced, we will be entitled
without bond, other security or proof of damages, to appropriate
equitable remedies with respect to breaches of such sections, in
addition to such other remedies as we may have.

 [B] You will hold us, our partners, contractors, employees and
agents harmless from damage, loss and expense arising directly
or indirectly from your acts and omissions in copying and
distributing the Program, including from any installation
routine that you may add.

 [C] With respect to every matter arising under this, you
consent to the exclusive jurisdiction and venue of the state and
federal courts sitting in Dallas, Texas, and to service by
certified mail, return receipt requested, or as otherwise
permitted by law.

 [D] You will not modify, reverse compile, disassemble, or
reverse engineer the Program, or use or disclose any
confidential information that it contains.

[V.03.07.94]
```

ORDER.FRM

The ORDER.FRM file is how you make money in shareware. If you want people to pay for your shareware, you must make it easy for them to do so. An ASCII file that they can print out and then mail or fax in will improve your registration rate. Here is a sample ORDER.FRM file, also from the RAPTOR program from Apogee. Notice how Apogee solicits sales of their other games at the same time they try to sell you RAPTOR.

APOGEE SOFTWARE ORDER FORM - FAX SHEET (Fax number: 214-278-4670)
PAGE 1 OF 2

*** Mark all games you wish to order ***
*** Also check out the special COMBO offers, listed further below ***

[ ] Raptor: Call of the Shadows – Best VGA shooter ever on the PC!	($34.95)
[ ] Blake Stone: Aliens of Gold – New action 3D game, 66 levels!	($59.95)
[ ] Blake Stone – Three mission version, 33 levels!	($39.95)
[ ] Halloween Harry – Totally awesome VGA action blast 'em game	($29.95)
[ ] Duke Nukem II – New VGA explosive action game	($34.95)
[ ] Duke Nukem I (the original) – Non-stop pure action!	($29.95)
[ ] Cosmo's Cosmic Adventure – Rescue Cosmo's parents on alien world	($34.95)
[ ] Monster Bash – Monstrous action/arcade adventure game	($34.95)
[ ] BioMenace – CIA weapons expert Snake Logan battles in Metro City	($29.95)
[ ] Wolfenstein 3-D All SIX EPISODES "Wolf-Pack"	($49.95)
[ ] Wolfenstein 3-D Hint Book (with all maps, story and secrets)	($10.00)
[ ] Wolfenstein 3-D "Spear of Destiny" – A Commercial Wolf3-D game	($34.95)
[ ] Major Stryker – Triple-parallaxed space adventure shoot 'em up!	($29.95)
[ ] Cmdr. Keen: Vorticons – The award-winning game from Id Software	($29.95)
[ ] Cmdr. Keen: Goodbye Galaxy – Id's amazing sequel to the classic	($34.95)
[ ] Cmdr. Keen: Aliens Ate My Baby Sitter – A commercial Keen game	($34.95)
[ ] Paganitzu – Puzzle/action game with great cinematics	($29.95)
[ ] Word Rescue – Highly-rated, award-winning educational game	($29.95)
[ ] Math Rescue – Another award-winning educational game	($29.95)
[ ] Secret Agent – Clever adventure/arcade scrolling action game	($29.95)
[ ] Crystal Caves – Similar to Commander Keen in style and action	($29.95)

[ ] other ____

*** THE FOLLOWING COMBO OFFERS WILL SAVE YOU BIG BUCKS! ***

[ ] Blast 'em COMBO: Raptor & Major Stryker (SAVE $15!)	($49.95)
[ ] Blake/Wolf 3-D COMBO: ALL EPISODES PLUS Wolf Hint Book (SAVE $30!)	($89.95)
[ ] Duke COMBO: Both Duke Nukem I & Duke Nukem II (SAVE $15!)	($49.95)
[ ] Duke/Cosmo COMBO: Both Duke Nukem's PLUS Cosmo (SAVE $30!)	($69.95)
[ ] Combat COMBO: Duke II/Halloween Harry/BioMenace (SAVE $25!)	($69.95)
[ ] Action COMBO: Secret Agent/Crystal Caves/Dark Ages (SAVE $40!)	($49.95)
[ ] Kid COMBO: Word Rescue & Math Rescue (SAVE $20!)	($39.95)
[ ] Cmdr. Keen V/G COMBO: Vorticons & Goodbye Galaxy (SAVE $15!)	($49.95)
[ ] Cmdr. Keen G/A COMBO: Goodbye Galaxy & Aliens (SAVE $10!)	($59.95)
[ ] Cmdr. Keen SUPER COMBO: ALL SIX KEEN EPISODES! (SAVE $30!)	($69.95)
[ ] CGA Space Action COMBO: CGA-Goodbye Galaxy & Monuments of Mars	($39.95)
[ ] CGA Adventurers COMBO: Pharaoh's Tomb & Arctic Adventure	($34.95)

DISK SIZE: [ ] 3.5" 1.44M [ ] 3.5" 720K [ ] 5.25" 1.2M (360k not supported)

GRAPHICS: [ ] SVGA [ ] VGA [ ] EGA [ ] Other:____________________

COMPUTER: [ ] PENTIUM/586 [ ] 486 [ ] 386 [ ] 286 [ ] Other:__________

SOUND CARD: [ ] Sound Blaster (SB) [ ] SB Pro [ ] SB 16 [ ] Ad Lib & Gold

[ ] PAS 16 [ ] GUS [ ] None [ ] Other:______________________

==

APOGEE SOFTWARE ORDER FORM - FAX SHEET (Fax number: 214-278-4670)
PAGE 2 OF 2

==

Name (please print)____

Address ____

Address ____

City ____________________ St./Prov. _______________ ZIP/Code __________

Country (if not USA) __________________ Phone/Fax ______________________

SHIPPING [ ] USA: $5. Each additional item add $1.
CHARGES: [ ] Canada & Mexico: $6. Each additional item add $1.
[ ] All other countries: $8. Each additional game add $2; shirts $4.

Total payment: $____________ (TEXAS residents MUST add correct sales tax.)
Note: Payment must be in U.S. dollars and drawn against a U.S. bank.
Please do not send cash!

Payment type: [ ] Visa [ ] MasterCard [ ] Discover [ ] Check [ ] Money Order

Card number: ____

Expiration date: _____/_____ (MM/YY) Signature: ________________________
*** Thank you! ***

Mail to: Apogee Software
P.O. Box 496389
Garland, TX 75049-6389

Order: 1-800-GAME123 (1-800-426-3123)
Phone: (214) 278-5655 (Foreign orders)
Visa, MasterCard, Discover welcome!

Make checks payable to “Apogee”. Allow up to two weeks for delivery.
All prices subject to change without notice. All items subject to availability.

Where do you get or buy Apogee shareware games (check favorite two only)?

[ ] Apogee’s home BBS: The Software Creations BBS
[ ] CompuServe
[ ] America Online
[ ] Other BBS – Please write name:
[ ] Shareware catalog – Please write name:
[ ] Work, a friend or a relative
[ ] Retail store, off a rack, in a box or other simple packaging

```
[ ] CD-ROM disk
[ ] Other:_______________________________________________

What do you like or dislike about Apogee, our games, business with us, etc.?

_____________________________________________________________________

_____________________________________________________________________

_____________________________________________________________________

Thank you!
```

Ratings

As of this writing, the games rating issue has not been sorted out yet. In December 1993, the U.S. Congress held hearings on the subject of violence and adult content in video games. They decided ratings in games were required, and instructed the game industry to come up with a plan for implementing them. Failing that, the Congress will implement a ratings bureaucracy for us.

A committee of industry leaders has been formed, and ratings strategies are under discussion. By the time you read this book, ratings may very well be necessary element of a computer game release. Most likely this will take the form of content labeling based on some well-defined criteria. Games will be labeled for violence, sexual content, and language. You will be need to fill out a form to determine your rating, and register the form with an agency. The rating will be voluntary, but some retailers will insist on carrying only rated games. If you are unsure about rating games, check with the major software trade associations, such as the SPA, STAR, and ASP for more information.

Copy Protection

Copy protection has fallen out of favor in recent years. When the industry was young, it was common to see *on-disk* copy protection. This method required that the original program disk be installed in the A: drive for the program to run. The game looked for a signature on the disk and would not run if the signature was not found. It's easy to see how users would not enjoy this kind of copy protection.

Another type of copy protection is a small hardware lock, called a *dongle*, which you attach to your computer's parallel port. I can't see any practical use of this kind of hardware requirement where games are concerned. If every game required a dongle, users would need to switch dongles frequently.

What could be less fun than unplugging your printer to attach a small metal device to your parallel port? There may be some classes of software where a dongle is appropriate, but a game is not one of them.

Some games have *manual-based* copy protection. The user is asked a question at the beginning of the game, such as what is the third word in the fourth paragraph on page 8 of the user's manual. If they type in the correct word, they may play the game. If they miss it, they must exit and restart the game.

This is not the way to make friends with your users. Put yourself in your user's shoes. Would you want to put up with this kind of aggravation?

Shareware games don't have copy protection because they don't need it. Shareware games are expected to be copied freely. Some commercial games still use copy protection, but it's less common than it used to be. In a competitive market, users seem to prefer to buy the games without copy protection.

When considering copy protection, let common sense be your guide.

Other Considerations

Styles in game design change over time so keep current with the industry. Watch what the other authors are doing so you can give your customers what they want. After all, you can't develop a game in a vacuum, and the most successful games seem to strike a balance between conformity and innovation. Pay attention to the details, and you'll produce better games.

Chapter 18

Your gaming career is taking off! What do you do now? Make some money, that's what!

Tips for Marketing Games

Now that you've finished your game, it's time to think about how you're going to sell it. After all, you just spent countless hours and your entire life savings perfecting your masterpiece. It would be nice to get a return on your investment. How can you make money as a game developer? Marketing. Let's talk about some of the ways games are marketed.

Retail Games

This is usually the first place game developers look to market games. The colorful boxes on the store shelves look very appealing. If you could get your product in one of those boxes, you would surely make a mint. Your friends would be jealous, your mom would be proud, and you could retire, right? Maybe. Let's look at the numbers.

Suppose a retail game publisher offers you 10-percent royalties. Is that a lot of money? Consider, however, that this is not 10 percent of retail, that's 10 percent of net. So if your game sells on the shelf for $39.95, the publisher is selling it to the distributor for a discount, say 50-percent off. So you're getting 10 percent of what the publisher gets, or $2 per box.

Suppose your game sells moderately well. You sell 10,000 copies the first quarter, 5,000 copies the second quarter, and then the game goes in the discount bin. After that, sales trickle in for a few months, then stop. How much money will you make?

```
10,000 x $2.00  =  $20,000 first quarter
 5,000 x $2.00  =  $10,000 second quarter
 1,000 x $ .50  =  $    500 third quarter
                   --------------------
                   $30,500 total returns
```

Thirty thousand dollars? Is that all you're going to make on your masterpiece? That doesn't seem like very much, especially if you've worked on your game for a year or more. You could easily invest that much money just in artwork and music. Unless we can improve those number, it's possible that you could actually lose money on a retail game.

The Royalty Equation

There are two parts to the royalty equation: the royalty percentage itself, and, just as important, the amount of distribution.

Game developers need to ask their publishers some important questions, most important are the ones about distribution:

- How is the distributor planning to distribute this game?
- What stores will it be in?
- How will it be advertised?
- Will there be promotions?

It's important to remember that the shelf life of a retail game is relatively short. If a game doesn't perform well in the first two quarters, chances are it will never perform well. It will be replaced by newer, hotter games. Sometimes it's the fault of the publisher that a game didn't perform well, other times, it's the fault of the game. For example, the game may not have been well designed or thoroughly tested, or it may have been rushed to market before it was ready.

A common mistake game programmers make is to sign an exclusive contract with a small publisher without bothering to find out what kind of distribution they can expect. Some publishers are optimistic about their ability to get a product on the shelves, even though they do not have a proven track record. It's heartbreaking for an author to have a retail game sell less than 5,000 copies because the distributor didn't do a competent job promoting and distributing the game.

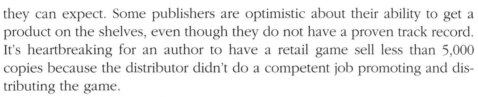

One way to make sure this doesn't happen to you is to ask for a performance guarantee. The contract can state that the author will make a minimum of $20,000 on the game in the first year or the publisher no longer has the exclusive right to market the program. For the exact wording of a performance guarantee, talk to a competent attorney.

Working with a Publisher

Not all retail publishers accept submissions from outside authors. Some game companies prefer to do all their development in-house. Others will accept "affiliated labels," and also do in-house development. It's hard for an outside developer to compete with in-house programming teams and their big budgets (often as much as $1 million or more), who have access to valuable resources, such as artists and musicians. If you're an independent developer, you may get some help, but you won't get the priority treatment the staff programmers get. If you're working with a publishing house as an outside developer, don't be afraid to ask for development money. If your game is good enough, you can get either an advance against royalties, or a straight development advance, which you won't have to pay back.

Perhaps your goal is to work as part of the in-house development team. This can be a rewarding career. You'll work with some of the best people in the industry, you'll have access to the latest technology and resources, and you'll have job security and benefits. However, there are some disadvantages. If you get a regular salary, your royalties may be small or nonexistent. It's also possible that you won't own the copyright on any of the software you develop, since it will be written on a work-for-hire basis. Further, you won't have creative control of your projects.

Be careful when you deal with retail publishers. Make sure they're reputable, and ask the important questions we discussed earlier. Talk to other authors who have published games with the company, and find out if they were happy with the results. Shop around a little. Look for a publisher that you can have a comfortable relationship with, so that when problems arise (as they always do) they can be worked out agreeably. If you feel friction between yourself and your publisher at the beginning, find a new publisher.

Shareware

Shareware is almost the direct opposite of retail software. As the author, you own the software, including all the copyrights, trademarks, and code, as well as the right to license the game to others. You make all the creative and marketing decisions, but you also shoulder the risks. You market your game yourself, fill the orders, do the technical support, but you also keep all the money. Games are not copy protected, but are passed around freely, and your customers participate in the distribution process.

Does Shareware Work?

Shareware has evolved over the years. These days, shareware distribution is more efficient than ever. Distribution networks can get your program on thousands of bulletin boards practically overnight. Shareware vendors are selling shareware on disks, CD-ROMs, pay-per-download services, vending machines, and every other distribution medium you can possibly imagine. Users are better educated than ever on the meaning of shareware and their responsibility to pay for it. The shareware industry is growing up.

On the other hand, it is entirely possible to make virtually no money in shareware. It happens frequently. An author will release a game, and registrations will trickle in at the rate of one or two per week for a period of years. Other authors will make a phenomenal amount of money in a very short period of time. Shareware, like all other marketing channels, yields mixed results, depending on the product. What are the characteristics of a successful shareware game? In my opinion there are five:

1. **Distribution.** Some people will tell you this is the most important part of shareware marketing. These people are usually shareware vendors who want your permission to sell your program. They will tell you the three most important factors to a shareware program's success are distribution, distribution, distribution. I would disagree with this emphasis. If a shareware game is good enough, it will automatically get excellent distribution. If it is a lame program, you can boost up the registrations by putting extra energy into the distribution, but you will reach a point of diminishing returns—you can spend more on uploading ZIP files and mailing out disks than you will get back in registrations. Distribution is important, but it will not make up for an inferior product, or a product without registration incentives.

2. **Quality.** As the shareware market becomes flooded, quality is more important than ever. Shareware users are becoming more sophisticated and pickier about the programs they register. A boring game with CGA graphics will not get any registrations, no matter how much distribution you get. Since all your users are trying your software before buying it, they will be a tougher audience than your average shelfware customer. Think about it this way. A software buyer who buys a game in a store will probably buy it based on how appealing the package is. They will take it home and install it, and they will try very hard to like it because they already paid for it. The shareware user, on the other hand, has gotten your game from a collection of several hundred or perhaps several thousand games. They get to try your game before committing themselves to buying it. If the game is not as good as they had hoped, they will simply download another one.
3. **Registration Incentives.** This is the trickiest part of the shareware equation. You want your users to register, and you must give them a reason to do so. The best reason is "more of the same." In the case of games, the winning strategy appears to be the trilogy method. This strategy, pioneered by Apogee software, splits a game into three episodes. Episode 1 is distributed freely through shareware channels and episodes 2 and 3 can be purchased by phone or mail order from the company. This strategy has been a phenomenal success for Apogee, but how much longer will it work? Now that there are so many games on the market, will the user buy episodes 2 and 3 from you, or just download episode 1 of somebody else's game?

   Withholding features in a shareware game in order to get more registrations is known in the industry as *crippling.* The word carries unfortunate negative connotations. Crippling can be carried to the extreme (register this word processor and get the vowels!) but there is ample evidence that giving away too much in a shareware program will have a negative impact on the author's profits. Use common sense when designing registration incentives. Give the user enough of a game to make it playable, and then offer something of value in exchange for registration.
4. **Program Design.** Timing is important with shareware games. You have about five minutes to hook the player's attention. Keep your opening cinematics brief, and let the player start playing right away. Early game levels should be and easy and addicting—success breeds addiction. Characters and artwork should be colorful and appealing. Your goal is to grab the player's attention and keep it.

How long the player plays is also important. If you give away too many levels in the shareware version, the player will play the game for several weeks, and then get tired of it. If you give the player too few levels, he will play the game for several hours and then decide registering it is not worth the money. Finding the right balance of difficulty, levels and playability is an art form, and if you can master it, you will do quite well at shareware.

5. **Legal Considerations.** The user is not the only person who you should concerned about. There are people who will want to sell your shareware game for their profit. The shareware vendors can be your best friend, or they can drive you crazy. Either way, you need to protect yourself. Have a legally binding license agreement distributed with your shareware game. I recommend game developers allow the shareware version to be distributed freely as long as no money is charged for it. Some shareware authors allow catalog and BBS distribution without permission required. However, these days, most authors require written permission before allowing shareware to be sold in stores. The reason for this is, many authors are getting royalties on versions of their games that are sold in stores, and they don't want to see non-royalty versions of their games competing with royalty versions. If you are not sure how you want to handle the retail distribution question, just have all the shareware vendors contact you before selling your game in stores, and negotiate each contract on an individual basis. Talk to other authors and see how they are handling vendor relations and retail contracts. If you have questions about copyrights and license agreements, talk to a lawyer.

Running Your Own Shareware Business

If you want to market your program as shareware, you had better be prepared to give your shareware business your long-term attention. You'll need to fill orders, answer technical support questions, interact with vendors and retail publishers, copy disks, mail out upgrades, and so on. These activities will continue indefinitely, because once you release a shareware game it's released for good. There's no way to recall a shareware game after it has been released.

Packaging for a shareware product is traditionally simple. Users like to receive a disk with an attractive printed label. A printed manual is nice, but not always necessary. A catalog of other games and related products is good for generating more sales.

The ability to accept credit cards over the phone will improve shareware registrations, as will a toll-free number and a technical support BBS. These things are not strictly necessary for a start-up company, though. Many authors have started out of their basement with nothing more than a dot-matrix printer and a personal phone line. Watching your shareware company grow from a tiny one-person startup to a major corporation will be very satisfying.

Running a shareware business is time consuming and will decrease the amount of time you can spend writing new code. The alternative to marketing your own shareware is to work with a shareware publisher. Apogee Software, Epic Megagames, and MVP Software all publish games in shareware and retail channels. If you have a good game and you're not sure you want to handle the details of marketing it yourself, you may want to submit your game to a shareware publisher.

Rackware

Rackware, also known as low-cost retail (LCR) software, is a relatively new phenomenon in the software publishing world. The LCR market evolved out of the shareware rack vending market. Shareware on racks in stores became controversial when the authors noticed huge numbers of disks were being sold, but they were not getting proportionally more registrations. Some authors speculated that it is too much to expect users to understand the concept of shareware sold in stores. When was the last time you bought a product in a store and brought it home only to discover you owed more money? Shareware vendors defended the practice, telling the authors to give it more time, and the shareware buying public would catch on. Maybe they have or haven't, but as of this writing shareware in stores appears to be decreasing and is being replaced by low-cost retail software.

LCR software is licensed programs, often the registered versions of shareware programs, that users can buy in stores in a low price range. LCR software has been compared to paperback books. The software is mass produced and sold in chain stores, book stores, grocery stores and gift shops—virtually anywhere that has room for a rack. The software sells in the $5.00-$10.00 price range, and the author gets a small royalty on each package sold, usually in the range of 40 or 50 cents per disk.

That may not sound like much, but the distribution is massive. Also, the shelf life of an LCR product tends to be longer than for regular retail games. Where a retail game may sell for six months, a rackware game may sell for years. This is a very favorable situation for the developer. Some authors are discovering they are making very good money on low-cost retail racks.

Another advantage of rackware publishing is the ownership of the program. The copyrights, trademarks, and code all belong to the author, as well as the right to license the game to others. In many cases, that means a game is not marketed exclusively through one publisher. The author may put the game on one rack or several racks, or may change racks, or may market the software simultaneously through shareware and rackware channels. A single program on a single rack will usually generate a small return for the author, but several programs on several racks can produce a very good income.

When designing a game for LCR distribution, keep your buying public in mind. The average K-Mart shopper will not spend a long time evaluating your program. They want something that catches their eye so they can throw the box in their cart and move on to the next aisle. Familiar games, like card games, do well. Family oriented games and children's games have a good market, as do shooting games. Screen shots on the outside of the box grab the buyer's attention. To be successful in LCR channels, a game must have mass-market appeal.

Rackware contracts can be exclusive or non-exclusive, shareware or non-shareware. The author should be careful when entering into exclusive LCR contracts. If an author signs an exclusive, non-shareware contract with an LCR publisher, then he should be sure that the level of distribution will justify giving up other marketing opportunities. The author should ask for a performance guarantee, with the understanding that if the vendor fails to sell a certain number of disks in a certain period of time, the exclusive contract becomes a non-exclusive one.

More Marketing Strategies

Opportunities build on opportunities. Typically, the author will submit a program to the rack vendor. If the vendor accepts the program, the vendor will arrange for packaging and distribution. Some authors pay careful attention to the packaging of their games. You can generate sales of related games by enclosing a coupon in the box. You can also write an online catalog of all your games and put it on the disk. *Don't ever pass up an opportunity to promote your other products!* You want to know who is buying your games, so you can sell them more games. Now you are in the mail-order business. The customer list you will build up this way will be a valuable asset.

You can market games in several channels simultaneously. You can release a shareware version of the game, and distribute that through shareware channels and also on royalty shareware racks. You can take the registered version, with more levels, and put it on all the non-exclusive LCR racks. You can make a special version, with different levels, and call it a deluxe or *private label* version, and put it on an exclusive LCR rack. You can change the name and the artwork, and re-release the game with new levels again the following year. You can mix several smaller games in game packs, and put different combinations on different product lines.

Sometimes you can find royalty CD-ROM deals. These involve putting several non-shareware games (or registered versions of shareware games) on a CD-ROM disk and selling it through mail order or retail. The vendor manufactures and markets the disk and sends a royalty check to the author. When a royalty is involved, this can be a favorable deal. When there is no royalty on CD-ROMs, watch out! Are you going to make any money? People who buy collections of 1000 or more shareware games on a CD-ROM may not be your best source of registrations. Instead of registering a game they like, they will just play it for a while and then move on to the next game. Some authors dislike shareware CD-ROMs, but cooperate with them anyway, because BBS sysops love them. And shareware authors depend on BBS sysops for distribution.

An innovative idea that seems to work well for some authors is the pay-per-download service. Users log into an online service, download the registered version of a shareware program, and the cost of the program is charged to their credit card. Prodigy offers such a service, and authors report being pleased with the results. Authors also report good results with CompuServe's SWREG service. This service takes registrations and charges the user's credit cards, then passes the information along to the author, who sends a disk to the user.

Where to Go for More Information

As you can see, there are many ways to market a game, each route has it's own special opportunities and pitfalls. The suggestions in this chapter will help you get started, but if you really want to be successful at marketing games, I suggest you look around for more information. One of the best sources of information is other game authors. You can meet them online in places like the CompuServe Gamers forum and the Software Creations BBS. There are also several trade associations that can provide information. Contact information for these resources is listed in Appendix C.

As a closing note, I would like to thank you for reading this book, and wish you success in your gaming career. I expect to see lots of wonderful games developed as a result of this book, and I hope yours turns out great! By all means, enter the contest presented in the back of this book—I'll be looking for your hot game! Good luck and happy gaming.

Appendix A

The Games on the Companion Disk

Three games are included on the companion disk, along with the source code for two of them. You can use these games to get ideas for your own games.

Playing *Tommy's Adventures*

To start *Tommy's Adventures*, go to the subdirectory where the game has been installed (the default is \FG\TOMMY) and type *tommy*. The *Tommy's Adventures* title screen will appear. Press any key to start playing the game. While in the game, you can use the keys shown in Table A.1.

Playing *Quickfire*

To start *Quickfire*, go to the subdirectory where the game has been installed (the default is \FG\QF) and type *qf*. The animated *Quickfire* title screen will appear. Press any key to start playing the game. While in the game, you can use the keys shown in Table A.2.

Table A.1 *Keys Used in the Tommy's Adventures Game*

Arrow Keys	Moves Tommy left, right, up, or down. The screen will scroll as Tommy moves to keep Tommy within a tolerance area.
Ctrl	Shoots. Tommy can shoot while standing, running, jumping, or falling.
Spacebar	Kicks. Tommy will do a forward spin kick when facing right, or a backward spin kick when facing left.
F1	Turns off the scoreboard. The scoreboard in the upper-left corner of the screen will disappear.
F2	Turns on the scoreboard.
Esc	Displays the status screen. When you see the status screen, you have the option of pressing Q for Quit, W for Warp, or any other key to continue with the game.
W	Warps (advances to the next level).

Because of disk space considerations, the sound effects and music for *Quickfire* were not included on the disk. If you want to hear the original *Quickfire* music from Rob Wallace, you can download a more complete version of *Quickfire* from our BBS at (702) 796-7134.

About Quickfire

Quickfire was written using the same general strategy as *Tommy's Adventures.* Video memory is resized in Mode X to support four-way scrolling. Sprites and levels were designed in the Fastgraph game editor. The objects (airplanes, bullets, and explosions) are controlled using action functions. The main differences between *Quickfire* and *Tommy's Adventures* are the continuously scrolling background, the lack of foreground tiles, and ignoring the tile attributes.

Several articles about the *Quickfire* source code were published in *PC TECHNIQUES* Magazine beginning with the December 1993/January 1994 issue.

Table A.2 *Keys Used in the Quickfire Game*

Arrow Keys	Moves the Quickfire airplane left, right, up, or down. The screen will constantly scroll to the right as the airplane moves, and will also scroll vertically and diagonally as needed to keep the airplane within the tolerance area.
Ctrl	Shoots. The Quickfire airplane will fire a series of bullets at the other airplanes. As other airplanes are hit, they will explode, and the score will be incremented.
Esc	Exits the *Quickfire* program. Upon exit, the frame rate will be displayed on the screen.

Playing Hedge Row

To start *Hedge Row*, go to the subdirectory where the game has been installed (the default is \FG\HEDGE) and type *hedge*. The *Hedge Row* title screen will appear briefly as the first maze is drawn. While in the game, use the mouse to maneuver your way through the maze. In addition, you can use the keys shown in Table A.3.

About Hedge Row

Hedge Row is included as an example of how to use the level editor to write a different kind of game. The maze tiles are stored in the file HEDGE.PCX, and the mazes are stored in files with LEV extensions. You can view and modify these files in the level editor. A GAME.DAT file on the disk lists the data files for each maze and can be used with the game editor. The source code for *Hedge Row* is also on the disk. More information about how *Hedge Row* works can be found on the disk in the file HEDGE.DOC.

Table A.3 *Keys Used in the Hedge Row Game*

C	Cheats. Displays the path through the maze.
N	Presents the next maze.
R	Uses the recursive maze solution. Watch the fascinating recursive algorithm in action as the computer attempts to solve the maze.
Esc	Exits *Hedge Row* and return to DOS.

Appendix B

Resources for the Game Developer

This guide provides information on useful resources that can greatly help you develop and market your own games. Here you'll find information on the best magazines, online services, tools, and other resources.

Magazines

Several magazines have information on developing and marketing games. Here are two of my favorites:

PC TECHNIQUES
7721 East Gray Road, Suite 204
Scottsdale, AZ 85260-6912
(602) 483-0192

Game Developer Magazine
600 Harrison Street
San Francisco, CA 94107-9602
(415) 905-2308

Online Services

One of the best ways to get information about developing and marketing games is to share ideas with other game developers. Here are a few of the better places I suggest you check out:

CompuServe Gamers Forum
To get to this forum, log on to CompuServe and use GO GAMERS, section 11. You'll find lots of software, games, and great advice.

Fastgraph Bulletin Board
Call our Fastgraph support bulletin board at (702) 796-7134.

Software Creations Bulletin Board
This board serves as a clearing house for thousands of game programmers around the U.S. You can reach this board by calling (508) 368-7139.

Music and Sound Libraries

All successful games require sound card support. The following programming toolkits will help you add music and sound effects to your game:

DigPak/MidPak
John Ratcliff
The Audio Solution
747 Napa Lane
St. Charles, MO 63304
(314) 939-0200 (BBS)

The DigPak/MidPak developers kit is free for non-commercial use, but there is a $1,000 fee for use in commercial products. To evaluate the toolkit, download the file DMKIT.ZIP from the BBS.

Sound Operating System
Human Machine Interfaces, Inc.
30 E. Broadway, Suite 180
Eugene, OR 97401
(503) 687-6509

The Sound Operating System is a high-end developers toolkit. The toolkit costs $399 with a licensing fee of $3,495 per title or $12,500 for a perpetual license, including source code.

Worx Toolkit
Mystic Software
1504 Encinal Avenue, Suite D
Alameda, CA 94501
(800) 697-8426

You can use the Worx toolkit for $79 with no royalties. Another toolkit, Worx Plus, is available for $199 and includes support for up to eight memory resident samples at the same time.

Artists

The following artists contributed to the software in this book:

Les Pardew
Cygnus Multimedia Productions, Inc.
4505 South 100 East, Suite 13
Pleasant Grove, UT 84062
(801) 785-5069

Mike Wall and Alfred Woo
Dub Media
75 Trapelo Road
Waltham, MA 02154
(617) 647-1101

Computer Game Developers Conference

The Computer Game Developers Conference is a valuable resource for game developers. It's held every year in April and is attended by some of the top talent in the industry. You can attend seminars and learn the secrets of developing and marketing games, and you can meet people in the industry who can help you bring your game to the marketplace. For more information about the Computer Game Developers Conference, contact:

Computer Game Developers Conference
555 Bryant Street, Suite 330
Palo Alto, CA 94301
(415) 856-4263

Information on Marketing Shareware

For more information on running a shareware business, you may want to join one of the shareware trade associations, such as the ASP or STAR.

Association of Shareware Professionals (ASP)
545 Grover Road
Muskegon, MI 49442-9427

Shareware Trade Association and Resources (STAR)
P.O. Box 13408
Las Vegas, NV 89112

It's also a good idea to interact with other shareware authors online, either on CompuServe, on other online services such as Genie or Prodigy, or on the online networks such as Ilink and RIME. Another good place to get shareware information is by attending an industry trade show. Currently, there are two annual shareware trade shows: the Summer Shareware Seminar, sponsored by Ziff-Davis Interactive, in Atlanta in August, and the Shareware Industry Conference in Indianapolis in June.

There are also some excellent books on shareware marketing. One of my favorites is *Writing and Marketing Shareware* by Steve Hudgik (Windcrest/ McGraw-Hill, 1992, ISBN 0-8306-2552-6).

Glossary

Action Arcade Game A game genre identified by tile-based backgrounds and animated sprites. Also known as a *platform game* or *side-scroller.*

Action Function A special type of function that controls the motion and characteristics of an object.

Animation A technique where successive still frames of a particular object appear to constitute a seamless sequence of movements.

Arcade Game A game with fast action where hand-eye coordination is the primary skill needed to beat the game.

Artificial Intelligence An algorithm by which the computer gives the illusion of thinking like a human. Also, the action of a character in a game as it reacts to other objects in the game.

Bit The smallest unit that can carry information in a computer—this is a base 2 number, equaling either 0 or 1.

BitBlt (**BIT BL**ock **T**ransfer) A bit string move, usually referring to moving the bits that represent an image from memory to display. Also known as a "blit."

Bitmap Arrays of data specifying the color of each pixel in a rectangular image of arbitrary size.

Blit To copy an image (or part of an image) from one place to another. See *BitBlt.*

Boss Enemy The biggest bad guy that must be killed in order to complete a level.

Cheat Code A keyboard sequence which, when used, gives the player an advantage in the game; for example, infinite ammunition, infinite lives, and the ability to walk through walls or fly.

Cinematics An animated sequence at the beginning of a game, or animated transition screens.

Clipping Cutting off parts of lines and/or shapes (sprites) that exceed the boundaries of a viewport or clipping region.

Clipping Region Rectangular area that defines where objects will be clipped.

Collision Detection Method of checking if two or more objects come in contact with each other.

Continue Another chance to play the game where you left off after you've lost all your lives.

Coordinate A location, or point in space, which may be addressed using arbitrary units.

Credits Listing of those involved in the development of a game, typically including the programmer, artist, musician, and producer.

Demo Mode A self-playing mode, showing off the features and artwork of a game.

Engine Code used as the basis for building a game, including the various utilities and a skeleton game.

Energy A scale representing how close a player is to death. Usually energy declines as a player collides with enemies, and increases when a player finds certain energy items, such as food.

Episode One portion of a shareware game series. Most often the first episode is used to interest the player in the game, while others are used as incentives to encourage registering the game. Sometimes different episodes have different plots.

Fastgraph High performance programmer's graphics library.

Fat Bit Editor A feature of an image editor that zooms in on an area of the image, and displays the individual pixels larger for easier editing.

Flipping Changing the display start address of video memory, so that a completely new part of video memory is visible. Also known as page flipping or page swapping.

Frame A sequence of events ending in a page flip. Also known as an *animation frame.*

Frame Rate Speed of animation, usually expressed in frames per second.

GIF An image file format where the image is compressed using LZW compression.

God Mode State of a game, usually triggered by a keystroke sequence, where the player cannot die, and may have other powers such as infinite ammunition or the ability to walk through walls. Also known as cheat mode.

Graphics Library Collection of functions that control the video ouput. Fastgraph is a graphics library.

Graphics Mode A PC mode where the screen is addressed in pixels.

Hidden Page A page-shaped area of offscreen video memory.

Keyboard Handler Functions or routines for programming and working with a keyboard. A *low-level* keyboard handler monitors keyboard activity so that special keys and key combinations can be detected.

LCR (**L**ow **C**ost **R**etail software) See rackware.

Layout Array An array holding information about which tiles in a level are covered by sprites and must be redrawn during a frame.

Layout Space A coordinate system based on the number of tiles on a page; for example, 22 tiles wide by 15 tiles high.

Level One continuous section of a platform game or other type of game. The goal of a game is to beat all the levels.

Level Editor A utility used for creating, viewing, and modifying levels.

Life More accurately referred to as a death, the unit for counting how many attempts a player has before a game is finished.

Mode X A 256-color planar or *tweaked* VGA graphics mode popularized by Michael Abrash.

One-Up An extra life, or the object that gives you an extra life.

Page An area of video memory or system RAM which holds enough data to fill the screen (or more) in the current graphics mode.

Page Flipping An animation technique that consists of writing to offscreen video memory, and then panning or flipping to that area. Also known as *page swapping*.

Panning Changing the screen origin to a different point in video memory.

Parallaxing An animation technique where the background is drawn in levels, and distant levels move at a slower speed than near levels, giving the illusion of depth.

PCX A popular image file format designed by Zsoft.

Pixel The smallest addressable unit on a computer screen.

Platform Game See *Action Arcade Game.*

Producer Someone who coordinates and supervises a game's development.

Publisher Anyone who markets games.

Rackware Games sold on racks in retail channels at a low price. Rackware may be shareware or non-shareware, exclusive or non-exclusive.

Registration Incentive A method of obtaining shareware registrations by offering something of value for money, such as more levels.

RLE An image stored using run-length encoding.

Resizing Changing the coordinate limits of video memory.

Resolution The number of pixels or character cells available on the screen.

Retrace A total screen update, usually happening at the rate of about 60 frames per second.

Royalties A method whereby a developer is paid for his or her work as a percentage of either net or gross receipts.

Score The cumulative number of points earned.

Scoreboard A graphical representation of the score, along with other items such as one-ups, energy, and ammunition.

Screen Origin The pixel coordinates of the upper left corner of the screen.

Scrolling Moving the screen smoothly in any direction.

Screen Space Coordinate system where object positions are identified as x,y positions in video memory.

Segue (pronounced "seg-way") A transitional device that helps one sequence flow smoothly into another. In a game, a segue usually occurs between levels and involves storyline development, often in the form of cinematics.

Shareware A method of marketing software where a program is distributed freely, and users may try it before paying for it.

Shelfware Software sold through regular retail channels, especially when marketed by an established commercial publishing house such as Electronic Arts.

Side-Scroller See *Action Arcade Game.*

Special Effect Any unusual or special visual image, sound, or music.

SPR File Fastgraph's **S**tandard **P**ixel **R**un image format. See *RLE.*

Sprite A bitmap of an arbitrary shape that can be moved across complex backgrounds without flicker or damage to the background image.

Sprite Editor A program for creating, viewing, and modifying sprites.

Sprite List Several related sprites, usually kept in a single file or buffer.

Storyline The setting for the game, including such things as an introduction to the characters, their location, and the reason they do what they do.

Text Mode A PC video mode where the screen is addressed in rows and columns of character cells. The default video mode of a PC when running DOS.

Tile A 16×16 image, usually blitted in sequence with other tiles to create levels.

Tile Attribute A one-byte value used to determine characteristics of a tile, such as *solid on top.*

Tile Editor A utility program used to create, view, and modify tiles.

Tile Library A collection of unique tiles used to build levels.

Tile Ripper A utility used to reduce one or several screens of artwork to unique tiles.

Tile Space A coordinate system based on the number of tiles in a level.

Title Screen The opening screen of a computer game, which includes the title and other information.

Transition The sequence between levels, often consisting of storyline development, special effects, or cinematics.

Transparent Pixels in a rectangular blit which are not displayed, so that the background shows through.

Trilogy A method of marketing games where a third of the game, known as an episode, is distributed as shareware, and the other two episodes are registered or purchased directly from the manufacturer.

TSR (**T**erminate and **S**tay **R**esident) A program that stays in memory after it returns control to the operating system, such as FGDRIVER.EXE.

VGA (**V**ideo **G**raphics **A**rray) Any of a collection of video modes; also the hardware that supports them.

Visual Page The page that is currently visible on the screen.

Warp Moving to an area in a game level, requiring a complete screen redraw; for example, going through a door or advancing to a new level.

Index

A

B

G

S

T

The Action Arcade Adventures Contest

Don't miss your chance to win over $2,500 dollars in hot game programming tools. Enter The Coriolis Group's Action Arcade Adventures Contest and show us the best fast-action applications that you've created with the tools, software, and files included in this book. All you need is your PC and your imagination.

Here are the prizes you can win:

1. The first place winner receives over $1,500 worth of game programming goodies like Borland C++ 4.0, Fastgraph Powerpack, Boxer/TKO, Borland Visual Solutions Pack, Phar Lap TNT DOS-Extender, SciTech's UniVBE, NuReality's Vivid 3D and 3D Plus, HMI's Sound Operating System, and Media Shop from Motion Works.
2. The first runner-up will receive $1,000 worth of game programming tools and add-on products from the list above.
3. The first 20 place winners will receive a free subscription to *PC TECHNIQUES* Magazine, their choice of a Coriolis Group Book, and a "way cool" Coriolis Group T-shirt.

What to Submit

Send your action arcade creation with source code to The Coriolis Group. Please make sure you include an entry form along with your software. Mark each disk with your name, phone number, and name of your game entry. If you need to archive your entry, submit it as a self-extracting archive. You may also submit your entry on CD-ROM or Syquest cartridge. You can submit as many entries as you like, but you must submit one entry at a time.

Contest Guidelines

1. All entries must be sent by **March 1, 1995.**
2. The entry must be created using the tools and products included in this book.

3. Each entry will be judged on the basis of content, creativity and design, user interface, usefulness, and educational and/or entertainment value, by a panel of judges from The Coriolis Group and the game development industry.
4. All winners will be notified by June 1, 1995. For the names of all winners, send a self-addressed, stamped envelope to The Coriolis Group, Action Arcade Adventures Contest, 7721 E. Gray Road, Suite 204, Scottsdale, AZ 85260.
5. The Coriolis Group will not return any entries unless a self-addressed envelope with sufficient postage is provided with the entry for return. The Coriolis Group is not responsible for lost or damaged entries.
6. The Coriolis Group reserves the right to demonstrate the winning entries in a future edition of the *Action Arcade Adventure Set* book and *PC TECHNIQUES* Magazine, and other national publications.
7. No purchase is necessary. This contest is subject to all federal, state, local, and provincial laws and regulations and is void where prohibited. This contest is not open to employees of The Coriolis Group, IDG, any Coriolis Group distributor, or the families of any of the above.

So what are you waiting for? Here's the perfect opportunity to show the world what you can do, have some fun, and win some valuable prizes.

Name ______________________ Daytime Phone ______________

Address ______________________________________

City ______________ State ________ Zip ____________

File Name ______________________________________

Brief Discription of Entry ______________________________

____

____

Send entries to: **Action Arcade Adventures Contest**
The Coriolis Group
7721 E. Gray Rd., Suite 204
Scottsdale, AZ 85260

I signify that the enclosed is my own original work and that I abide by all rules described here.

Signature ______________________________________

Adventure Set License Agreement

Please read this Coriolis Adventure Set software license agreement carefully before you buy this product and use the software contained on the enclosed disk.

1. By opening the accompanying software package, you agree that you have read and agree with the terms of this licensing agreement. If you disagree and do not want to be bound by the terms of this licensing agreement, return this product in whole for refund to the source from which you purchased it.
2. The entire contents of the disk and the compilation of the software contained therein are copyrighted and protected by both U.S. copyright law and international copyright treaty provisions. Each of the programs, including the copyrights in each program, is owned by the respective author, and the copyright in the entire work is owned by The Coriolis Group, Inc. You may copy any or all of this software to your computer system.
3. The disk contains source code presented in the book, utilities, tools and pictures. You may use the source code, utilities, tools and pictures presented in the book and included on the disk to develop your own applications for both private and commercial use unless other restrictions are noted in the book or on the disk by the author of the file.
4. You may not decompile, reverse engineer, disassemble, create a derivative work, or otherwise use the programs except as stated in this agreement.
5. The Coriolis Group, Inc., and the author specifically disclaim all other warranties, express or implied, including but not limited to warranties of merchantability and fitness for a particular purpose with respect to defects in the disk, the program, source code, and sample files contained therein, and/or the techniques described in the book, and in no event shall The Coriolis Group and/or the author be liable for any loss of profit or any other commercial damage, including but not limited to special, incidental, consequential, or other damages.
6. The Coriolis Group, Inc. will replace any defective disk without charge if the defective disk is returned to The Coriolis Group, Inc. within 90 days from the date of purchase.